Embedded Programming In Ada®

Embedded Programming In Ada®

Theodore F. Elbert
The University of West Florida
Pensacola, Florida

VNR VAN NOSTRAND REINHOLD COMPANY
New York

Library of Congress Catalog Card Number 85-29464
ISBN 0-442-22350-1

Manufactured in the United States of America

Published by Van Nostrand Reinhold Company Inc.
115 Fifth Avenue
New York, New York 10003

Van Nostrand Reinhold Company Limited
Molly Millars Lane
Wokingham, Berkshire RG11 2PY, England

Van Nostrand Reinhold
480 Latrobe Street
Melbourne, Victoria 3000, Australia

Macmillan of Canada
Division of Gage Publishing Limited
164 Commander Boulevard
Agincourt, Ontario M1S 3C7, Canada

15 14 13 12 11 10 9 8 7 6 5 4 3 2 1

Library of Congress Cataloging-in-Publication Data

Elbert, Theodore F.
Embedded programming in Ada[R].

Includes index.
1. Ada (Computer program language) I. Title.
QA76.73.A16E43 1986 005.13′3 85-29464
ISBN 0-442-22350-1

PREFACE

Embedded Programming in Ada is intended for the practicing programmer or for the advanced engineering or computer science student. The presentation of the material presumes a certain level of sophistication on the part of the reader, so general concepts normally found in introductory programming texts are not covered. Some familiarity with operating systems is also presumed, and a basic knowledge of some block-structured language such as PL/1 or Pascal is recommended. The material is presented with a bias toward embedded-system programming, but the basic concepts apply, of course, in any context.

The Ada language has similarities to other block-structured languages—notably Pascal. It also has a wealth of additional features not found in most other languages—not even in real-time languages targeted particularly to embedded computer applications. The organization of this book reflects these similarities and differences, in the manner in which the material is presented. Chapter 1 presents a general overview of the language and its features. Because of the interaction among many of the language features, it is necessary for the reader to have an overvall concept of the language structure as specific details are presented. For this reason, Chapter 1 should be read by anyone not already familiar with the language structure. Material in this chapter also sets the stage for the software engineering flavor of the remaining material. Chapter 1 also introduces the reader to the *language reference manual*. Because the reference manual is the ultimate reference for the syntax and semantics of the Ada language, close association with the reference manual is maintained throughout the text.

Chapter 2 contains a brief history of the development of the Ada language. Some knowledge of this history is useful in understanding the reasons behind some of the language features. As with Chapter 1, this material may be skipped by the reader already familiar with the basic language structure.

In Chapter 3, by far the longest chapter in the text, those concepts of the Ada language that are similar to those of other block-structured languages are covered. Included here are complete discussions of data types and data objects, and of their declaration. Basic syntax in terms of expressions and statements is covered, and Ada's subprograms are considered in detail. In addition, the exception-handling features of the language are discussed. By the end of this chapter, the reader should be able to write Ada programs using subprogram units. Although there is a large amount of material in Chapter 3, it can be covered rapidly because of the similarities to other block-structured languages such as Pascal.

Beginning with Chapter 4, the more advanced features of the language are presented. In Chapter 4, the Ada package feature is developed, and the generic unit is discussed in Chapter 5. The coverage of these features is rather complete, and several short programming examples are provided.

The input-output aspects of the Ada language are discussed in Chapter 6. Again, the coverage is complete, stressing the use of the generic input-output packages and of the functions and procedures exported by these packages.

Chapter 7 covers the tasking feature of the language. Task initialization, rendezvous, and termination are treated in detail, and several short programming examples are given.

In Chapter 8, those topics not covered in previous chapters are discussed. These topics include overloading, renaming, pragmas, and other topics that did not easily fit into any previous chapter.

Finally, Chapter 9 includes a very brief discussion of the design and life-cycle support implications of the Ada language. The Ada Programming Support Environment (APSE) is introduced here.

A basic principle applied in the writing of this text was to avoid, to the extent possible, the use of forward references. Obviously, this concept bears heavily on the order in which material is presented. For example, exceptions are introduced in Chapter 3, but their use in packages and tasks is covered in Chapters 4 and 7, respectively. In certain instances the principle is violated, but it is done so with appropriate apology to the reader.

Throughout the text the reader will find short programming examples or code segments designed to stress the particular point being presented. To the extent possible, these programs have been tested using the Telesoft-Ada partial implementation of the language. There may remain some instances of incorrect code, and for this the author must assume the blame.

Several people were instrumental in the production of this work at the University of West Florida. Lurleyne Terry, Sharon Darnley and Lucy Perrow shared the word processing task, while Dennis Coats and Steve Wolniewicz proofed the manuscript and tested most of the programs.

Bill Brykczynski of the Institute for Defense Analysis also helped proof the manuscript. My wife Barbara provided the inspiration and also assisted in arranging the entire manuscript. Without such assistance, the project would never have been brought to completion.

THEODORE F. ELBERT

Pensacola, Florida

CONTENTS

Embedded Programming In Ada®

Chapter 1
INTRODUCTION TO ADA

1.1 GENERAL OVERVIEW

The Ada language is a modern, high-order, programming language that was developed under the sponsorship of the United States Department of Defense for one specific purpose: to reduce the life-cycle software costs for embedded computer systems. *Embedded computer systems* are usually defined to be those computer systems that constitute a part of a larger system whose primary function is other than computational. In the case of the Department of Defense, the application is clearly to weapon systems and other military uses, but the general concept of an embedded computer system applies equally well to process control, to communications systems, and to many other nonmilitary uses of computers. In fact, the development of the Ada language has produced a superior, state-of-the-art, general-purpose programming language that incorporates most of the modern principles of software engineering.[1] Indeed, many of the features of Ada may seem strange and even cumbersome to an experienced programmer who is not familiar with modern software engineering principles such as *information hiding, abstraction, modularity,* and *localization,* among others. Modern software design methodologies, such as *structured programming, top-down design,* and *object-oriented* design, are fully supported by the Ada language.

Although the development of the Ada language was directed specifically toward the embedded computer system, the resulting language is well suited to other applications as well. Other areas such as

- general systems programming
- industrial process control applications requiring real-time concurrent processing
- general applications programming
- scientific computation

can all benefit from the modern features of the language. In the educational field, the Ada language has been adopted by some institutions as the primary language of instruction because its features force the user to apply good programming practice.

The Ada language is a modern algorithmic language with control structures similar to those of other modern block-structured languages such as Pascal. The Ada language also provides the user with the ability to define his own data types and subprograms, in a manner analogous to that found in Pascal. It provides for modularity by a unique feature called a *package,* in which data, data types, subprograms, and other packages can be encapsulated. Modularity is supported in a physical sense as well by the *separate compilation* facilities of the language. Special real-time programming features of the language include concurrently executing threads of code called *tasks* and the ability to handle exceptions directly within the high-order language. Synchronization of and communication among concurrently executing tasks are provided within the language itself, making it unnecessary for the program to effect calls to the underlying operating system in order to provide such features. Also provided within the language is precise control over the representation of data in the underlying hardware, as well as access to system-dependent features. Finally, the *generic facilities* of the Ada language permit parameterization of subprograms and packages, a process by which a template of the subprogram or package is compiled, but without some essential details. These details are provided later as parameters in a process called *instantiation.* A given generic unit can be instantiated any number of times in an Ada program, with the use of a different set of parameters for each instantiation.

The Ada language is *strongly typed,* meaning that data objects of a given type may be assigned only those values appropriate to the type. Furthermore, only certain predefined operations may be performed on data of a given type. Type checking is performed at compile time, thus providing early detection of errors associated with data typing. A unique Ada data type, the *private type,* provides the programmer with the ability to create *abstract data types.* Data abstraction is a modern software engineering concept by which details of an implementation are hidden from the user, while at the same time mechanisms for the use of the implementation are provided. In this manner, the software equivalent of a "black box" can be created.

1.1.1 Criteria for the Language Design

It is important for the student of the Ada language to be aware of the design goals of the language developers. Many of the language's most visible features may seem cumbersome or even counterproductive to those not aware of the intended application domain or to those unfamiliar with the more modern concepts of software engineering. The application domain was that of the Department of Defense embedded computer system. In general, embedded computer systems have definite characteristics, as listed below and indicated in Figure 1.1.

- Programs tend to be large, often on the order of tens of thousands or even hundreds of thousands of lines of code.
- They are in service for extended periods, perhaps up to 20 years.
- They must be fault-tolerant, recovering from faults or gracefully degrading to a lower level of performance. This includes software response to exceptions in the processing.
- They undergo continuous field changes, including software updates due to design improvements or changing operational requirements.
- They must have high reliability, both in hardware and in software.
- There are usually physical constraints in terms of hardware size or processing speed, implying a requirement for efficiency in the software.
- Input-output requirements are usually specialized.
- There is usually a requirement for concurrent processing.
- There is usually a requirement for real-time processing, in that the system must respond to physical stimuli in real time.
- There is normally a host-target relationship, with software development taking place on a large host computer equipped with software development tools, while the actual application is on the embedded target computer containing only those features required for mission functionality.

This particular domain of embedded systems was targeted by the Department of Defense because the preponderance of its software costs

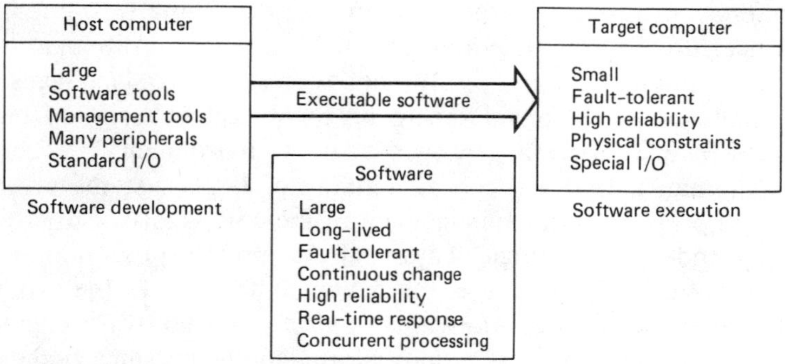

Figure 1.1. The host-target environment of embedded systems.

were incurred in programming for embedded systems, and because software life-cycle costs were rapidly becoming by far the major contributor to overall system costs. Furthermore, software maintenance costs were often exceeding those of initial software development, sometimes by an order of magnitude or more. Thus, the potential was there for an enormous savings in system life-cycle costs if a programming language could be developed that would provide features specifically oriented to life-cycle cost reduction. The reader should note at this point that minimization of life-cycle costs may well produce initial development costs well above minimum as maintenance-enhancing features are incorporated into the software design.

To accomplish Ada's design goal of minimizing life-cycle software costs of Department of Defense embedded computer systems, the language was developed with three primary concerns:

1. reliability and maintainability of the resulting software
2. efficiency in terms of execution time and machine resources
3. the realization that programming is a human activity, and that the language features must take into account human limitations

These concerns were fundamental in the design of the language; the reader should keep this in mind as the various language features are explored in later chapters.

Because of the emphasis placed on features that promote reliability and maintainability, it is not surprising that the language emphasizes program readability—often at the expense of ease of writing. A properly written Ada program is almost self-documenting, since the syntax rules permit English-like constructs. The strong typing features of the language enhance program reliability, and the incorporation of exception handlers into the language enhance run-time reliability. The separate compilation features also support the maintainability of programs written in the language.

Efficiency in terms of execution time and machine resources was a key concern during the development of the language. Although the Ada language contains several features not found in other languages, none of the features were considered to be exorbitant in terms of machine resources or of execution time in the target environment.

As a human activity, the programming of large systems presents a perplexing problem—the management of the complexity of the resulting software. Indeed, this single feature of the modern programming environment has been identified as the major contributor to the production of poor-quality software. Many features of good software engineering practice—those such as abstraction, information hiding, and modularity—

have as one of their purposes the management of complexity. The Ada language design incorporates these and other features that tend to reduce the complexity of the resulting software. The Ada language also provides features, such as separate compilation, that provide the ability to assemble a program from independently produced software components. The independent production of software components is characteristic of the development of large programs.

1.1.2 Software Engineering Principles

In general, the term *software engineering* implies a disciplined approach to software development—the application of principles completely analogous to those of long-standing practice in engineering design. This process, in turn, calls for the delineation of a set of operational requirements, together with the specification of general characteristics of the resulting software. While the operational requirements are specific to the particular software project, the general characteristics to which all software development should aspire have been detailed.[2] These general characteristics, which when adopted become general design goals, are modifiability, efficiency, reliability, and understandability. In addition to these general design properties, the Department of Defense embedded system should exhibit the properties of portability (of both software and programmers) and reusability.

As indicated in Figure 1.2, the Ada language design was driven by the need to provide these general design goals in Ada software. This need, in turn, was met by incorporating into the language the means of applying

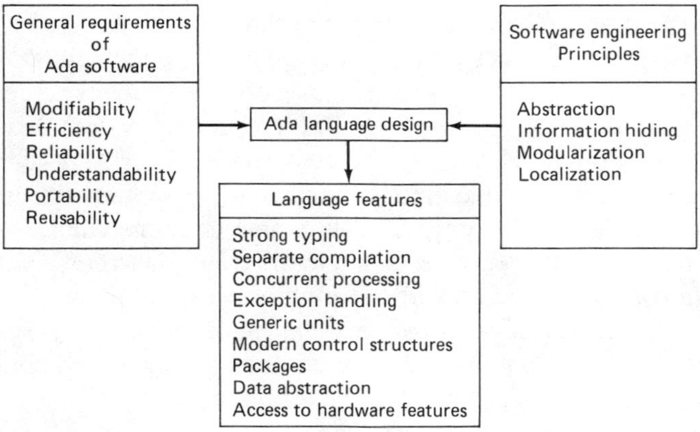

Figure 1.2. The Ada language design.

the software engineering principles of abstraction, information hiding, modularization, and localization. The resulting language features—strong typing, separate compilation, and others as indicated in Figure 1.2—all support the attainment of these general design goals in software developed through use of the Ada language. Each of the general design goals—modifiability, efficiency, reliability, understandability, portability, and reusability—is examined below.

1.1.2.1 Modifiability. As the name implies, *modifiability* refers to the ease with which controlled change may be incorporated into existing software. Embedded computer systems in particular have a need for software with this property, because of the many modifications made to operational software over the life cycle of the system. Important to achievement of modifiability are

- controlled change—the absence of side effects that cause unexpected modification of program behavior
- self-documentation—the software itself should reflect the underlying algorithmic design
- management of complexity—software modifications should not increase the complexity of the solution represented by the software

Typically, modification to software is performed by programmers other than those involved with the original design, and it may be performed at a site other than that at which the original design was developed. The Ada language features of strong typing, generic units, packages, and separate compilation serve to enhance the modifiability of software.

1.1.2.2 Efficiency. The term *efficiency,* in this context, refers to the use of hardware resources and execution time by compiled code. While compiler efficiency—referring to the use of time and resources by the compiler—may be of some interest, the embedded-system programmer is much more concerned with the execution characteristics of compiled code on the target machine. In the embedded-system environment, optimization with respect to either execution time or computational resources may be required. Furthermore, a single program may require execution time optimization in one part of the program and resource optimization in another. In the development of the Ada language, any proposed feature for which efficient implementation could not be clearly envisioned using standard compiler design techniques was rejected.

1.1.2.3 Reliability. The general concept of *reliability,* as applied to software, concerns the question of whether the software will perform its intended function accurately under normal conditions, and whether it will do so consistently. Abnormal conditions should never result in erroneous performance masked as proper performance. Instead, the software should be able to recover from such conditions or, at the very least, to continue execution with reduced effectiveness, a characteristic known as *graceful degradation*. Thus, the software should avoid catastrophic failure which results in program abandonment by the underlying operating environment.

The reliabilty of software is dependent upon the correctness of the design specifications, upon the correctness of the mapping of the design to the software implementation, and upon the ability of the software to recover from exceptional conditions if they should arise. For large programs, it is often difficult or impossible to produce a requirements specification which is complete and invariant, simply because of the sheer complexity of the problem. Furthermore, in the case of embedded systems, the hardware design may be taking place concurrently with the software design, or the system operational requirements may be in a state of almost constant change. In this situation, the correctness of the design is a nebulous concept; one can never be sure of absolute reliability, even if the mapping of the design to the software implementation is known to be correct. A realistic definition of software reliability is "that a program should meet its specifications, should never produce 'incorrect' output regardless of the input, should never allow itself to be corrupted, should take meaningful and useful action in unexpected situations, and it should completely fail only when further progress is completely impossible."[3]

Achievement of a high level of reliability in software nearly always requires a reduction in code efficiency, since features such as data checking and exception handling require a large amount of extra code and usually entail an increase in execution time. It is generally conceded, however, that reliability is cost-effective in the modern embedded-system application. Some of the reasons for this concession follow:

- The cost of system failure could be immense, not only in terms of equipment failure but also in terms of human lives.
- The tendency today is toward increased hardware capability at lower cost and smaller size.
- It is much more difficult to improve an unreliable system than it is to improve an inefficient system.
- Inefficiency is immediately apparent. Reliability problems are much more insidious and therefore are more capable of causing damage.
- As a market consideration, unreliable software will not sell, regardless of the efficiency.

As the reader progresses through this book, he will see several features of the Ada language which promote reliability in Ada software. Language features such as strong typing and separate compilation tend to ensure the correctness of the mapping from the design to the software, while the exception-handling capability of the language permits a program to recover from unexpected situations.

1.1.2.4 Understandability. The *understandability* of software relates to the extent that an observer can grasp both the functional aspects of the software and the relationship between the software and other system components. In order for software to be understandable, its very form must imply to an observer the structure of the design being implemented. This concept extends well beyond the mnemonic use of meaningful data names and the use of ample commenting. It includes the use of a meaningful coding style, the use of an appropriate structured design methodology, careful selection of how data is structured, and the incorporation of other features that respect the role of programming as a human activity. The ease of maintenance of a program obviously depends upon the property of modifiability—that change can be incorporated easily, without harmful side effects and without an increase in complexity—and upon the property of understandability—that the manner in which the design is mapped to the software implementation is easily comprehended.

The understandability of a software implementation can be highly dependent upon the implementation language. Since one of the primary concerns of the Ada language development effort was the realization that programming is a human activity, one finds in the language many features which can serve to enhance the understandability of Ada software. The strong typing, the modern control structures, and the data abstraction features of the language are examples.

1.1.2.5 Portability. *Portability* refers to the ease with which software can be moved from one computer to another. In an era of rapidly escalating software costs, it seems only reasonable to incorporate features that factor portability into the software design, even at the expense of increased development costs. The idea of portability is not new, of course, since any high-order language is portable to some extent. Only assembler programs are perpetually tied to specific hardware. The degree of portability differs among high-order languages, however, and it often depends upon the particular implementation of the language on the underlying machine. In the embedded-system environment in particular, a program written in a high-order language often must depend upon assembler language subprograms to exploit some feature of the underlying hardware, or upon the underlying operating system for features like task synchronization and exception handling. Current practice is to enhance the portability of programs by isolating those sections of code that are dependent upon either the underlying hardware or the underlying operating system. The most prevalent method of achieving this isolation is through the use of replaceable subprograms. Moving of the software from one machine to the other then requires replacement only of these subprograms.

A high degree of portability is inherent in all programs written in the Ada language, because they are virtually independent of the underlying hardware and of the underlying operating system. Access to features both of the underlying hardware and of the operating system is provided in the Ada language itself. The burden of providing this access is borne by the Ada compiler and run-time support software. Furthermore, the Ada language itself has been protected against the use of subsets or extensions by the fact that the name Ada has been copyrighted. Before any compiler can be called an Ada compiler, it must be validated by the Department of Defense; such validation requires that a compiler successfully pass a battery of some 2500 different tests designed to validate conformance with the language specifications.

Not only do these features enhance program portability, they also ensure that programming skills are portable from one working environment to the other—an important consideration to the highly mobile professionals in the defense industry. To further enhance the commonality of work environments, a standard Ada Programming Support Environment (APSE) has been defined, so that the programmer, in addition to being provided a common language, is also provided a standard set of program development tools.

1.1.2.6 Reusability. While *portability* refers to the ease with which software can be moved from one machine to the other, the term *reusability* is used to describe how well software components lend themselves to use by different programs. The concept of reusable software is not new by any means. For some time, programmers have made use of subprograms called from standard support libraries to achieve the implementation of commonly used algorithms. In the development of reusable subprograms, care must be taken to preserve the integrity of the calling environment and to provide an efficient interface between the subprogram and the calling environment. But the concept of reusability can be extended beyond the reuse of a subprogram, which is usually the implementation of an algorithm. Such things as data structures, groups of constants, or data itself can be viewed as reusable resources. In the Ada language, the concept of reusability is given wide applicability through the package and generic unit features of the language.

1.1.3 Ada's Program Units

There are five general classes of programming languages: (1) basic assembly languages, (2) systems implementation languages, (3) static high-level languages, (4) block-structured languages, and (5) dynamic high-level languages. These general classes differ in the way in which they relate to the underlying machine, in the manner in which storage is allocated, and in the run-time support required.

Assembly languages are unique to the machine upon which the resulting code is to be executed. In general, there is a one-to-one relationship between assembly statements and machine language instructions, although most assembly languages today permit the use of macroinstructions—which are equivalent to a number of basic assembly instructions—and some of the modern control constructs such as if-then-else and basic loop structures. Storage allocation is static, in that all required data storage is allocated at assembly time. Assembly language programs do not reflect the basic fabric of the program design, as do programs written in a high-order language, so the reliability and modifiability of the resulting software suffers. Because assembly languages are unique to the underlying hardware, assembly language programs are not portable. They are, however, usually efficient.

Systems implementation languages—of which the language C is an example—provide facilities such as control structures and type checking, but they preserve some of the direct access to the underlying hardware so useful in assembly languages. Statements in these languages translate to many machine code instructions.

Static high-order languages provide control structures and the declaration of variables, but the underlying machine is completely transparent. This fact enhances the portability of programs written in high-order languages, but forces the use of assembly language subprograms when access to the underlying machine features is required. Storage allocation is static and is made at compile time. COBOL and FORTRAN are the best-known static high-level languages.

Block-structured languages are distinguished from static high-order languages principally by their ability to provide a limited form of dynamic storage allocation called block structuring. The program is divided into program blocks—clearly delineated areas of the program, such as subprograms. Execution of a program requires a run-time support system which allocates storage upon entry into a block and deallocates the same storage when the block is exited. Upon entry to each block, program execution is interrupted so that the run-time support system can allocate the required storage. Thus, the storage requirements are not known at compile time. Furthermore, since storage allocation is dynamic, variables of the program are actually created and destroyed as the program executes—thus creating areas of the program in which certain variables exist and other areas in which they do not. This fact underlies the concept of the *scope* of a variable or of some other program entity. Block-structured languages are also characterized by the ability to classify program objects as being of a certain type. Like the languages ALGOL and Pascal, from whch it was derived, Ada is a block-structured language.

Finally, *dynamic high-order languages* are distinguished by the feature that all storage allocation is done dynamically. Execution of individual statements in a dynamic high-order language can cause storage allocation or deallocation. The LISP language, now coming into wide use in artificial intelligence applications, is an example of a dynamic high-order language.

It is important to recognize the fact that the Ada language is a block-structured high-order language, as indicated in Figure 1.3, for then many of the language features become more understandable. For example, blocks in the Ada language are represented by the three basic program units—subprograms, packages, and tasks. Each of these program units may have a declarative region in which objects requiring storage are declared. Execution of code within these blocks is preceded by dynamic allocation of the storage required for execution of the block—or at least an implementation of the language must behave as though dynamic storage allocation takes place in this manner. The process by which a declaration achieves its effect in the Ada language is termed *elaboration*. It is important to note that elaboration takes place during program execution, not at compile time.

The basic functional entity in the Ada language is the *program unit*. An Ada program is composed of one or more of these program units. Each program unit can be independently written, compiled, tested, and stored in a program library. A program unit, in turn, normally consists of two parts: the specification, which contains information pertinent to the interfacing of the program unit with other program units, and the

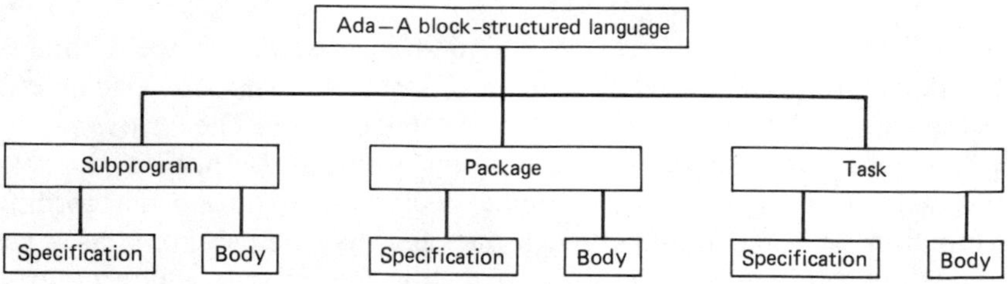

Figure 1.3. Ada's program units.

body, which contains the implementation details in terms of executable statements. The specification and body of a subprogram or package may themselves be separately compiled, further enhancing the capability of developing a large program as a set of nearly independent software components. This feature of the Ada language is key to the management of software complexity, and in turn contributes to the reliability, modifiability, and reusability of Ada software.

1.1.3.1 Subprograms. As in other languages, the Ada subprogram is normally used to implement an algorithm. There are two basic kinds of subprograms—procedures and functions. Procedures produce a series of actions by the use of executable statements, and they may communicate with the calling environment through the use of parameters. The procedure is normally the basic executable unit of an Ada program—that is, the main program is normally a procedure. Functions, on the other hand, are used to compute a value, which is then returned to the calling environment under the function name. All of this sounds very much like the description of subprograms in other languages, but in the Ada language the concept of a subprogram is coupled with strong type checking and other features which tend to enhance the modifiability, reliability, and reusability of Ada software.

Additional features of Ada's subprograms include the ability to separately declare and compile the specification and the body of the subprogram. The specification constitutes the interface of the subprogram with other program units, so that, once the specification is compiled, other program units—in the process of their compilation—may reference the subprogram, even if the body of the subprogram has not yet been compiled. The body, on the other hand, is the actual implementation of the algorithm expressed by the subprogram. It contains the executable code comprising the process implied by the algorithm. Because the interface with the calling environment is affected only by the specification, the body of a properly designed Ada subprogram may be modified and recompiled without requiring recompilation of other program units.

1.1.3.2 Packages. Packages are unique to the Ada language, although a similar feature exists in the Modula-2 language. The Ada package is used to encapsulate groups of logically related entities. The term *logically related entities* refers to any set of program entities—subprograms, packages, tasks, type declarations, or object declarations—grouped according to function or application. Thus, a package may be as simple as a set of constant declarations, such as English-to-metric conversion factors, or it may be a set of subprograms and an associated set of type and

object declarations, such as a subprogram package designed to perform complex matrix manipulation.

Ada's packages also may have separately compilable specifications and bodies, with the specification representing the interface between the package and other program units by which it is referenced. The ability to compile the specification prior to compiling the body—or for that matter, even prior to writing the body—enhances the functionality of the package concept in the large system design environment, in which several programming teams may be working more or less independently on different software components of the same system. The package concept also enhances the modifiability of software, since package bodies may be modified at will and, as long as the specification remains intact, the interfacing of the package to other program units remains unchanged.

Ada's packages are also important to the concept of reusable software. They hold promise for a "black-box" approach to software development, analogous to the effect that large-scale integration has had on hardware development. Packages that implement certain algorithms, for example, can be marketed by specifying only the input-output relationships of the package. The actual implementation—represented by the body of the package and analogous to the semiconductor chip in an integrated circuit package—is of no importance to the user. Only that information contained in the specification—analogous to the pin-out configuration of an integrated circuit package—need be known to the user, together with a general description of the algorithm that is implemented. Indeed, Ada's package concept, combined with the portability provided by other language features, offers promise of a software industry long needed but never really provided by other languages.

1.1.3.3 Tasks. Concurrent processing in sequential machines—the process by which there is more than one related set of sequential statements being executed simultaneously, either on separate processors or time-sliced on a single processor—is not a unique requirement of embedded systems. For many years large mainframe systems have provided multiprogramming or multiprocessing features to enhance processor utilization and to provide a multiuser environment. More recently, operating systems for microprocessor-based machines have provided this capability, even in computers of modest size. In the embedded-system environment, concurrent processing is used not so much for processor efficiency as it is to satisfy the requirement that the system respond to stimuli from its environment in what is termed *real time*. That is, the response generated by the system to a set of input stimuli must be produced in a time frame appropriate for the response. Since there may be several—or even many—

sets of stimuli requiring attention by the computer, and since they gene occur at random times, it is often necessary to resort to concurrent processing in order to ensure appropriate real-time processing of the input data. In systems using languages other than the Ada language, the synchronization of and communication among concurrently executing sections of code is accomplished in one of two ways. For those programs written in assembler, an executive routine of some sort—probably interrupt-driven—is written to provide the synchronization function. For those programs written in a high-order language, a run-time support package—termed a *real-time operating system*—is linked with the program and the result loaded into the target computer memory. These real-time operating systems normally provide an interface with the underlying hardware at a primitive level. These primitive system functions usually include provisions for input-output, for synchronization of and communication among concurrently executing code segments, and for management of memory resources. While the use of a real-time operating system relieves the programmer of the necessity for dealing with the underlying hardware at a primitive level, it still requires him to step out of the high-order language and into the operating system by use of operating system calls. Since these system calls are specific to the particular real-time operating system, and since the operating system itself is often machine specific, the portability of the resulting program suffers.

Concurrent processing in the Ada language is provided by the task structure. A task is a set of instructions, together with associated type and object declarations, which is executed concurrently with other tasks either through multiprocessing or through time-slicing on a single processor. Tasks, like subprograms and packages, have a specification and a body, but task specifications and bodies cannot be separately compiled. The advantage that Ada's tasks provide is the fact that task synchronization and intertask communication can be effected directly in the high-order language, thus precluding the necessity for explicit interaction with the underlying operating system. Such interaction is still present in an Ada program, of course, but it is implicitly provided as a response to the execution of statements in the high-order language. The process by which synchronization of and communication among concurrently executing tasks are accomplished is called the *rendezvous*. A rendezvous is produced when certain statements are executed in the two communicating tasks.

1.1.3.4 Generic Units. A very powerful feature of the Ada language, and one that is made necessary as a result of the strong typing characteristics of the language, is its capability of providing generic program units. This feature permits the programmer to parameterize either a package or a subprogram in a manner that can best be explained by use of a simple example. Suppose a requirement exists in a program for a subprogram that will sort the elements of an array. The array elements may be either integers or characters. In many languages, a single sort subprogram could be used for this purpose, since the algorithm is the same in either case. In the Ada program, however, the strong typing characteristics of the language prohibit the assignment of character values to objects of type INTEGER, or the assignment of integer values to objects of type CHARACTER. Thus, two sort programs will be required—one for an integer array and one for a character array. A preferred alternative would be to provide a generic sort subprogram, complete in every detail except for the type of the element of the array to be sorted. A copy of the generic subprogram can be obtained, with the missing type provided, by a single Ada statement providing what is termed an *instantiation* of the generic subprogram. The generic subprogram may be instantiated any number of times, creating any number of copies. Furthermore, different types may be provided for each instantiation. There are restrictions on the types which can be specified at instantiation, but the utility of this feature is immediately evident.

Ada's generic units comprise generic subprograms and generic packages, as indicated in Figure 1.4. They are usually considered to be templates from which corresponding subprograms or packages can be obtained through the process of instantiation. The generic unit may be parameterized, as in the example above, and the parameters may be types, they may be objects (i.e., they may be variables or constants), or they may be subprograms. The program unit resulting from instantiation of a generic unit is called an *instance* of the generic unit. An instance of a generic subprogram is a subprogram, an instance of a generic package is a package. Generic units are not executable, but instances of generic units are executable.

Ada's generic facility aids greatly in helping the programmer accommodate the strong typing feature of the language, but its usefulness

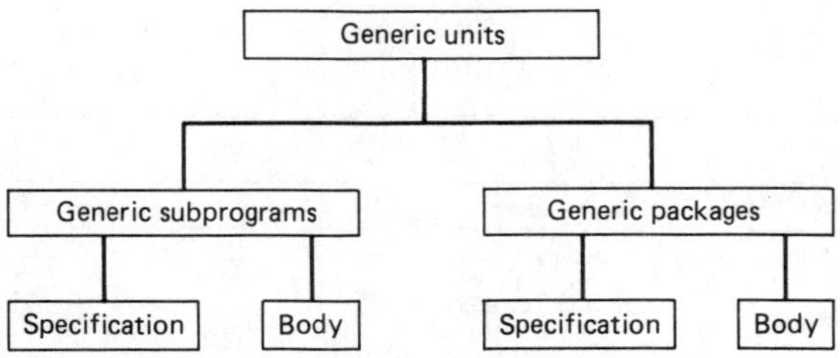

Figure 1.4. Ada's generic units.

extends much further. The utility of the application of generic units to the implementation of reusable software seems quite evident.

1.1.4 Ada's Data Types

Data objects in the Ada language belong to a type that specifies the values that may be assigned to the object and the operations that apply to the object. Ada's data types usually have an identifier associated with them, but there may be objects whose type has no name, in which case the object is said to be of an *anonymous* data type. The strong typing features manifest themselves in the fact that the type of an object is checked whenever any operation is applied to the object, in order to ensure that there is type compatibility between the object and the operation. Type checking is done primarily at compile time, but there are occasions in which it may occur at elaboration time.

The strong typing feature of the Ada language is much more pronounced than in other languages such as Pascal because, for reasons to be explored later, nearly all objects in a properly designed Ada program are of user-defined data types of some kind. Furthermore, two objects that can assume the same values—for example, integer values—can be of distinctly different types and therefore cannot be mixed in any kind of arithmetic operation. To the experienced programmer encountering the Ada language for the first time this feature may seem rather outrageous, but some reflection should indicate that the reliability and modifiability of a program are enhanced by strong typing. Typing conflicts usually indicate some underlying problem in the program design, and these conflicts in an Ada program are detected at compile time. For this reason languages that are not so strongly typed, or that provide implicit type conversion when typing conflicts are detected, produce less reliable software.

While a given Ada program may have many different data types declared within the program, these data types all fall into one of four general classes, as indicated in Figure 1.5: (1) scalar data types, (2) composite

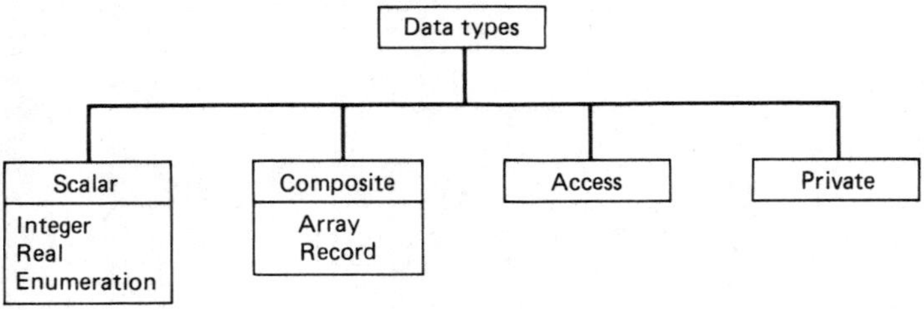

Figure 1.5. Ada's data types.

data types, (3) access data types, and (4) private data types. It is important to note that these are classes of data types. For example, there is no Ada data type named SCALAR, but in an Ada program there may be declared any number of named data types of this class, all of which are generically called scalar data types.

1.1.4.1 Scalar Data Types. The class of scalar data types has three subclasses: (1) integer data types, (2) real data types, and (3) enumeration data types. As with the primary classes, there are no data types named REAL or ENUMERATION, although there is a predefined INTEGER type. Rather, a program may declare named types belonging to one of these classes. Two different types belonging to the same class—for example, integer types—have the same properties but are distinctly different types. Two integer data types, for example, have common arithmetic operations defined, but objects of these types cannot be mixed in an arithmetic operation.

Integer data types have associated with them a set of values which is a consecutive range of integers. The Ada language provides flexibility in the declaration of an integer type in that a range of values must be specified, and values outside the range are not permitted to be assigned to objects of that type.

Real data types in any programming language represent only approximations to the real numbers, since a finite number of bits must be used to represent the mantissa of a real data type. For example, if the mantissa—expressed as a fractional part always less than one—is represented by 24 bits, then there are only 2^{24} different mantissa values that objects of the type can assume. Real values that are not precisely equal to one of these representable values are, by necessity, approximated by one of the representable values. The result, of course, is that the representation of real numbers in any machine is actually discrete; thus, the representation belies the continuous character of the real numbers. Most programming languages ignore this fact, leaving the consideration of the accuracy with which real numbers are represented to the programmer. The Ada language, on the other hand, explicitly recognizes the fact that real numbers are represented by a range of discrete values. The language rules are specific about how real data types are represented by these discrete values, which are called *model numbers*. The net result is that a programmer may declare real data types with a minimum guaranteed error bound in the representation of real numbers, a feature which greatly enhances the portability of Ada software. Error bounds are defined in terms of the model numbers of the type.

Real data types are further divided into two categories: (1) floating-point types, which provide a relative representation error bound, and (2) fixed-point types, which provide an absolute representation error bound. Floating-point types are analogous to real data types in any other language. They are represented by a fractional mantissa and an exponent, thus making the representation error bound a function of the value. That is, the model numbers are very close together for small values, but they become farther apart as the value increases. Fixed-point types, on the other hand, are represented by integer multiples of a basic increment, making the model numbers equally spaced over the entire range of values. This flexibility in the representation of real numbers, together with the explicit recognition of errors that may be inherent in the representation, provide the Ada programmer with a great deal of control over the numeric properties of his solution.

Enumeration data types in the Ada language are almost identical to those found in Pascal and in other modern languages. The programmer, in effect, declares his own data type by explicitly listing the values that objects of the type may assume. The values are simply identifiers or character literals, and they are termed *enumeration literals*. The purpose of enumeration data types is to increase the readability, and hence the understandability and modifiability, of the software. In languages such as FORTRAN, for example, the setting of a switch would be represented by two integer values, whereas in an Ada program an enumeration data type with the values ON and OFF can be declared and used to represent the switch position.

1.1.4.2 Composite Data Types. The class of composite data types in the Ada language contains two subclasses: arrays and records. There are no data types called ARRAY or RECORD in an Ada program, but rather a program may declare named types belonging to these classes. Composite data types are those types that comprise combinations of components in some specific format. Array types and record types in the Ada language are very similar to their counterparts in other languages. In an array, all components must be of the same data type, whereas a record may have components of differing types. In an array, the components are indexed, whereas in a record they are named. Components of records and arrays can be of virtually any data type, permitting complex data structures such as arrays of records, records with array components, records with record components, and so on. The features of—and operations on—composite data types in Ada are much richer than those found in virtually any other language.

1.1.4.3 Access Data Types. The access type in the Ada language is analogous to the pointer type in other languages such as Pascal. There is no data type named ACCESS, but rather a program may declare named types belonging to this class. Ada's access types permit the programmer to accommodate situations in which dynamic storage allocation—allocation made during execution as the need is perceived by the program—is required. For example, a number of records, unknown at compile time, may be required in an on-line system. The use of access types will permit record objects to be created—that is, storage to be allocated by the run-time support system—as the need arises in program execution.

In the example just cited, the record objects created at run time are not access-type objects; rather, they are of a record type. Objects of an access type *designate* other objects—in this case, record objects—which are identified by no other means; that is, the designated objects have no name. Objects designated by access-type objects can also be deallocated, thus releasing the storage for further allocation by the run-time support system. In fact, such deallocation is often automatically effected under certain specified conditions in a process termed *garbage collection*.

1.1.4.4 Private Data Types. Ada's private data types may seem strange to experienced programmers encountering the Ada language for the first time. A type defines a set of values and a set of operations for the type. The ususal concept of a data type implies that the user is cognizant of the structure of the type and the set of values that objects of the type may assume. Private data types provide the programmer the ability to make useless to the user of a type any information regarding the structure and values of the type, and to limit operations on objects of the type to an explicit set of operations. This ability may not, at first consideration, seem to be of any particular advantage. However, the ability to declare private data types has one very important feature of permitting a programmer to produce abstract data types of his own design. An example may help clarify this statement.

In Pascal there is a data type named SET. In certain applications, this data type is very useful since objects of type SET have most of the characteristics of mathematical sets. Pascal objects of type SET have defined for them certain operations such as union, intersection, and others that relate to manipulation of mathematical sets. The user is aware of these permissible operations on objects of type SET, but just how the objects are implemented by the language is hidden. It is not that the language implementer did not want the user to know how objects of type SET are implemented—this information could be obtained by examining the compiler. It is just that such knowledge is useless to the user because it can in no way affect how a program involving the use of the SET type is written. Type SET is an abstract data type—objects of the type can be declared and manipulated using a specified set of operations, but the implementation details are hidden from the user. Ada's private data types have precisely this feature, and therefore they enable the programmer to create abstract data types with features specifically tailored to his particular application. For example, an abstract data type equivalent in every way to Pascal's SET type can be created in an Ada program by use of the private data type.

1.1.5 Ada's Control Structures

The control structures in the Ada language are similar to those found in any modern language. The if and case statements constitute the conditional control statements. The case statement has a slightly different syntax than that found in languages such as Pascal, but the basic function is the same. The if statement has the usual if-then-else format, with nested if's included by the reserved word **elsif.**

The iterative structure in the Ada language is the loop, which is bounded by the reserved words **loop** and **end loop.** Controlled looping is provided by either a while or a for condition. An Ada loop can be exited from any location by execution of an exit statement.

1.2 THE ADA STANDARD

The name Ada is a registered trademark of the United States Government, Department of Defense, Under Secretary for Research and Engineering. The use of the Ada trademark is administered by the Ada Joint Program Office (AJPO). The Department of Defense freely makes use of the term Ada—under a set of very mild conditions—available to those who use it to indicate conformance with the standard specification of the Ada language. This specification is formalized as both a Military Standard (MIL-STD) and as a standard of the American National Standards Institute (ANSI). The document defining the standard is for sale by the Superintendent of Documents, U.S. Government Printing Office, and is entitled *Reference Manual for the Ada Programming Language,* ANSI/MIL-STD-1815A-1983—referred to here as the language reference manual, or LRM. The suite of test programs used in validation of a candidate Ada implementation tests the candidate implementation against the specification of the language contained in the language reference manual.

1.2.1 The Extent of the Standard

The standard specifies language features, but does not specify how these features are produced in any given implementation. In particular, the standard specifies

- the form of an Ada program unit
- the effect of translating and executing an Ada program unit
- the manner in which Ada program units may be combined to form Ada programs
- the predefined program units that an implementation must provide
- the permissible variations within the standard and the manner in which they must be specified
- those violations of the standard that must be detected
- the effect of attempting to translate or execute a program containing detected violations of the standard
- those violations of the standard that need not be detected.

On the other hand, the standard does not specify

- the means by which an Ada program unit is transformed into executable object code
- the means by which translation or execution of an Ada program unit is invoked
- the size of the object code resulting from the translation of Ada source code
- the relative execution speeds of different language constructs
- the form or content of any listings produced by an implementation
- the form or content of error or warning messages
- the effect of executing a program unit that contains a violation of the standard not required to be detected
- the maximum size of a program or program unit

The general concept is one of specifying what *effect* an implementation must produce, but leaving open the precise manner in which this effect is produced. This approach leaves implementation details up to the compiler designer and promotes a competitive approach to compiler development.

Because the language standard is not specific in how certain features are implemented, it may be possible for a program to execute differently in two different implementations, if the program requires a particular implementation technique for proper operation. In general, the Ada standard requires that programs themselves conform with certain rules that are specified throughout the text. Conformance with these rules ensures that a program does not depend upon some optional implementation feature for proper operation, and thus it promotes the portability of Ada software. Programs that violate these rules are said to be *erroneous*. Compilers are not required to provide either compile-time or run-time detection of an erroneous program, nor are they required to properly execute erroneous programs.

Similarly, during execution of particular Ada code constructs certain actions are specified to occur, but the order in which the actions are performed is not specified by the language standard. Thus, an implementation may perform these actions in any order, so long as the net result is in conformance with the standard. Any program that depends upon a specific order for proper operation will not be portable. Such programs are said to exhibit *incorrect order dependencies*. An Ada compiler is not required to provide either compile-time or run-time detection of incorrect order dependencies. Thus, it is the programmer's responsibility to ensure that his program is not erroneous and does not depend upon incorrect order dependencies for proper operation. Either of these characteristics can remain undetected in what is apparently a properly operating program, until the program is ported to a different implementation.

1.2.2 Conformity with the Standard

In order to be in conformance with the standard, an Ada implementation must

- correctly translate and execute correct Ada programs, so long as the storage capacity of the implementation is not exceeded
- reject all program units that exceed the capacity of the implementation
- reject all programs containing violations whose detection is required by the standard
- supply all predefined program units required by the standard
- contain no variations except where such variations are explicitly permitted by the standard
- specify, in the manner prescribed by the standard, all permitted variations included in the implementation

The purpose of the validation procedures is to ensure that a candidate implementation conforms with the standard in the manner just described.

1.2.3 The Language Reference Manual

The primary purpose of the language reference manual (LRM) is to provide the Ada standard to those involved in implementing the language. Nevertheless, it also serves as the ultimate reference document for Ada programmers. The LRM contains 14 chapters and three annexes, and it constitutes the standard for the Ada language.

Chapter 1	Introduction
Chapter 2	Lexical Elements

Chapter 3	Declarations and Types
Chapter 4	Names and Expressions
Chapter 5	Statements
Chapter 6	Subprograms
Chapter 7	Packages
Chapter 8	Visibility Rules
Chapter 9	Tasks
Chapter 10	Program Structure and Compilation Issues
Chapter 11	Exceptions
Chapter 12	Generic Units
Chapter 13	Representation Clauses and Implementation-Dependent Features
Chapter 14	Input-Output
Annex A	Predefined Language Attributes
Annex B	Predefined Language Pragmas
Annex C	Predefined Language Environment

There are also three appendices—containing a glossary, a syntax summary, and the specification of how implementation-dependent characteristics must be documented.

Because the LRM is the final authority in questions relating to composition rules for and the effect of constructs in Ada code, the reader will undoubtedly need to develop a familiarity with the LRM. For this reason, and because some systematic manner of specifying Ada syntax will be required in the sequel, it will be the policy in this book to describe the form of Ada constructs by use of the same context-free syntax as is used in the LRM. This policy will permit the reader to refer to the LRM without change of syntax notation. The notation used is a modified Backus-Naur-form, in which

- Meaningful words written in lowercase letters are used to represent general categories of syntax. For example:

```
simple_name
expression
discriminant_part
```

  Embedded underlines are used to emphasize that syntax notation is implied
- Reserved words are written in lowercase boldface. For example:

```
procedure
array
record
if
```

- Optional terms are enclosed in square brackets. For example,

```
return_statement ::= return[expression]
```

indicates that the syntax of a return statement is the reserved word **return,** optionally followed by an expression.

- Terms that may be repeated zero or more times are enclosed in braces. For example,
```
identifier_list ::= identifier {,identifier}
```
indicates that the syntax of an identifier list is at least one identifier, followed by zero or more identifiers separated by commas.
- A vertical bar separates alternative items. For example,
```
real_type_definition ::=
floating_point_constraint | fixed_point_constraint
```
indicates that the syntax of a real-type definition is a floating-point constraint or a fixed-point constraint. A vertical bar occurring immediately after an opening brace implies the actual occurrence of a vertical bar.

A complete example will serve to further clarify the concept. The syntax notation for a loop statement is

```
loop_statement ::=
   [loop_simple_name:]
      [iteration_scheme)] loop
         sequence_of_statements
      end loop [loop_simple_name];
```

This notation implies that a loop may be preceded by an optional name, that there may be an optional iteration scheme preceding the reserved word **loop,** that a sequence of statements must follow the reserved word **loop,** and that the sequence of statements must be followed by the reserved words **end loop,** which in turn may optionally be followed by the optional loop name.

Further clarification of the iteration scheme is given by the syntax notation

```
iteration_scheme ::= while condition
| for loop_parameter_specification
```

indicating that either a **while** or a **for** loop can be implemented. Finally, the syntax notation

```
loop_parameter_specification ::=
   identifier in [reverse] discrete_range
```

implies that the **for** loop executes the sequence of statements once for each value of the discrete range, optionally in reverse order.

The syntax notation is indented in a manner that conforms to the recommended style of writing Ada programs. The indentation and paragraphing contained in the syntax notation are not required. Only the semicolon delimiter is significant.

In order to assist the reader in referencing previously developed material, syntax notation will be identified by syntax numbers. For example, Statement (3.21) will identify syntax notation 21 in Chapter 3.

1.3 PREDEFINED LANGUAGE ENVIRONMENT

Several references have already been made to the *predefined environment* of the Ada language. This term arises from the fact that the language standard requires that an implementation provide certain predefined program units. These predefined units are

- package STANDARD
- package CALENDAR
- generic procedure UNCHECKED_DEALLOCATION
- generic function UNCHECKED_CONVERSION
- generic package SEQUENTIAL_IO
- generic package DIRECT_IO
- package TEXT_IO
- package IO_EXCEPTIONS
- package LOW_LEVEL_IO

The predefined units provide support to any Ada program needing the kind of service provided by the unit. The fact that they are included in the language specification makes such support standard across all Ada implementations. Discussion of the functions served by each of the predefined program units will not be presented in detail at this point, but instead will be deferred until the unit is encountered in the proper context. A brief discussion of a few of the predefined units is necessary here, however, because these units will be used to provide examples of some of the features of the language in subsequent chapters. The predefined program units can be found in Appendices A and C.

1.3.1 Package STANDARD

Ada has no data types built into the language itself. Instead, those types that are predefined in Ada are declared in the predefined package named STANDARD. Since package STANDARD is a program unit, type declarations within the package conform to all Ada syntax rules. All data types used in an Ada program must either be declared in the program itself or be declared in package STANDARD or in one of the other predefined units. The predefined types declared in package STANDARD are

- BOOLEAN
- INTEGER
- FLOAT
- CHARACTER
- STRING
- DURATION

Certain exceptions are also predefined in package STANDARD.

Just as there are no data types built into the language, neither are there operations, such as mathematical or logical functions, integral to the language itself. These operations are also provided by package STANDARD as subprograms declared for each of the predefined data types. Thus, the listing of the specification of package STANDARD serves as the ultimate reference for Ada's predefined types and for operations on those predefined types.

1.3.2 Other Predefined Program Units

It is not possible to discuss in any detail the remaining predefined program units until the reader has mastered some of the features of the language. At this point, only the following very general overview can be given:

- Package CALENDAR—provides the basic time function for an Ada program. Time intervals and second, hour, day, month, and year—together with associated operations—are provided by the package.
- Package SYSTEM—provides definitions of certain configuration-dependent characteristics. The contents of this package are implementation-dependent, but it must contain information relating to data representation capability of the implementation.
- Generic procedure UNCHECKED_DEALLOCATION—relates to the manner in which storage allocated to objects designated by an access type can be deallocated.
- Generic function UNCHECKED_CONVERSION—relates to the manner in which explicit conversion from one data type to another is accomplished.
- Generic package SEQUENTIAL_IO—provides operations for the input and output of sequential files. There is no input-output facility inherent in the language; there is only that capability provided by the predefined program units.
- Generic package DIRECT_IO—provides operations for the input and output of direct-access files.

- Package TEXT_IO—provides operations for the input and output of text files.
- Package IO_EXCEPTIONS—provides predefined exceptions for input-output operations.
- Package LOW_LEVEL_IO—provides implementation-dependent input and output operations acting on physical devices.
- Package MACHINE_CODE—provides for the embedding of machine code instructions within an Ada program.

One final comment is in order regarding input-output in the Ada language. With most languages, the executable module produced by the compilation and linking of programs is burdened with a comprehensive set of input-output routines, some of which may not be required by the specific program being executed. By providing input-output capability through the use of predefined program units which are optionally included in the compilation of an Ada program, the language promotes efficiency of resources. This feature is particularly effective in the host-target environment usually employed in embedded-system program development. The host computer, on which program development takes place and which must support software development tools, usually has an input-output requirement vastly different from that of the target machine, on which the operational program must eventually execute. By judicious use of the predefined input-output packages, a program designer can ensure that the target system software bears the burden only of the required input-output facilities.

REFERENCES

1. Ross, D. T., Goodenough, J. B., and Irvine, C. A., Software Engineering: Process, Principles, and Goals, *Computer: 65* (May 1975).
2. Ibid.
3. Sommerville, I., *Software Engineering* (Reading, Mass.: Addison-Wesley, 1982).

EXERCISES

1. Give your interpretation of the term *software engineering*.
2. Define the following terms: information hiding; abstraction; modularization; localization.
3. Discuss how each of the characteristics of Exercise 2 can affect the reliability of software.
4. Discuss how each of the characteristics of Exercise 2 can affect the modifiability of software.
5. Discuss how each of the characteristics of Exercise 2 can affect the understandability of software.

6. What is meant by the term *graceful degradation?*
7. Distinguish between the meaning of the term *portability* and that of the term *reusability*.
8. List the general characteristics of the Ada language that are related to the fact that it is a block-structured language.
9. List the differences between subprograms and packages.
10. Discuss the differing requirements leading to the need for concurrent processing in operating systems and in embedded systems.
11. Discuss the relationship between the strong typing feature of the Ada language and Ada's generic units.
12. Distinguish between Ada's fixed-point and floating-point data types.
13. Compare Ada's data types to those of Pascal.
14. Compare Ada's control structures to those of Pascal.
15. Explain how trademarking of the term Ada enhances the standardization of the language.
16. Explain what is meant by the term *erroneous* when applied to an Ada program.
17. Explain what is meant by the term *incorrect order dependencies* when applied to an Ada program.
18. List the data types that are declared in package STANDARD.
19. Discuss the difference between the manner in which input-output support is achieved in Ada and that in which it is achieved in most other languages.
20. Discuss the concept of an abstract data type.
21. Describe the host-target environment as it applies to embedded computer systems.

Chapter 2
HISTORY OF THE ADA LANGUAGE

2.1 THE PROBLEM IN SOFTWARE DEVELOPMENT

A legitimate question asked by the experienced programmer when first encountering the Ada language is, "Why must we have yet another language, and one that is such a radical departure from current programming practice?" The answer to this question—and indeed a deeper appreciation of many features of the Ada language—can be obtained by examining the history behind the development of the language within the Department of Defense, and by examining the general status of software development in the early 1970s. By the late 1960s, it was clear to perceptive individuals in the programming field that the exploding computer technology was not making software development easier by providing more capable hardware—in fact, just the opposite trend was occurring. As the computational power of computers grew at an explosive rate—a phenomenon still occurring today—the applications for computers grew in proportion, and it was the software development capability that became the critical shortcoming of the industry. As Dijkstra put it in his classic Turing Award Lecture in 1972,

> . . . when we had a few weak computers, programming became a mild problem, and now that we have gigantic computers programming has become an equally gigantic problem. In this sense, the electronic industry has not solved a single problem, it has only created them—it has created the problem of using its products.[1]

If the capability of modern computers inspired Dijkstra to make this comment in 1972—two years before the term microprocessor was even coined—think of its appropriateness today.

The primary problem manifesting itself was the reliability of software, and this fact first emerged from the Conference on Software Engineering held in Garmisch in October 1968. Again in the words of Dijkstra,

> . . . it is generally recognized that the design of any large sophisticated system is going to be a very difficult job, and whenever one meets people responsible for such undertakings, one finds them very much concerned about the reliability issue, and rightly so.[2]

In addition to the machines getting more powerful, they were getting less expensive, a trend that has been even more pronounced since the introduction of the microprocessor. Since programming is a labor-intensive activity with ever-increasing costs, the result has been a steady increase in the proportion of system development cost allocated to software development. When one considered life-cycle costs, the tendency was even more pronounced, since poor reliabililty was making software maintenance very costly. It has been estimated that 60% of life-cycle software costs are incurred by software maintenance,[3] making software reliability and modifiability prime factors in determining life-cycle costs.

The United States Department of Defense is the world's largest user of computers. The mounting problem in software development is of critical concern to the Department of Defense for two reasons. First, of course, is the fact that software reliability directly affects weapon system reliability—a critical concern to defense planners. The second reason involves the ever-present budgetary consideration—software costs are becoming the principal factor in embedded computer costs, and those related to embedded computers are becoming an appreciable part of the total cost of any modern weapon system. It is also known that embedded-system software costs are by far the major contributor to the overall software budget within the Department of Defense. Perhaps the most condemning indictment of the state of software development in the mid 1970s is given in a requirements report for what turned out to be the Ada language: Problems "appear in the form of software that is non-responsive to user needs, unreliable, excessively expensive, untimely, inflexible, difficult to maintain, and not reusable."[4] The same report assesses the role of programming languages in addressing software development problems: "Programming languages are neither the cause nor the solution to software problems, but because of the central role they play in all software activity, they can either aggravate existing problems or simplify their solution."[5] This concept was one of the driving forces behind the development of the Ada language.

2.1.1 The Proliferation of Languages

Several studies conducted in the early 1970s indicated that the software problems in the Department of Defense were being compounded by a proliferation of languages being used. Not only were a great number of languages in use, but on many projects custom languages were being developed. These specialized languages were often of poor quality, and they often led to language and compiler problems late in the system development cycle. The Department of Defense, in response to the language proliferation problem, established the High Order Language Working Group (HOLWG) with the goal of standardizing to a few well-specified, well-maintained languages in order to ensure the availability of production-quality compilers for Department of Defense computers.

The initial step was to standardize on a set of seven existing languages, which was made official policy by the Department of Defense Directive 5000.31 in November 1976. The seven languages were

- FORTRAN
- COBOL
- TACPOL
- CMS-2
- SPL/1
- JOVIAL J3
- JOVIAL J73

While FORTRAN and COBOL are familiar to any experienced programmer as the standards for scientific computation and data processing, respectively, the remaining five languages may not be recognized by those not involved with programming for computers embedded in weapon systems. TACPOL is an army-sponsored embedded computer language, CMS-2 and SPL/1 are navy-sponsored, and JOVIAL is an air force language.

2.1.2 The Need for a New Language

Although standardization to the seven specified languages was a useful interim step, the Department of Defense management was convinced that none of these languages was adequate for the long term, principally because of the more fundamental problems arising in software development. In fact, when the interim language standardization was implemented, all three services were proposing new languages to overcome inadequacies in those languages on the interim list. Embedded-system language requirements not well supported by existing languages included concurrent processing, exception handling, real-time input-output, interfacing to special hardware, and access to the underlying operating system. Furthermore, it was recognized that, if the numbers of approved languages could be reduced, the reusability of software could be enhanced and training costs could be minimized.

The primary task of the High Order Language Working Group was the specification of the requirements for Department of Defense embedded computer programming languages. The first attempt at defining the requirements of a new high-order language was aptly termed STRAWMAN and was published in April 1975. The STRAWMAN requirements were circulated through the military, industrial, and academic communities for comment. Responses from the STRAWMAN review were incorporated into the second iteration, termed WOODENMAN, which was then circulated for further comment in August 1975. Finally, the TINMAN requirements were published in June 1976 and represented the standard with which a Department of Defense embedded computer programming language should conform.

Once the TINMAN requirements were specified, it was known what capabilities a high-order language should exhibit. The next step was to compare currently viable languages to the requirements. Twenty-three high-order languages were examined, including the seven on the interim list and the well-known languages PL/1, ALGOL 60, ALGOL 68, and Pascal. When no existing language satisfied more than 75% of the requirements, it was apparent that only two alternatives existed: Subset the requirements for identifiable application areas, or develop a new, more capable language to meet the requirements.

The first alternative was eliminated when studies indicated that only a small percentage of the requirements could be eliminated for any specific application area. The real problem was, as had been expressed earlier by Dijkstra, that advancements in hardware technology were taxing existing software capabilities. Additional impetus for the development of a new language was provided by three independent economic analyses, all of which indicated that economies on the order of tens of billions of dollars could be provided through the turn of the century by the development and use of a common high-order language.

2.2 THE DEVELOPMENT OF ADA

From the 23 languages reviewed by the High Order Language Working Group, three were selected as being appropriate base languages for the development of a new language. These languages were Pascal, ALGOL 68, and PL/1. The Request for Proposal for the design of the new language, which had been given the name DoD-1, was issued in April 1977. Four successful bidders were selected to participate in a competitive, six-month, first-phase design contract. Each of these four bidders had selected Pascal as the base language, which is significant in the fact that Pascal has become the most widely used vehicle for teaching software engineering methodology and structured programming principles.

The first-phase language designs were color coded to ensure anonymity in the evaluation process. The four designs were

- Blue—SoftTech
- Red—Intermetrics
- Yellow—SRI
- Green—Honeywell/Honeywell Bull

On the basis of evaluation of the first-phase design efforts, two designs were selected for further development in the second phase. These two were the Red and Green designs. In the meantime, further modification to the requirements document resulted in the IRONMAN requirements, issued in January 1977, and the revised IRONMAN in July 1977. The final requirements document, STEELMAN, was issued in June 1978. In March 1979, the Red and Green second-phase language designs were completed, and in May the Green language was selected as the common, embedded computer, high-order programming language of the Department of Defense. The green covers found on both the language reference manual and *Ada Letters*—the bimonthly publication of SIGADA, the Ada Special Interest Group within the Association of Computing Machinery (ACM)—remain today to attest to the fact the Honeywell Bull's winning design was coded green.

2.2.1 The Ada Language Definition

The final language design represented the culmination of six years of effort on the part of the Department of Defense. There were five refinements of the technical requirements; there was scientific cooperation among military, industrial, and academic communities unprecedented in any previous language design effort; there was an integration of international interests, with representatives of 15 countries involved; and the design process was open to continuous, public, scientific scrutiny. The Ada language was developed to meet specific design requirements, making it the first language to be designed using well-defined principles of software engineering.

The only tangible result of this design effort was the language reference manual. There was no compiler—only a manual specifying precisely what a compiler must and must not do. Since the language reference manual was published, several Ada compilers have been developed, both under government contract and through funding by private industry.

The name Ada was officially applied to the new language in 1979, replacing the interim name DoD-1. The name is not an acronym, as are FORTRAN and COBOL for example, but rather is a proper name. The language was named in honor of Ada Augusta, Countess of Lovelace (1815–1852), only daughter of the romantic poet Lord Byron and Lady Anabella Milbanke. Ada was a mathematician who, at an early age, became fascinated with Charles Babbage's difference engine—so much so that she spent the rest of her relatively short life involved in Babbage's work. She is recognized today as the world's first programmer.

2.2.2 The Ada Programming Support Environment

The proliferation of high-order languages had a second, more subtle, effect on software development. The greater the number of languages supported, the fewer software tools (debuggers, full capability editors, etc.) were developed, simply because of the dilution of resources. It was quickly realized that the adoption of a single high-order language would make possible a standard support environment, and in July 1978, a document outlining some technical and managerial issues of an Ada Programming Support Environment (APSE) was issued, under the name SANDMAN. This document was followed by PEBBLEMAN in December 1978, and then by the final requirements document, STONEMAN, in February 1980.[6] The STONEMAN document provides criteria for assessment and evaluation of APSE designs and offers guidance for APSE designers and implementers.

The purpose of the APSE is to support the development of Ada software and to support the maintenance of that software throughout its life cycle. The three principal features of the APSE are

1. The data base, which contains all information associated with a software project throughout its life cycle. This data relates to both technical and management issues.
2. The interface, which includes a control language for access to the data base and to software tools in the toolset.
3. The toolset, which includes tools for program development, maintenance, and configuration control.

Also addressed by the STONEMAN requirements is the portability of user programs and software tools, which is accomplished by giving requirements for two lower levels within the APSE—the Kernel Ada Programming Support Environment (KAPSE) and the Minimum Ada Programming Support Environment (MAPSE). The APSE is discussed further in Section 9.2.

2.2.3 The Ada Language Standard

The term Ada was copyrighted by the Department of Defense in 1981, soon after the requirements were developed by Honeywell Bull, with registration number 1,179,900. In December 1980, the requirements were approved as MIL-STD-1815. In February 1983, after a massive coordination effort and some slight modification to the standard, the language reference manual was issued as an ANSI standard—ANSI/MIL-STD-1815A. The history is summarized in Figure 2.1.

The Ada Joint Program Office (AJPO), within the Office of Under Secretary for Research and Engineering, U.S. Department of Defense, was established in December 1980, and was charged with promotion of the Ada language. Since that time the AJPO has assumed several responsibilities, not the least of which is the establishment of the Ada Validation Office, tasked with the validation of proposed Ada compilers.

2.3 DEPARTMENT OF DEFENSE SUPPORT OF ADA

After having spent six years in the development of a state-of-the-art, high-order programming language that holds promise of vast economies

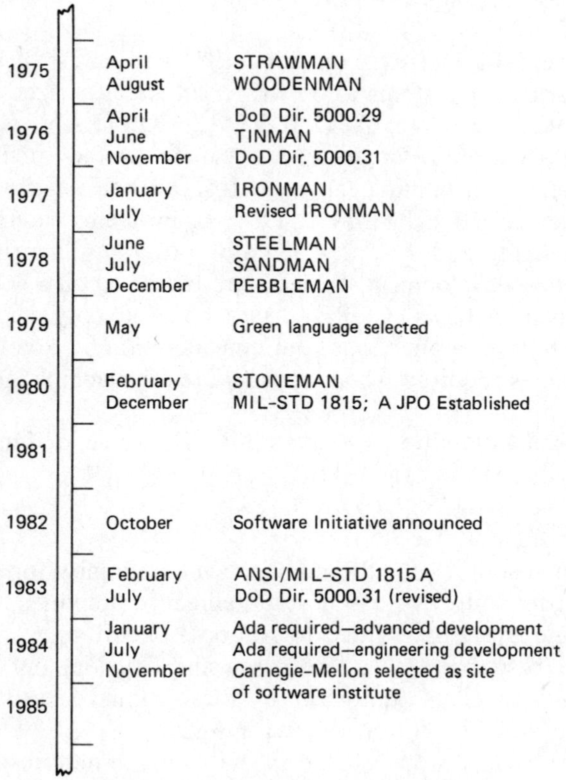

Figure 2.1. History of the Ada language.

in software life-cycle costs, the Department of Defense initiated a systematic approach to the promotion of the language. The establishment of the Ada Joint Program Office was the first step, but decisive actions were necessary to bring the three services and their contractors into the process.

2.3.1 Department of Defense Directives

Since the Department of Defense first became concerned about the software development problem in the mid-1970s, it has issued several directives that directly affect software development. Two of the more important directives are listed here.

1. Directive 5000.29, April 1976—required the use of a DoD-approved high-order language in defense systems. This directive curtailed the use of assembler languages.
2. Directive 5000.31, November 1976—reduced the list of DoD-approved high-order languages to seven.

   Directive 5000.31 (revised), June 1983—requires all software for mission-critical systems to be written in an authorized language, of which there are five: Ada, JOVIAL, FORTRAN, COBOL, and ATLAS. The Ada language is specified as the single, common, computer programming language for Defense mission-critical applications, effective January 1, 1984, for programs entering advanced development, and July 1, 1984, for programs entering full-scale engineering development. Waivers are permitted on a specific system or subsystem basis. COBOL is to be used only for business or administrative applications, but consideration of Ada for these applications is required where appropriate for machine independence.

Mission Critical Computer Resources (MCCR) are defined in accordance with 10 U.S.C. 2315[7] as follows:

A. Intelligence Systems:
   Computer resources for the intelligence community for the research and development of or use in its intelligence activities.
B. Cryptologic Systems Related to National Security:
   Computer resources for the research and development of or use in cryptologic activities authorized by the National Security Agency.
C. Command and Control of Military Forces:
   Computer resources in or used in the research and development of

1. the National Military Command and Control Systems, and
2. Worldwide Military Command and Control Systems, and
3. DoD Component Command and Control systems.

D. Integral Part of a Weapon System:
Computer resources
1. physically a part of, dedicated to, or essential in real time to performance of weapon systems,
2. used for specialized training, diagnostic testing and maintenance, simulation, or calibration of weapon systems, and
3. used for research and development of weapon systems.

E. Critical to the Direct Fulfillment of Military or Intelligence Missions:
Computer resources in or used in the research and development of
1. systems that will be deployed as mission support in a combat environment,
2. war planning systems,
3. environmental systems supporting military missions (e.g., weather, oceanographic, or satellite systems),
4. projects the existence of which is classified,
5. warning, surveillance, reconnaissance, and electronic warfare systems,
6. mapping, charting, and geodesy systems,
7. airlift, sealift, and port facilities,
8. military communications systems, and
9. logistics systems that provide direct support to operating forces on maintenance of weapons systems (organic supply, software support facilities for weapons systems, etc.).

These documents serve to indicate the support that Ada is receiving within the Department of Defense. Their content is summarized in Figure 2.2.

Department of Defense Directive 5000.31 June 1983
Specifies Ada as the single, common, computer programming language for Defense mission-critical systems: • Intelligence systems • Cryptologic systems • Command and control systems • Weapon systems • Other critical uses

Figure 2.2. Department of Defense policy on the use of Ada.

2.3.2 Department of Defense Software Initiative

The infusion of a new, more capable programming language into the software development process will not solve the basic problem identified by Dijkstra in 1972—that programs must be intellectually manageable. Programming is a human activity, and therefore the complexity of a program design must be managed. This does not mean that programs must be kept small, but rather that large programs must be designed in a manner that accommodates the human limitation on complexity. There are well-defined software engineering techniques for managing complexity of software—those of abstraction, information hiding, modularity, and localization. Ada was designed with these concepts in mind; it remains to develop methodologies that exploit the full capabilities of the language.

In late 1982, the Department of Defense announced its Software Initiative,[8] a program intended to improve the state of the art in software technology and to exploit the advantages of computer technology through software. The Software Initiative complements hardware initiatives within the Department of Defense, principally the Very High Speed Integrated Circuit (VHSIC) program—which holds promise for greatly improved hardware performance through the use of sub-micron feature size semiconductor technology—and the Defense Advanced Research Projects Agency (DARPA) supercomputer project. Simply stated, the goal of the initiative is to "improve software productivity while achieving greater system reliability and adaptability."[9]

To obtain its stated goal, the Software Initiative will focus on three major objectives: (1) improving personnel resources, (2) increasing the power of software tools, and (3) increasing the use of software tools. Eight specific areas have been targeted by the initiative:

1. measurement
2. human resources
3. project management
4. systems issues
5. application-specific demonstrations
6. software acquisition
7. human engineering
8. support systems

The Ada language development represents a base upon which the initiative will be developed. Through the efforts of the initiative, the full capabilities of the language will be exploited.

Two other facets of the Software Initiative have emerged. In November 1984, Carnegie-Mellon University was selected as the site of the Software Engineering Institute, established by the Department of Defense to serve as a focus for applied research and technology transfer within the initiative.

One of the primary responsibilities of the institute will be the development and integration of workstations into the software development environment. There will be a significant emphasis on knowledge-based artificial intelligence support systems[10] and on design methodologies.

The other development has been the initiation of the Software Technology for Adaptable Reliable Systems (STARS) program within the initiative. The STARS program will target improvement in the acquisition, management, development, and support of software for military systems.

These developments are also summarized in Figure 2.1.

2.4 LIABILITIES OF ADA

The Ada language has its critics, not the least of which is the eminent computer scientist C. A. R. Hoare, whose concern over the "plethora of features and notational conventions" prompted the title of his 1980 Turing Award lecture, "The Emperor's Old Clothes." So concerned was Hoare over what he perceived to be problems with the Ada language, that he wrote

> . . . And so, the best of my advice to the originators and designers of Ada has been ignored. In this last resort, I appeal to you, representatives of the programming profession in the United States, and citizens concerned with the welfare and safety of your country and of mankind: Do not allow this language in its present state to be used in application where reliability is critical, i.e., nuclear power stations, cruise missiles, early warning systems, anti-ballistic missile defense systems. The next rocket to go astray as a result of a programming language error may not be an exploratory space rocket on a harmless trip to Venus: It may be a nuclear warhead exploding over one of our own cities. An unreliable programming language generating unreliable programs constitutes a far greater risk to our environment and our society than unsafe cars, toxic pesticides, or accidents at nuclear power stations.[11]

Strangely enough, one of Hoare's primary targets was exception handling—usually considered an enhancement of run-time reliability—which he considered to be dangerous. Hoare believed that a powerful subset of the language should be selected, and that extensions should be specially designed when necessary. Subsets and extensions, of course, were counter to the design goals of the language.

Other critics expressed their views when the ACM position on the ANSI standardization of the Ada language was presented.[12] Again, the question of subsets was predominant. Many of the criticisms have been addressed by a member of the Ada design team,[13] who concludes that the Ada language can be made simpler by reducing its facilities, but it is doubtful that the resulting language would be useful to the user community in the long term.

2.5 THE FUTURE OF THE ADA LANGUAGE

The Ada language is considered by many to be the language of the future—not only for military computer systems, but for industrial and commercial applications as well. It is a state-of-the-art general-purpose language that addresses the complexity problems first identified in the early 1970s. The language provides a rich set of capabilities for use in the application of modern software engineering techniques to enhance the understandability, modifiability, and portability of software. It has the full support of the Department of Defense, both through the protection of the integrity of the design and through the support represented by the Software Initiative. There is no reason that the Ada language could not replace FORTRAN in scientific computation or COBOL for commerical software, other than the very large investments already made in software using these languages.

There can be no doubt about the Department of Defense intentions with respect to the Ada language. It will be the language used in the programming of Mission Critical Computer Resources. This, in turn, will force the language to mature as more compilers become available and as a pool of Ada programming talent develops. Since the same basic software development problems appear in military, commercial, and scientific applications, and since the Ada language and Ada technology will aid in solving these problems, there is no doubt that inroads will be made into the COBOL and FORTRAN domains. The Ada language is tailored to the characteristics of modern hardware, and hardware capabilities may well be the deciding factor.

Embedded computer systems abound outside the military arena, and these systems have many of the same requirements as military systems. Such areas as process control, factory automation, robotics, artificial intelligence, and knowledge-based systems hold promise for commercial exploitation of the language. Even in areas such as word processing and office automation—or any application in which software must be portable, or must respond to real-time stimuli, or are large and long-lived and must evolve through several generations of field changes—the Ada language holds promise offered by no other language.

REFERENCES

1. Dijkstra, E. W., "The Humble Programmer," *Communications of the ACM,* **15**(10):861 (1972).
2. Ibid.
3. Boehm, B. W., "Software Engineering," *IEEE Transactions on Computers,* **SE-5**(1):6–15 (January 1977).
4. Fisher, D. A., "A Common Programming Language for the Department of Defense—Background and Technical Requirements," Institute for Defense Analysis Report P-1191, June 1976.
5. Ibid.
6. "Requirements for Ada Programming Support Environments," U.S. Department of Defense, "STONEMAN," February 1980.
7. *Ada Information Clearinghouse Newsletter,* **II**(4) (November–December 1984), Rome, New York.
8. Emery, David E., "The Department of Defense Software Initiative, A Summary," *Ada Letters,* A Bimonthly Publication of SIGAda, the ACM Special Interest Group on Ada, **II**(4) (January, February 1983).
9. Ibid.
10. Evers, Johnny, M. S. Thesis, "A Top Down Software Documentation Procedure Using Ada," University of West Florida, 1985.
11. Hoare, C. A. R., "The Emperor's Old Clothes," given as the 1980 Turing Award Lecture, *Communications of the ACM,* **24**(2):75–83 (February 1981).
12. "Ada and the ACM Position on Standardizations," *Communications of the ACM,* **25**(6) (June 1982).
13. Wechmann, Brian A., "Is Ada Too Big? A Designer Answers the Critics," *Communications of the ACM,* **27**(2): 98–103 (February 1984).

EXERCISES

1. Describe the manner in which life-cycle cost of software can be affected by a programming language. What positive effects should the Ada language have?

2. Relate the issues of complexity of large systems to the consideration of programming as a human activity.

3. Give the reasons why a common support environment is advantageous, and why the introduction of a common language can make possible a common support environment.

Chapter 3
BASIC CONCEPTS OF THE ADA LANGUAGE

3.1 BASIC SYNTAX

Source code for a computer program is comprised of characters, which in turn form the *lexical elements* of the language in which the program is written. Lexical elements, in turn, form statements and declarations. The entire program consists of a set of characters which are interpreted by the compiler in accordance with a strict set of syntax rules. Thus, the syntax rules are fundamental to the use of the language. The Ada language is rich in syntax, and for this reason the introduction of constructs by example can often leave the reader without a full appreciation of this richness. The approach to be used in this book is to present the full syntax initially and then to illustrate use of the construct by example. Where possible, syntax notation will follow the language reference manual (LRM).[1] The hope is that any syntax notation can be followed through underlying notation to the basic character set. Terminology in the syntax notation is also important if correspondence to the LRM is to be maintained.

3.1.1 Ada's Character Set

The basic character set of the Ada language is that of the American Standard Code for Information Interchange (ASCII), subdivided into *basic* and *nonbasic* sets. The basic character set contains

- uppercase letters: A–Z
- decimal digits: 0–9
- special characters: "# & ' ( ) * + , − . / : ; < = > _ |
- the space character

Any Ada program can be written using only this basic set of characters and the horizontal tabulation, vertical tabulation, carriage return, line feed, and form feed characters, which are termed format effectors.

The remaining ASCII characters may be used in writing an Ada program. These are

- lowercase letters: a–z
- other special characters: ! $ % ? [\ ] ^ ` { } ~

Lowercase letters have the same effect as the corresponding uppercase letters, except when appearing within string and character literals. The other special characters can be transliterated into the basic character set by a method to be discussed later. Special characters in this set may be used only in character or string literals, with three exceptions involving the exclamation mark, the colon, and the percent character.

The reader is invited to examine package ASCII within the predefined package STANDARD in Appendix A for some hint as to how the other special characters are handled if an implementation supports only the basic character set.

The syntax statement for basic characters is simple, but it represents the final point of resolution to which any other syntax statement can be reduced:

```
basic_character ::=
    basic_graphic_character | format_effector   (3.1)
```

Here, the term graphic character is used to represent those ASCII characters that are printable, as opposed to the ASCII control characters such as carriage return (CR) and line feed (LF). The syntax statement is completed by:

```
basic_graphic_character ::=
    upper_case_letter | digit
  | special_character  | space_character    (3.1.1)
```

For graphic characters, the syntax statement is

```
graphic_character ::= basic_graphic_character
    | lower_case_letter | other_special_character  (3.2)
```

The reader should note that Statement (3.1) can be reduced to the character set of

- uppercase letter
- digit
- special character
- space character
- format effector

by use of Statement (3.1.1). Similarly, Statement (3.2) can be reduced to the character set

- uppercase letter
- digit
- special character
- space character
- lowercase letter
- other special character

Any syntax statement presented in this book can eventually be reduced to combinations of this character set and the format effectors.

3.1.2 Identifiers

Identifiers are groups of contiguous characters bounded on either side by a separator. A separator is a space character, a format effector, or the end of a line. Identifiers are used as names—of objects, types, subprograms, etc.—and as reserved words. The permissible characters used in forming identifiers are uppercase and lowercase letters, digits 0–9, and the underline character. The syntax statement for an identifier is

```
identifier ::=
   letter {[underline] letter_or_digit}      (3.3)
```

where

```
letter_or_digit ::= letter | digit       (3.3.1)
```

and

```
letter ::= upper_case_letter | lower_case_letter
                                           (3.3.2)
```

This combination of syntax statements implies that the first character in an identifier must be an uppercase or lowercase letter, and that it may be followed by an optional underline, in turn followed by an uppercase letter, a lowercase letter, or a digit. The sequence within the braces may be repeated any number of times, so long as the end of a line is not encountered. The brackets indicate that the underline is optional. Thus, the following represent valid identifiers:

```
EAST_VELOCITY         master_arm_position   X32
DYNAMIC_PRESSURE      Line_Count            VEL_36
BEST_OF_THREE         LineCount             S3692
```

Some examples of invalid identifiers are

```
EAST__VELOCITY    --contiguous underlines not permitted
3_TEST            --first digit must be letter
EAST VELOCITY     --space character is a separator
CR:LF             --special characters not permitted
EAST_VELOCITY_    --underline cannot be last character
```

Because lowercase letters have the same effect as uppercase letters, the following sets of identifiers are equivalent:

```
EAST_VELOCITY, East_Velocity, EAST_velocity,
BEST_OF_THREE, Best_of_Three, best_of_three,
```

and so on.

Finally, since the underline character is significant, the identifiers

```
EAST_VELOCITY, DYNAMIC_PRESSURE, and Line_Count
```

are distinct, respectively, from the identifiers

```
EASTVELOCITY, DYNAMICPRESSURE, and LineCount.
```

Statement (3.3) indicates that Ada's identifiers can be of any length, so long as they fit on a single line.

3.1.3 Literals

In a programming language, the term literal applies to an object that represents a value literally—that is, by means of letters or other characters. In the Ada language, literals are one of four following types: (1) numeric literals, (2) character literals, (3) string literals, and (4) enumeration literals. Discussion of the enumeration literal must be deferred until the enumeration type is considered in Section 3.4.1.

3.1.3.1 Numeric Literals. Numeric literals are groups of characters that represent numbers. The syntax statement is

```
numeric_literal ::= decimal_literal | based_literal
                                                    (3.4)
```

Here, a decimal literal is simply a decimal number, whose syntax is given by

```
decimal_literal ::= integer [.integer] [exponent]
                                                    (3.4.1)
```

where

```
      integer ::= digit {[underline] digit}     (3.4.2)
```

and

```
     exponent ::= E {+} integer | E - integer   (3.4.3)
```

This set of syntax statements indicates that a decimal literal must begin with an integer—even if it is zero—and may contain a decimal point followed by another integer, which in turn may be followed by an exponent. The term integer refers to a continuous set of digits, possibly with inserted underlines. The exponent consists of the letter E—uppercase or lowercase—preceded by an optional plus sign for positive exponents and by a required minus sign for negative exponents. No spaces are permitted, even in the exponent, because a space character is a separator. A zero exponent is allowed for an integer literal, but an exponent in an integer literal cannot have a minus sign.

The term based literal refers to a literal expressed in a number system other than decimal. The syntax statement is

```
based_literal ::=
   base#based_integer [.based_integer]#[exponent]
                                                  (3.4.4)
```

where

```
    base ::= integer                               (3.4.5)

    based_integer ::=
       extended_digit {[underline]extended_digit}
                                                  (3.4.6)

    extended_digit ::= digit | letter              (3.4.7)
```

The base and exponent are in decimal, and the exponent syntax is given by Statement (3.4.3). The base is the number system in which the based literal is expressed, and it must lie between 2 and 16. The only letters allowed in Statement (3.4.7) are the hexadecimal digits A–F.

Examples of numeric literals are given below.

Decimal literals:

```
0           2_143_678        1.732e-10
56          2_647.346_795    2647.346795
1.732E-10   0.27536E30       0.27536e30
5E20        0.0              0.3752
6.3E-5      0.000063         0.63E-4
```

Based literals:

```
16#7A5D#                8#6057#
16#7_A5D#               2#1011.1110_1011#
2#101110011110#         16#FC07.27FE#
2#1011_1001_1110#       16#F.FF#E+2.
```

In the last example, it should be noted that the exponent is in decimal. The equivalent decimal value of the based number is 4095.0. Also note that the embedded underlines do not affect the numeric value of the literal, and that no underlines are permitted in the exponent.

Numeric literals in the Ada language are of the data types universal-integer or universal-real and are unbounded in the values that they may assume or the precision with which they are considered to be expressed. Before a value expressed by a numeric literal is assigned to an object, it is implicitly converted to the type appropriate for the object. This concept will be discussed further when assignment is considered.

3.1.3.2 Character Literals. A character literal is a single character enclosed by two apostrophe characters. Its value is the character itself. The syntax statement is

```
character_literal ::= 'graphic_character'     (3.5)
```

The graphic character syntax is given by Statement (3.2). Examples are

'X'   'x'   '3'   '+'   '''   '{'   ' '

The last example is the space character.

3.1.3.3 String Literals. A string literal is a contiguous set of graphic characters enclosed by two quotation characters. The syntax statement is

```
string_literal ::= "{graphic_character}"     (3.5.1)
```

where the graphic character syntax is given by Statement (3.2). Thus, string literals can contain any printable ASCII character, as well as the space character. However, since the end of a line is a separator, a string literal cannot be continued to the following line. Examples of string literals are given below:

```
"PUSH TO TEST"            "LAUNCH {7}"
"ENTER WAYPOINT #6"       "Left to heading 320"
```

It is possible to concatenate string literals to form longer string objects and to embed ASCII control characters into string objects. This subject will be considered further in Section 3.6.1.7.

3.1.3.4 Comments. The understandability of software is enhanced by commenting, which is supported by nearly all programming languages. Ada's comments begin with two adjacent hyphens and extend to the end of the line. Comments may occupy an entire line or may follow the semicolon delimiter on a line containing a statement. Examples are

```
-- This section contains the coordinate transformation
INDEX := INDEX + 1; -- increment index
```

The rich use of comments is, in the Ada language as it is in other languages, highly recommended as a means of enhancing the readability—and hence the understandability—of software.

3.1.4 Reserved Words

Reserved words, sometimes called key words in other languages, are identifiers that have particular meaning to the compiler. As a consequence, reserved words must never be used as identifiers within an Ada program. Ada's reserved words are given in Table 3.1. Reserved words are identified in this book, as in the LRM, by the use of boldface lowercase letters. While the use of reserved words as identifiers is prohibited, their use in string literals or comments is permitted.

Table 3.1 Ada's Reserved Words

abort	**declare**	**generic**	**of**	**select**
abs	**delay**	**goto**	**or**	**separate**
accept	**delta**		**others**	**subtype**
access	**digits**	**if**	**out**	
all	**do**	**in**		**task**
and		**is**	**package**	**terminate**
array			**pragma**	**then**
at	**else**		**private**	**type**
	elsif	**limited**	**procedure**	
	end	**loop**		
begin	**entry**		**raise**	**use**
body	**exception**		**range**	
	exit	**mod**	**record**	**when**
			rem	**while**
		new	**renames**	**with**
case	**for**	**not**	**return**	
constant	**function**	**null**	**reverse**	**xor**

3.1.5 Delimiters

Certain special characters have specific meaning to the compiler, depending upon the context in which they are used. These special characters are called *delimiters* and are either *simple* or *compound delimiters*. Simple delimiters are given in Table 3.2, and compound delimiters in Table 3.3.

Table 3.2 Simple Delimiters

&	ampersand	.	dot, point, or period
'	apostrophe	/	slash, divide
(	left parenthesis	:	colon
)	right parenthesis	;	semicolon
+	plus	=	equal
,	comma	>	greater than
−	minus	|	vertical bar
*	star, multiply		

Table 3.3 Compound Delimiters

=>	arrow	>=	greater than or equal
..	double dot	<=	less than or equal
**	double star, exponentiate	<<	left label bracket
:=	assignment ("becomes")	>>	right label bracket
/=	inequality ("not equal")	<>	box

The precise meaning of these delimiters will be detailed when they are discussed in the context of their application. The semicolon delimiter, for example, terminates an Ada statement.

3.2 DECLARATIONS

All entities within an Ada program must be declared—in most cases explicitly—before they can be used. Entities are declared by a basic declaration, for which the syntax statement is

```
basic_declaration ::=
   object_declaration        | number_declaration
  | type_declaration         | subtype_declaration
  | subprogram_declaration   | package_declaration
  | task_declaration         | generic_declaration
  | exception_declaration    | generic_instantiation
  | renaming_declaration     | deferred_constant_declaration
                                                      (3.6)
```

The reader will no doubt recognize most of the entities within this syntax statement from the introductory remarks of Chapter 1. Eventually, each of these basic declarations will be discussed in detail; the current interest is in the type, subtype, object, and number declarations.

Declarations must occur in specified regions of an Ada program called *declarative parts*. Declarations are not executable statements in the true sense of the word, because they do not cause an action to be performed by the program in the same sense as does an executable statement. Rather, declarations are instructions to the run-time system to make the declared entity available to the program—a process called *elaboration*. How elaboration is accomplished by an implementation is not specified by the LRM, but the implementation must satisfy the rules of scope—to be discussed later—with respect to elaboration. In an efficient implementation, elaboration of certain entities implies dynamic storage allocation by the run-time system. It is important to note that, while type checking is done at compile time, elaboration is a run-time effect in an Ada program.

3.2.1 Type Declarations

A type in the Ada language is characterized by a permissible set of values and a set of operations. The four classes of types were discussed in Section 1.1.4. They are (1) scalar, (2) composite, (3) access, and (4) private. These are classes of types, not types themselves. In the sequel, an object whose type belongs to the class of scalar types will be termed a scalar object. A similar notation applies to the other three classes. Types are created by the elaboration of type declarations at run time. After a type declaration is elaborated, a program may then declare objects of the type. Objects are the Ada entities that contain values, and may be either variables or constants. The syntax statement for a type declaration is

```
type_declaration ::= full_type declaration
  | incomplete_type_declaration | private_type_declaration
                                                        (3.7)
```

where

```
full_type_declaration ::=
   type identifier [discriminant_part] is
      type_definition;                     (3.7.1)
```

and

```
type_definition ::=
   enumeration_type_definition | integer_type_definition
 | real_type_definition         | array_type_definition
 | record_type_definition       | access_type_definition
 | derived_type_definition                      (3.7.2)
```

The syntax for the various type definitions will be detailed when the types themselves are discussed.

3.2.2 Subtype Declarations

A subtype is a type with an associated constraint. The particular form of the constraint may be one of several kinds, depending upon the type. A commonly encountered constraint is a *range constraint,* by which the permissible values associated with the type are constrained to lie within a prescribed range. A subtype is not a new type, but instead gives a new name to a constrained subset of the original type. The original type used in a subtype declaration is called the *base type* of the subtype. Since no constraint at all is considered to be one of the possible constraints, types themselves can be considered to be subtypes. The base type of a type is the type itself.

The syntax statement of a subtype declaration is

```
subtype_declaration ::=
   subtype identifier is subtype_indication;   (3.8)
```

where

```
subtype_indication ::= type_mark [constraint]
                                                (3.8.1)

type_mark ::= type_name | subtype_name          (3.8.2)
```

and

```
constraint ::=
   range_constraint  | floating_point_constraint
 | index_constraint  | discriminant_constraint  (3.8.3)
```

The syntax for and use of the various constraints will be detailed when subtypes are discussed. Syntax is given by Statements (3.14.2), (3.18.1), (3.22.5), and (3.26.1), respectively.

3.2.3 Derived Type Declarations

A derived type in the Ada language is a type whose definition, as used in Statement (3.7.2), defines a new type for which the characteristics—values and set of operations—are derived from some previously declared type called the *parent type*. The parent type itself may be a subtype or a derived type. A derived type is a new type, distinct from the parent type, so that objects of a derived type cannot be combined with objects of the parent type. For example, if the parent and derived types are integer types, objects of the derived type cannot be added to objects of the parent type.

The syntax statement for the derived type definition in Statement (3.7.2) is

```
derived_type_definition ::= new subtype_indication
                                                (3.9)
```

The subtype indication is given in accordance with Statement (3.8.1) and defines the parent subtype of the derived type. Note that the subtype indication may contain a range constraint. The parent type of the derived type is the base type of the parent subtype. The parent subtype may be the base type itself, since a type is an unconstrained subtype of itself.

3.2.4 Anonymous Type Declarations

Those types declared in accordance with Statements (3.7), (3.7.1), and (3.7.2) are named types—that is, they can be referenced by the name specified by the identifier of Statement (3.7.1). These names can be used, for example, as the type name in subtype declarations corresponding to Statements (3.8), (3.8.1), and (3.8.2), or as the subtype indication in the definition of a derived type corresponding to Statement (3.9). Similarly, the derived types and subtypes obtained from declarations corresponding to Statements (3.7) and (3.8) are named types. There are occasions in which a data type is implicitly declared, in which case there is no name associated with the type. Such types are called *anonymous types,* and they will be so identified as they occur in discussion.

3.2.5 Object Declarations: Variables and Constants

In the Ada language, the term *object* applies to any entity that can be assigned a value. Objects are either *variables* or *constants* as implied by Figure 3.1, and they are created in one of several ways: through elaboration of a specific object declaration, as a parameter of a subprogram, as a generic object, as a loop parameter, as an object designated (pointed to) by an access object, or as a component of a compound object. Of particular interest here is the syntax of an explicit object declaration:

```
object_declaration ::=
    identifier_list : [constant] subtype_indication
    [:= expression];
| identifier_list : [constant]
constrained_array_definition [:= expression];      (3.10)
```

where

```
identifier_list ::= identifier {, identifier.}
                                                  (3.10.1)
```

If the optional assignment delimiter (:=) and the following expression appear in the declaration, an initial value is assigned at elaboration time. Otherwise, the value is undefined until an explicit assignment is made by execution of a statement. If the optional reserved word **constant** does not appear, then the value of the object may be changed by program

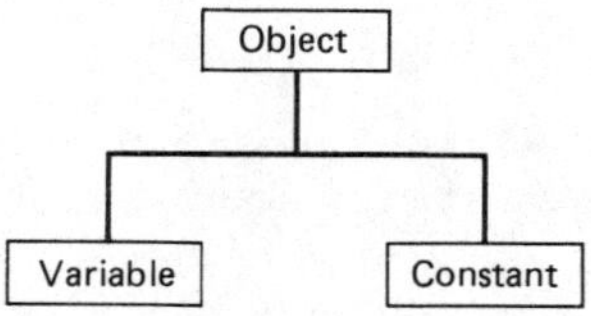

Figure 3.1. Ada objects.

execution, and the object is termed a variable. If the reserved word **constant** appears in the declaration, then the assignment delimiter and its expression must also appear. The value of the expression is assigned to the object upon elaboration and is static throughout execution; that is, its value cannot be changed. In this case, the object is termed a constant. It should be noted that the initializing expression need not be static in either case above; that is, it can contain variables.

The particular form of object declaration by which constant objects with numerical values are declared is called a *number declaration*. The syntax for a number declaration is a special form of Statement (3.10):

```
number_declaration ::=
  constant := universal_static_expression;
                                              (3.10.2)
```

Examples are

```
PI            : constant := 3.141_592_654;
FOOT_TO_METER : constant := 0.3048006;
KILOBYTE      : constant := 2**10;
```

The initializing values are of type universal_real and universal_integer. Objects declared by number declarations are called named numbers. Further examples of object declarations are deferred until specific data types are discussed.

3.2.6 Attributes

Objects and types in the Ada language have a set of named characteristics known as attributes. These attributes have values, either numeric or boolean, which can be obtained under the attribute name at run time. Appendix B contains the required set of attributes that must be provided by an implementation. Additional attributes may be provided in accordance with the conformity requirement of Section 1.2.2.

The syntax statement for an attribute is

```
attribute ::= prefix'attribute_designator    (3.11)
```

where

```
attribute_desigator ::= simple_name
[(universal_static_expression)]             (3.11.1)
```

The prefix is the entity—usually a type or an object—to which the attribute applies, and simple_name is the name of an attribute from

Appendix B. Examples of attributes will be given with the discussion of specific types. The formal syntax for a prefix is given in Statement (3.31).

3.3 DATA TYPES

There has been considerable discussion of the fact that the Ada language is strongly typed, implying a high degree of required type compatibility in the assignment of values to objects and in the mixing of objects in expressions. Both objects and values belong to specific types, and no value can be assigned to an object unless the two are type compatible. Only certain prescribed operations are permitted on objects of a given type. The set of permitted operations includes those operations predefined for the type and any explicitly declared subprograms that have a parameter or a result of the type. The Ada language has certain predefined types that must be provided by any implementation. These predefined types are declared in package STANDARD and include the types BOOLEAN, INTEGER, FLOAT, CHARACTER, STRING, and DURATION, and subtypes NATURAL and POSITIVE. Package STANDARD also includes the declarations of the predefined operations associated with these types.

One particular set of predefined types requires consideration at this point. These are the so-called *universal types*—universal_integer, universal_real, and universal_fixed. The universal_integer type is considered to have no constraints whatsoever on the size of the value, whereas the universal_real and universal_fixed types have no size constraint and are represented with an infinitely fine accuracy. These data types are conceptual in nature, of course, because data types with these characteristics could never be represented in hardware. They are a necessary conceptualization, however, if values with these types are to be assigned to entities such as numeric literals. For example, there is no limit on how large an integer literal can be, but there are definite limits on values of type INTEGER. In the case of real literals, the expression

```
0.1  really means  0.10000000 . . .
```

That is, an infinitely fine precision is implied; but such precision is not attainable in a computer with a finite word length. The Ada language deals with the practical limitation on the precision of representation of real numbers by defining a set of *model numbers*—a finite set of real numbers with exact representation—for each real data type. Real literals, then, are considered to be of the anonymous type universal_real—implying the infinitely fine precision required—and must be converted to a machine-representable type before they can be assigned as values of objects. Similarly, integer literals are considered to be of the unbounded anonymous type universal_integer, and they must be converted to a declared type before assignment. The type universal_fixed is also an infinite precision anonymous real type defined in conjunction with Ada's fixed-point data types, which are discussed in Section 3.5.3.

In addition to their uses as numeric literals, universal types are found in the values returned by some attributes and in values of named numbers. The conversion of values of universal types to declared types is, in most cases, implicitly performed by the language, but it may also be explicitly specified by the program. Type conversion is discussed in Sections 3.7.3 and 3.7.4. The concept of model numbers is developed thoroughly in Section 3.5.

The syntax of a type declaration has been discussed previously. In the remainder of this section, three of the four classes of types—scalar types, composite types, and access types—will be considered. The first of these classes—scalar data types—contains three subclasses, as implied by Figure 1.5: (1) enumeration types, (2) integer types, and (3) real types. The scalar types comprise two other groupings: the discrete data type, which comprises the integer and enumeration types, and the numeric data type, which comprises the integer and real data types. This grouping is depicted in Figure 3.2. The two discrete data types are similar in that the permissible values are discrete, have a well-defined ordering, and are a precise representation.

The real data types, on the other hand, represent real numbers, which are not discrete in nature. Real types are, however, by virtue of their representation in the underlying hardware, necessarily an approximation to the real numbers. Real data types are further divided into floating-point types and fixed-point types, as indicated in Figure 3.3. These two real data types differ in one very important characteristic—the error bound with which they represent approximation to the real numbers. In most languages, real data types are implemented by use of exponentials,

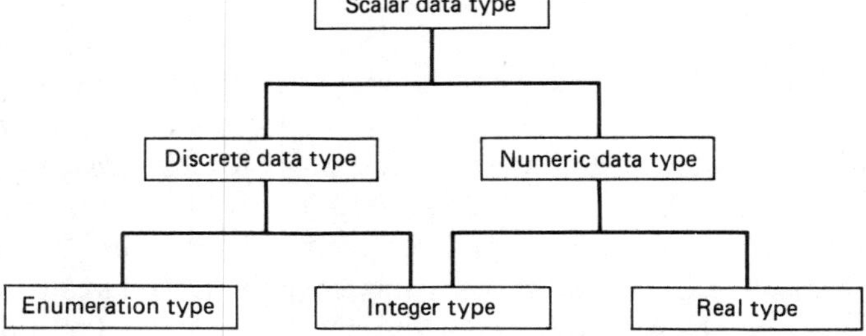

Figure 3.2. Scalar data types.

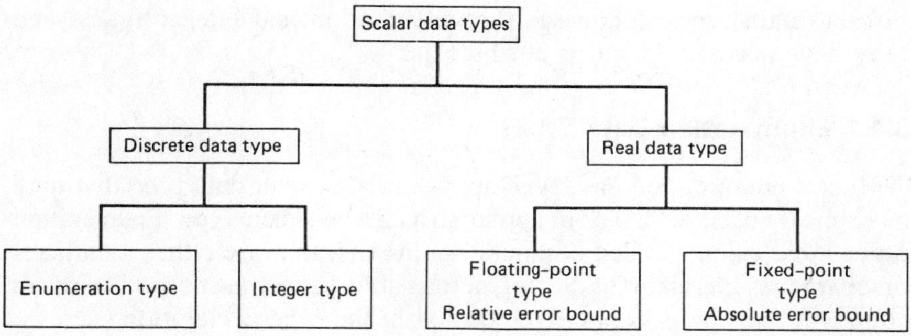

Figure 3.3. Grouping of scalar data types.

with real numbers represented by a fractional mantissa and an exponent. The size of the exponent determines the range of the representation—the smallest to the largest number—while the size of the mantissa determines the precision with which the real number is represented. One effect of this kind of representation is that the accuracy with which real numbers are approximated by an implementation with a specified precision—that is, with a specified number of bits in the mantissa—is a function of the size of the real number being represented. The Ada language has two representations for real numbers, as implied by Figure 3.3. The floating-point type is equivalent to the representation found in most other languages; that is, it has a relative error bound. The fixed-point type, on the other hand, has an error bound that is specified as an absolute value—that is, the error bound is not a function of the value of the real number being represented.

Because of the characteristics outlined above, scalar data types will be grouped as follows for the purpose of discussion: discrete data types—integer and enumeration types—and real data types—floating-point and fixed-point types. This grouping is represented by Figure 3.3. The reader is again reminded that there are no data types with the names SCALAR, ENUMERATION, REAL, FIXED_POINT, FLOATING_POINT, or DISCRETE. These terms apply to general classes of data types. The data types themselves must be explicitly declared in the Ada program itself, or predefined in package STANDARD or some other part of the predefined environment discussed in Appendix C.

3.4 DISCRETE DATA TYPES

Discrete data types are those types whose permissible values are discrete and are associated with integer-valued position numbers. The class of discrete data types comprises the enumeration and integer types, and they have a common set of attributes.

3.4.1 Enumeration Data Types

The term enumeration data type applies to a class of data type that may be explicitly declared in an Ada program as a named data type. Enumeration types have values, called enumeration literals, that are either identifiers or character literals. The set of permissible values associated with an enumeration type is explicitly specified in the type declaration.

The syntax statement for the declaration of an enumeration type is given by Statements (3.6), (3.7), (3.7.1), and (3.7.2) by the path

```
        type_declaration ::= type identifier is
                enumeration_type_definition;          (3.12)
```

where

```
    enumeration_type_definition ::=
            (enumeration_literal_specification
            {, enumeration_literal_specification })
                                                      (3.12.1)

 enumeration_literal_specification ::= enumeration_literal
                                                      (3.12.2)
```

and

```
  enumeration_literal ::= identifier | character_literal
                                                      (3.12.3)
```

The enumeration type definition which can contain an unlimited number of identifiers and/or character literals, is a complete listing of the values that objects of the type may be assigned. The enumeration literals must be distinct, and the order in which they are listed determines the position numbers of the values, starting with zero.

Examples of enumeration type declarations are, in accordance with Statement (3.12),

```
type THREAT    is (NIL, LOW, MEDIUM, HIGH, URGENT);
type FIGHTER   is (F14, F18, F15, F16, F20);
type WEATHER   is (CLEAR, PCLDY, CLDY, OVCAST);
type HEXDIGIT  is ('1','2','3','4','5','6',
    '7', '8', '9', 'A', 'B', 'C', 'D', 'E', 'F');
type HETERO    is ('1', '2', 'X', 'Z', 'OTHERS');
```

After elaboration of the above type declarations in an Ada program, and subject to the rules of scope of the language, objects of the types may be declared in accordance with Statements (3.10), (3.10.1), and (3.10.2). For example, the type declarations above permit the following object declarations:

```
AC_1, AC_2, AC_3  :  FIGHTER;
EVALUATION        :  THREAT;
PRIM_COVER        :  FIGHTER  := F14;
HEX_COUNT         :  HEXDIGIT := 'F';
```

The last two examples illustrate the initialization of an object at elaboration time.

Subtypes of these types may be declared using the range constraint in accordance with Statements (3.8), (3.8.1), (3.8.2), and (3.8.3) by the following path:

```
subtype_declaration ::=
    subtype identifier is type_name
    [range_constraint];                          (3.13)
```

where

```
range_constraint ::= range range         (3.13.1)
```

and

```
range ::= range_attribute
    | simple_expression..simple_expression  (3.13.2)
```

In general, the form of a simple expression can be quite detailed. The general syntax is given by Statement (3.34.2), and the general discussion is contained in Section 3.7.2. For the present discussion, only enumeration literals will be considered. Examples in this case are

```
subtype AF_FIGHTER is FIGHTER range F15..F20;
subtype GOOD_WX    is WEATHER range CLEAR..PCDY;
subtype NUMB       is HETERO  range 1..2;
```

Note that the range must consist of contiguous values of the enumeration literals from the type declaration. Objects of these subtypes can then be declared. For example, the object declarations

```
BLUE_1, BLUE_2 : AF_FIGHTER;
```

declare two objects of the subtype AF_FIGHTER. If the same identifier or character literal is used as an enumeration literal for more than one enumeration type definition, then the enumeration literal is said to be *overloaded.* Because of the strong typing of the Ada language, the type of the enumeration literal must be apparent from the context in which it appears. If an ambiguity exists that cannot be resolved, a qualified expression—to be discussed in Section 3.7.6—must be used. The general concept of overloading is discussed in Section 8.2.1.

There are two predefined enumeration types whose characteristics can be obtained from package STANDARD. These are type BOOLEAN and type CHARACTER. From package STANDARD, the following type declaration is obtained:

```
type BOOLEAN is (FALSE, TRUE);
```

There are also ten functions declared for operations on objects of type BOOLEAN. Similarly, type CHARACTER is declared in package STANDARD as the 128 ASCII characters, including control characters. The graphic characters are defined as character literals.

3.4.1.1 Operations. The set of operations predefined for enumeration data types are given in Table 3.4. Some of these operations have not yet been discussed, but it can be seen that there are no mathematical operators. Only those operations concerned with assignment and ordering of values make any sense for enumeration types.

Table 3.4 Operations Associated with Enumeration Types

OPERATION	SYMBOL
assignment	:=
membership	**in** **not in**
qualification	
relational	= /= < <= > >=

3.4.1.2 Attributes. The minimum set of predefined attributes of enumeration types is

- BASE
- FIRST
- IMAGE
- LAST
- POS
- PRED
- SIZE
- SUCC
- VAL
- VALUE
- WIDTH

In addition, objects of an enumeration type have the attributes

• ADDRESS • SIZE

The reader is referred to Appendix B for a precise description of these attributes. It should also be noted that some attributes are evaluated at run time, and that they may be used in declarations or in executable statements. Some examples of attributes and their values, based upon the declarations of Section 3.4.1, are

```
FIGHTER'LAST          --F20
THREAT'FIRST          --NIL
HEXDIGIT'SUCC('A')    --'B'
AC_1'ADDRESS          --returns address of AC_1
```

Use of attributes is illustrated in later examples.

3.4.2 Integer Data Types

Integer data types are declared in accordance with Statements (3.7), (3.7.1), and (3.7.2) through the path

```
type_declaration ::= type identifier is
        integer_type_definition;                    (3.14)
```

where

```
integer_type_definition ::= range_constraint
                                                  (3.14.1)
```

and where the range constraint is given by Statements (3.13.1) and (3.13.2) through the path:

```
range_constraint ::=
            range simple_expression..simple_expression
                                                  (3.14.2)
```

The expression used in the range constraint must be static. In general, the form of a simple expression can be rather detailed. The general syntax is given by Statement (3.34.3), and the general discussion is contained in Section 3.7.2. For the present discussion, only single numeric literals or single objects will be used. Negative bounds are permitted.

An implementation must provide at least one predefined integer type as a declaration in package STANDARD. This type has the name IN-

TEGER. An implementation is free to provide other predefined integer types, such as the recommended types SHORT_INTEGER and LONG INTEGER. All integer type declarations within a program are derived from the predefined integer types in the following manner. An integer type declaration corresponding to Statements (3.14), (3.14.1), and (3.14.2) has the general form

```
                    type T is range L..R;                 (3.15)
```

where T is the type name, and L and R are the lower and upper bounds, respectively, of the range constraint. The effect of this declaration is equivalent to the following declarations:

```
type integer_type is new predefined_integer_type;
subtype T is integer_type
             range integer_type(L)..integer_type(R);
                                                  (3.15.1)
```

Here, integer_type is an anonymous type—that is, there is no name associated with the type. The predefined integer type is one of the integer types which is defined in package STANDARD, and which is implicitly selected by the implementation. This selection must be made so that the predefined integer type contains within its range of values the bounds specified by L and R in the declaration of Statement (3.15). If there is no predefined integer type satisfying this requirement, the compiler must detect this fact at compile time. The terminology

```
          integer_type(L)..integer_type(R)          (3.16)
```

in Statement (3.15.1) implies a case of explicit type conversion of the bounds L and R to the anonymous integer type. Explicit conversion is discussed in Section 3.7.3.

The equivalency of Statements (3.15) and (3.15.1) clearly indicate that any integer type declared by the use of the general form of Statement (3.15) is a constrained subtype of a derived type whose parent type is the predefined integer type. Thus, according to the rules applicable to subtypes and derived types contained in Sections 3.2.2 and 3.2.3, the type T of Statement (3.15) is a type distinct from any other integer type, with the same properties—that is, with the same set of applicable operations—as the predefined integer type. Since the Ada standard requires all predefined integer types to have the same set of applicable operations as does the predefined type INTEGER, the type T of Statement (3.15) has all the properties of the predefined type INTEGER, yet it is a distinct type.

One may comment that this discussion is not important from a practical viewpoint, but the implicit dependence of user-declared integer types—as obtained from declarations corresponding to Statement (3.15)—upon the predefined integer types declared in package STANDARD is a critical one, because the range of a type declaration is restricted to lie within that of the predefined integer type from which it is derived. An analogous concept applied to real data types is even more critical.

Examples of integer type declarations are

```
type RANGE_MARK is range 0..10_000;
type VEL_COUNT  is range 0..1024;
type X_MIL      is range -1000..1000;
```

Examples of subtype declarations, in accordance with Statements (3.8), (3.8.1), (3.8.2), and (3.8.3) are

```
subtype FINE_RANGE_MARK is RANGE_MARK range 0..10;
subtype X_MILL_2        is X_MILL     range 0..512;
subtype LIMITED_INTEGER is INTEGER    range -100..100;
subtype NATURAL         is INTEGER    range 0..INTEGER'LAST;
```

The last two subtype declarations have the predefined type INTEGER as the base type. The last subtype declaration is actually taken from package STANDARD. In this declaration, INTEGER'LAST is an attribute which has as its value the largest value associated with type INTEGER.

3.4.2.1 Operations. The operations associated with integer data types are derived from the predefined type INTEGER. These operations are given in Table 3.5. Most of these operations are identical to those found in other languages. Those readers accustomed to the use of **mod** in Pascal

Table 3.5 Operations Associated with Integer Types

OPERATION	SYMBOL
addition	+
assignment	:=
division	/ **rem** **mod**
exponentiation	**
explicit conversion	
membership	**in** **not in**
multiplication	*
qualification	
relational	= /= < <= > >=
unary	+ − **abs**

should use caution, because Ada's **mod** operation produces a different result from Pascal's **mod** in some instances.

3.4.2.2 Attributes. The predefined attributes of integer data types are identical to those of enumeration types, because integer and enumeration types are both discrete data types. The attributes are

- BASE
- FIRST
- IMAGE
- LAST
- POS
- PRED
- SIZE
- SUCC
- VAL
- VALUE
- WIDTH

Objects of type INTEGER have the attributes

- ADDRESS
- SIZE

The reader is referred to Appendix B for precise descriptions of these attributes. Examples of attributes based on the declarations of Section 3.4.2 are

```
RANGE_MARK'LAST     --10_000
X_MIL'FIRST         --0
INTEGER'LAST        --the largest value associated
                      with the predefined type
                      INTEGER
```

The last example is found in Section 3.4.1.2, and also in package STANDARD, where the attribute is used as an upper limit on a range constraint, as indicated below:

```
subtype NATURAL is INTEGER range 0..INTEGER'LAST;
```

If the object X_RANGE is declared as an object of type RANGE_MARK,

```
X_RANGE : RANGE_MARK;
```

then the attribute

```
X_RANGE'SIZE
```

will yield the number of bits allocated to the object X_RANGE.

3.5 REAL DATA TYPES

Real data types provide representation of real numbers. As distinct from the representation of integer numbers—which is precise, that is, there are no errors inherent in the representation—the representation of real numbers is necessarily an approximation. The two classes of real data types, the floating-point and fixed-point types, differ in the manner in which the error bounds associated with this approximation are specified. Before proceeding with a discussion of Ada's real data types, it is important for the reader to recognize the effect that precision of representation has on the portability of software. Computation involving real numbers—or rather, involving the approximation to real numbers afforded by computers—is subject to a myriad of subtle effects because of the limitations imposed on the precision with which real numbers are represented. An algorithm that works well on one machine may fail completely on another machine in which real numbers are represented with a lesser precision. Since one of the goals of the Ada language development was portability of software, Ada's real data types are provided with a guaranteed minimum precision. A program must explicitly specify, in the declaration of a real data type, the minimum precision with which objects of that data type will be represented in any machine for which the program is to be compiled. An implementation may provide more precision than that specified in the type declaration, but it must provide at least the specified precision. Thus, a programmer can specify the minimum precision with which real numbers must be represented in order for any particular algorithm to function properly, and he can be assured of at least that precision in any implementation that successfully compiles the program.

Floating-point types are real data types that have the minimum guaranteed precision specified by explicitly stating in the type declaration the minimum number of significant decimal digits to be provided for the representation of objects of the type. This approach provides a relative error bound—that is, the error bound is a function of the value, being relatively small for small values and relatively large for large values.

Fixed-point types, on the other hand, have a minimum guaranteed precision specified by explicitly stating in the declaration the maximum increment separating two values. This approach provides an absolute error bound—that is, the error bound is the same for all values of the real number being represented. These concepts are illustrated in Figure 3.4.

The syntax statement for the declaration of a real data type is obtained from Statements (3.7), (3.7.1), and (3.7.2) through the path

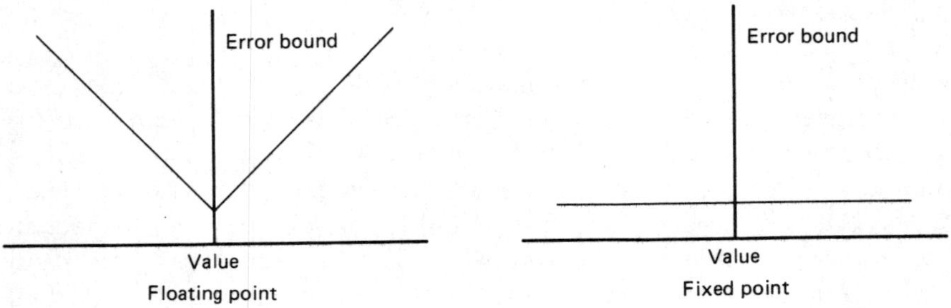

Figure 3.4. Representational error bounds for real data types.

```
type_declaration ::=
        type identifier is real_type_definition;
                                                  (3.17)
```

where

```
real_type_definition ::=
     floating_point_constraint | fixed_point_constraint
                                                  (3.17.1)
```

Examples will be given in the following sections, where floating-point and fixed-point types are considered.

3.5.1 Model Numbers

The Ada language achieves its control over the error bounds in the representation of real numbers by explicitly recognizing that, although real numbers themselves form a continuum with infinitely many values within any finite range, their representation in any computer is discrete. That is, there is a finite number of values that the representation of a real number can assume, and any real number must be represented by one of these values. Real numbers in this finite set of numbers are represented exactly, but real numbers not in the set must be approximated by one of the numbers in the set. In the Ada language, this inherent characteristic of the representation of real numbers is formalized by the concept of model numbers. Each real data type—floating-point and fixed-point—has an associated set of model numbers which represent the finite set of values that objects of the type can assume. The set of model numbers associated with a given type is implicitly specified by the type declaration. An implementation must represent these model numbers exactly. The concept of model numbers as they apply specifically to floating-point and to fixed-point types will be treated in detail when the types themselves are considered.

The set of model numbers is determined by the type declaration, and the model numbers are therefore portable from one implementation to another. An implementation may provide more than the minimum required set of numbers that can be exactly represented, creating what is called a set of *safe numbers*. The set of safe numbers is implementation-dependent—and therefore not portable—but must contain at least the set of model numbers of the type.

3.5.2 Floating-Point Data Types

Floating-point data types represent real numbers by use of the standard exponential form

```
± mantissa * (radix ** exponent)
```

The mantissa is a fractional number—less than one—expressed in a number base given by the radix, and the exponent is an integer number. The range of the representation is determined by the range of the exponent, and the precision of the representation is determined by the number of digits in the mantissa. The minimum number of bits that an implementation must provide for the mantissa and for the exponent is determined by the type declaration. The syntax statement for the declaration of a floating-point type is obtained from Statement (3.17) and (3.17.1) through the path

```
type_declaration ::=
        type identifier is floating_point_constraint;
                                                    (3.18)
```

where

```
floating_point_constraint ::=
        floating_accuracy_definition {range_constraint}
                                                  (3.18.1)
```

and

```
floating_accuracy_definition ::=
        digits static_simple_expression   (3.18.2)
```

The syntax for the optional range constraint is given by Statement (3.14.2).

In general, the form of a simple expression can be rather detailed. The general syntax is given by Statement (3.34.3), and the general discussion is contained in Section 3.7.2. For the present discussion, only single numeric literals will be used.

An implementation must provide a predefined floating-point type named FLOAT, which is declared in package STANDARD. The precision with which type FLOAT is implemented in package STANDARD is implementation-dependent. An implementation may provide other predefined floating-point types, such as the recommended LONG_FLOAT and SHORT_FLOAT, with more and less precision than FLOAT. All floating-point type declarations within a program are derived from the predefined floating-point types in the following manner. A floating-point type declaration corresponding to Statements (3.18), (3.18.1), and (3.18.2) has the general form

```
type T is digits D [range L..R];          (3.19)
```

where T is the type name, D is the static simple expression specifying the number of decimal digits of precision, and L and R are the lower and upper bounds, respectively, of the optional range constraint. The effect of this declaration is equivalent to that of the following declarations:

```
type floating_point_type is new
        predefined_floating_point_type;
subtype T is floating_point_type digits D
  [range floating_point_type(L) ..
        floating_point_type(R)];          (3.19.1)
```

Here, floating_point_type is an anonymous type—that is, there is no name associated with the type. The predefined floating-point type is one of the floating-point types which is declared in package STANDARD—possibly type FLOAT—and which is implicitly selected by the implementation so that its model numbers include the set of model numbers required by the digits specification D. If there is no predefined floating-point type satisfying this requirement, the compiler must detect this fact at compile time. Furthermore, if the optional range constraint is supplied, then both L and R must belong to the range of safe numbers.

The equivalency of statements (3.19) and (3.19.1) clearly indicates that any floating-point type declared by use of the general form of Statement (3.19) is a subtype of a derived type whose parent type is either FLOAT or some other predefined floating-point type. Thus, according to the rules applicable to derived types and subtypes contained in Sections 3.2.2 and 3.2.3, the type T of Statement (3.19) is a type distinct from any other floating-point type and has the same set of applicable operations as the predefined floating-point type from which it is derived. Since the Ada standard requires all predefined floating-point types to have the same set of applicable operations as does the predefined type FLOAT, the type T of Statement (3.19) has all the properties of the predefined type FLOAT, yet it is a distinct type.

3.5.2.1 Model Numbers. The digits specification D of Statement (3.19) is the minimum number of decimal digits required in the fractional mantissa. This value, in turn, defines the number of bits necessary to represent the mantissa. If the number of digits is D, then the number of bits B is given by

```
B = D (log 10/log 2) + 1 = 3.32D + 1
```

rounded up to the next integer value. The range of the exponent is specified by the language standard to be

```
-4B to 4B.
```

The model numbers are then obtained as those numbers having exactly B bits in the mantissa and an exponent in the above range. The portability of the floating-point type derives from the fact that any implementation is required to provide this same set of model numbers. An implementation may also provide a set of safe numbers which must include the set of model numbers. Thus, an algorithm written to rely only on the minimum numerical properties guaranteed by the set of model numbers—or, equivalently, by the specified number of significant digits D—will be portable from one implementation to another. That is, an implementation may provide more precision than specified by D, but never less than that specified.

A simple example will serve to illustrate this point. Consider the following floating-point declaration, made in accordance with Statement (3.19):

```
type MASS_READING is digits 2;
```

The number of bits in the mantissa is obtained as

```
B = 3.32D + 1 = 7.64 => 8 bits
```

The exponent range is then

```
-32 to 32.
```

The model numbers associated with type MASS_READING are now specified. The nonnegative model numbers are

MANTISSA	DECIMAL VALUE
0_2	0.0
$(.00000001)_2$	$0.00390625 \times 10^{-32}$
	$0.00390625 \times 10^{-31}$
	$0.00390625 \times 10^{-30}$
	.
	.
	.
	$0.00390625 \times 10^{31}$
	$0.00390625 \times 10^{32}$
$(.00000010)_2$	$0.0078125 \times 10^{-32}$
	$0.0078125 \times 10^{-31}$
	$0.0078125 \times 10^{-30}$
	.
	.
	.
	0.0078125×10^{31}
	0.0078125×10^{32}
$(.00000011)_2$	$0.01171875 \times 10^{-32}$
	$0.01151875 \times 10^{-31}$
	$0.01171875 \times 10^{-30}$
	.
	.
	.
	$0.01171875 \times 10^{31}$
	$0.01171875 \times 10^{32}$
and so on, until finally,	
$(.11111111)_2$	$0.9960375 \times 10^{-32}$
	$0.99609375 \times 10^{-31}$
	$0.99609375 \times 10^{-30}$
	.
	.
	$0.99609375 \times 10^{31}$
	$0.99609375 \times 10^{32}$

The total number of model numbers is

```
[255] [2 (32) + 1] + 1 = 16,576
```

The reader should note that 1.0×10^{32} and 1.0×10^{-32} are not model numbers. All implementations of the Ada language are required to provide this set of model numbers for type MASS_READING. Specific model numbers that will be useful later are

```
0.2421875      0.60546875
0.24609375     0.609375
0.3125         0.61328125
2.5            0.6171875
```

The precision specified by the digit specification D is the minimum required of all implementations. That is, an implementation may provide more precision than that specified, but never less. The reason an implementation would provide more precision than required can be seen from consideration of Statement (3.19.1). The floating-point type MASS READING has an anonymous base type which, in turn, is derived from a parent type which is type FLOAT or some other predefined floating-point type. Suppose, for the sake of argument, that type FLOAT is the only predefined floating-point type, and that type FLOAT is implemented with nine bits in the mantissa. Then type MASS_READING will also be implemented with nine bits in the mantissa and a minimum exponent range of −36 to 36. This result is a direct consequence of Statement (3.19.1). The set of nonnegative values associated with type MASS_READING is then

MANTISSA	DECIMAL VALUE	
0_2	0.0	
$(.000000001)_2$	$0.00193125 \times 10^{-36}$	
	$0.00193125 \times 10^{-35}$	
	.	
	.	
	.	
	$0.00193125 \times 10^{36}$	
$(.000000010)_2$	$0.00390625 \times 10^{-36}$	
	$0.00390625 \times 10^{-35}$	
	.	
	.	
	.	
	$0.00390625 \times 10^{-32}$	model numbers
	.	
	.	
	.	
	$0.00390625 \times 10^{-32}$	
	.	
	.	
	.	
	$0.00390625 \times 10^{36}$	
$(.000000011)_2$	$0.005859375 \times 10^{-36}$	
	$0.005859375 \times 10^{-35}$	
	.	
	.	
	.	
	$0.005859375 \times 10^{36}$	

$(.000000100)_2$ $\quad 0.0078125 \times 10^{-36}$

$0.0078125 \times 10^{-35}$

.

.

.

$0.0078125 \times 10^{-32}$ } model numbers

.

.

.

0.0078125×10^{32}

.

.

.

$0.0078125 \times 102+(36)$

and so on, until finally,

$(.111111110)_2$ $\quad 0.99609375 \times 10^{-36}$

$0.99609375 \times 10^{-35}$

.

.

.

$0.99609375 \times 10^{-32}$ } model numbers

.

.

.

$0.99609375 \times 10^{32}$

.

.

.

$(.111111111)_2$ $\quad 0.998046875 \times 10^{-36}$

$0.998046875 \times 10^{-35}$

.

.

.

$0.998046875 \times 10^{36}$

Thus, the provision of additional range and additional precision is the result of a lack of a predefined floating-point type with an eight-bit mantissa. These additional values are part of the set of safe numbers associated with type MASS_READING.

In the example just considered, the predefined type FLOAT had nine bits in its mantissa, requiring an exponent range of

```
-4B to 4B
```

yielding

```
-36 to 36.
```

The model numbers for type FLOAT then range from

$$0.00193125 \times 10^{-36} \text{ to } 0.998046875 \times 10^{36}$$

and comprise the safe numbers of type MASS_READING. Since type FLOAT is implemented with the minimum required exponent range, its set of safe numbers is the same as its set of model numbers.

An implementation may provide an exponent range in excess of that required for the model numbers. Suppose that, in the current example, the exponent range provided for the predefined type FLOAT is

$$-40 \text{ to } 40.$$

Then, the safe numbers of type FLOAT range from

$$0.00193125 \times 10^{-40} \text{ to } 0.998046875 \times 10^{40}$$

and, of course, include the model numbers.

The set of safe numbers associated with the floating-point type MASS_READING, in the current example, is the same as that associated with type FLOAT, from which MASS_READING is derived. This result is a direct consequence of Statement (3.19.1). Thus, the set of safe numbers associated with a floating-point type differs from the set of model numbers of the type as a result of two possible influences:

1. The predefined floating-point type from which the type is derived, in accordance with Statement (3.19.1), has more than B bits in its mantissa. This affects both the mantissa and exponent values of the safe numbers.
2. The predefined floating-point type from which the type is derived has more than the minimum required exponent range. This affects only the exponent values of the safe numbers.

Since the precision and range of the predefined floating-point type FLOAT—and those of other optionally predefined floating-point types—are implementation-dependent, there is a limit to the precision with which floating-point types can be declared. Thus, portability of even these types can be affected. The point is that the compiler will reject a declaration that exceeds its capabilities for floating-point precision. Those implementation-dependent characteristics that determine the limits of range and precision of numeric data types are defined in a predefined package named SYSTEM, which is part of the predefined environment listed in

Appendix C. Within package SYSTEM, the following named numbers are declared:

- `MIN_INT` --the most negative value of all predefined integer types
- `MAX_INT` --the largest value of all predefined integer types
- `MAX_DIGITS` --the largest value allowed for the number of significant decimal digits in a floating-point constraint

These concepts are important, because a casual reading of many Ada language texts may imply greater compiler flexibility, in terms of how floating-point types are implemented, than is actually required by the Ada standard.

The net effect of the floating-point declaration is that the programmer can specify the minimum required precision for a floating-point type. The compiler will compare these precision requirements with those provided by the predefined floating-point types which, in turn, are characteristic of the implementation and perhaps of the target computer. If these precision requirements cannot be met by any of the predefined floating-point types, then the compiler must reject the declaration. Otherwise, the compiler selects the most appropriate predefined type to represent the declared type through the use of Statement (3.19.1). The additional precision and range, if any, provided by the predefined type selected by the compiler is represented by the safe numbers of the declared type.

Any program with critical floating-point precision requirements, and that is to be portable from one target computer to another, should contain its own floating-point type declarations, rather than depending upon predefined types such as FLOAT. In this manner, any attempt to retarget the software—that is, to move it from one target computer to another—will result in a compiler error if the required precision cannot be provided. On the other hand, use of predefined types such as FLOAT will result in successful compilation even though the inherent precision requirements are not met.

3.5.2.2 Operations. The predefined operations associated with floating-point data types are derived from the predefined floating-point type FLOAT, and are listed in Table 3.6.

The minimum accuracy that an implementation must provide for any predefined operation producing a floating-point result, and for the result of any predefined relational operation between floating-point operands, is defined in terms of the model numbers of the particular floating-point type involved. Specifically, the range of real numbers associated with a

Table 3.6 Operations Associated with Floating-Point Types

OPERATION	SYMBOL
addition	+
assignment	:=
division	/
exponentiation	**
explicit conversion	
membership	**in** **not in**
multiplication	*
qualification	
relational	= /= < <= > >=
subtraction	−
unary	+ − abs

floating-point data type is considered to be divided into *model intervals*—intervals whose bounds are model numbers. For any operation that yields a floating-point result, the minimum required error bounds on the result are defined in the following manner:

- The model interval associated with a model number is the model number itself.
- The model interval of a value is the smallest model interval that includes the value.
- The result model interval is the smallest model interval of the result type that includes the minimum and maximum of all values produced by the precise mathematical operation when the operand(s) assume any values in their respective model intervals.
- If an operand is itself the result of another operation, the result model interval of the operation is the operand model interval.

An implementation is free to assign, as the result of an operation, any value contained in the result model interval. Some simple examples should serve to illustrate these points.

Consider again the floating-point type MASS_READING declared as

```
type MASS_READING is digits 2;
```

There are 16,576 model numbers specified by this declaration—that is, by the floating-point constraint **digits** 2—and these model numbers are listed in the previous section. Suppose now that three objects are declared, in accordance with Statements (3.10) and (3.10.1),

```
SCALE_1, SCALE_2, SCALE_3 : MASS_READING;
```

Suppose also that these objects have been assigned values. These values must be model numbers; suppose that they are

```
SCALE_1 = 0.78125
SCALE_2 = 0.3125
SCALE_3 = 2.5
```

The model intervals for these three values are the values themselves, since they are model numbers. If the following expression is evaluated,

```
SCALE_1 * SCALE_2
```

the result model interval is the smallest model interval of the result—in this case, of the type MASS_READING—that contains all results obtained from the precise multiplication of all values in the model intervals of SCALE_1 and SCALE_2. In this case, there is only a single value in each model interval, and the range of result values is a single number:

```
0.78125 * 0.3125 = 0.244140625
```

The *result model interval* is the smallest model interval of the result type which includes this value. In this case, the model interval—as obtained from Section 3.5.2.1—is

```
0.2421875 to 0.24609375.
```

These values are two contiguous model numbers of type MASS_READING that are implied, but not actually shown, in the previous section. An implementation may assign any model number in this interval, of which there are only two—the two endpoints. Thus, the result could be 0.24421875 or 0.24609375. In either case, the two-digit precision has been maintained.

Suppose now that the expression to be evaluated is

```
SCALE_1 * SCALE_2 * SCALE_3
```

and further suppose that the expression is evaluated by first multiplying SCALE_1 by SCALE_2, and then multiplying the result by SCALE_3. The result model interval of the first operation is, from above

```
0.2421875 to 0.24609375
```

which becomes one of the operand model intervals of the second multiply operation. The other operand model interval of the second multiply operation is the model number itself, 2.5. The result model interval for the second multiply operation is the smallest model interval of the type MASS

READING that contains the minimum and maximum of all possible values obtained when the two operands are assigned any value in their respective model intervals. In this case, the minimum and maxmum are

```
0.2421875 * 2.5 = 0.60546875
```

and

```
0.24609375 * 2.5 = 0.615234375.
```

The smallest model interval of type MASS_READING that includes these two numbers is

```
0.60546875 to 0.6171875
```

which contains four model numbers,

```
0.60546875    0.61328125
0.609375      0.6171875
```

An implementation is free to assign any of these four values to the final result.

If safe numbers are provided by an implementation, then the error bounds for safe numbers follow the same rules as are specified for model numbers. The concept of model intervals is extended to define safe intervals, and procedures analogous to those outlined above are defined for safe numbers.

3.5.2.3 Attributes. The attributes of floating-point types fall into three general groups, as shown below.

1. Attributes that are general or that relate to model numbers:

• ADDRESS	• LARGE
• BASE	• LAST
• DIGITS	• MANTISSA
• EMAX	• SIZE
• EPSILON	• SMALL
• FIRST	

2. Attributes that relate to safe numbers:

• SAFE_EMAX	• SAFE_LARGE
• SAFE_SMALL	

3. Machine-dependent attributes not related to model numbers or safe numbers:

   - MACHINE_EMAX
   - MACHINE_EMIN
   - MACHINE_MANTISSA
   - MACHINE_OVERFLOWS
   - MACHINE_RADIX
   - MACHINE_ROUNDS

In addition, there are two attributes defined for objects of a floating-point type:

- ADDRESS
- SIZE

The reader is referred to Appendix B for detailed descriptions of these attributes.

Examples here are based on the type MASS_READING, which was developed in Section 3.5.2.1. The type declaration is

```
type MASS_READING is digits 2;
```

and it is assumed that the only predefined floating-point type is type FLOAT, with nine bits in its mantissa and an exponent range of −36 to 36. The model numbers and some of the safe numbers are listed in Section 3.5.2.1. With regard to this example, then, the following attribute values apply:

```
MASS_READING'DIGITS     --2
MASS_READING'MANTISSA   --8
MASS_READING'SMALL      --0.00390625  x 10^-32
MASS_READING'LARGE      --0.99609375  x 10^32
MASS_READING'EMAX       --32
MASS_READING'SAFE_MAX   --0.998046875 x 10^36
MASS_READING'SAFE_SMALL--0.00193125  x 10^-36
MASS_READING'SAFE_EMAX --36
```

The use of attributes such as these can permit an algorithm to adjust itself to the characteristics of the implementation or to those of the machine on which it is executing.

3.5.3 Fixed-Point Data Types

Fixed-point data types represent real numbers by use of integer multiples of a specified positive real number called *small,* and in the following manner:

$$\pm \text{ mantissa } * \text{ small}$$

where the mantissa is a positive integer. The range of the representation is determined by the range of the mantissa, and the precision of the representation is determined by the value of small. The syntax statement for the declaration of a fixed-point type is obtained from Statements (3.17) and (3.17.1) through the path

```
type_declaration ::= type identifier is
          fixed_point_constraint;                (3.20)
```

where

```
fixed_point_constraint ::=
          fixed_accuracy_definition [range constraint]
                                                 (3.20.1)
```

and

```
fixed_accuracy_definition ::=
          delta static_simple_expression   (3.20.2)
```

The syntax for the range constraint is given by Statement (3.14.2). In general, the form of a simple expression can be rather detailed. The general syntax is given by Statement (3.34.3), and the general discussion is contained in Section 3.7.2. For the present discussion, only single numeric literals or single objects will be used.

An implementation must provide at least one anonymous predefined fixed-point type, but it may provide more than one. The range and precision of these predefined types is implementation-dependent. All fixed-point declarations within a program are derived from the predefined anonymous types in the following manner. A fixed-point type declaration corresponding to Statements (3.20), (3.20.1), and (3.20.2) has the general form

```
type T is delta D range L..R;          (3.21)
```

where T is the type name, D is the value of the static simple expression that specifies the error bound, and L and R are the lower and upper bounds of the range constraint. In most instances, the range constraint is required—the only exception occurs in a subtype declaration. The effect of this declaration is equivalent to that of the following declarations:

```
type fixed_point_type is new
      predefined_fixed_point_type;
subtype T is fixed_point_type
      range fixed_point_type(L).. fixed_point_type(R);
                                                 (3.21.1)
```

Here, fixed-point-type is an anonymous type, and predefined-fixed-point-type is one of the anonymous predefined fixed-point types provided by the implementation. The anonymous predefined fixed-point type is implicitly selected by the implementation so that its model numbers include the model numbers required by the fixed-point constraint. If there is no predefined fixed-point type satisfying this requirement, the compiler must detect this fact at compile time.

The equivalency of Statements (3.21) and (3.21.1) clearly indicates that any fixed-point type declared by use of the general form of Statement (3.21) is a subtype of a derived type whose parent type is an anonymous predefined fixed-point type. Thus, according to the rules applicable to derived types and subtypes, as outlined in Sections 3.2.2 and 3.2.3, the type T of Statement (3.21) is a type distinct from any other fixed-point type, and it has the same set of applicable operations as the predefined fixed-point type from which it is derived.

3.5.3.1 Model Numbers. The **delta** specification of Statement (3.21) is the upper bound on the representation error of the declared floating-point type. The number small defined in the previous section is derived from **delta** as the largest power of two—including negative powers—that is less than or equal to **delta.** The model numbers are then obtained as all multiples for which the mantissa has exactly B bits, where the value of B is chosen as the smallest number for which each bound of the range constraint is either a model number or lies within a value of small from a model number. Thus, an algorithm written to depend only on the minimum numerical properties guaranteed by the set of model numbers—or, equivalently, by the value of **delta** and the range constraint—will be portable from one implementation to another. That is to say, an implementation may provide more precision than specified by **delta,** but it may never provide less than that specified. A simple example will serve to illustrate this point. Consider the following fixed-point declaration, made in accordance with Statement (3.21):

```
type CURRENT_MEASUREMENT is delta 0.025
                          range -100.0..100.0;
```

Ideally, the model numbers would be

```
-100.0, 99.975, 99.95, . . . , 0.025, 0, -0.025,
                . . . , -100.0.
```

However, the Ada standard states that the value of small shall be selected as the largest power of two less than or equal to **delta**—in this case, small would be chosen as

$$small = 2^{-6} = .015625$$

The nonnegative model numbers are then defined as

```
                    0.0
(1)(.015625)      = 0.015625
(2)(.015625)      = 0.03125
                  .
                  .
                  .
(6399)(.015625) = 99.984375
(6400)(.016525) = 100.0
```

The number of bits B required for the mantissa is 13, since 6400 lies between 2^{12} and 2^{13}.

In this example, the bounds were model numbers themselves. Such is not always the case, as is illustrated by the declaration

```
type CURRENT MEASUREMENT is delta 0.025
        range 0.0 to 99.3;
```

As before,

$$\text{small} = 2^{-6} = .015625.$$

The model numbers are

```
    0.0
(1)(.015625)      = 0.015625
(2)(.015625)      = 0.03125
                  .
                  .
                  .
(6354)(.015625) = 99.28125
(6355)(.015625) = 99.296875
```

and possibly

```
(6356)(.015625) = 99.3125
```

The Ada standard requires that each bound of the specified range must either be a model number or lie at most a distance small from a model number. Thus, the value 99.3125 may be included in the set of model numbers, in which case the actual range constraint is

```
0.0 to 99.3125
```

or it may not be included, in which case the actual range constraint is

```
0.0 to 99.296875
```

Fixed-point data types, like their floating-point counterparts, have associated with them a set of safe numbers that must include the model numbers. Examination of Statement (3.21.1) reveals that the safe numbers of a fixed-point type are the model numbers of the predefined fixed-point type from which it is derived. For example, if the fixed-point type CURRENT_MEASUREMENT is declared as

```
type CURRENT_MEASUREMENT is delta 0.025
        range -100.0..100.0;
```

then the model numbers are as described above. Suppose that the anonymous predefined fixed-point type used to derive type CURRENT_MEASUREMENTS, through the syntax of Statement (3.21.1), is implemented with

$$\text{small} = 2^{-8} = 0.00390625$$

Then, the nonnegative model numbers of the anonymous predefined type lying within the range constraint of type CURRENT_MEASUREMENT are

```
-(25,600)(.00390625) = -100.0
-(25,599)(.00390625) = -99.99609375
-(25,598)(.00390625) = -99.9921875
-(25,597)(.00390625) = -99.98828125
-(25,596)(.00390625) = -99.984375
-(25,595)(.00390625) = -99.98046875
-(25,594)(.00390625) = -99.9765625
-(25,593)(.00390625) = -99.97265625
-(25,592)(.00390625) = -99.96875
                     .
                     .
                     .
 (25,596)(.00390625) = 99.984375
 (25,597)(.00390625) = 99.98828125
 (25,598)(.00390625) = 99.9921875
 (25,599)(.00390625) = 99.99609375
 (25,600)(.00390625) = 100.0
```

These numbers constitute the safe numbers for type CURRENT_MEASUREMENT. Notice that every fourth safe number is a model number.

It is possible for the programmer to specify the value of small by use of a length clause, which is considered in detail in Section 8.3.2. Thus, he can specify that small equal **delta,** so that the **delta** can then be interpreted literally as the bound on the representation error of the fixed-point type. Such specification may be inefficient in terms of memory and execution time, however.

3.5.3.2 Operations. The predefined operations associated with fixed-point data types are the same as those listed for floating-point types in Section 3.5.2.2. Similarly, the minimum accuracy that an implementation must provide for any predefined operation producing a fixed-point result is determined in a manner completely analogous to that prescribed for floating-point types. Specifically, the range of real numbers associated with a fixed-point data type is considered to be divided into model intervals—intervals whose bounds are model numbers. For fixed-point data types, the model intervals are all of the same width, whereas for floating-point types the model interval width increases with the value of the real number being represented. For any operation that yields a fixed-point result, the minimum required error bounds on the result are defined in the following manner:

- The model interval associated with a model number is the model number itself.
- The model interval of a value is the smallest model interval that includes the value.
- The result model interval is the smallest model interval of the result type that includes the minimum and maximum of all values produced by the precise mathematical operation when the operands assume any values in their respective model intervals.
- If an operand is itself a result of another operation, the result model interval of the operation is the operand model interval.

An implementation is free to assign, as the result of an operation, any value contained in the result model interval. There are some special characteristics of multiplication and division of fixed-point values that differ from their floating-point counterparts. These characteristics will be discussed in Section 3.7.2.3.

3.5.3.3 Attributes. The attributes of fixed point types fall into three general categories:

1. Attributes that are general or that relate to model numbers:

- AFT
- DELTA
- FIRST
- FORE
- LARGE
- LAST
- SIZE
- SMALL

2. Attributes that relate to safe numbers:

- SAFE_SMALL
- SAFE_LARGE

3. Machine-dependent attributes not related to model numbers or safe numbers:

- MACHINE_OVERFLOWS
- MACHINE_ROUNDS

The reader is referred to Appendix B for a detailed description of these attributes.

The examples here are based upon the example of Section 3.5.3.1. The type declaration is

```
type CURRENT_MEASUREMENT is delta 0.025
        range -100.0..100.0;
```

and the anonymous predefined fixed-point type used to derive type CURRENT_MEASUREMENT is implemented with

$$\text{small} = 2^{-8} = 0.00390625$$

The model numbers and some of the safe numbers are listed in Section 3.5.3.1. With respect to this example, then, some attribute values are

```
CURRENT_MEASUREMENT'AFT          -- 2
CURRENT_MEASUREMENT'DELTA        -- 0.025
CURRENT_MEASUREMENT'FIRST        -- -100.0
CURRENT_MEASUREMENT'FORE         -- 4
CURRENT_MEASUREMENT'LARGE        -- 100.0
CURRENT_MEASUREMENT'LAST         -- 100.0
CURRENT_MEASUREMENT'SMALL        -- 0.015625
CURRENT_MEASUREMENT'SAFE_SMALL -- 0.00390625
CURRENT_MEASUREMENT'SAFE_LARGE -- 100.0
```

It should be noted that the selection of the value of small—and therefore of the model numbers—and the selection of safe numbers is not under the control of the programmer. But it should also be noted that knowledge of these selections can be obtained from the attributes of the type itself.

3.6 COMPOSITE DATA TYPES

Ada's composite data types comprise arrays and records. As is the case with Pascal and other modern languages, complex data structures can be represented by arrays and records, since the components of an array can themselves be arrays or records—as can the components of a record. Composite data types in the Ada language, however, are more versatile than those of other languages, principally because of the Ada language's provision for *unconstrained* array types—array types for which the type declaration does not specify the number of elements—and for *discriminated* records, in which some characteristic of the record type is not specified in the declaration. The missing characteristics of unconstrained array and discriminated record types are provided by each object declaration of the type. This situation is depicted in Figure 3.5.

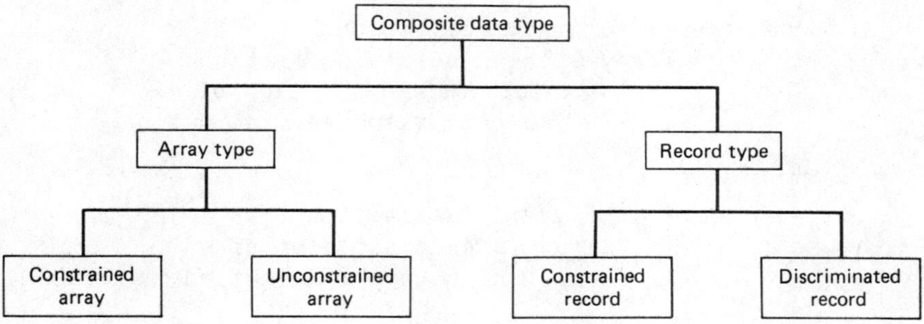

Figure 3.5. Composite data types.

The Ada language also provides for reference to contiguous elements of a one-dimensional array—by means of an object called a *slice*—and for assignment of values to arrays and records through the use of an *aggregate*. These concepts will now be examined in detail.

3.6.1. Array Data Types

Nearly all programming languages provide a composite object called an array. An array is an indexed grouping of objects of the same data type into a single data structure. Arrays in the Ada language can be simple one-dimensional arrays, or they can be multidimensional arrays. Associated with any Ada array data type are two additional data types, that of the index, which must be a discrete type, and that of the component, which can be of virtually any data type. As will be discussed later, one can even declare an array of task objects. There are some operations applicable to an entire array, but more commonly array objects are manipulated by accessing single components or by manipulating groups of contiguous components called slices.

An array data type is declared in accordance with Statements (3.7), (3.7.1), and (3.7.2) through the path

```
type_declaration ::=
        type identifier is array_type_definition;
                                                  (3.22)
```

where the following syntax statements apply:

```
array_type_definition ::=
        unconstrained_array_definition
        | constrained_array_definition      (3.22.1)

unconstrained_array_definition ::=
        array (index_subtype_definition
        {, index_subtype_definition}) of
                component_subtype_indication
                                            (3.22.2)

constrained_array_definition ::=
        array index_constraint of
        component_subtype_indication        (3.22.3)

index_subtype_definition ::= type_mark range <>
                                            (3.22.4)

index_constraint ::= (discrete_range {, discrete_range})
                                            (3.22.5)

discrete_range ::= discrete_subtype_indication | range
                                            (3.22.6)
```

The syntax for a range is given by Statement (3.13.2). For an unconstrained array definition, the index—or indices for a multidimensional array—is defined as a subtype of a declared discrete data type, in accordance with Statement (3.22.4). The symbol <> is called *box notation,* and it represents the index constraint to be supplied when objects of the type are declared. For a constrained array type, the indices are given by an index constraint as indicated in Statement (3.22.5). For both constrained and unconstrained arrays, the component type is explicitly stated.

3.6.1.1 Constrained Arrays. When a constrained array type is declared, the range of the index—or indices in the case of a multidimensional array—is specified in the type declaration. This specification is the index constraint of Statement (3.22.5). All array objects of this type that are declared in a program have the same index constraint—as opposed to unconstrained arrays, for which the index constraints are specified when each array object is declared and may vary from one array object to another. The syntax of a constrained array type declaration is obtained from Statements (3.22), (3.22.1), (3.22.3), (3.22.5), and (3.22.6).

The reader should note that the indices of arrays need only be of a discrete data type. Thus, in addition to integer types, any enumeration type may be used as an array index. Use of enumeration types as array indices often enhances the readability of Ada code.

Examples of constrained array type and object declaration are given below. For the sake of completeness, assume the following enumeration type declarations to be in effect:

```
type IFF is (FRIEND, UNKNOWN, FOE);
type TGT_MACHINE is (UYK_7, M68000, Z8000, AF1750A
                     MIL_7000, R1666B);
type ANG_VEL is (ROLL_RATE, YAW_RATE, PITCH_RATE);
subtype POSITIVE is INTEGER range 1..INTEGER'LAST;
```

The last declaration is actually contained in package STANDARD. Examples of constrained array type declarations are then:

```
type TARGET_THREAT is array(1..100) of IFF:
      --a one-dimensional, 100-component array whose
        components are of type IFF, and whose index
        is a constrained integer

type MEMORY is array(TGT_MACHINE) of POSITIVE;
      --a one-dimensional, six-component array whose
        components are of type POSITIVE and whose
        index is an enumeration type

type MATRIX_3 is array(1..3, 1..3) of FLOAT;
      --a 3 x 3 square array whose components are of
        type FLOAT and whose indices are constrained
        integers

type ANG_VEL_VECTOR is array(ANG_VEL) of FLOAT;
      --a one-dimensional, three-component array
```

```
        whose components are of type FLOAT and whose
        index is an enumeration type
```

Array objects are declared in accordance with Statement (3.10); examples are

```
TARG_1, TARG_2, TARG_3         : TARGET_THREAT;
MEM_VALUE                      : MEMORY;
ROT_MATRIX_1, ROT_MATRIX_2     : MATRIX_3;
VEL_STATE                      : ANG_VEL_VECTOR;
```

In addition, anonymous constrained array types can be implicitly declared in object declarations, in accordance with Statements (3.10) and (3.22.3). Examples are given below:

```
BUFFER     : array(1..1000) of CHARACTER;
TEMP_STORE : array(1..1000) of CHARACTER;
   --these two objects are of two separate anonymous
     types; that is, the types have no names. Even
     though the form is the same for both anonymous
     types, they are nevertheless distinct types.
VEL_ARRAY : array (1..10) of ANG_VEL_VECTOR;
   --a ten-component array of an anonymous type,
     whose components are three element arrays of
     type ANG_VEL_VECTOR.
```

Constrained arrays are the only objects for which the type can be explicitly declared in the object declaration. For all other objects, the type must first be declared in an explicit type declaration, and then objects of that type declared in object declarations.

3.6.1.2 Unconstrained Arrays. In many instances it is desirable to declare two or more array objects of the same type, but with different index constraints. The Ada language provides this feature by means of the unconstrained array. The declaration of an unconstrained array type leaves open the value of the index constraints, which are then provided for each object of the type at the time that the object is declared. The syntax of an unconstrained array type declaration is given by Statements (3.22), (3.22.1), (3.22.2), and (3.22.4). The compound delimiter <> in Statement (3.22.4) is called box notation and represents an undefined range whose bounds are to be provided by the specific object declarations. As with constrained arrays, the index need only be of a discrete data type, implying that enumeration types as well as integer types can be used for the type mark in Statement (3.22.4).

Examples of unconstrained array type declarations are given below. For the sake of completeness, asume the following type declarations to be in effect:

```
type CONTROL is (AILERON, RUDDER, ELEVATOR, THROTTLE);
type NEW_INDEX is range 1..500;
type MONTH_KEY is (JAN, FEB, MAR, APR, MAY, JUN, JUL
                  AUG, SEP, OCT, NOV, DEC);
type LOCATION_KEY is (LOS_ANGELES, CHICAGO, NEW_YORK,
                     DENVER, DALLAS);
type PIXEL_VALUE is delta 0.0125 range -12.5..12.5;
```

Examples of unconstrained array type declarations are then:

```
type BUFFER is array(NEW_INDEX range <>)
                  of CHARACTER;
     --An unconstrained one-dimensional array
       type whose components are of the
       predefined type CHARACTER, and whose index
       is an integer type NEW_INDEX. The range of
       NEW_INDEX is to be specified by the object
       declaration.
type ARRIVAL_DATA is array(LOCATION_KEY range <>,
                    MONTH_KEY range <>) of NATURAL;
     --an unconstrained two-dimensional array
       whose components are of the predefined type
       NATURAL, and whose indices are of
       enumeration types LOCATION_KEY and MONTH_
       KEY. The ranges of these indices are to be
       specified by the object declaration.
type PICTURE is array(INTEGER range <>,
                  INTEGER range <>) of PIXEL_VALUE;
     --an unconstrained two element array whose
       components are of the type PIXEL_VALUE, and
       whose indices are of the predefined type
       INTEGER. The ranges of the indices are to
       be specified by the object declaration.
type CONTROL_VALUE is array(CONTROL range <>)
                        of FLOAT;
     --a one-dimensional array whose components
       are of the predefined type FLOAT, and whose
       index is of type CONTROL. The range of the
       index is to be specified by the object
       declaration.
```

The index constraints for unconstrained arrays are specified in each object declaration, and they apply only to the declared object. Examples of object declarations based upon the above type declarations are

```
LO_MESSAGE_BUFFER : BUFFER(0..127);
     --declares a 128-component array object of type
       BUFFER. The index range is 0..127.
HI_MESSAGE_BUFFER : BUFFER(128..255);
     --declares a 128-component array object of type
       BUFFER. The index range is 128..255.
LOW_RES            : PICTURE(1..64, 1..128);
     --declares a 64 x 128 component, two-dimensional
       array object of type PICTURE.
HI_RES             : PICTURE(1..256, 1..512);
     --declares a 256 x 512 component, two-dimensional
       array object of type PICTURE.
SHORT_REPORT       : ARRIVAL_DATA(NEW_YORK..DALLAS,
                                  JAN..JUN);
     --declares a 3 x 6, two-dimensional array object
       of type ARRIVAL_DATA. The indices are NEW_
       YORK, DENVER, and DALLAS, and JAN, FEB, MAR,
       APR, MAY, JUN.
LONG_REPORT        :ARRIVAL_DATA(LOS_ANGELES..DALLAS,
                                 JAN..DEC);
     --declares a 5 x 12, two-dimensional array object
       of type ARRIVAL_DATA.
```

An array constraint can also be provided in a subtype declaration. The applicable syntax is given by Statements (3.8), (3.8.1), (3.8.2), and (3.8.3), for the case in which the constraint supplied is an index constraint. For example, the declaration

```
subtype LO_RES_PIX is PICTURE(1..64, 1..128);
```

declares 64×128, two-dimensional constrained array type—in this case, a subtype—with the same properties as type PICTURE. An object declaration such as

```
LO_RES          : LO_RES_PIX;
```

then declares a 64×128 element, two-dimensional array object.

The relationship between constrained and unconstrained arrays is implied by the fact that a constrained array type declaration is equivalent to an unconstrained array type declaration followed by a subtype declaration that provides the range constraint. For example, the declaration of the previous section

```
type TARGET_THREAT is array(1..100) of IFF;
```

is equivalent to the succession of declarations

```
subtype index_subtype is INTEGER range 1..100;
type array_type is array(index_subtype range <>) of Iff;
subtype TARGET_THREAT is array_type(index_subtype);
```

where index_subtype and array_type are anonymous types. Similar implied declarations apply to multidimensional arrays.

3.6.1.3. Array Slices. In most languages array components must be manipulated individually as scalar objects. Often, the need arises to manipulate, as a group, a selected sequence of components of an array. In the Ada language, a sequence of consecutive components of a one-dimensional array is called a slice, which is itself an object. The type of a slice is the type of the array of which it is a slice. The syntax for a slice is given by

```
slice ::= prefix(discrete_range)          (3.23)
```

where the discrete range is given by Statement (3.22.6). The prefix is the name of a one-dimensional array object of which the slice is a sequence of components. The formal syntax for a prefix is given by Statement (3.31). Examples of slices, using the declaration of the two previous sections, are

```
TARG_1(1..50)   --the first 50 components of the 100-
                  component array TARG_1
TARG_1(26..50)  --25 components (as indicated) of the
                  100-component array TARG_1
MEM_VALUE(M68000..AF1750A) --a three-component slice of
                             the six-component array
                             MEM_VALUE
```

These examples illustrate the use of the range option of Statement (3.22.6). The discrete subtype indication option of Statement (3.22.6) is exemplified by the following declarations:

```
subtype LOW_INDEX is INTEGER range 1..50;
subtype MID_INDEX is INTEGER range 26..50;
subtype GROUP_1 is TGT_MACHINE range M68000..1750A;
```

Then, the slices

```
TARG_1(LOW_INDEX)
TARG_1(MID_INDEX)
MEM_VALUE(GROUP_1)
```

are equivalent to the slices given above. It is important to note that

```
TARG_1(5..5)
```

is a one-component slice of the array TARG_1 and, as such, is of the same type as TARG_1. The name

```
TARG_1(5)
```

on the other hand denotes a component of the array TARG_1, and consequently is of type IFF.

Also, it should be pointed out that the prefix in Statement (3.23) can itself be a slice, since a slice is of the same type as the array from which it is obtained. For example, the slice

```
TARG_1(MID_INDEX)(30..35)
```

consists of the indicated components of the array object TARG_1.

Slices are defined only for one-dimensional arrays. There is no analogous concept applicable to multidimensional arrays. However, because array elements can themselves be arrays, multidimensional arrays can alternatively be declared by a sequence of one-dimensional array declarations, in which case slices of each of the one-dimensional arrays can be used.

3.6.1.4 Array Aggregates. One of the operations that can be performed on array objects, as is discussed in the following section, is that of assignment. If assignment of array objects—as opposed to assignment of the individual components—is to be performed, then some means of representing a value for an array must be provided. In the Ada language, a basic operation that combines component values into a composite value is called an aggregate. Aggregates are applicable both to the value of an array object and to the value of a record object. The syntax for an aggregate is

```
aggregate ::=
        (component_association {, component_association)
                                                  (3.24)
```

where

```
component_association ::=
        [choice {| choice} = >] expression
                                              (3.24.1)
```

and

```
choice ::= simple_expression
         | discrete_range | others
         | component_simple_name          (3.24.2)
```

The syntax for the discrete range is given by Statement (3.22.6). Thus, an aggregate is a group of expressions for the component values of a value of an array object or of a record object. The components may be identified by positional association—in which the position of the component in the aggregate corresponds to the position of the component in the array or record—or by named component association, using the compound delimiter =>. In the latter case, the index is specified as well as the value, as shown in the following examples based on the array object TARG_1 of Section 3.6.1.1:

```
(1 => FRIEND)
(3|4|5 => FOE)
(1 => FRIEND, 3|4|5 => FOE, others => UNKNOWN
```

In these examples, the vertical bar means "and," while the reserved word **others** refers to all components not already named. Specific rules apply to array aggregates and to record aggregates. In either case, however, the type of an aggregate must be apparent from the context in which it is used, which often requires some further clarification in the form of a qualified expression, which is discussed in Section 3.7.6. The concern here is the array aggregate.

Array aggregates are of a specific type which must match the type of the array or slice to which they are to be assigned. If the aggregate is of a one-dimensional array type, then each choice of Statement (3.24.1) must specify the index value—either through positional association or named component association—and the expression must be of the component type. In the example array MEM_VALUE of Section 3.6.1.1, which is declared in the following manner,

```
type TGT_MACHINE is (UYK_7, M68000, Z8000, AF1750A,
                     MIL_7000, R1666B);
```

```
type MEMORY is array (TGT_MACHINE) of POSITIVE;
MEM_VALUE : MEMORY;
```

an aggregate containing a value of the array object MEM_VALUE, using positional association, might be

```
(65_536, 262_144, 131_072, 16_384, 32_768, 64_536)
```

The same aggregate using named component association would be

```
(UYK_7 => 65_536, M68000 => 262_144, Z8000 => 131_072,
AF1750A => 16_384, MIL_7000 => 32_768, R1666B =>
64_536)
```

When named component association is used, the order of the components is not important. It is not permissible to mix positional association and named component association in the same array aggregrate.

A second example is provided by the array object TARG_1 of Section 3.6.1.1, which was declared in the following manner:

```
type IFF is (FRIEND, UNKNOWN, FOE);
type TARGET_THREAT is array(1..100) of IFF;
TARG_1, TARG_2, TARG_3 : TARGET THREAT;
```

The aggregate

```
(1 => FRIEND, 3|4|5 => FOE, others => UNKNOWN)
```

is a possible value of the array objects TARG_1, TARG_2, or TARG_3 with the component of index 1 equal to FRIEND; with components of indices 3, 4, and 5 equal to FOE; and with all remaining components equal to UNKNOWN. This aggregate, of course, uses named component association. The **others** choice can also be used with positional notation. For example, the above aggregate can also be expressed as

```
(FRIEND, UNKNOWN, FOE, FOE, FOE, others => UNKNOWN).
```

An aggregate can also be a value of an array slice. Examples are provided by the slice TARG_1(1..50) or, equivalently, TARG_1(LOW_INDEX), from Section 3.6.1.3. An aggregate representing a value for this slice might be

```
(1 => FRIEND, 3|4|5 => FOE, others => UNKNOWN)
```

or, alternatively,

```
(FRIEND, UNKNOWN, FOE, FOE, FOE, others => UNKNOWN)
```

Here, the **others** choice refers to components with indices 2, and 6 through 50. A second example is provided by the slice MEM_VALUE (M68000..1750A) or, equivalently, MEM_VALUE(GROUP_1), for which an aggregate might be

```
(M68000 => 262_144, Z8000 => 131_072, AF1750A => 16_384)
```

in named component association, or

```
(262_144, 131_072, 16_384)
```

using positional association.

Discussion to this point has been limited to aggregates whose type is that of a one-dimensional array. If the type of an aggregate is that of a multidimensional array, then it is written as a series of enclosing one-dimensional array aggregates. That is, an N-dimensional aggregate is written as a one-dimensional aggregate whose components are N − 1 dimensional aggregates, which in turn are called *subaggregates*. If the first subaggregate is multidimensional, then the process is repeated until a one-dimensional subaggregate with components that are of the component type of the aggregate is reached. In this manner, multidimensional array aggregates are formulated using a series of one-dimensional array aggregates, all of which conform to the principles discussed above. Examples are taken from Section 3.6.1.1, and relate to the following declarations:

```
type MATRIX_3 is array(1..3, 1..3) of FLOAT;
ROT_MATRIX_1, ROT_MATRIX_2 : MATRIX_3;
```

An array aggregate containing a value of the array object ROT_MATRIX_1 might be

```
((0.36, 0.78, 0.77), (0.27, 0.03, 0.56), (0.21, 0.96, 0.47))
```

using positional association, or

```
(1 => (0.36, 0.78, 0.77), 2 => (0.27, 0.03, 0.56),
 3 => (0.21, 0.96, 0.47))
```

using a combination of positional and named component association, or

```
(1 => (1 => 0.36, 2 => 0.78, 3 => 0.77), 2 => (1 => 0.27,
 2 => 0.03, 3 => 0.56), 3 => (1 => 0.21, 2 => 0.96,
 3 => 0.47))
```

using all named component association. The **others** choice can also be used in multidimensional aggregates in the same context as it can for one-dimensional arrays. For example

```
(others => (others => 0.0))
```

is an aggregate of zero values for the array object ROT_MATRIX_1.

The bounds on the indices of an array aggregate must be evident from the context in which the aggregate is used. The discussion of this topic relates to one-dimensional aggregates, but it applies equally to the enclosing one-dimensional aggregates used to represent a multidimensional aggregate. If there is an **others** choice in the aggregate, it is not clear from the aggregate itself what bounds are to be applied to the index. This difficulty can be seen in the example aggregate of values for the array object TARG_1 and the example aggregate of values of the slice TARG_1(1..50). In the former case, the **others** choice refers to components with indices 2, and 6 through 100, while in the latter case it refers to components with indices 2, and 6 through 50. The question must be resolved by the context in which the aggregate appears, implying that the context must define the index constraint. For this reason, the **others** choice is allowed only if the aggregate appears in one of the following contexts:

- as the expression on the right-hand side of an assignment statement
- as an actual parameter of a generic unit
- as an actual parameter of a subprogram
- as the result expression of a function
- as the operand of a qualified expression
- as the expression of the component association of an enclosing aggregate (either an array or record aggregate).

In the first two cases, named component association is not allowed if there is an **others** choice present. While some of these concepts have not yet been discussed, the basic idea is clear—the context in which the aggregate appears determines precisely what the **others** choice implies. For example, for an aggregate appearing as the expression on the right-hand side of an assignment statement, the bounds on the array index are evident from the type of object on the left-hand side of the assignment statement.

If an array aggregate does not have an **others** choice, then the following rules apply:

- If the aggregate uses named component association, then the bounds are the smallest and largest choices given.
- If the aggregate uses positional association and appears in one of the contexts specified above in the discussion of the use of the **others** choice, then the bounds are determined from the context.
- If the aggregate uses positional association but the bounds are not evident from the context, the lower bound is the first index.

The use of aggregates enhances the capabilities of operations available for array objects, since it is not necessary to resort to operations on the components themselves in order to manipulate the array object. Some examples of operation using aggregates will be given in the following section.

3.6.1.5 Operations. In considering the manipulation of values of an array object, it is important to recognize the difference between manipulating the value of an array by use of operations on the entire array as an array object, and manipulating the array by operations on the components of the array. For example, the declarations

```
type VECTOR is array(1..3) of FLOAT;
FORCE : VECTOR;
```

produce a one-dimensional array object with three components of type FLOAT. Thus, the three components

```
FORCE(1), FORCE(2), and FORCE(3)
```

are scalar objects of type FLOAT and can be manipulated as such. For example, the assignment statements

```
FORCE(1) := 1.0;
FORCE(2) := 2.0;
FORCE(3) := 3.0;
```

assign a value to the array object FORCE by manipulation of the components. On the other hand, the assignment statement

```
FORCE := (1.0, 2.0, 3.0);
```

assigns the value of the aggregate to the array object FORCE by manipulation of the entire array. While the operations available for the components are those defined for the predefined floating-point type FLOAT, those available for the entire array object are much more limited. In general, the basic operations defined for an array type are given in Table 3.7. The relational operators = and /= consider the array as a whole, and they return a scalar result of type BOOLEAN. The relational operators <, <=, >, >= return a BOOLEAN result obtained from an element-by-element operation on the two operand arrays. Specific details of predefined operations will be presented in Section 3.7.2.

Table 3.7 Operations Associated with Array Types

OPERATION	SYMBOL
aggregate	
assignment	:=
explicit conversion	
indexing of components membership	**in** **not in**
qualification	
limited relational	= /=
logical	**and** **or** **xor** **not**
unary	**not**
If the array component type is a discrete type:	
relational	< <= > >=
If the array is one-dimensional:	
concatenation	&

3.6.1.6 Attributes. The following predefined attributes apply to both array types and to array objects, except that they are not allowed for unconstrained array types.

- FIRST
- FIRST(N)
- LAST
- LAST(N)
- RANGE
- RANGE(N)
- LENGTH
- LENGTH(N)

Array objects, in addition, have the attributes

- ADDRESS
- SIZE

while array types, including unconstrained array types, have the attributes

- BASE
- SIZE

The reader is referred to Appendix B for specific information about these attributes.

The examples below are based on array types and array objects declared in Section 3.6.1.1. Specifically:

```
type TGT_MACHINE is (UYK_7, M68000, Z8000, AF1750A,
                     MIL_7000, R1666B);
type MEMORY is array(TGT_MACHINE) of POSITIVE;
type MATRIX_3 is array(1..3, 1..3) of FLOAT;
MEM_VALUE   : MEMORY;
ROT_MATRIX_1, ROT_MATRIX_2 : MATRIX_3;
```

Then, the following attribute values for array objects are obtained:

```
MEM_VALUE'FIRST          --UYK_7
MEM_VALUE'LAST           --R1666B
MEM_VALUE'RANGE          --UYK_7..R1666B
MEM_VALUE'LENGTH         --6
ROT_MATRIX_1'FIRST(2)    --1
ROT_MATRIX_1'LAST(2)     --3
```

Similar attributes are obtained for the array types. For example,

```
MEMORY'FIRST        --UYK_7
MATRIX_3'FIRST(2)   --1
```

and so on.

It is evident, from examination of Appendix B, that the attributes FIRST and FIRST(1) yield the same result, as do the corresponding pairs LAST and LAST(N), RANGE and RANGE(N), and LENGTH and LENGTH(N).

3.6.1.7 Strings. String-handling capabilities in Ada are provided by the predefined, one-dimensional, unconstrained array type STRING declared in package STANDARD. The declaration can be obtained from Appendix A as

```
subtype POSITIVE is INTEGER range 1..INTEGER'LAST;
type STRING is array(POSITIVE range <>) of CHARACTER;
```

Thus, the type STRING is an unconstrained array with an index type that is the set of positive integers, and with components of type character. In addition to the operations presented in Section 3.6.1.5 for array types, the predefined type STRING has additional operations provided by predefined functions declared in package STANDARD. Since string objects are one-dimensional arrays in every sense of the word, albeit with a few additional operations specific to the type, no special discussion of their use is necessary. Examples of string declarations are

```
WAYPOINT_MESSAGE : STRING(1..255);
        --declares a string object with 255 characters
TEMP_WARNING     : constant STRING := "OVERTEMP";
        --declares a string constant using a string
          literal
QUERY            : STRING(1..12) := "WHAT WEAPON?";
        --declares a string object with an initial value
```

Since type STRING is an unconstrained array type, the index constraint must be provided in the object declaration, as illustrated in the declaration of the string objects WAYPOINT_MESSAGE and QUERY above. The exception to this requirement is a constant string declaration, in which the index constraint is evident from the value.

A string literal, discussed previously in Section 3.1.3.4, is actually an operation that combines the sequence of characters contained in the string into a value of a one-dimensional array of type CHARACTER. For example, the string literal "WHAT WEAPON?" is converted to a one-dimensional array aggregrate

```
('W','H','A','T',' ','W','E','A','P','O','N','?')
```

which is then assigned as an initial value to the string object QUERY. This representation also requires that the number of characters—including spaces—in a string literal precisely match the number of components in a string object to which it is to be assigned.

Because of their character as one-dimensional arrays, objects of type STRING can also have their components manipulated independently as scalar objects of type CHARACTER. For example, the object QUERY(3) has the value 'A' after the object declaration above. The assignment

```
QUERY(3) := I;
```

is legitimate and results in the indicated change in the string value.

3.6.2 Record Data Types

While an array is a grouping of objects of the same data type into a single data structure in which the components are identified by index values, the record permits grouping of objects of different data types into a single data structure in which the components are identified by names. Record types in the Ada language are made very flexible through the use of *variant records* and *record discriminants,* which make the actual structure of a record type variable from one object declaration to another. The syntax for a record type follows from Statements (3.6), (3.7), (3.7.1), and (3.7.2) through the path

```
type_declaration ::= type identifier
    [discriminant_part] is type_definition;     (3.25)
```

where

```
record_type_definition ::=
      record
        component_list
      end record                               (3.25.1)
```

with

```
component_list ::=
     component_declaration {component_declaration}
   | {component_declaration} variant_part
   | null;                                     (3.25.2)
```

```
component_declaration ::=
     identifier_list : component_subtype_definition
                          [:= expression];     (3.25.3)
```

and

```
component_subtype_definition ::= subtype_indication
                                               (3.25.4)
```

The syntax for a subtype indication is given by Statements (3.8.1), (3.8.2), and (3.8.3). The record definition of Statement (3.25.1) uses the reserved words **record** and **end record** to bound the declaration of the component list, in which the individual named components are declared.

The first examples to be considered will not contain discriminants or variant parts, which are discussed later. A record type is useful when data of differing types are associated with a single entity of some kind. For example, the position and velocity of an aircraft could be specified by the following declarations:

```
type VELOCITY is digits 10;
type POSITION is digits 8;
type STATE is
    record
       X_VEL : VELOCITY;
       Y_VEL : VELOCITY;
       Z_VEL : VELOCITY;
       X_POS : POSITION;
       Y_POS : POSITION;
       Z_POS : POSITION;
    end record;
```

In this example, the component list consists of the six scalar object declarations. Record objects of type STATE can be declared in the usual manner. For example,

```
AC1, AC2, AC3 : STATE;
```

declares three record objects of type STATE.

A second example is a record type that contains the date and time of an event. It is specified by the following declarations:

```
type MONTH_NAME is (JAN, FEB, MAR, APR, MAY, JUN,
                    JUL, AUG, SEP, OCT, NOV, DEC);
type YEAR_NAME is range 1900..2000;
type DAY_NAME  is range 1..31;
type HOUR_NAME is range 0..23;
type MIN_NAME  is range 0..59;
type SEC_NAME  is range 0..59;
type EVENT is
     record
        YEAR  : YEAR_NAME;
        MONTH : MONTH_NAME;
        DAY   : DAY_NAME;
        HOUR  : HOUR_NAME;
        MIN   : MIN_NAME;
        SEC   : SEC_NAME;
        ID    : STRING(1..25) := (1..25 => '*');
     end record;
```

Each of the record components is of a distinct type, even though five of them are integer types. The component ID is of type STRING and has an initial value, as provided by Statement (3.25.3), that is implemented as an aggregate. It should be noted that the record type EVENT as declared above is different from that declared as

```
type EVENT is
      record;
         YEAR   : INTEGER range 1900..2000;
         MONTH  : MONTH_NAME;
         DAY    : INTEGER range 1..31;
         HOUR   : INTEGER range 0..23;
         MIN    : INTEGER range 0..59;
         SEC    : INTEGER range 0..59;
         ID     : STRING(1..25) := (1..25 => '*');
     end record;
```

In this case, the components YEAR, DAY, HOUR, MIN, and SEC are all of the same type—the predefined INTEGER. This representation does not have the protection afforded by Ada's strong typing rules.

Objects of type EVENT can be declared in the normal manner. If there are to be a large number of events, it may be desirable to declare an array of records, such as

```
EVENT_LIST : array(1..500) of EVENT;
```

which declares an array object of an anonymous type with 500 components, each of which is a record of type EVENT. Or, an array type may be declared,

```
type EVENT_ARRAY is array(1..100) of EVENT;
```

after which any number of objects can be declared, such as

```
POLITICAL_EVENT  : EVENT_ARRAY;
MILITARY_EVENT   : EVENT_ARRAY;
SCIENTIFIC_EVENT : EVENT_ARRAY;
```

each of which is a 100-component array.

A component of a record may also be an array, or it may be another record. For example, one way in which a circular buffer for objects of type CHARACTER can be implemented is by use of an array and two pointers as components of a record, as indicated in Figure 3.6. The declarations are

```
type BUFFER_INDEX is range 1..500;
type BUFFER_ARRAY is array(BUFFER_INDEX) of CHARACTER;
type BUFFER_RECORD is
     record
        FIRST : BUFFER_INDEX;
        LAST  : BUFFER_INDEX;
        LIST  : BUFFER_ARRAY;
     end record;
```

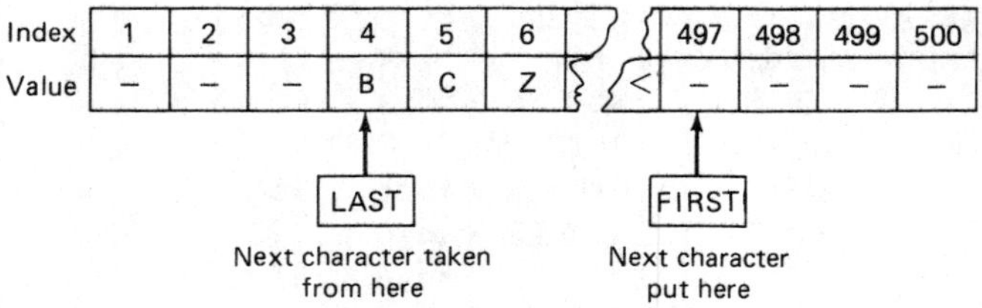

Figure 3.6. Circular buffer implemented as an array.

Objects can then be declared:

```
TERMINAL_BUFFER : BUFFER_RECORD;
PRINTER_BUFFER  : BUFFER_RECORD;
```

or even

```
ALL_BUFFERS     : array(1..10) of BUFFER_RECORD;
```

declaring a one-dimensional, ten-element array of an anonymous type, whose components are records of type BUFFER_RECORD.

The data structuring flexibility of the Ada language can be further illustrated by using the circular buffer to store records. For example, if it is desired to declare a circular buffer of records of type EVENT, the only change required in the above declarations is

```
type BUFFER_ARRAY is array(BUFFER_INDEX) of EVENT;
```

The result is a record data type (BUFFER_RECORD), one of whose components (LIST) is an array whose components, in turn, are records of type EVENT. Objects of type BUFFER_RECORD can be declared in this case; for example:

```
type EVENT_TYPE is (POLITICAL, MILITARY, SCIENTIFIC);
ALL_EVENTS : array(EVENT_TYPE) of BUFFER_RECORD;
```

Here, the array object ALL_EVENTS is of an anonymous type with components

```
ALL_EVENTS(POLITICAL)
ALL_EVENTS(MILITARY)
ALL_EVENTS(SCIENTIFIC)
```

Each of these components is itself a record (of type BUFFER_RECORD) in which components include an array (of type BUFFER_ARRAY) whose components, in turn, are records (of type EVENT) which themselves have an array component in the form of a string. This kind of structuring can go on almost indefinitely.

There is one limitation to the use of arrays as record components. The Ada language does not allow an array object of an anonymous type as a record component. For example, the declaration

```
type BUFFER_RECORD is
     record
        FIRST : BUFFER_INDEX;
        LAST  : BUFFER_INDEX;
        LIST  : array (BUFFER_INDEX) of CHARACTER;
     end record;
```

would not be allowed because the type of array object LIST is anonymous.

3.6.2.1 Record Discriminants. Flexibility in the declaration of record objects is provided by the use of record discriminants. A record discriminant is a component of a record that determines certain features of the remaining components. The discriminant must be of a discrete data type. In particular, record discriminants can specify

- part of the default expressions for record components
- the bound in an index constraint of a record component
- a discriminant value in a discriminant constraint
- a discriminant name in a variant part

The first two uses should be evident, and examples will be given below. The latter two uses will be discussed in the following sections.

The syntax for the declaration of a discriminated record—that is, a record with a discriminant—is given by Statement (3.25), in which

```
discriminant_part ::=
   (discriminant_specification { ; discriminant_
    specification})                               (3.25.5)
```

and

```
discriminant_specification ::=
   identifier_list : type_mark [ := expression]
                                                  (3.25.6)
```

and where the syntax for the identifier list is given by Statement (3.10.1):

```
identifier_list ::= identifier { , identifier}
```

It can be seen that there may be more than one discriminant specification, and each specification can contain more than one discriminant. Each discriminant can be provided with a default value given by the expression in Statement (3.25.6). However, if default expressions are provided for any discriminant, they must be provided for all discriminants. In the declaration of each object of the discriminated record type, the value of the discriminant can be explicitly specified by means of a discriminant constraint. The syntax for an object declaration with a discriminant constraint is given by Statements (3.10), (3.10.1), (3.8), (3.8.1), and (3.8.3), through the path

```
object_declaration ::=
     identifier_list : type_mark [discriminant
      constraint];                                  (3.25.7)
```

where the syntax for the type mark is given by Statement (3.8.2). The optional discriminant constraint must be used in the object declaration if no default value is provided in the type declaration. If the type declaration does contain a default value, then the optional discriminant constraint may or may not be provided in the object declaration. If provided, the value in the type declaration overrides the default value. The syntax for a discriminant constraint is

```
discriminant_constraint ::=
   (discriminant association {, discriminant_association})
                                                    (3.25.8)
```

where

```
discriminant_association ::=
   [discriminant simple_name
    {| discriminant_simple_name} =>] expression
                                                    (3.25.9)
```

This syntax implies that discriminant values can be expressions and that positional association or named association can be used.

There is a subtle implication to the use of default values of the discriminant in a record object declaration, as opposed to the specification of the discriminant value by a discriminant constraint. In the latter case, the record object becomes constrained in the sense that the value of the discriminant cannot be changed by later assignment. That is, the record object has a fixed value for the discriminant, even though the remaining components can be altered by appropriate operations. Such a record object is said to be a constrained record, in the same sense that array objects are constrained. On the other hand, if the discriminant value is not specified by an index constraint in the record object declaration, then the default value applies and the record object is unconstrained—that is, the value of the discriminant can be changed by assignment during execution. However, the only way in which the value of the discriminant can be changed is by assigning a value to the entire record. While this discussion relates to the case of a single discriminant, the same principles apply to the situation in which there are multiple discriminants.

Constrained subtypes of an unconstrained record type can also be declared, using the syntax of Statements (3.8) through (3.8.3), through the path

```
subtype_declaration ::=
     subtype identifier is type_mark discriminant_
      constraint                                    (3.25.10)
```

Objects of the subtype are then declared without specification of the discriminant constraint, because the subtype is constrained.

Several examples of the use of record discriminants are given below. These examples relate only to the use of discriminants to provide default expressions for record components and to provide the bound for an index constraint. Examples of the remaining two uses—with discriminant constraints and with variant parts—will be given in the following sections.

Consider the declarations:

```
type BUFFER_INDEX is range 1..500;
type BUFFER_ARRAY is array(BUFFER_INDEX range <>)
                              of CHARACTER;
type BUFFER_RECORD(BUFFER_LENGTH : BUFFER_INDEX := 500) is
    record
        FIRST : BUFFER_INDEX;
        LAST  : BUFFER_INDEX;
        LIST  : BUFFER_ARRAY(1..BUFFER_LENGTH);
    end record;
      --This is a discriminated record in which the record
        discriminant specifies the index constraint of the
        component LIST, an array object of type character.
```

This example converts the circular buffer of the previous section, which is of a fixed length of 500, to a circular buffer with a variable length determined by the value of the discriminant BUFFER_LENGTH. If the value of BUFFER_LENGTH is not provided in the object declaration as a discriminant constraint, then the default value of 500 is used. Thus, object declarations might be as given below:

```
TERMINAL_BUFFER  : BUFFER_RECORD(128);
    --declares a record object of type BUFFER_RECORD in
      which the value of the discriminant BUFFER_LENGTH
      is 128. Positional association is used. The record
      is constrained.
PRINTER_BUFFER   : BUFFER_RECORD(BUFFER_LENGTH => 512);
    --declares a record object of type BUFFER_RECORD in
      which the value of the discriminant BUFFER_LENGTH
      is 512. Named association is used. The record is
      constrained.
MAX_BUFFER       : BUFFER_RECORD;
    --declares a record object of the type BUFFER_
      RECORD in which the value of the discriminant
      BUFFER_LENGTH initially has the default value of
      500. The record is unconstrained.
```

In the last declaration, MAX_BUFFER is unconstrained, meaning that the value of 500 initially assigned to the discriminant BUFFER_LENGTH can be changed by later assignment. In the two former declarations, the discriminant BUFFER_LENGTH is fixed at values of 128 and 512, respectively.

As a second example, consider the following declarations:

```
type BOOLEAN_MATRIX is array(INTEGER range <>,
                              INTEGER range <>) of BOOLEAN;
type SQUARE_BOOLEAN_MATRIX(DIMENSION : INTEGER) is
  record
     MATRIX : BOOLEAN_MATRIX(1..DIMENSION, 1..DIMENSION);
  end record;
      --declares a discriminated record type which has
        only one component, a two-dimensional square
        array of dimensions given by the value of the
        discriminant DIMENSION. The components of the
        array are of type BOOLEAN.
```

Object declarations must provide the value of the discriminant DIMENSION through the use of a discrminant constraint. Thus,

```
BIT_MAP : SQUARE_BOOLEAN_MATRIX(256);
  --declares an object of type SQUARE_BOOLEAN_MATRIX
    which contains as its only component a 256 x 256
    component boolean array of type BOOLEAN_MATRIX.
```

```
DOT_MAP : SQUARE_BOOLEAN_MATRIX;
 --is not a permitted declaration, because there is no
   default value for the discriminant DIMENSION and it
   is not specified by a discriminant constraint in the
   object declaration.
```

As yet a third example, consider a revision of the record type STATE presented in Section 3.6.2. The revised declarations are

```
type VELOCITY is digits 10;
type POSITION is digits 8;
type STATE (XV, YV, ZV : VELOCITY; XP, YP, ZP : POSITION)is
    record
        X_VEL : VELOCITY : = XV;
        Y_VEL : VELOCITY : = YV;
        Z_VEL : VELOCITY : = ZV;
        X_POS : POSITION : = XP;
        Y_POS : POSITION : = YP;
        Z_POS : POSITION : = ZP;
    end record;
     --declares a discriminated record type with six
       scalar components of floating-point types. There
       are six discriminants--XV, YV, ZV, XP, YP, and ZP--
       which provide the initializing values for the
       floating-point components.
```

Object declarations must specify the discriminant values by means of a discriminant constraint. Examples are

```
AC_1 : STATE(1.27654E4, 3.62975E3, 8.97466E3,
             6.2759468E2, 2.6397428E1, 7.9742768E2);
    --declares a record object of type STATE with the
      discriminant values--and therefore initializing
      values--as indicated. Positional association is
      used. The record object is constrained.
AC_2 : STATE(XV|YV|ZV => 1000.0, XP|YP|ZP => 1000.0);
    --declares a record object of type STATE with the
      discriminant values as follows:
           XV, YV, and ZV = 0.0
           XP, YP, and ZP = 1000.0
      Named association is used. The record object is
      constrained.
AC_3 : STATE
    --is not a permitted declaration, because there
      are no default values for the discriminants,
```

```
and the object declaration does not have a
discriminant constraint.
```

Even in a situation such as this, in which the record discriminants provide initializing values to record components, the discriminants themselves may have default values. For example, the declaration

```
type STATE (XV, YV, ZV : VELOCITY := 0.0;
            XP, YP, ZP : POSITION := 0.0) is
  record
  ---
  end record;
```

provides default values for the discriminants and would make the declaration of AC_3 above permissible. The record object, in this instance, is unconstrained.

A constrained subtype declaration, as outlined in Statement (3.25.10), can be used to declare constrained subtypes of the unconstrained type STATE. For example, the declaration

```
subtype ZERO_STATE is STATE(0.0, 0.0, 0.0, 0.0, 0.0, 0.0);
```

declares the constrained record type ZERO_STATE. Object declarations such as

```
AC_3 : ZERO_STATE;
```

are now permitted, because type ZERO_STATE is constrained.

A final example shows how a discriminated record can be used to make string processing more convenient in Ada programs. A problem arises from the fact that strings are represented as one-dimensional arrays of type CHARACTER, as discussed in Section 3.6.1.7. Hence, if a string object is declared as

```
QUERY : STRING(1..12);
```

then values assigned to the string object QUERY must have precisely 12 characters. That is, the assignment

```
QUERY := "WHAT WEAPON?";
```

is permissible, while the assignment

```
QUERY := "TEST OK?";
```

is not permissible. Instead, the string literal must be padded with spaces to produce 12 characters. Thus, the assignment

```
QUERY : "   TEST OK?";
```

is permissible. Such padding can be tedious and can lead to errors. An alternative is to declare a discriminated record type, such as in the declaration

```
type STRING_LENGTH is range 0..132;
type VAR_STRING(LENGTH : STRING_LENGTH := 0) is
    record
       STRING_VALUE : STRING(1..LENGTH);
    end record;
```

Thus, the discriminant provides the length of the string, which is permissible because type STRING is an unconstrained array type. The string length is variable from zero to 132, and has an initializing value of zero. Objects of type VAR_STRING can then be declared:

```
QUERY_1 : VAR_STRING(10);
 --declares a record object whose only component is a
   ten-element string. The record is constrained.
QUERY_2 : VAR_STRING(12);
 --declares a record object whose only component is a
   12-element string. The record is constrained.
```

So far, it seems that nothing has been gained, since both records are constrained. However, if unconstrained record objects are declared, such as

```
QUERY_1, QUERY_2 : VAR_STRING;
```

then the default value of zero is used for the record discriminant LENGTH, but the records are unconstrained. Therefore, the discriminant can be changed by complete record assignment. Then the assignments

```
QUERY_1 := (12, "WHAT WEAPON");
QUERY_2 := (7, "TEST OK");
```

are both permissible. The expressions on the right-hand sides are record aggregates—which will be discussed shortly—in which the first component is the record discriminant. Furthermore, an assignment such as

```
QUERY_1 := QUERY_2;
```

is also permissible, because the discriminant is assigned along with the record component.

3.6.2.2 Variant Records. The variant record in Ada is nearly identical to that found in other languages such as Pascal. In essence, a variant record has a variant part—which is a list of components—that can be different for different record objects of the type. The particular form of the variant part is determined by the value of a record discriminant. The syntax for a variant record is given by Statements (3.25) through (3.25.6), with the additional syntax

```
variant_part ::=
     case discriminant_simple_name is
          variant
          {variant}
     end case;                                  (3.25.11)
```

and

```
variant ::=
     when choice {| choice} =>
          component_list                (3.25.12)
```

The syntax for choice is given by Statement (3.24.2) and that for the component list by Statement (3.25.2). The variant part is in the form of a case statement, which is discussed later in Section 3.8.3.

The usual typing rules apply to variant parts; that is, each choice must be of the same type as the discriminant. Each possible value of the discriminant—that is, each value associated with the type of the discriminant—must occur once and only once in the set of choices of the variant part, and no other value is permitted. The simple expressions and ranges used as choices must be static, that is, their values cannot be variable. The **others** choice stands for all possible values of the discriminant not specified by previous choices; if used, it must occur as the only choice in the last variant. A component simple name is not permitted as a choice of a variant.

The discriminant used in variant records is identical to that used in discriminated records. Thus, the discriminant may have a default value, in which case an object declaration may produce either a constrained or an unconstrained record object, depending upon whether or not the object declaration contains a discriminant constraint. If there is no default value declared for the discriminant, then all object declarations must have a discriminant constraint, and all objects are constrained records—in that the form of the variant part of an object cannot be changed during execution. The form of the variant part of unconstrained variant records, on the other hand, can be changed by assignment of different values to the discriminant, but such assignment can occur only as part of an entire record assignment.

Several examples of the use of variant records are given below. The first example is given by the following declarations:

```
type DIST is digits 6;
type DEGREE is digits 6;
type FIX_TYPE is (RADAR, LORAN, SATELLITE);
type FIX(SOURCE : FIX_TYPE := RADAR) is
    record
        LATITUDE  : DEGREE;
        LONGITUDE : DEGREE;
        HOUR      : INTEGER range 0..23;
        MINUTE    : INTEGER range 0..59;
        SECOND    : INTEGER range 0..59;
        case SOURCE is
            when RADAR =>
                RANGE     : DIST;
                BEARING   : DEGREE;
                GEO_POINT : STRING(1..24);
            when LORAN =>
                STATION_PAIR_1 : STRING(1..10);
                STATION_PAIR_2 : STRING(1..10);
            when SATELLITE
                PASS_NUMBER : POSITIVE;
                SAT_NAME    : STRING(1..7);
        end case;
    end record;
     --declares a variant record type whose variant
       part contains three choices. The discriminant is
       the enumeration object SOURCE, which has a
       default value of RADAR.
```

In this example, all objects of type FIX will have components LATITUDE, LONGITUDE, HOUR, MINUTE, SECOND, and will have one of the sets of components associated with the three choices—that is either

```
RANGE      or  STATION_PAIR_1  or  PASS_NUMBER
BEARING        STATION_PAIR_2      SAT_NAME
GEO_POINT
```

depending upon the value assigned to the discriminant SOURCE. Example declarations are given below:

```
FIX_1 : FIX(LORAN);
 --declares a record object of type FIX in which the
   discriminant SOURCE has the value LORAN. The
   variant part of the record is that associated with
   the choice LORAN. The record object is constrained.
FIX_2 : FIX;
 --declares a record object of type FIX in which the
   discriminant SOURCE has the default value RADAR.
   The variant part of the record is that associated
   with the choice RADAR. The record object is
   unconstrained.
```

The fact that the object FIX_2 is unconstrained implies that the value of the discriminant SOURCE can be changed by assignment during program execution. Such assignment, however, can only be made as part of an entire record assignment, as discussed in the previous section. The object FIX_1, on the other hand, is a constrained record, implying that the value of the discriminant SOURCE is fixed and cannot be changed by record assignment. For example, the assignment

```
FIX_2 := FIX_1;
```

is permitted, because FIX_2 is unconstrained, but the assignment

```
FIX_1 := FIX_2;
```

may or may not be permitted, depending upon the discriminant value of FIX_2.

A constrained subtype of type FIX can be declared, in accordance with Statement (3.25.10). For example, the declaration

```
subtype LORAN_FIX is FIX(LORAN);
```

declares a constrained record type LORAN_FIX. Objects of type LORAN_FIX can then be declared. For example, the declaration

```
FIX_3 : LORAN_FIX;
```

declares record object FIX 3, which has the same structure as that produced by the object declaration

```
FIX_3 : FIX(LORAN);
```

using the variant record type FIX.

A second example involves the following declarations:

```
type TEMP  is digits 4;
type PRESS is digits 5;
type SENSOR_LOCATION is (COMPRESSOR_INLET,
     COMPRESSOR_OUTLET, TURBINE_INLET, TURBINE_OUTLET,
     FAN_INLET, FAN_OUTLET, NOZZLE);
type SENSOR_VALUES (LOCATION: SENSOR_LOCATION) is
     record
         STATIC_PRESSURE : PRESS;
         TEMPERATURE     : TEMP;
         case LOCATION is
            when TURBINE_OUTLET | NOZZLE =>
               DYNAMIC_PRESSURE : PRESS;
            when others =>
               null;
         end case;
     end record;
      --declares a variant record type whose variant
        part contains two choices. The discriminant is
        the enumeration object LOCATION, which has no
        default value specified.
```

In this example, all objects of type SENSOR_VALUES will have the two components named STATIC_PRESSURE and TEMPERATURE. In addition, if the value of the discriminant LOCATION is either TURBINE_OUTLET or NOZZLE, there will be an additional component named DYNAMIC_PRESSURE. Since there is no default value for the discriminant, all object declarations must contain a discriminant constraint. Hence, all objects of type SENSOR_VALUE are constrained records. This example illustrates the use of the **others** choice to eliminate the necessity for explicitly listing the remaining choices.

3.6.2.3 Record Aggregates. Just as array component values can be combined into a composite value called an array aggregate, so also can record component values be combined to form a record aggregate. The syntax for an aggregate is given by Statements (3.24), (3.24.1), and (3.24.2), and is applicable to both array aggregates and record aggregates. In the case of a record aggregate, the choices are the components of the record; the discriminants, if any, must be included. The value of a discriminant that specifies a variant part must be given by a static expression. If the choice **others** is used, it must represent at least one component. Either positional or named association can be used. If named association is used, the component values, including those of the discriminants, can be in any order. If positional association is used, the discriminant values must appear first and, if there is more than one discriminant, the values must appear in the same order as they appear in the discriminant part of the record type declaration. Some examples of aggregates based on the record declarations of Sections 3.6.2, 3.6.2.1, and 3.6.2.2 are given below.

Two aggregates representing values of record objects of type EVENT, from Section 3.6.1, are

```
(1985, NOV, 7, 13, 27, 56, "REACTOR TEST #1          ")
 --uses positional association. The string literal is
   padded with blanks.
```

and

```
(YEAR => 1969, MONTH => JUL, DAY => 20, HOUR => 13
 MIN => 19, SEC => 40, ID => "APOLLO---EAGLE HAS
 LANDED")
 --uses named association. These values could occur
   in any order.
```

The positional and named associations may be mixed, but once a named association is used, all remaining associations must be named. For example,

```
(1969, JUL, 20, ID => "APOLLO--EAGLE HAS
LANDED", SEC => 40, MIN => 19, HOUR => 13)
```

is also a permissible form of the aggregate above.

The second example involves aggregates representing values of discriminanted record objects of type SQUARE_BOOLEAN_MATRIX, as declared in Section 3.6.2.1. A possible aggregate value is given below:

```
(2, ((TRUE, FALSE), (FALSE, TRUE)))
 --the discriminant value is 2, implying a 2 x 2
   array. The array values are specified by an array
   aggregate. Positional association is used.
```

Alternate forms of this aggregrate are given below:

```
(2, (1 => (TRUE, FALSE), 2 => (TRUE, FALSE)
(DIMENSION => 2, ((TRUE, FALSE), (TRUE, FALSE))).
```

And there are other forms combining positional and named associations.

Aggregate values for discriminated record objects of type VAR_STRING, also declared in Section 3.6.2.1, are represented by the following examples:

```
(12, "WHAT WEAPON?")
 --the discriminant LENGTH is assigned the value 12,
   and the component STRING_VALUE is assigned the 12-
   character string literal as indicated. Positional
   association is used.

(LENGTH => 7, STRING_VALUE => "TEST OK")
 --the discriminant LENGTH is assigned the value 7, and
   the component STRING_VALUE is assigned the seven-
   character string literal as indicated. Named
   association is used.
```

The three examples above relate to the discriminated record types of Section 3.6.2.1. Examples of aggregate values of objects of the variant record types of Section 3.6.2.2 are given below.

Examples of aggregates representing values of variant record objects of type FIX are

```
(RADAR, 32.63, 117.47, 13, 26, 52, 200.0,
 332.0, "POINT REYES                ")
 --the discriminant SOURCE is assigned the value RADAR,
   which in turn determines that the variant part
   contains the three components RANGE, BEARING, and
   GEO_POINT, to which the last three components of the
   aggregate assign values. Positional association is
   used.

(SOURCE => SATELLITE, LATITUDE => 47.36, LONGITUDE =>
 12.76, HOUR => 23, MINUTE => 03, SECOND => 13,
 PASS_NUMBER => 1623, SAT_NAME => "TRANSIT")
 --the discriminant SOURCE is assigned the value
   SATELLITE, which in turn determines that the variant
   part contains the two components PASS_NUMBER and
   SAT_NAME. Named association is used.
```

As a final example, aggregate values for a variant record object of type SENSOR_LOCATION, declared in Section 3.6.2.2, might be

```
(COMPRESSOR_INLET, 56.75, 1235.7)
 --the discriminant LOCATION is assigned the value
   COMPRESSOR_INLET, which is part of the others
   choice. Thus, the variant part is null; that is,
   it contains no components. Positional association
   is used.
```

```
(NOZZLE, 364.27, 723.6, 1075.6)
 --the discriminant LOCATION is assigned the value
   NOZZLE, which then determines that the variant part
   contains the additional component DYNAMIC_PRESSURE.
   Positional association is used.
```

Named association, or a combination of positional and named association, could be used in any of these example aggregates.

While record aggregates can be used to represent composite values, which can then be assigned to the entire record object, the individual record components—with the exception of any discriminants—can themselves be manipulated as the data objects that they are, in a manner completely analogous to the manipulation of array components. Reference to record components must be made using selected component notation, as described in Section 3.7.1.2.

3.6.2.4 Operations. The predefined operations associated with record types are as given in Table 3.8. Specific details of these operations will be presented later, although the general concept of several of the operations is fairly evident.

Table 3.8 Operations Associated with Record Types

OPERATION	SYMBOL
assignment	:=
aggregate	
explicit conversion	
membership	**in** **not in**
qualification	
relational	= /=
selection of components	

3.6.2.5 Attributes. The following predefined attributes are associated with record types:

- BASE
- SIZE

Record objects have the attributes

- ADDRESS
- SIZE
- CONSTRAINED

In addition, record components have the attributes

- FIRST_BIT
- LAST_BIT
- POSITION

The reader is referred to Appendix B for specific details of these attributes.

3.6.3 Access Data Types

In the Ada language, dynamic storage allocation—that is, the capability of allocating and releasing storage independently of the block-structured environment—is provided by the access data type. The access type is equivalent to the pointer type in Pascal and provides a mechanism for the dynamic creation of objects during the execution of a program. This concept is completely different from the creation of objects by object declarations, which can occur only during elaboration of the declarative parts of program units, and which occurs in the same manner each time the declaration is elaborated. Dynamic creation of objects is achieved during program execution by means of an entity called an *allocator*, which may be evaluated any number of times depending upon the structure and execution of the program.

An access object—that is, an object of an access type—has no function other than to designate, or point to, another object that itself has no name. That is, the designated object can be referenced only through the access object, which can be considered to contain the address of the designated object. This relationship is illustrated in Figure 3.7. Each object of a particular access type will either designate no object—called a **null** access—or designate an object of a specific type identified in the type declaration of the access type. The syntax for the declaration of an access type is given by Statements (3.7), (3.7.1), and (3.7.2) through the path

```
type_declaration ::=
        type identifier is access_type_definition;
                                                  (3.26)
```

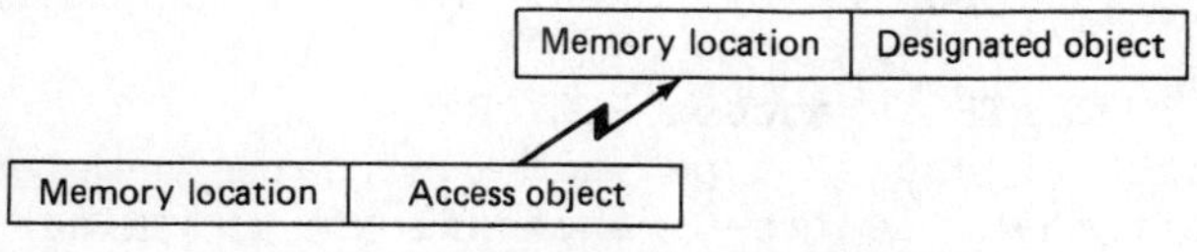

An access object "points to" a designated object.

Figure 3.7. Access objects.

where

```
access_type_definition ::= access subtype_indication
                                                    (3.26.1)
```

and where the syntax for the subtype indication is given by Statement (3.8.1). In the subtype indication, the only constraints permitted after the name of an access type are range constraints and discriminant constraints. Otherwise, there is no restriction on the use of constraints. The subtype indication identifies the designated type, that is, the type of the object designated by objects of the access type. The conglomeration of all objects designated by objects of a particular access type forms a collection of objects associated with the access type. It is permissible for more than one access object to designate the same object.

If an access object is a constant—declared as indicated in Section 3.2.5—then its value cannot be changed. That is, it always designates the same object, as opposed to access variables whose values can be changed by assignment. However, the value of the designated object need not remain constant; its value can be changed by assignment using the selected component notation described in Section 3.7.1.2.

Examples of access type declarations are given below. Some of these examples refer to type declarations of previous sections:

```
type MESSAGE is access STRING;
 --declares an access type that designates nameless
   objects that are unconstrained character strings. The
   index constraint must be provided by either the
   allocator or the object declaration.

type FIXED_MESSAGE is access STRING(6);
 --declares an access type that designates nameless
   objects that are constrained character strings of six
   components. The index constraint is provided.

type THREAT_PTR is access TARGET_THREAT;
 --declares an access type that designates nameless
   objects that are one-dimensional, 100-component
   arrays of type TARGET_THREAT. See Section 3.6.1.1.

type PICTURE_PTR is access PICTURE;
 --declares an access type that designates nameless
   objects that are two-dimensional unconstrained arrays
   of type PICTURE as declared in Section 3.6.1.2. Index
   constraints must be provided by either the allocator
   or the object declaration.
```

```
type AC_STATE is access STATE;
 --declares an access type that designates nameless
   objects that are records of type STATE, as declared
   in Section 3.6.2.

type TEMP_STORAGE is access BUFFER_RECORD;
 --declares an access type that designates nameless
   objects that are discriminated records of type
   BUFFER_RECORD, as declared in Section 3.6.2.1. The
   discriminant constraint may be provided either by the
   allocator, the object declaration, or the default
   value.

type FIX_PTR is access FIX;
 --declares an access type that designates nameless
   objects that are variant records of type FIX, as
   declared in Section 3.6.2.2. The discriminant
   constraint may be provided by either the allocator,
   the object declaration, or the default value.
```

These are type declarations; access objects are declared in the usual manner:

```
MESS_1          : MESSAGE;
 --declares an access object that designates a STRING
   object. The index constraint must be supplied by the
   allocator.

MESS_2          : FIXED_MESSAGE;
 --declares an access object that designates a six-
   component STRING object.

EVAL            : THREAT_PTR;
 --declares an access object that designates a one-
   dimensional, 100-component array object of type
   TARGET_THREAT.

FRAME           : PICTURE_PTR;
 --declares an access object that designates a nameless
   unconstrained array object of type PICTURE. The
   index constraint must be supplied by the allocator.

AC1             : AC_STATE;
 --declares an access object that designates a nameless
   record object of type STATE.
```

```
DATA_RECORDS : TEMP_STORAGE;
 --declares an access object that designates a nameless
   unconstrained record of type BUFFER_RECORD. The
   discriminant BUFFER_LENGTH may be provided by the
   allocator or by the default value.

SAT_POSIT     : FIX_PTR(SOURCE => SATELLITE);
 --designates an access object that designates a
   nameless constrained variant record of type FIX. The
   discriminant SOURCE is provided by the object
   declaration.
```

While the elaboration of access objects such as these actually creates the access objects, the objects themselves have an initial value of **null**—that is, they designate nothing—until a value is provided through the evaluation of an allocator or by the assignment of some other access value. In fact, the **null** initial value of an access object is the only initialization of any object provided by the Ada language. The value of an object of any other type is undefined until the object is assigned a value, unless a default initial value is included in the object declaration, as indicated by Statement (3.10).

3.6.3.1 Allocators. When access objects are created by elaboration of their declaration, the type of the objects which they designate has already been established—specifically, they are established by the access type declarations. Upon elaboration, however, the access value is **null,** as indicated in the previous section. Not only does the **null** value imply that no object is designated, it also implies that memory has not been allocated to store the designated object. The evaluation of an allocator creates the designated object—causes memory to be allocated—and produces an access value that designates the object. This access value may then be assigned to an access object of the proper type. The syntax for an allocator is

```
allocator ::=
   new subtype_indication | new qualified_expression  (3.27)
```

where the syntax for a subtype indication is given by Statement (3.8.1). The syntax for a qualified expression will be presented in Section 3.7.6. Because access objects may designate unconstrained arrays or unconstrained records, their allocators in such instances must supply the required index constraint or discriminant constraint. Specification of these constraints is effected by the syntax of Statement (3.27) through the path

```
allocator ::= new subtype_indication    (3.27.1)
```

where the syntax of a subtype indication is obtained from Statements (3.8.1) and (3.8.3). Specifically, the syntax is

```
subtype_indication ::= type_mark constraint
                                                  (3.27.2)
```

where

```
constraint ::= index_constaint | discriminant constraint
                                                  (3.27.3)
```

The index and range constraints are the only constraints permitted in an allocator.

Examples of the use of allocators, based upon the example type declarations of the previous section, are given below:

```
new TARGET_THREAT;
 --creates a nameless object that is a 100-element
   array of type TARGET_THREAT. The object is not
   initialized. An access value designating the object
   is produced.

new STATE;
 --creates a nameless object that is a record of type
   STATE. The object is not initialized. An access
   value designating the object is produced.
```

The access values produced by these allocators can be assigned to access objects of the corresponding types. One way to assign values is by means of an assignment statement. For example, execution of the statement

```
EVAL := new TARGET_THREAT;
```

assigns the access value produced by evaluation of the allocator on the right-hand side of the assignment delimiter to the access object on the left-hand side. This process is illustrated in Figure 3.8. Of course, type compatibility must be maintained in such an assignment. In this case, EVAL has been declared as an object of type THREAT_PTR which, in turn, was declared as an access type designating an object of type TARGET_THREAT.

```
EVAL: THREAT_PTR;
  -- Access object EVAL is created
```

```
EVAL: = new TARGET_THREAT;
 -- Allocation creates designated object, which
    is a 100-component array. Component values
    are undefined. Assignment operator assigns
    access value to EVAL.
```

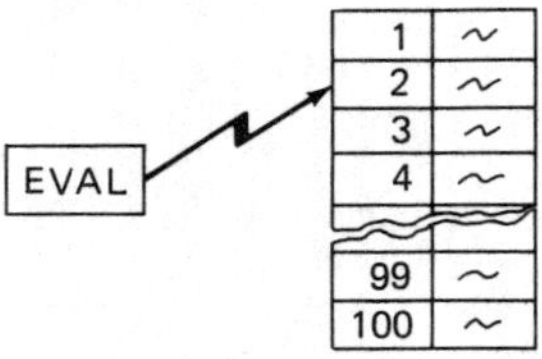

Figure 3.8. Allocation.

A second example is the assignment statement

```
AC1 := new STATE;
```

which assigns the access value produced by evaluation of the allocator on the right-hand side to the access object AC1.

In the two examples above, the designated objects were constrained; that is, TARGET_THREAT was a constrained array type, and STATE was a constrained record type. In the event that the designated object is not constrained, then the constraint must be provided by the allocator. Three examples from the previous section serve to illustrate this point; they are based on the following declarations:

```
type PICTURE_PTR  is access PICTURE;
type TEMP_STORAGE is access BUFFER_RECORD;
type FIX_PTR      is access FIX;
FRAME          : PICTURE_PTR;
DATA_RECORDS : TEMP_STORAGE;
```

The first access type, PICTURE_PTR, designates a two-dimensional unconstrained array. The remaining two access types designate unconstrained records—a discriminated record in the case of TEMP_STORAGE and a variant record in the case of FIX_PTR. Allocators creating designated objects must provide the missing constraints. For example, in the assignment statement

```
FRAME := new PICTURE(1..256, 1..256);
```

the allocator on the right-hand side provides the index constraint and creates a 256 × 256 nameless array of type PICTURE. It also provides an access value designating this array, which is assigned to the access object FRAME. Similarly, for the second example above, the assignment statement

```
DATA_RECORDS := new BUFFER_RECORD(128);
```

provides the required discriminant constraint, causing the allocator to create a nameless record of type BUFFER_RECORD that has as one component a 128-component array named LIST. In the final example above, an allocator might be

```
new FIX(SOURCE => SATELLITE)
```

in which the discriminant constraint is provided using named association, as contrasted to the positional association used in the two previous examples. The designated object in all three cases, of course, is constrained.

3.6.3.2. Initialization. When the evaluation of an allocator creates a designated object, the value of the object is undefined, as is the case for any object declaration that does not include an initializing value. The exception, of course, is the access object, which is provided with the initial value **null.** Values can be assigned to designated objects in a manner to be discussed later. It is possible, however, to initialize the designated object at the time of allocation. Initialization is achieved by use of an Ada construct called a *qualified expression*. The subject of qualified expressions is covered later in Section 3.7.6, but their use in this situation is fairly simple, using the syntax of Statement (3.27) in the following form:

```
allocator ::= new qualified_expression      (3.28)
```

where

```
qualified_expression ::=
        type_mark'expression | type_mark'aggregate
                                              (3.28.1)
```

The form of the qualified expression used in this case is an aggregate preceded by the type of the designated object. For example, the allocator

```
new TARGET_THREAT'(1..100 => UNKNOWN)
```

not only creates a nameless designated 100-component array object, but it also assigns the value UNKNOWN to all components. Similarly, in the assignment statement

```
AC1 := new STATE'(0.0, 0.0, 0.0, 0.0, 0.0, 0.0);
```

the allocator creates the designated object—in this case a record of type STATE with six components—and initializes all the components to 0.0. Use of the alternative form of the qualified expression—that involving an expression—permits initialization by use of expressions of the designated type, if appropriate.

In the event that the designated object is unconstrained, it is not necessary to explicitly provide the constraint, since it is implicitly contained in the initial value assigned. For example, an allocator creating a designated object of type BUFFER_RECORD with initialization is

```
new BUFFER_RECORD'(BUFFER_LENGTH => 256,
    FIRST => 0, LAST => 0, LIST => (1..256 => '*'))
```

In the case of a discriminated record such as BUFFER_RECORD, the discriminant value appears in the aggregate. Notice that named association is used here. The same allocator, using positional association in the aggregate, is

```
new BUFFER_RECORD'(256, 0, 0, (1..256 => '*'))
```

If the designated object is a variant record, the same concept applies. For example, an allocator creating a designated object of type FIX, with initialization, is

```
new FIX'(RADAR, 32.63, 117.47, 13, 26, 52,
              200.0, 332.0, "POINT REYES    ")
```

Positional association is used here.

In the event that the designated object is an unconstrained array, the index constraint is implied by the initial value assigned. For example, in the assignment statement

```
FRAME := new PICTURE'(1..256 => (1..256 => 0.0));
```

the allocation not only creates a 256 × 256 nameless array of type PICTURE, it also initializes all components to zero. It is not necessary to explicitly provide the index constraint, because it is implied by the initial value assigned. The array aggregate in this case is formed according to the discussion of Section 3.6.1.4.

3.6.3.3 Incomplete Type Declarations. One of the most common uses of access types is in the building of linked lists, trees, and other linked data structures. For example, a singly linked list can be represented by a collection of records. The records themselves are designated objects, and the first record in the list is designated by an access object called the head of the list. Each nameless record in the list has a link component that designates the next record in the list. The final record has a **null** link field. Thus, the entire linked list of records is, in effect, designated by the head of the list. In order to create such a structure, it is necessary to circumvent an inherent characteristic of the Ada language—that no entity can be used before its declaration is elaborated. The provision of the language that permits this circumvention is the incomplete type declaration. The syntax for an incomplete type declaration is given by Statement (3.7) with the alternative

```
    type_declaration ::= incomplete_type_definition
                                                          (3.29)
```

where

```
  incomplete_type_definition ::= type identifier
                                   [discriminant_part];
                                                        (3.29.1)
```

The reader will note that only an identifier, and an optional discriminant part, follows the reserved word **type.** The most important part, the type definition, is missing. When an incomplete type declaration is used, there must subsequently be a corresponding full type declaration with the same identifier. A discriminant part must be provided by the full type declaration if, and only if, the corresponding incomplete type declaration provides a discriminant part. The syntax for a discriminant part is given by Statements (3.25.5) and (3.25.6). Before the full type declaration is elaborated, the only permitted use of a type declared by an incomplete type declaration is in the declaration of an access type. That is, it can only appear as the type mark in the subtype indication of an access type definition, as given by Statements (3.26), (3.26.1), and (3.8.1). The only form of constraint permitted in this subtype indication is a discriminant constraint.

The need for the incomplete type definition can be illustrated by examining the declarations required for a simple linked list. Consider the following declarations:

```
type ELEMENT;
type LINK    is access ELEMENT;
type ELEMENT is
   record
        WORD : STRING(1..12);
        NEXT : LINK;
   end record;
```

Here, the first statement is an incomplete type declaration of the type ELEMENT. It must be provided prior to the elaboration of type LINK, because the declaration of type LINK refers to type ELEMENT. By the same reasoning, the declaration of type LINK must precede the declaration of type ELEMENT—in this case, the full declaration of type ELEMENT. The requirement for the incomplete type definition of ELEMENT is cleary evident. A simple linked list comprised of records of type ELEMENT is illustrated in Figure 3.9.

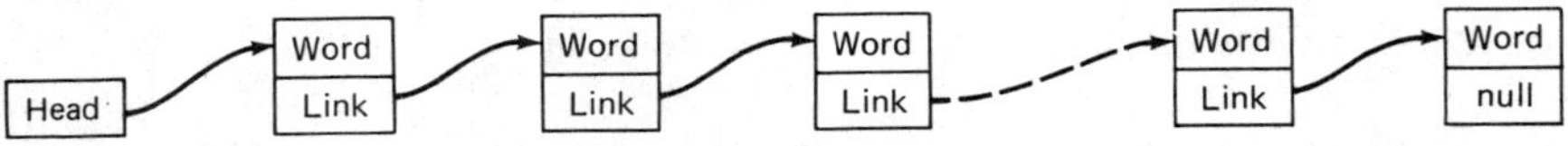

Figure 3.9. A simple linked list.

In general, there is no limitation on the type of an object designated by an access object. The type of a component of a composite designated object can be another access type, in which case there is a mutual dependency between the access types, or it can be the same access type, as in the linked list example above. In the latter case, the access type is recursive.

3.6.3.4 Operations. The predefined operations associated with access types are given in Table 3.9. Some of these operations are not apparent from the discussion to this point, but they are listed here for later reference.

Table 3.9 Operations Associated with Access Types.

OPERATION	SYMBOL
association	
asignment	:=
explicit conversion	
membership	**in** **not in**
qualification	
relational	= /=
selection of components	
If the designated object is an array:	
indexing	
slices	

3.6.3.5 Attributes. The following predefined attributes apply to access types:

- BASE
- STORAGE_SIZE
- SIZE

If the designated object is an array, the following additional attributes are predefined:

- FIRST
- FIRST(N)
- LAST
- LAST(N)
- LENGTH
- LENGTH(N)
- RANGE
- RANGE(N)

These attributes yield values associated with the designated array. Finally, an access object has the attributes:

- ADDRESS
- SIZE

The reader is referred to Appendix B for details of these attributes.

3.7 NAMES AND EXPRESSIONS

The discussion to this point has assumed some basic familiarity on the part of the reader with the concepts of names and expressions as they apply to data objects. In this section, this assumed familiarity is formalized and some new concepts are introduced.

3.7.1 Names

In any programming language, the objects are usually associated with names, formulated in accordance with some specific rules. In the Ada language, a name can represent declared entities—including types, objects, subprograms, and so on. The precise format of a name and how it relates to that of an identifier is given by the following syntax:

```
name ::= simple_name
    | character_literal   | operator_symbol
    | indexed_component   | slice
    | selected_component  | attribute          (3.30)
```

where

```
        simple_name ::= identifier          (3.30.1)
```

and the syntax for an identifier is given by Statement (3.3). Thus, a simple name is the identifier associated with an entity in its declaration. In the case of components of composite types—indexed components and selected components in Statement (3.30)—and of slices and attributes, the names include a prefix to identify the particular composite object. The syntax for a prefix is

```
prefix ::= name | function_call.            (3.31)
```

The syntax for a name, of course, is given by Statement 3.30; the function call is discussed later in Section 3.10.4. Of the alternatives in Statement (3.30), only the indexed component, selected component, and operator symbol have not been previously considered. Here, indexed component and selected component notation is formalized.

3.7.1.1 Indexed Components. While certain operations are associated with array types, these operations are fairly limited in scope. Detailed manipulation of an array often must be accomplished by means of operations on the individual components. The name of an array component is an indexed component, for which the syntax is

```
indexed_component ::= prefix(expression {, expression}).
                                                   (3.32)
```

The prefix is the name of the array object, and the expression(s) specifies the index value(s) for the component of interest. This notation is common to most other languages. For example, some of the components of the arrays declared in Section 3.6.1.1 have the following names:

```
TARG_1(10)              ROT_MATRIX_1(2,3)
TARG_2(36)              ROT_MATRIX_2(1,3)
TARG_3(97)              VEL_STATE(YAW_RATE)
MEM_VALUE(M68000)
```

The indexed components need not be scalars. For example, in Section 3.6.2 the following array object—of an anonymous type—is declared:

```
ALL_EVENTS : array(EVENT_TYPE) of BUFFER_RECORD;
```

The components of this array, named by the indexed components

```
ALL_EVENTS(POLITICAL)
ALL_EVENTS(MILITARY)
ALL_EVENTS(SCIENTIFIC)
```

are themselves complex data structures. Each component is a record containing a component which itself is an array of records.

If the array object is nameless and designated by an access object then the prefix in Statement (3.32) is the name of the access object. For example, the declarations

```
type BALLISTIC_TABLE is array(1..100, 1..100) of FLOAT
type BAL_TAB_PTR is access BALLISTIC_TABLE;
MK2_TABLE : BAL_TAB_PTR;
```

followed by the assignment statement

```
MK2_TABLE := new BALLISTIC_TABLE;
```

create a nameless 100 × 100 component array designated by the value of the access variable MK2_TABLE. Components of this array have names such as

```
MK2_TABLE(1,1), MK2_TABLE (1,2)
```

and so on.

3.7.1.2 Selected Components. The names of record components and record objects designated by access values are given by a construct called a selected component. The syntax for a selected component is

```
selected component ::= prefix.selector     (3.33)
```

where

```
selector ::= simple_name
   | character_literal | operator_symbol | all
                                            (3.33.1)
```

and where the syntax for a prefix is given by Statement (3.31). This syntax is also used in forming an expanded name used to reference an entity outside its region of direct visibility. This concept is discussed in Section 3.11.2.

The name of a record component must have a simple name—the identifier associated with the particular component—as the selector. The prefix is the name of the record object. If the record object is nameless and designated by an access object, the prefix is the name of the access object. When it is desired to denote an entire designated object, the selector **all** is used.

Some simple examples are given here. Consider the record declaration

```
type CONTROL_EFFORT is
   record
        AILERON   : FLOAT;
        ELEVATOR  : FLOAT;
        RUDDER    : FLOAT;
        THROTTLE  : FLOAT;
   end record;
```

and the object declaration

```
NEUTRAL_CONTROL : CONTROL_EFFORT;
```

Then, the following names denote the components of the record object NEUTRAL_CONTROL:

```
NEUTRAL_CONTROL.AILERON    NEUTRAL_CONTROL.RUDDER
NEUTRAL_CONTROL.ELEVATOR   NEUTRAL_CONTROL.THROTTLE
```

Each of these objects is of type FLOAT, and any floating-point attribute or operation may be applied to it. If an access type is declared, along with an object of the type

```
type CNTRL_PTR is access CONTROL_EFFORT;
CONTROL_UPDATE : CNTRL_PTR;
```

then the assignment statement

```
CONTROL_UPDATE := new CONTROL_EFFORT;
```

creates a nameless record of type CONTROL_EFFORT, whose components have the names

```
CONTROL_UPDATE.AILERON    CONTROL_UPDATE.RUDDER
CONTROL_UPDATE.ELEVATOR   CONTROL_UPDATE.THROTTLE
```

Again, these objects are of type FLOAT, and any floating-point operation or attribute may be applied to them. On the other hand, the designated object itself has the name

```
CONTROL_UPDATE.all.
```

It is important to recognize the difference between the object denoted by the name CONTROL_UPDATE and that denoted by the name

CONTROL_UPDATE.**all**. The former is an access object, while the latter is a record object designated by the access object.

Logical application of the concepts of indexed components and selected components can be used to access any part of a data structure. As an example, consider the following declarations from Section 3.6.2:

```
type EVENT is
   record
        YEAR  : INTEGER range 1900.2000;
        MONTH : MONTH_NAME;
        DAY   : INTEGER range 1..23;
        HOUR  : INTEGER range 0..159;
        MIN   : INTEGER range 0..59;
        SEC   : INTEGER range 0..59;
        ID    : STRING(1..25) := (1..25 => '*');
   end record;
type BUFFER_INDEX is range 1..500;
type BUFFER_ARRAY is array(BUFFER_INDEX) of EVENT;
type BUFFER_RECORD is
   record
        FIRST : BUFFER_INDEX;
        LAST  : BUFFER_INDEX;
        LIST  : BUFFER_ARRAY;
   end record;
type EVENT_TYPE is (POLITICAL, MILITARY, SCIENTIFIC);
```

with the additional declaration

```
type EVENT_ARRAY is array(EVENT_TYPE) of BUFFER_RECORD;
```

Then, EVENT_ARRAY is a three-component array type. Each component of EVENT_ARRAY is a record of type BUFFER_RECORD. Records of type BUFFER_RECORD have three components, one of which is an array of type BUFFER_ARRAY. Arrays of type BUFFER_ARRAY have 500 components; each component is a record of type EVENT. Records of type EVENT have seven components, one of which is a one-dimensional, 25-component array in the form of a string. If the object ALL_EVENTS is declared as

```
ALL_EVENTS : EVENT_ARRAY;
```

then the following names, among others, are defined:

```
ALL_EVENTS(POLITICAL)
ALL_EVENTS(MILITARY)
```

```
ALL_EVENTS(SCIENTIFIC)
--these names denote the components of the array object
  ALL_EVENTS. They are record objects of type
  BUFFER_RECORD.
ALL_EVENTS(POLITICAL).FIRST
ALL_EVENTS(POLITICAL).LAST
ALL_EVENTS(POLITICAL).LIST
--these names denote the components of the record object
  ALL_EVENTS(POLITICAL). The first two are of integer
  type BUFFER_INDEX. The last is an array of type BUFFER_
  ARRAY.
ALL_EVENTS(POLITICAL).LIST(1)
ALL_EVENTS(POLITICAL).LIST(2)
                    .
                    .
                    .
ALL_EVENTS(POLITICAL).LIST(500)
--these are components of the array ALL_EVENTS(POLITI-
  CAL).LIST. They are record objects of type EVENT.
ALL_EVENTS(POLITICAL).LIST(1).YEAR
ALL_EVENTS(POLITICAL).LIST(1).MONTH
ALL_EVENTS(POLITICAL).LIST(1).DAY
ALL_EVENTS(POLITICAL).LIST(1).HOUR
ALL_EVENTS(POLITICAL).LIST(1).MIN
ALL_EVENTS(POLITICAL).LIST(1).SEC
ALL_EVENTS(POLITICAL).LIST(1).ID
--these are the components of record object
  ALL_EVENTS(POLITICAL).LIST(1). The first six are
  scalar objects. The last is an array object of the
  predefined type string, with 25 components.
ALL_EVENTS(POLITICAL).LIST(1).ID(1)
ALL_EVENTS(POLITICAL).LIST(1).ID(2)
                    .
                    .
                    .
ALL_EVENTS(POLITICAL).LIST(1).ID(25)
--these are the components of the string array
  ALL_EVENTS(POLITICAL).LIST(1).ID.
```

Although names such as these are cumbersome, they do reflect the underlying structure of the data, and hence they enhance the understandability of Ada code. The Ada language does provide a renaming capability by which long names such as these can be denoted by simple names. Renaming is discussed in Section 8.2.2.

3.7.2 Expressions

An expression is an entity formed of operations and operands that can be evaluated to yield a value. In the Ada language an expression has a type, which depends upon the operands and operations contained in the expression. Ada's strong typing rules apply both in the evaluation of an expression and in the assignment of the resulting value. The general syntax for an expression is

```
expression ::=
     relation {and relation} | relation {and then relation}
 | relation {or relation} | relation {or else relation}
 | relation {xor relation}                              (3.34)
```

where

```
        relation ::=
               simple_expression [relational_operator
                                  simple_expression]
        | simple_expression [not] in range
        | simple_expession{not] in type_mark          (3.34.1)
```

and

```
     simple_expression ::= [unary_adding_operator] term
                           {binary_adding_operator term}
                                                     (3.34.2)
```

with

```
        term ::= factor {multiplying_operator factor}
                                                     (3.34.3)

         factor ::= primary [**primary} | abs primary
                  | not primary                      (3.34.4)

     primary ::=
        numeric_literal | null | aggregate | string_literal
               | name | allocator | function_call
               | type_conversion | qualified_expression
               | (expression).                       (3.34.5)
```

The primaries are the fundamental constituents of an expression. Each primary has a value and a type. The only names permitted are named numbers, attributes that yield values, and names denoting objects or denoting values. Examples below are based on the following declarations:

```
PI          : CONSTANT := 3.141_592_65;
SUM         : FLOAT;
LINE_COUNT  : INTEGER;
VEL         : FLOAT;
EVALUATION  : THREAT;
HEX_COUNT   : HEXDIGIT;
ARMED       : BOOLEAN;
```

Examples of primaries are given below:

```
PI                 -- a named number
SUM                -- a name for an object
INTEGER'LAST       -- an attribute
4.7                -- a numeric literal
null               -- the value null
(1..25 => '*')     -- an array aggregate
(LINE_COUNT + 1)   -- a parenthesized expression
new THREAT         -- an allocator
```

Examples of the remaining primaries—function calls, type conversions, and qualified expressions—will be given when the primaries themselves are discussed.

Examples of expressions are

```
VEL                      -- a primary
not ARMED                -- a factor
16.2 * VEL               -- a term
4.7                      -- a simple expression
-3.2 + VEL               -- a simple expression
VEL ** 2 + 10.0 * SUM    -- a simple expression
LINE_COUNT in 3..20      -- a relation
```

The details of operations and of some of the primaries are treated in the remainder of this section.

3.7.2.1 Predefined Operations. The operations provided by the Ada language are similar to those provided by most other languages. There are six classes of operators, for which the syntax is listed below in the order of decreasing precedence:

```
highest_precedence_operator ::= ** | abs | not                 (3.35)
multiplying_operator        ::= * | / | mod | rem              (3.36)
unary_adding_operator       ::= + |                            (3.37)
binary_adding_operator      ::= + | - | *                      (3.38)
relational_operator         ::= = | /= | < | <= | > | >=
                                                               (3.39)
logical_operator            ::= and | or | xor                 (3.40)
```

The rules of combining operators in the Ada language are similar to those of other languages. They can be formalized here, in terms of the various alternatives in the syntax statements associated with Statement (3.34). Specifically, the rules are as given below.

For an expression, a relation, a simple expression, or a term, operations are performed in the order of their precedence, in the absence of parentheses imposed for specific associations. When the expression has been reduced to operations of the same precedence, and all parenthesized expressions have been evaluated, the remaining operations are performed in textual order from left to right. Free use of parentheses is permitted to force associations that counter the rules of precedence.

3.7.2.2 Highest-Precedence Operations. The highest-precedence operators are exponentiation, absolute value, and logical negation. Their characteristics are summarized in Table 3.10. The **not** operation applied to a boolean array simply negates all components. Exponentiation with a real exponent is not predefined—not because real exponents do not occur in embedded-system programming, but because the precision required

Table 3.10 Highest-Precedence Operations

OPERATION	OPERATOR	OPERAND TYPE		RESULT TYPE
absolute value	**abs**	any numeric type		same numeric type
logical negation	**not**	any boolean type		same boolean type
		one-dimensional array of boolean components		same array type
		LEFT	RIGHT	
exponentiation	**	any integer type	INTEGER	same as left
		any floating-point type	INTEGER	same as left

in real exponentiation may vary from one application to another. Ada's package and generic unit features encourage the development of customized operations for applications such as real exponentiation. Exponentiation with an integer exponent is predefined for both floating-point and integer values. When the exponent—that is, the right operand—is positive, exponentiation is equivalent to repeated multiplication for both integer and floating-point types. A negative exponent can be used with a floating-point type, but it cannot be used with an integer type because the result would not be an integer.

3.7.2.3 Multiplication Operations. The multiplication operators in the Ada language are multiplication, division, modulus, and remainder. Their characteristics are summarized in Table 3.11. The typing rules of the Ada language become apparent in characteristics such as these, for the language rules are specific in that the two operands of the "*" operator, for example, must be of the same type, and that the result is of the same type. The operands, of course, are not restricted to being objects—they can be virtually any expression, as implied by Statements (3.34) through (3.34.5).

The **rem** and **mod** operators differ in a distinct way. The **rem** operator returns the remainder of an integer division. That is, the value returned by the operation

```
A rem B
```

where A and B are objects of an integer type, is

```
A - (A / B) * A
```

Thus, A **rem** B is always of the same sign as A and has an absolute value that is less than that of B. The **mod** operator, on the other hand,

Table 3.11 Multiplication Operations.

OPERATION	OPERATOR	OPERAND TYPE	RESULT TYPE
multiplication	*	any integer type any floating-point type	same integer type same floating-point type
integer division	/	any integer type	same integer type
floating-point division	/	any floating-point type	same floating-point type
modulus	**mod**	any integer type	same integer type
remainder	**rem**	any integer type	same integer type

returns a value that corresponds to modular arithmetic in basic number theory. That is, the operation

```
A mod B
```

where A and B are objects of an integer type, returns a value that has the sign of B and an absolute value less than that of B, and such that the relation

```
A = B * N + (A mod B)
```

is satisfied. This formulation of the modulus operation differs from that of Pascal.

Fixed-point types, because of the way in which their model numbers are formed, have predefined multiplication and division operations that are not compatible with the general strong typing features of the language. These operations are summarized in Table 3.12. Note that multiplication and division operations can involve operands that are of two different fixed-point types, and also that one operand may be of a fixed-point type while the other is of an integer type. The same model number properties that make multiplication and division by objects of type INTEGER reasonable also produce difficulty in multiplication and division when both operands are fixed-point types. For this reason, the result type of these operations is the predefined type universal_fixed. Such a result must be explicitly converted to some other numeric type for use. Explicit type conversion is discussed in Section 3.7.3; it is sufficient here to note that any result of type universal_fixed requires explicit conversion on the part of the programmer before it can be used. This feature, while cum-

Table 3.12 Fixed-Point Multiplication

		OPERAND TYPE		
OPERATION	OPERATOR	LEFT	RIGHT	RESULT TYPE
multiplication	*	any fixed-point type	INTEGER	same as left
		INTEGER	any fixed-point type	same as right
		any fixed-point type	any fixed-point type	universal_fixed
division	/	any fixed-point type	INTEGER	same as left
		any fixed-point type	any fixed-point type	universal_fixed

bersome, ensures explicit control of the accuracy of the computation, since the type universal_fixed is exact.

3.7.2.4 Unary Adding Operations. The unary adding operators constitute what is normally considered to be the algebraic sign of a numeric object. Formally, the properties of these operations are given in Table 3.13.

Table 3.13 Unary Adding Operations.

OPERATION	OPERATOR	OPERAND TYPE	RESULT TYPE
identity	+	any numeric type	same numeric type
negation	−	any numeric type	same numeric type

3.7.2.5 Binary Adding Operations. The binary adding operations are addition, subtraction, and catenation. Their characteristics are summarized in Table 3.14.

Table 3.14 Binary Adding Operations.

		OPERAND TYPE		
OPERATION	OPERATOR	LEFT	RIGHT	RESULT TYPE
addition	+	any numeric type	same numeric type	same numeric type
subtraction	−	any numeric type	same numeric type	same numeric type
catenation	&	any one-dimensional array type	same array type	same array type
		any one-dimensional array type	the component type	same array type
		the component type	any one-dimensional array type	same array type
		the component type	the component type	any one dimensional array type

The catenation operator, provided primarily for string manipulation, is predefined for any one-dimensional array type. The four catenation operations provide for

1. catenation of two arrays to form a single array whose length is the sum of the lengths of the two operands

2. affixing an additional component as the highest indexed component
3. affixing an additional component as the lowest indexed component
4. combining two components to form a two-component array

In each case, the components of the result comprise the components of the left operand followed by the components of the right operand.

3.7.2.6 Relational Operations. The relational operators are divided into two groups characterized by their applicability. These groups are listed below:

1. the equality operators = and /=
2. the ordering operators <, <=, >, and >=

The characteristics of these operators are summarized in Table 3.15. For discrete types, equality is defined as equality of the values. For two operands of a real type, for which the values may be only approximately equal, equality is defined as the overlapping of the model intervals containing the values. For composite types, equality is defined as equality of all components.

Table 3.15 Relational Operations.

OPERATION	OPERATOR	OPERAND TYPE	RESULT TYPE
equality, inequality	= /=	any type	BOOLEAN
ordering tests	< <= > >=	any scalar type	BOOLEAN
		any one-dimensional discrete array type	BOOLEAN

The ordering operators are defined for scalar types and for one-dimensional, discrete array types. For discrete types, the ordering is based on the position numbers. For one-dimensional discrete arrays, the ordering is based on the position numbers of the component values, starting with the first component. If the first components are equal, then the second components are checked, and so on. This feature is designed to facilitate string handling, but the operations are valid for arrays of any discrete type.

3.7.2.7 Membership Tests. The membership tests are **in** and **not in** and are defined for all data types; they return a value of type BOOLEAN. The syntax for a membership test is given in Statement (3.34.1). The syntax for the range and type mark are given by Statements (3.13.2) and (3.8.2), respectively. In the case of a type mark, the simple expression must have the same base type as the type mark. The membership test is whether the operand value belongs to the subtype denoted by the type mark. In the case of a range, the test is limited to scalar types and determines whether the operand value lies within the given range. The membership tests **in** and **not in** are complements.

3.7.2.8 Logical Operations. Logical operations in the Ada language are similar to those in other languages, with the possible exception of the *short-circuit* operators. The characteristics of the basic logical operations are summarized in Table 3.16. Array operations are performed on a component-by-component basis. In all cases, both operands must be of the same type. The short-circuit forms of the logical operators **and** and **or** simply eliminate unnecessary evaluation of the right operand. The **and then** operator will not evaluate the right operand if the left operand evaluates to FALSE, since the value of the logical operation **and** is then FALSE regardless of the result of the evaluation of the right operand. Similarly, the **or else** operator will not evaluate the right operand if the left operand evaluates to TRUE. The short-circuit forms can be useful in operations such as

```
B /= 0.0 and then A / B >= 12.0
```

in which case the right operand is not evaluated if the left operand evaluates FALSE, thus avoiding a numeric exception caused by dividing by zero.

Table 3.16 Logical Operations.

OPERATION	OPERATOR	OPERAND TYPE	RESULT TYPE
conjunction	**and**	any boolean type	same boolean type
	and then	any one-dimensional boolean array type	same array type
inclusive disjunction	**or**	any boolean type	same boolean type
	or else	any one-dimensional boolean array type	same array type
exclusive disjunction	**xor**	any boolean type	same boolean type
		any one-dimensional boolean array type	same array type

3.7.2.9 Static Expressions. The concept of a static expression has been used several times in reference to the declaration of numeric types. The general idea is that a static expression has a value that is fixed; that is, the value cannot be modified during execution of the program. This property in turn implies that the value of a static expression can be determined at compile time. Formally, an expression of a scalar type is static if its primaries (see Section 3.7.2) consist solely of the following:

- enumeration literals
- named numbers
- certain function calls, attributes, and qualified expressions that have static values
- numeric literals
- constants whose initialization is static

Static constraints and static ranges are constraints and ranges specified by static expressions.

3.7.3 Explicit Type Conversion

The rigid type-checking rules of the Ada language may preclude the orderly implementation of a desired algorithm in which, for example, the programmer may want to multiply the value of a floating-point object by the value of an integer object to obtain a floating-point result. In many other languages, type conversion in cases such as this is implicitly performed, so that a possibility exists that an invalid program may be made executable—yet incorrect—by the compiler, without the knowledge of the programmer. In the Ada language such conversion is possible, but it must be explicitly specified by the programmer. The syntax for an explicit type conversion is

```
type_conversion ::= type_mark(expression)    (3.41)
```

where the syntax for a type mark and that for an expression are given by Statements (3.8.2) and (3.34), respectively. The operand is the expression, which is first evaluated and then converted to the type specified by the type mark. If the type mark is a subtype, the actual conversion is to the base type—called the *target* type—followed then by a check of the subtype constraints. The operand expression cannot be an allocator, an aggregate, or a string literal.

Explicit type conversion is permitted only between closely related types, as defined below:

- Numeric types—conversion is permitted between any two numeric types, including the anonymous types universal_integer, universal_real, and universal_fixed. The conversion of a real type to an integer type rounds to the nearest integer.

- Derived types—conversion is permitted between a derived type and its parent; or between two types derived from the same parent.
- Array types—conversion is permitted between two array types if the following conditions are met:
  - both types have the same dimensionality
  - the index types are the same, or can be explicitly converted
  - the component types are the same

  If the conversion is to an unconstrained array, the index bounds are determined by the operand type.

In general, if a conversion from one type to another is permitted, then the inverse conversion is also permitted. In any conversion, of course, subtype constraints are respected. No conversion between a subtype and its base type is required, because a subtype is not a type distinct from its base type.

Several examples of explicit type conversion are given below, based on the following declarations:

```
type COUNT    is range 1..5000;
type CURRENT  is delta 0.025 range - 100.0..100.0;
type VOLTAGE  is delta 0.01 range - 500.0..500.0;
type POWER    is digits 6;
type WEIGHT   is digits 6;
type MATRIX_3 is array(1..3, 1..3) of FLOAT;
type INDEX    is new COUNT;
type ROT_MATRIX  is new MATRIX_3;
type VECTOR   is array(INTEGER range < >) of FLOAT
subtype VECTOR_6 is VECTOR(1..6);
type LONG_VECTOR is array(1..36) of FLOAT;
NO_ROUNDS    : COUNT;
READING      : INDEX;
CUR_MEAS     : CURRENT;
VOLT_MEAS    : VOLTAGE;
ROTATE_1     : MATRIX_3;
ROTATE_2     : ROT_MATRIX;
TEMP_VECTOR  : LONG_VECTOR;
```

The examples of explicit type conversions are

```
WEIGHT(3 * NO_ROUNDS)          -- integer value is
                                  converted to floating
                                  point.
```

```
INTEGER(CUR_MEAS)              -- real value is rounded to
                                  nearest integer.
INDEX(NO_ROUNDS)               -- converts value of type
                                  COUNT to value of type
                                  INDEX. COUNT and INDEX
                                  are distinct integer
                                  types.
POWER(CUR_MEAS * VOLT_MEAS)    -- converts universal_fixed
                                  result to floating-point
                                  type POWER. See Section
                                  3.7.2.3.
ROT_MATRIX(ROTATE_1)           -- converts value of 3 x 3
                                  array ROTATE_1 to type ROT
                                  MATRIX.
VECTOR(TEMP_VECTOR)            -- converts value of array TEMP
                                  VECTOR to type VECTOR,
                                  and constrains the value
                                  to the index bounds of TEMP
                                  VECTOR.
VECTOR(TEMP_VECTOR(11..20))    -- converts value of array
                                  slice TEMP_VECTOR(11..20)
                                  to type VECTOR, and
                                  constrains the index
                                  bounds to (11..20).
VECTOR_6(TEMP_VECTOR(11..16))  -- converts value of array
                                  slice TEMP_VECTOR(11..16)
                                  to type VECTOR_6. The
                                  array bounds are (1..6),
                                  those of VECTOR_6.
```

By requiring explicit conversion of types, the Ada language ensures that overriding of the typing rules is an overt action on the part of the programmer, rather than a covert action on the part of the compiler.

3.7.4 Implicit Type Conversion

There are some subtle implicit type conversions in the Ada language relating to the anonymous predefined types universal_integer, universal real, and universal_fixed. Universal types in the Ada language are predefined anonymous types with no bounds and, for universal_real or universal_fixed types, an infinite precision. Obviously, these data types are conceptual in nature, and values of universal types must be converted to some numeric type before they can be assigned. Such conversion is implicit in the case of a numeric literal, a named number, or an attribute. In other cases, the conversion must be explicitly accomplished, in accordance with the developments of the previous section.

There is yet another situation in which implicit conversion takes place. A constrained array value may be assigned to a constrained array object if they both have the same length and are objects of the same unconstrained array type. The implicit conversion is from one subtype of an unconstrained array type to another with the same number of elements. The net effect of this implicit conversion is that the assignment is made on a component-by-component basis, starting with the first component and proceeding to the last, without regard for the actual index range of the expression.

Examples of implicit type conversion are given below, based on the following declarations:

```
type COUNT     is range 1..100;
type VALUE     is digits 8     range 0.0..120.0;
type READOUT   is delta 0.01   range 0.0..12.0;
type FLOW_DATA is array(COUNT range < >) of READOUT;
INDEX       : COUNT;
FLOW_RATE   : VALUE;
METER_READ  : READOUT;
TOTAL_READ  : FLOW_DATA(1..100);
FIRST_READ  : FLOW_DATA(1..5);
SEC_READ    : FLOW_DATA(6..10);
```

Examples of implicit type conversion are

```
INDEX := 32;                 -- conversion from universal_
                                integer to integer type COUNT.
FLOW_RATE := 0.8;            -- conversion from universal_real
                                to floating-point type VALUE.
METER_READ := 6.3;           -- conversion from universal_real
                                to fixed-point type READOUT.
FIRST_READ :=                -- subtype conversion of
    TOTAL_READ(11..15);         slice TOTAL_READ(11..15).
SEC_READ := FIRST_READ;      -- subtype conversion of
                                FIRST_READ.
INDEX :=                     -- conversion of attribute value
    TOTAL_READ'LENGTH;          from universal_integer to
                                integer type COUNT.
```

The reader should note the difference between the *implicit* array subtype conversion considered here and the *explicit* type conversion of the previous section. In the examples there, the array to be converted is of a distinctly different type than the type to which it is to be converted. The implicit conversion considered here involves subtypes of the same unconstrained array type.

3.7.5 Universal Expressions

The predefined anonymous types universal_integer and universal_real were described in Section 3.3 as conceptual data types with no underlying representation. Before values of these types—such as those specified by numeric literals—can be assigned, they must be converted to some numeric type. Normally, such conversion is implicitly performed according to details outlined in the previous section. There are instances, however, in which operations on values of these two universal types may be required. For example, consider the declarations:

```
PI                  : CONSTANT := 3.141_592_653;
RADIUS_TO_AREA      : CONSTANT := PI ** 2 / 2.0;
RADIUS_TO_CIRCUM : CONSTANT := 2.0 * PI;
```

The values of these named numbers are of type universal_real, and conversion does not take place until they are assigned or used in an expression of some kind.

The conceptual idea is that any operations predefined for integer types are also predefined for the anonymous type universal_integer, and that any operation predefined for floating-point types are also predefined for the anonymous type universal_real. In addition, multiply and divide operations involving combinations of universal_real and universal_integer types are defined and are summarized in Table 3.17. The evaluation of a universal_real expression must be exact, unless the expression is not static. Again, the evaluation is conceptual in that what is really required is that the value before conversion be exact. But the value before conversion can never be used, so that the only requirement of the implementation is that the conversion appear to be derived from an exact evaluation.

Even though universal arithmetic needs to be performed only in concept, it is possible—using Ada's package structure—to actually implement

Table 3.17 Additional Operations for Universal Types.

		OPERAND TYPE		RESULT
OPERATION	OPERATOR	LEFT	RIGHT	TYPE
multiplication	*	universal_real	universal_integer	universal_real
		universal_integer	universal_real	universal_real
division	/	universal_real	universal_integer	universal_real

unlimited precision arithmetic.[3] In this case, the universal types are no longer anonymous but instead are declared types with their own associated operations.

3.7.6 Qualified Expressions

The strong typing rules of the Ada language require that the type of an expression be proper for the context in which it is used. In many cases, the type of an expression is not unambiguously implied by the context; thus some method of explicitly stating the type is required. The qualified expression is provided for this purpose. The syntax of a qualified expression is

```
qualified_expression ::=
        type_mark'(expression) | type_mark'aggregate
                                                    (3.42)
```

The syntax for the type mark, expression, and aggregate is given by Statements (3.8.3), (3.34), and (3.24), respectively. The operand—the expression or the aggregate—must have the same base type as is specified by the type mark, since a qualified expression is merely a way to resolve ambiguities rather than a mechanism for type conversion.

Examples of qualified expressons are given below, based upon the following declarations:

```
type IFF is (FRIEND, UNKNOWN, FOE);
type TARGET_THREAT is array(1..100) of IFF;
type PICTURE is array(INTEGER range < >,
                      INTEGER range < >) of FLOAT;
type PICTURE_PTR is access PICTURE;
type IDENT is (FOE, NATO, US, JAP, OTHER);
TARG_1 : TARGET_THREAT;
FRAME  : PICTURE_PTR;
```

Examples of the use of qualified expressions are

```
TARG_1 := TARGET_THREAT'(1..10 => FRIEND,
                         others => UNKNOWN);
 -- aggregate requires qualification because the use of
   others makes the index range ambiguous.

FRAME  := new PICTURE'(1..256 => (1..256 => 70.0));
 -- qualified aggregate used as initializing value for
    an allocator. See Section 3.6.3.2.
```

```
IDENT'(FOE)
IFF'(FOE)
 -- qualification needed to determine which enumeration
    literal FOE is intended. See Section 3.4.1.
```

In general, the use of a qualified expression is required whenever the type of an expression or of an aggregate is not determinable from the context in which it is used.

3.8 STATEMENTS

Whereas declarations are the means by which an Ada program creates types and objects, statements are the means by which data is manipulated. While declarations are elaborated, statements are executed. In this section, those statements of the Ada language that are conventional in nature—that is, those statements that are similar to statements found in other modern languages such as Pascal—will be discussed. Specifically, consideration will center on the following statements:

- assignment
- exit
- goto
- if
- loop
- case
- block

Two other statements

- procedure call
- return

will be considered when subprograms are discussed in Section 3.9. The remaining statements

- delay
- raise
- entry call
- abort
- code
- accept
- select

apply to the more advanced concepts of the Ada language and will be discussed at the point at which these concepts are introduced.

A statement in an Ada program is either a *simple statement* or a *compound statement*. A compound statement can enclose simple statements or other compound statements. The general syntax for a statement is

```
statement ::=
   {label} simple_statement | {label} compound_statement
                                                  (3.43)
```

where

```
   simple_statement ::= null_statement
   | assignment_statement | procedure_call_statement
   | exit_statement       | return_statement
   | goto_statement       | entry_call_statement
   | delay_statement      | abort_statement
   | raise_statement      | code_statement        (3.43.1)
```

and

```
         compound_statement ::=
           if_statement       | case_statement
         | loop_statement     | block_statement
         | accept_statement   | select_statement    (3.43.2)
```

with

```
         label ::= << label_simple_name >>         (3.43.3)

              null_statement ::= null;             (3.43.4)
```

Any statement may have a label, which serves as a symbolic address for the statement. The syntax for a simple name is given by Statement (3.31)—it is simply an identifier.

The Ada language permits a sequence of statements to appear anywhere a single statement may appear, a feature that enhances the maintainability of Ada code because it permits the insertion of statements without the insertion of the **begin** and **end** delimiters required in other languages such as Pascal. Instead, the Ada language uses the **begin** and **end** delimiters to designate sequences of statements that may have associated *declarative regions*—regions in which object and type declarations may appear. The semicolon delimiter is used as a statement terminator, implying that every statement, both simple and compound, must end with a semicolon.

3.8.1 The Assignment Statement

An object that is not a constant is called a *variable,* implying that its value can be changed during execution of the program. There are two ways in which the value of a variable can be changed: (1) directly, by an assignment, and (2) indirectly, when the variable is updated by some other means, such as a procedure call. Directly changing the value of a variable is accomplished by use of the assignment statement. The syntax of the assignment statement is

```
assignment_statement ::=
        variable_name := expression;          (3.44)
```

where the syntax for a name and that for an expression are given by Statements (3.30) and (3.34), respectively. The effect of the execution of an assignment statement is simply that the expression is evaluated and the resulting value is assigned to the variable. The typing rules of the Ada language require that the type of the expression match the subtype of the variable. Thus, both types and constraints are checked. One exception to this rule is the situation in which the variable is an array, in which case the implicit subtype conversion discussed in Section 3.7.4 applies.

3.8.2 The If Statement

One of the two conditional control statements in the Ada language is the if statement. As in most other languages, the if statement is used to specify which of several alternative courses of action will be taken, depending upon the value of one or more boolean expressions. The general syntax of an if statement is

```
if_statement ::=
   if condition then
         sequence_of_statements
   {elsif condition then
         sequence_of_statements}
[else
         sequence_of_statements]
end if;
```

where

```
condition ::= boolean_expression    (3.45.1)
```

and

```
sequence_of_statements ::= statement {statement}
                                                  (3.45.2)
```

and the syntax for an expression is given by Statement (3.34). The general effect of an if statement is that the conditions are evaluated, starting with the condition following the reserved word **if** and continuing until one of the conditions evaluates as TRUE. The sequence of statements associated with that condition is then executed, and control then passes to the statement following the **end if,** unless a branch out of the if statement is effected. If none of the conditions evaluate to TRUE, then the **else** part, if present, is executed. If no conditions evaluate to TRUE and there is no **else** part, then control passes to the statement following the **end if.** The net effect of the alternatives and optional parts in Statement (3.45) is to produce four general forms of the if statement:

```
if_then_statement ::=
   if condition then
      sequence_of_statements
   end if;                                   (3.45.3)

if_then_else_statement ::=
   if condition then
      sequence_of_statements
   else
      sequence_of_statements
   end if;                                   (3.45.4)

if_then_elsif_statement ::=
   if condition then
      sequence_of_statements
   {elsif condition then
      sequence_of_statements}
   end if;                                   (3.45.5)
```

The fourth form is the complete form given by Statement (3.45). Each one of these forms produces slightly different results, as indicated below:

- if_then_statement—If the condition evaluates as TRUE, the sequence of statements is executed, followed by the execution of the statement following the **end if.** If the condition evaluates as FALSE, execution continues with the statement following the **end if.**
- if_then_else_statement—If the condition evaluates as TRUE, then the first sequence of statements is executed, followed by execution of the statement following the **end if.** If the condition evaluates as FALSE, the second sequence of statements is executed, followed by execution of the statement following the **end if.**

- if_then_elsif_statement—If the first condition evaluates as TRUE, then the first sequence of statement is executed, followed by execution of the statement following the **end if.** If the first condition evaluates as FALSE, the second condition is evaluated. If this result is TRUE, the second sequence of statements is executed, followed by execution of the statement following the **end if.** If the second condition evaluates FALSE, then the third condition is evaluated, and so on. If no condition evaluates TRUE, execution continues with the statement following the **end if.**

The general form of Statement (3.45) might be termed the if_then_elsif_else statement. The reader should note that the use of the **elsif** makes certain kinds of nested if statements much more readable than is the case in most other languages. The use of **end if** also serves to enhance the understandability, and hence the modifiability, of Ada code.

Some examples of if statements are given below, based on the following declarations:

```
type EVAL is (POSITIVE, POSSIBLE, NEGATIVE);
type HIT_COUNT is range 0..20;
type COUNT is range 1..200;
type HIT_ARRAY is array(COUNT) of HIT_COUNT;
TARGET_HITS : HIT_ARRAY;
DETECT      : array(COUNT) of EVAL;
NO_TARGETS  : COUNT;
```

Examples of the use of the if statement are

```
if TARGET_HITS(1) > 12 then
   DETECT(1)   := POSITIVE;
   NO_TARGETS := NO_TARGETS + 1;
end if;
--example of the if_then construct.
  If the condition evaluates FALSE, then
  execution continues after the end if.

if TARGET_HITS(6) > 12 then
   DETECT(6)   := POSITIVE;
   NO_TARGETS := NO_TARGETS + 1;
else
   NO_TARGETS := NO_TARGETS - 1;
end if;
--example of if_then_else construct.
```

```
    If the condition evaluates FALSE, then
    the else part is executed.

  if TARGET_HITS(15) > 12 then
     DETECT(15) := POSITIVE
     NO_TARGETS := NO_TARGETS + 1;
  elsif TARGET_HITS(15) > 6 then
     DETECT(15) := POSSIBLE;
  end if;
  --example of if_then_elsif construct.

  if TARGET_HITS(97) > 12 then
     DETECT(97) := POSITIVE;
     NO_TARGETS := NO_TARGETS + 1;
  elsif TARGET_HITS(97) > 6 then
     DETECT(97) := POSSIBLE;
  else
     NO_TARGETS := NO_TARGETS - 1;
  end if;
  --example of the if_then_elsif_then_else construct.
    The else part is executed only if all conditions
    evaluate FALSE.
```

The number of **elsif**s is unlimited. For example, if the declaration of EVAL were

```
type EVAL is (POSITIVE, PROBABLE, POSSIBLE, NEGATIVE);
```

the last if statement could read

```
if TARGET_HITS(97) > 15 then
   DETECT(97) := POSITIVE;
   NO_TARGETS := NO_TARGETS + 1;
elsif TARGET_HITS(97) > 10 then
   DETECT(97) := PROBABLE;
   NO_TARGETS := NO_TARGETS + 1;
elsif TARGET_HITS(97) > 5 then
   DETECT (97) := POSSIBLE;
else
   NO_TARGETS := NO_TARGETS - 1;
end if;
```

The reader familiar with Pascal should code the equivalent of this statement in Pascal in order to illustrate the usefulness of the **elsif** construct.

3.8.3 The Case Statement

The remaining conditional control statement in the Ada language is the case statement, which is used to select one of a number of alternative sequences of statements. The selection is based on the value of an expression, which must be of a discrete type; that is, it must be either of an integer type or of an enumeration type. The syntax of a case statement is

```
case_statement ::=
   case expression is
       case_statement_alternative
       {case_statement_alternative}
   end case;                                        (3.46)
```

where

```
case_statement_alternative ::=
   when choice {| choice} =>
       sequence_of_statements                       (3.46.1)
```

The syntax for a choice is given by Statement (3.24.2). That for an expression is given by Statement (3.34), but in this case the expression is limited to values of a discrete type. Each choice must be of the same discrete type as the expression, and each value of the type must occur once and only once in the set of choices. The simple expressions and discrete ranges—from Statement (3.24.2)—must be static; that is, their values must not be subject to change during program execution. Enumeration literals, numeric literals, named numbers, and constants are static, as are expressions containing only static primaries. A component simple name—see again Statement (3.24.2)—is not permitted as a choice in a case statement.

The **others** choice is permitted, but only in the last alternative, and only as the single choice in the last alternative. In some cases, the **others** choice is required. Specifically, it is required when the type of the expression is the anonymous predefined type universal_integer, since the use of the **others** choice is the only way to include the infinity of values of this conceptual type.

Examples of the use of the case statements are based on the declarations of the previous section, and are as follows:

```
case TARGET_HITS(97) is
   when 0..5 =>
      NO_TARGETS := NO_TARGETS - 1;
```

```
   when 6..10 =>
      DETECT(97) := POSSIBLE;
   when 11..15 =>
      DETECT(97) := PROBABLE;
      NO_TARGETS := NO_TARGETS + 1;
   when 16..20 =>
      DETECT(97) := POSITIVE;
      NO_TARGETS  := NO_TARGETS + 1;
end case;
--choices are discrete ranges. All values 0..20 are
  represented.

case DETECT(1) is
   when POSITIVE | PROBABLE =>
      NO_TARGETS := NO_TARGETS + 1;
   when POSSIBLE =>
      null;
   when NEGATIVE =>
      NO_TARGETS := NO_TARGETS - 1;
   end case;
--one alternative has multiple choices, one has a null
  statement.
```

The **others** choice could have been used as the last alternative in either case above, but its real usefulness is in representing a large number of remaining choices that cannot be represented as a discrete range.

3.8.4 The Loop Statement

The ability to execute a sequence of statements repeatedly, forming what is commonly called a *loop,* is vital to the implementation of most practically useful computer programs. The Ada construct provided to perform looping is appropriately termed the loop statement, and it has been designed to encourage and promote good structured programming practice. The loop statement will cause a sequence of statements to be executed repeatedly for a specified number of times—which may be zero or infinite—or until a certain condition is met. The syntax of the loop statement is

```
loop_statement ::=
   [loop_simple_name :]
      [iteration_scheme] loop
         sequence_of_statements
      end loop [loop_simple_name];        (3.47)
```

where

```
iteration_scheme ::= while condition
   | for loop_parameter_specification     (3.47.1)
```

and

```
loop_parameter_specification ::=
    identifier in [reverse] discrete_range (3.47.2)
```

The syntax for a condition is given by Statement (3.45.1); it is a boolean expression. The syntax for a discrete range is given by Statement (3.22.6).

The alternatives and optional parts of Statements (3.47) and (3.47.1) produce three forms of the loop statement:

```
basic_loop_statement ::=
   [loop_simple_name :]
      loop
         sequence_of_statements
      end loop [loop_simple_name];       (3.47.3)

while_loop_statement ::=
   [loop_simple_name :]
      while condition loop
         sequence_of_statements
      end loop [loop_simple_name];       (3.47.4)

for_loop_statement ::=
   [loop_simple_name :]
      for identifier in [reverse] discrete_range
         sequence_of_statements
      end loop [loop_simple_name];       (3.47.5)
```

The first form is called the *basic loop* and implies that the sequence of statements is executed repeatedly an infinite number of times. Endless loops such as this are not uncommon in process control applications, or in other instances of embedded computer systems in which it is necessary to continually perform some operation in a repeated fashion. However, the Ada language also provides a way of exiting an endless loop—or any loop, for that matter—either conditionally or unconditionally, without regard for the number of times the loop has been executed. The means of exiting a loop in this manner is the exit statement, which is considered below.

The second form, the *while loop,* executes the loop statements repeatedly so long as the condition evaluates TRUE. Before each loop begins, the condition is evaluated. If the condition evaluates as FALSE, execution continues at the statement following the **end loop.** A while loop will execute zero number of times if the condition evaluates FALSE upon entry into the loop statement.

The third form of the loop statement is called a *for loop,* and it involves the implicit declaration of a *loop parameter* denoted by the identifier following the reserved word **for.** The type of the loop parameter is the base type of the discrete range. The loop is executed once for each value of the discrete range, and, prior to each iteration of the loop, the succeeding value of the discrete range—in increasing order—is assigned to the loop parameter. If the optional reserved word **reverse** is present, values of the loop parameter are assigned in decreasing order. The loop will be executed zero times if the discrete range is a null range; that is, if the upper bound is less than or equal to the lower bound. Within the loop, the loop parameter is a constant, implying that its value cannot be changed. Thus, the loop parameter cannot appear on the left-hand side of an assignment statement or in any circumstance in which its value would be changed. The loop parameter is the only object for which the language does not require an explicit declaration. The scope of a loop parameter is the loop statement itself.

Any loop can be named by use of the optional loop simple name. If the name is used at the beginning of the loop, then it must also follow the reserved words **end loop.**

Any loop can contain an exit statement which, when executed, causes the loop to be completed; that is, the next statement executed is that following the reserved words **end loop.** Thus, a while loop may be exited even though the condition never evaluates FALSE, and a for loop may be exited even though the discrete range is not completely spanned. The syntax of the exit statement is

```
exit_statement ::=
   exit [loop_name] [when condition];        (3.48)
```

where the syntax for a condition is given by Statement (3.45.1). An exit statement using the optional loop name is permitted to appear only in a loop with the same name, and it causes an exit from the named loop. An exit statement without a loop name causes an exit from the innermost enclosing loop, even if the innermost loop is named. A loop may contain any number of exit statements.

If the optional condition is used, the loop is exited only when the condition evaluates to TRUE. Otherwise, execution continues at the statement following the exit statement. If the optional condition is not used, the loop is exited unconditionally.

Examples of the basic loop statement are given below. Because this kind of loop usually performs some task that interacts with data outside the loop, such as would occur in the reading of a file or in the scanning of sensor values, the sequence of statements within the loop is abstracted as a series of dots.

```
PRESSURE_LOOP:
   loop
      . . . . .
      read pressure sensors
      . . . . .
   end loop PRESSURE_LOOP;
   --endless loop that is named. Endless loops such as
     this may be common in a multitasking environment.

   loop.
      . . . . .
      read temperature sensor
      exit when TEMP > MAX_TEMP;
      . . . . .
   end loop
   --endless loop with exit statement. The loop is not
     named.
```

Examples of the while loop are shown below:

```
FACTORIAL : FLOAT;
INT       : INTEGER range 0..60;
. . . . . .
FACTORIAL := 1.0;
while INT /= 0 loop
   FACTORIAL := FACTORIAL * FLOAT(INT);
   INT       := INT - 1;
end loop;
--computes the factorial of an integer. Explicit
  type conversion from integer to FLOAT is used.
  The loop is not named.

type HIT_COUNT is range 1..20;
type COUNT     is range 1..200;
type HIT_ARRAY is array(COUNT) of HIT_COUNT;
```

```
TARGET_HITS : HIT_ARRAY;
INDEX       : COUNT1;

. . . . .
INDEX := 1;
FIRST_ZERO:
   while HITS /= 0 loop
      HITS  := TARGET_HITS(INDEX);
      INDEX := INDEX + 1;
   end loop FIRST_ZERO;
   --determines the index of the first zero
     component of array TARGET_HITS. This is a
     named loop.
```

Examples of the for loop are shown below:

```
type VECTOR_50 is array(1..50) of FLOAT;
WEIGHTS : VECTOR_50;
TOT_WGHT, PART_WEIGHT : FLOAT;
   . . . . .
TOT_WGHT := 0;
for INDEX in reverse 1..50 loop
   TOT_WGHT := TOT_WGHT + WEIGHTS(INDEX);
end loop;
--sums all components of array WEIGHTS.
  The loop is traversed in reverse order.

PART_WEIGHT := 0;
for INDEX in 1..10 loop
   PART_WEIGHT := PART_WEIGHT + WEIGHTS(INDEX);
end loop;
--sums first ten components of array WEIGHTS.

type MATRIX_3 is array(1..3, 1..3) of FLOAT;
COST_MATRIX : MATRIX_3;
TOTAL_COST  : FLOAT;
TRACE       : FLOAT;
. . . . .
TRACE := 0.0;
for INDEX in 1..3 loop.
   TRACE := TRACE + COST_MATRIX(INDEX, INDEX);
end loop;
--loop computes the trace of the 3 x 3 matrix
  COST_MATRIX.
```

```
TOTAL_COST := 0;
for ROW_INDEX in 1..3 loop
   for COL_INDEX in 1..3 loop
      TOTAL_COST := TOTAL_COST + COST_MATRIX
                    (ROW_INDEX, COL_INDEX);
   end loop;
end loop;
--nested loops to determine the sum of the
  elements of the 3 x 3 matrix COST_MATRIX.
```

Only one example of an exit statement is shown above. To illustrate further some of the ramifications of the exit statement, consider the rather abstract set of nested loops—some of them named—shown below.

```
OUTER_LOOP:
   loop
      ..... outer loop
   exit;                           -- exits OUTER_LOOP
   .....
   loop
      ..... first inner loop
      exit;                        -- exits first inner loop
      .....
      exit OUTER_LOOP              -- exits OUTER_LOOP
      .....
         INNER_2:
            loop
               ..... named loop
               exit;               -- exits INNER_2
               .....
               exit INNER_2;       -- exits INNER_2
               .....
               exit OUTER_LOOP;    -- exits OUTER_LOOP
               .....
            end loop INNER_2;      -- control to here when
                                      exiting INNER_2
      .....
   end loop;                       -- control to here when
                                      exiting first inner
                                      loop
end loop OUTER_LOOP;               -- control to here when
                                      exiting OUTER_LOOP
```

It should be noted that the use of an exit statement within a while loop or within a for loop detracts from the structuring of the program in that the loop no longer has a single exit point. Good programming practice dictates that exit statements should be used with reluctance, particularly if some other control structure that adheres to the structuring concept will suffice.

3.8.5 The Block Statement

The Ada language is *block structured;* that is, each program unit—subprogram, package, or task—may contain a declarative part and a sequence of statements. Declarations of types, objects, and other entities can occur in the declarative part of these units. This combination of a declarative part and a sequence of statements is called a *block* and forms the basis of the block structuring of the language. Whereas blocks used as subprograms are common to other block-structured languages such as Pascal, in the Ada language the block structure can be caused to occur anywhere within the sequence of executable statements by use of the block statement. The primary reason for the use of a block statement is related to the scope of declared entities; because the scope rules of the Ada language are not discussed until later, consideration here must be limited to syntax.

The syntax for a block statement is

```
block_statement ::=
   [block_simple_name :]
      [declare
         declarative_part]
       begin
         sequence_of_statements
      [exception
         exception_handler
          {exception_handler}]
      end [block_simple_name];              (3.49)
```

The declarative part of a block statement is discussed below; the exception part is considered in Section 3.9.4. As can be seen from Statement (3.49), a block statement may have a name; if the block is named, then the name must appear after the reserved word **end.** The declarative part is also optional, as is the exception part, implying that the simplest form of a block statement is a sequence of statements bracketed by the reserved words **begin** and **end.**

The declarative part, if present, contains any declarations made in the block. The syntax for the declarative part is

```
declarative_part ::=
   {basic_declarative item}{later_declarative_item}
                                                  (3.50)
```

where

```
    basic_declarative_item ::= basic_declaration
       | representation_clause | use_clause      (3.50.1)

later_declarative_item ::= body
   | subprogram_declaration | package_declaration
   | task_declaration       | generic_declaration
   | use_clause             | generic_instantiation
                                                 (3.50.2)

         body ::= proper_body | body_stub        (3.50.3)

         proper_body ::= subprogram_body
            | package_body | task_body           (3.50.4)
```

The complexity of this set of syntax statements indicates the richness of the Ada language features. About the only item above that has been discussed to this point is the basic declaration, whose syntax is given by Statement (3.6). Each of the declarative items seen in Statements (3.50) through (3.50.4) will eventually be discussed in detail. There are contained in Statements (3.50) through (3.50.4) some implied restrictions on the order in which certain declarations can appear in a declarative part. These restrictions result from the fact that all *basic declarative items* must appear before the *later declarative items*. By comparing Statements (3.50.1) and (3.6) to Statements (3.50.2) through (3.50.4), it can be seen that the only later declarative items that are not also basic declarative items are subprogram, package, and task bodies and body stubs. The net result of these restrictions is that, once a body or a body stub appears, only later declarative items may occur from that point. Stated more directly, the following declarations, if present, must appear prior to the first body or body stub:

- object declarations
- type declarations
- exception declarations
- deferred constant declarations
- number declarations
- subtype declarations
- renaming declarations

After the first body or body stub appears, declarations are limited to

- other bodies
- package declarations
- generic declarations
- use clauses
- subprogram declarations
- task declarations
- generic instantiation

The syntax for a declarative part is important to the use of the block statement, but its implications extend much further. The bodies of subprograms, packages, and tasks may all contain declarative parts, and the discussion of these program units will reference Statement (3.50) and the detail of the declarative part contained in this section.

Examples of block statements, some with declarative parts, are given below:

```
begin
   if ANGLE >= 0.0   then
      RESULT := TRUE;
   else
      RESULT := FALSE;
   end if;
end;
--a block statement containing only a sequence of
  statements.

declare
   POWER      : INTEGER := 1;
   TERM       : FLOAT;
   MULTIPLIER : FLOAT;
begin
   if VALUE > 0.0 then
      while POWER <= SERIES_LIMIT loop
         MULTIPLIER := 1.0 / FLOAT(POWER);
         TERM       := ((VALUE - 1.0) / (VALUE + 1.0))
                       ** POWER;
         RESULT     := RESULT + (MULTIPLIER * TERM);
         POWER      := POWER + 2;
      end loop;
   end if;
   RESULT := 2.0 * RESULT;
end;
--a block statement with a declarative part. The
  sequence of statements computes the natural
  logarithm by use of a power series. The declarative
  part contains only basic declarations--
  specifically, it contains only object declarations.
```

```
ROUND:
   declare
      INT : INTEGER;
   begin
      INT    := INTEGER(VALUE);
      RESULT := FLOAT(INT);
   end ROUND;
   --a named block statment containing a declarative
     part. The statements round an object of type
     FLOAT to the nearest whole number.
```

In each of these examples, the object RESULT is global; that is, it is declared in the enclosing program units.

Since blocks occur in subprograms and other program units, further examples of both blocks and declarative parts abound in later chapters.

3.8.6 The Goto Statement

The goto statement has been shown to be theoretically unnecessary in a programming language.[4] Arguments have been made pro and con for the retention of the goto construct in modern programming languages,[5,6] and the pros prevailed in the design of the Ada language. The syntax of a goto statement is

```
go_to_statement ::= goto label_name        (3.51)
```

where the syntax of a label is given by Statements (3.43) and (3.43.3). The execution of a goto statement causes explicit transfer of control from the goto statement to a *target statement* specified by the label name. There are limitations on the relative positions of the goto statement and of the target statement. Specifically, the innermost sequence of statements that contains the target statement must also contain the goto statement. The term *sequence of statements* refers to the syntactic category referenced as sequence_of_statements in syntax such as Statements (3.45), (3.46), (3.47), and (3.49). Other occurrences will be seen in developments to follow.

Since one sequence of statements may enclose another sequence of statements, the rule outlined above permits transfer of control to a target statement in a sequence that encloses a second sequence that contains the goto statement. The reverse transfer, however, is not permitted because the innermost sequence containing the target statement does not contain the goto statement. For example, a goto can transfer control out of a loop, but cannot be used to transfer control into a loop. The same concept holds for if statements, loop statements, case statements, and block statements.

3.9 EXCEPTIONS

In the discussion of Chapter 1, it was pointed out that one of the usual requirements of an embedded computer system is a high degree of reliability—in both hardware and software. The reliability of software relates first to whether or not the software actually implements the desired algorithm correctly under all conditions, and second to how the software responds to those situations in which a properly designed program cannot continue execution because of some exceptional condition that arises. In the first case, the Ada language promotes software reliability by its myriad of features that support sound software engineering practice. In the second case, which refers to the run-time reliability of the software, the Ada language enhances software reliability by providing for the declaration of exceptions and exception handlers. While exception handling is nothing new in embedded-system programming, those programs written in languages other than Ada must resort to primitive operating system calls to properly handle exceptions. This fact, of course, is detrimental to the portability of software. In the Ada environment, exceptions and exception handling are part of the language itself, and all exceptions can be handled without resort to explicit operating system access.

In an Ada program, an *exceptional situation* is an event that causes suspension of normal program execution. An exception is a name given to such events, and raising an exception is an action that draws attention to the fact that the situation exists. In general, there are two classes of exceptions:

1. predefined exceptions—These exceptions are declared in package STANDARD and can be raised by the run-time system in response to exceptional conditions detected by the system.
2. user-defined exceptions—These exceptions are declared in an Ada program, just as other entities such as types and objects are declared, and they are raised by an executable statement called a raise statement.

The only difference between these two classes of exceptions is the way in which they may be raised. Once an exception has been raised, the ensuing actions are identical in either case.

3.9.1 Predefined Exceptions

The following exceptions are declared in package STANDARD and are thus predefined in the language:

- CONSTRAINT_ERROR—raised when a constraint of some kind is violated. Included are violations of range constraints and index constraints, and attempts to use a record component that does not exist with the current discriminant value. It is also raised if an attempt is made to use a component of an object designated by an access object whose value is **null.**
- NUMERIC_ERROR—raised when a predefined numeric operation cannot produce the correct result or, in the case of operations whose result type is real, when the operation cannot produce a result with the accuracy declared for the type.
- PROGRAM_ERROR—raised when some program function cannot be properly performed. Such functions include subprogram calls, generic instantiation, and task activation. This exception is a catchall, often being used when all else fails.
- STORAGE_ERROR—raised when some limitation on memory allocation is reached, such as will occur when the dynamic storage allocated to a task is exceeded, when the space available for the collection of objects designated by an access object is exhausted, or when there is insufficient memory available for elaboration of a declarative item.
- TASKING_ERROR—raised when exceptions occur during intertask communication.

These exceptions can be raised by the run-time system in response to the exceptional situations specified above. They can also be explicitly raised by the execution of a raise statement.

3.9.2 User-Defined Exceptions

A properly operating program may encounter a situation in which the value of a certain object, while not causing an exceptional condition for which program execution cannot continue, nevertheless represents a situation to which the programmer wishes to draw attention. For this purpose the Ada language provides the programmer with the capability to declare his own exceptions and to raise those exceptions by an explicit executable statement. The syntax for the declaration of an exception is

```
exception_declaration ::= identifier_list : exception;
                                                 (3.52)
```

where the syntax for an identifier list is given by Statement (3.10.1). An exception denoted by an exception name is determined at compile time and is the same no matter how many times the exception declaration is elaborated. This feature is in direct contrast to other declared entities such as types and objects, for which each elaboration produces a distinct entity. These characteristics are discussed in detail later when the scope rules of the Ada language are considered.

3.9.3 The Raise Statement

The action of abandoning normal program execution in response to an exception, and then calling attention to the fact that such a situation has occurred, is called *raising the exception*. Predefined exceptions are raised by the run-time system in response to exceptional situations which preclude continued execution, and they can also be explicitly raised by a raise statement. User-defined exceptions can only be raised by use of a raise statement. The syntax for a raise statement is

```
raise_statement ::= raise [exception_name];     (5.53)
```

The effect of the execution of a raise statement is to raise the named exception. A raise statement without an exception name is permitted only within an exception handler. Its effect is to raise again the exception in whose handler it appears.

Examples of the declaration of user-defined exceptions, and of the use of raise statements, are given below.

```
OVER_TEMP           : exception; -- declaration of exception
RADAR_INT, IR_INT   : exception; -- declaration of two
                                    exceptions
raise OVERTEMP;                  -- raises exception
raise NUMERIC_ERROR;             -- raises predefined
                                    exception
raise;                           -- permitted only in
                                    exception handler
```

The raise statement may appear anywhere an executable statement may appear.

3.9.4 Exception Handlers

In contrast to most other languages, which require communications with the underlying run-time system at a primitive level when an exception occurs, the Ada language provides for programmer-defined response to exceptions within the language itself. The language feature that provides this capability is the exception handler. An exception handler can appear as the last part of a block statement, as indicated by Statement (3.49). The inclusion of an exception handler in a block statement is optional. Exception handlers can also appear in other blocks, that is, in the sequence of statements in a subprogram, package, or task. The syntax of an exception handler is

```
exception_handler ::=
   when exception_choice {|exception_choice} =>
        sequence_of_statements                        (3.54)
```

where

```
exception_choice ::= exception_name | others    (3.54.1)
```

Since exception handlers can appear in block statements and in the sequence of statements in a subprogram, package, or task, confusion is avoided if the discussion centers on a construct called a *frame*, and which has the following syntax:

```
begin
   sequence_of_statements
exception
   exception_handler
   {exception_handler}
end;
```

Thus, the block statement specified by Statement (3.49) contains a frame. The bodies of subprograms, packages, and tasks will be shown to also contain a frame.

The handling of an exception consists of two distinct actions. First, the exception is lowered; that is, it is no longer raised. Second, the sequence of statements in the exception handler are executed. The first action makes possible the second, since no statements can be executed with an exception raised. The second action, the execution of the sequence of statements, normally performs some function demanded by the condition that raised the exception. Because the exception is lowered upon entering an exception handler, the raise statement without an exception name, as described in the previous section, is provided. By use of this statement, the exception handler can contain a sequence of statements and then raise again the exception.

The exception handlers contained in the exception part of a frame handle exceptions that are raised by the sequence of statements within the frame. Only those exceptions that are named as exception choices in Statement (3.54) are handled. When the **others** choice is used, it is only allowed in the last exception handler in the frame, and as the only choice in the last exception handler. It represents all exceptions not contained as choices in other exception handlers in the frame. In general, there is no limitation on the kinds of statements that can be included in the sequence of statements of an exception handler.

Examples of exception handlers are presented below:

```
begin
   ..... sequence of statements
exception
   when NUMERIC_ERROR | CONSTRAINT_ERROR =>
        RESULT := 0;
end;
--provides handlers for two predefined exceptions
  that may occur in the execution of the sequence
  of statements.

begin
   ..... sequence of statements
exception
        when RADAR_INT =>
           WARNING := "RADAR INTERCEPT";
        when IR_INT =>
           WARNING := "IR INTERCEPT    ";
        when others =>
           WARNING := "ARTIFACT        ";
           raise;
end;
--provides handlers for two user-defined
  exceptions. All other exceptions, whether user-
  defined or predefined, are raised again by the
  raise statement in the others choice.
```

In general, when an exception is raised in a frame, the remainder of the frame is abandoned and control passes to the exception part of the frame. Just what happens then depends on whether the frame is part of a block statement, of a subprogram, of a package, or of a task. In this section, only the case of exceptions raised within block statements is considered; other cases are considered when the appropriate program units are discussed.

When an exception is raised during the execution of the sequence of statements in a block statement, execution of the remaining statements is abandoned and control passes to the exception part of the frame. If a handler is provided for the exception, either by name or by an **others** choice, then the sequence of statements associated with the exception handler is executed, after which control passes to the statement immediately following the reserved word **end**—with the exception no longer raised. If no exception handler is provided, or if no exception part is present, control passses directly to the statement following the reserved word **end**—with the exception still raised. The enclosing program unit then responds to the exception in the manner just described.

Because the Ada language provides for initialization in object declarations, it is possible for predefined exceptions to be raised during the elaboration of the declarative part of a block statement. If this occurs, the elaboration is abandoned and control passes directly to the statement following the reserved word **end,** with the exception still raised. The sequence of statements is not executed, nor is the exception part of the frame searched for an appropriate exception handler.

Finally, an exception may be raised during the execution of an exception handler. Since an exception handler itself may contain block statements and subprogram calls, such exceptions may be handled within local frames contained in the exception handler itself. If an exception is not handled within a local frame, then control passes to the statement following the reserved word **end** with the second exception raised. The enclosing program unit then responds to the second exception in the manner described above.

To illustrate the handling of exceptions raised in block statements, consider the following skeletal code segment containing a nested block statement:

```
OUTER_BLOCK:
 begin
   ..... first part of sequence of statements of
         OUTER_BLOCK
      INNER_BLOCK:
          declare
             INDEX : COUNT := NEW_COUNT;
          begin
             ..... sequence of statements
```

```
            exception
               when CONSTRAINT_ERROR =>
                    .....
            end INNER_BLOCK;
    ..... remainder of sequence of statements of
          OUTER_BLOCK
    exception
            when CONSTRAINT_ERROR =>
                    .....
            when NUMERIC ERROR =>
                    .....
  end OUTER_BLOCK;
```

In this example, there are several places where the exceptions CONSTRAINT_ERROR and NUMERIC_ERROR can be raised. Particular situations and their results are given below:

CONSTRAINT_ERROR occurring in sequence of statements in OUTER_BLOCK	—handled by CONSTRAINT_ERROR exception handler in OUTER_BLOCK. Remaining part of OUTER_BLOCK is abandoned.
NUMERIC_ERROR occurring in sequence of statements in OUTER_BLOCK	—handled by NUMERIC_ERROR exception handler in OUTER_BLOCK. Remaining part of OUTER_BLOCK is abandoned.
CONSTRAINT_ERROR occurring in the initialization of object INDEX in the declarative part of INNER_BLOCK	—handled by CONSTRAINT_ERROR exception handler in OUTER_BLOCK. All of INNER_BLOCK is abandoned, including the exception handler.
CONSTRAINT_ERROR occurring in the sequence of statements in INNER_BLOCK	—handled by CONSTRAINT_ERROR exception handler in INNER_BLOCK. Remaining part of INNER_BLOCK is abandoned.

NUMERIC_ERROR occurring in the sequence of sequence of statements in INNER_BLOCK	—handled by NUMERIC_ERROR exception handler in OUTER_BLOCK. Remaining part of INNER_BLOCK is abandoned, and the remainder of OUTER_BLOCK is abandoned.

Finally, if some other exception is raised within INNER_BLOCK, then control passes to the statement directly following the **end** statement of OUTER_BLOCK, since no exception handler is found in either INNER_BLOCK or OUTER_BLOCK.

3.10 SUBPROGRAMS

Subprograms are found in virtually every programming language, so much so that the basic machine code instruction set of nearly every computer contains instructions dealing with subprograms. In most languages, however, subprograms are considered useful only because they permit an algorithm that is used repeatedly in a program to be coded only once as a subprogram, rather than repeatedly each time it is used. In the Ada language, subprograms also provide a means of applying the software engineering design features of modularity, information hiding, and abstraction of the particular algorithm implemented by the subprogram. Subprograms in the Ada language comprise two forms that differ principally in the manner in which they communicate with the environment from which they are called. These forms are

1. procedure—communicates with the calling environment through the use of parameters
2. function—receives information from the calling environment by the use of parameters, but can return information only as a value of the function name

The process of invoking a subprogram—that is, causing the subprogram to be executed—is termed a *subprogram call.* A call to a procedure is made by an executable statement termed a *procedure call.* A function call, on the other hand, is an expression whose evaluation requires execution of the function and the return of a value denoted by the function name.

3.10.1 Subprogram Specifications

As with all other entities in an Ada program, subprograms must be declared, and the declaration can only appear within the declarative part of some other program unit—another subprogram, a package, a task, or a generic unit—or within the declarative region of a block statement. A subprogram specification can also be separately compiled as a compilation unit, as is discussed in Section 3.11.3. The declaration of a subprogram has the following syntax:

```
subprogram_declaration ::= subprogram specification;
                                                    (3.55)
```

where

```
subprogram_specification ::=
    procedure identifier [formal_part]
  | function designator [formal_part] return type_mark
                                                  (3.55.1)
```

and

```
designator ::= identifier | operator_symbol      (3.55.2)

        operator_symbol ::= string_literal      (3.55.3)

formal_part ::=
   (parameter_specification {; parameter_specification})
                                                  (3.55.4)

parameter_specification ::=
   identifier_list : mode type_mark [:= expression]
                                                  (3.55.5)

          mode ::= [in] | in out | out           (3.55.6)
```

The syntax for an identifier list and that for an expression are given by Statements (3.10.1) and (3.34), respectively, and that for a string literal is given by Statement (3.6). The only string literals permitted as operator symbols are those containing as their only graphic characters the operator symbols listed in Statements (3.35) through (3.40).

A subprogram declaration consists of the *specification* of the subprogram, for which the syntax is given by Statement (3.55.1). The specification of a procedure gives the name of the procedure and the parameters of the procedure, if there are any. The specification of a function gives the designator—or, more loosely, the name—of the function, the parameters of the function, and the type of the returned value, termed the *result type*. Thus, the specification contains the information that a user must have in order to invoke the subprogram. The actual implementation of the subprogram—that part containing the executable code—is called the *body* of the subprogram.

3.10.2 Subprogram Bodies

The actual implementation of a subprogram is contained in the subprogram body, which comprises the subprogram specification and a block. The syntax for a program body is

```
subprogram_body ::=
   subprogram_specification is
      [declarative_part]
   begin
      sequence_of_statements
   [exception
      exception_handler
      {exception_handler}]
   end [designator];                        (3.56)
```

where the syntax for a subprogram specification is given by Statement (3.55). The syntax for a declarative part, that for a sequence of statements, and that for an exception handler are given by Statements (3.50), (3.45.2), and (3.54), respectively. If the optional designator is used, it must be the same designator appearing in the specification.

A point to be noted is that a subprogram declaration consists solely of the specification of the subprogram, and that the body of the subprogram also contains the specification. Such repetition may seem redundant, but it has very definite use that will be evident when the concept of scope is discussed later. This redundancy does make the declaration of a subprogram optional in certain instances. If there is no declaration, then the specification contained in the body has the same effect as a declaration. If there is a declaration, then the specification contained in the declaration and in the body must be identical. Of course, for each subprogram declaration there must be a corresponding subprogram body—unless the subprogram is written in another language. Subprograms written in other languages are made accessible through the use of pragma INTERFACE, which is discussed in Section 8.2.3.4.

3.10.2.1 The Return Statement. The return statement is provided for use in subprogram bodies to complete the execution of the subprogram. The syntax of a return statement is

```
return_statement ::= return [expression];    (3.57)
```

where the syntax for an expression is given by Statement (3.34). When used in the body of a function, a return statement must include the expression, since the return statement is the only means by which a return value is specified. When used in a procedure, a return statement must not include the expression.

The effect of a return statement is identical in both procedures and functions—the procedure or function is completed and a return to the calling environment is effected. Thus, a procedure may be completed in one of two ways—through execution of a return statement or by executing to the end of the procedure body. A function body, on the other hand, should never execute to the end of the function, since completion through the execution of a return statement should be effected prior to reaching the end of the function. Otherwise, no return value is assigned to the function, and the predefined exception PROGRAM_ERROR will be raised.

3.10.2.2 Separate Compilation. Ada's separate compilation features permit the specification of a subprogram and the body of a subprogram to be compiled separately as compilation units. Thus, the specification, which contains all information necessary for use of the subprogram, can be compiled even before the body is written, making possible the logical use of the subprogram even before the actual implementation is written—or, for that matter, before it is even conceived. This feature exemplifies the abstraction of what might be a rather complex operation into a relatively simple subprogram specification. Separate compilation is also important to the development, by teams of programmers, of large-scale programs, since users of a subprogram need only the abstraction provided by the specification to ensure logical compatibility. This topic is discussed in detail in Section 3.11.3.

3.10.3 Subprogram Parameters

Information is passed from the calling environment—which is a sequence of statements within a subprogram, package, task, or generic unit—to a subprogram through the use of subprogram parameters. In addition, in the case of a procedure, information can be returned to the calling environment through the use of parameters. Functions can return information to the calling environment only in the form of a value denoted by the function name.

There are two forms of subprogram parameters, depending upon their use:

1. formal parameters—parameters that appear in the subprogram specification and that are used in statements within the subprogram body
2. actual parameters—parameters that appear in the subprogram call

When a subprogram is called, the values of the actual parameters are assigned to the formal parameters before the subprogram body is executed. The precise manner in which this assignment is made depends upon the parameters themselves, and possibly upon the implementation. Formal parameters will be discussed here; actual parameters will be considered when subprogram calls are discussed in the following section.

A formal parameter of a subprogram has one of three different modes, which is declared in the specification of the subprogram as indicated in Statements (3.55.5) and (3.55.6). These modes are

in —implies that information flow is from the calling environment to the subprogram only. Parameters specified as **in** parameters are treated like constants within the sub-program; their value cannot be changed and any attempt to do so will cause a compilation error.

out —implies that information flow is from the subprogram to the calling environment only. Parameters specified as **out** parameters must have a value assigned within the sub-program, or their value upon return is undefined.

in out—implies that information flow is both from the calling environment to the subprogram and from the subprogram to the calling environment. Values of **in out** parameters can be both used and assigned within the subprogram.

While procedures may have any combination of **in, out,** and **in out** parameters, functions are restricted to **in** parameters, thus restricting the information flow from the function to the calling environment to the value denoted by the function name. If no mode is specified, the mode of a parameter defaults to **in.**

Examples of subprogram specifications and subprogram bodies are given below:

```
function ROUND(VALUE : FLOAT) return FLOAT;
   --declaration of function ROUND. Default mode of
     the formal parameter is in.

procedure SLANT_RANGE(RANGE, ELEV : in FLOAT;
                      RESULT : out FLOAT);
   --declaration of procedure SLANT_RANGE with both in
     and out formal parameters.

procedure SWAP_BITS(BIT_1, BIT_2 : in out BOOLEAN);
   --declaration of procedure SWAP_BITS. Both formal
     parameters are in out.

function ROUND(VALUE : FLOAT) return FLOAT is
   RESULT :  FLOAT;
   INT    :  INTEGER;
begin
   INT    := INTEGER(VALUE);
   RESULT := FLOAT(INT);
return RESULT;
end ROUND;
   --body of function ROUND, having a declarative part.
     Returned values are determined by the return
     statement.

procedure SWAP_BITS(BIT_1, BIT_2 : in out BOOLEAN) is
     TEMP : BOOLEAN;
begin
   TEMP  := BIT_1;
   BIT_1 := BIT_2;
   BIT_2 := TEMP;
end SWAP_BITS;
   --body of procedure SWAP_BITS. Both formal parameters
     are of mode in out.
```

The specification of the subprograms ROUND and SWAP_BITS can be seen in both the declaration and the body of these subprograms, as discussed in Section 3.10.2. The declaration is not required but, if it is present, it can be compiled separately from the body. The terms *declaration* and *specification* are often used synonymously to denote the declaration of a subprogram as a separate entity from the body. Such use is justified by the implication of Statement (3.55).

3.10.4 Subprogram Calls

The elaboration of a subprogram body has no other effect than to establish the fact that the subprogram can be invoked by a subprogram call, which is the only means by which the subprogram body can be executed. The procedure call is an executable statement for which the syntax is

```
    procedure_call ::=
       procedure_name [actual_parameter_part];          (3.58)
```

where

```
    actual_parameter_part ::=
       (parameter_association {, parameter_association})
                                                      (3.58.1)

       parameter_association ::=
          [formal_parameter =>] actual_parameter       (3.58.2)

      formal_parameter ::= parameter_simple_name       (3.58.3)

  actual_parameter ::=
     expression | variable_name | type_mark(variable_name)
                                                      (3.58.4)
```

and where the syntax for an expression and that for a type mark are given by Statements (3.45.2) and (3.8.2), respectively.

For a function call, the syntax is

```
        function_call ::=
           function_name [actual_parameter_part]       (3.58.5)
```

where the syntax for the actual parameter part is given by Statement (3.58.1). A function call is a primary, as described by Statement (3.34.5) and the discussion of Section 3.7.2.

A procedure call is an executable statement, whereas a function call is a constituent of an expression. In either case, the effect of the subprogram call is identical. Each formal parameter is associated with the corresponding actual parameter, after which the declarative part of the body is elaborated and the sequence of statements of the body is executed. The association of formal and actual parameters can be either positional or named—as implied by Statement (3.58.2)—in much the same manner as values are associated with aggregate components.

Examples of subprogram calls are given below, based upon the example subprogram declarations of the previous section.

```
EXTENT := 2.0 * ROUND(LENGTH);
--function call to function ROUND. Formal
  parameter VALUE is associated with actual
```

```
    parameter LENGTH. Positional association is
    used.

SLANT_RANGE(RANGE => DIST, ELEV => ANGLE);
--call to procedure SLANT_RANGE, using named
    parameter association.

SWAP_BITS(ZERO_BIT, ONE_BIT);
--call to procedure SWAP_BITS, using positional
    parameter association.
```

Named associations can appear in any order, so that the call to procedure SLANT_RANGE could also be written as

```
SLANT_RANGE(ELEV => ANGLE, RANGE => DIST);
```

with no change in effect. However, the procedure call

```
SLANT_RANGE(DIST, ANGLE);
```

is different from the procedure call

```
SLANT_RANGE(ANGLE, DIST);
```

A subprogram call can use both named and positional association, in which case the positional associations must occur first. The net result is that once a named association is used, all remaining associations must be named.

3.10.4.1 Parameter Association. The manner in which parameter associations are made depends upon the mode of the parameter and upon the type of the parameter. The strong typing features of the Ada language require that each actual parameter have the same type as the associated formal parameter. An actual parameter associated with an **in** formal parameter may be an expression, for which the syntax is given by Statement (3.34), since the only function of an **in** parameter is to provide information to the subprogram. If the formal parameter has a mode of **out** or **in out,** the actual parameter must be the name of a variable because the actual parameter will be assigned a value upon return from the subprogram, which in this case can only be a procedure.

For scalar parameters, the association is by *value*. That is, for parameters of mode **in** or **in out,** the value of the actual parameter is assigned to the associated formal parameter. Upon return from the subprogram, then, for those parameters of mode **out** or **in out,** the value of the formal parameter is assigned to the associated actual parameter.

For parameters that are access objects, association by value is used for parameters of all three modes upon subprogram entry, and also for **out** and **in out** parameters upon return.

For parameters of a composite type—arrays and records—the association may be either by *value* or by *reference*. An association by reference simply means that every use of the formal parameter within the subprogram is actually a use of the associated actual parameter. Since **in** parameters cannot be changed within the subprogram, and since **out** and **in out** parameters have values assigned upon return, whether association by value or by reference is used is transparent to the user.

3.10.4.2 Default Parameter Values. The syntax of Statement (3.55.5) implies that default values may be applied to the formal parameters in a subprogram specification by use of the optional assignment operator and associated expression. Default values are permitted only with **in** parameters, and they have the following effect. If a parameter specification includes the optional default value, the program call need not include an actual parameter for association with the affected formal parameter. Instead, the default value is assigned to the formal parameter. However, if an actual parameter is provided, then the value of that parameter overrides the default value and is assigned to the formal parameter.

If an actual parameter is omitted in the subprogram call, then the remainder of the parameters cannot use positional association, because then the particular parameter for which the default option is intended would be ambiguous. The rule for the use of default parameters permits the use of positional association up to the position of the omitted parameter, and requires named association from that position on.

The reader should note that the default value is obtained from an expression that may be dynamic. That is, it can contain objects that are variables. The default expession is not evaluated when the specification of a subprogram is elaborated, but rather when the subprogram is called and executed.

Examples of a subprogram specification using default expressions are given below.

```
procedure SLANT_RANGE(RANGE : FLOAT; ELEV : FLOAT := 0.0);
--the default value for formal parameter ELEV is 0.0.
  The mode of both parameters is in, the default mode.

SLANT_RANGE(DIST, 0.0);
SLANT_RANGE(DIST);
SLANT_RANGE(RANGE => DIST);
--three equivalent calls to procedure SLANT_RANGE. The
```

```
  latter two use the default value of formal parameter
  ELEV.

SLANT_RANGE(DIST, ANGLE);
--subprogram call that overrides the default value of
  formal parameter ELEV with the value of the actual
  parameter ANGLE.
```

3.10.5 Exception Handling in Subprograms

As implied by the syntax of Statement (3.56), a subprogram body may contain an exception part. The sequence of statements of a subprogram body constitutes a frame, in the sense of the discussion of Section 3.9.4. Thus, the exception handlers contained in the exception part of a subprogram body handle exceptions that are raised within the sequence of statements of the subprogram body. Only those exceptions that are named as exception choices in the syntax of Statement (3.54) are handled. In general, when an exception is raised in a frame, the remainder of the frame is abandoned and control passes to the exception part of the frame, if one is present. In the case of a subprogram, if a handler is provided by the exception part, either by name or by an **others** choice, then the sequence of statements associated with the exception handler is executed. A normal return to the calling environment is then effected, with the exception no longer raised. If no exception handler is provided, or if no exception part is present, then a return to the calling environment is made with the exception still raised. The calling program unit then responds to the exception in the manner just described. That is, the remainder of that frame is abandoned and control passes to the exception part, if one is present. This process continues until the exception is handled or until the main program is abandoned.

If an exception is raised during the elaboration of the declarative part of a subprogram, the entire subprogram is abandoned and a return to the calling environment is made with the exception raised. This procedure is mandated because exception handlers within the frame of the subprogram body may depend upon declarations contained in the declarative part of the subprogram.

Finally, an exception may be raised during the execution of an exception handler. Since an exception handler may contain block statements and subprogram calls, such exceptions may be handled within local frames contained in the exception handler itself. If an exception is not handled within a local frame, then a return to the calling environment is made with the second exception raised.

3.10.6 Subprogram Features

The block structuring of the Ada language provides two features usually required of embedded-system languages. Ada subprograms support *recursion,* and they are *reentrant.* By recursion is meant the ability of a subprogram to call itself. In languages such as FORTRAN, recursion is not supported because a subprogram, in calling itself, overwrites its own parameter values. In a block-structured language such as Ada, each time a subprogram is called the declarative part is elaborated, thus allocating memory for declared objects. Therefore, if a program calls itself recursively, a new set of object declarations is elaborated for each call, thereby maintaining the integrity of the parameter values of prior calls.

The term reentrant refers to a characteristic of a language that supports concurrent processing—as does the Ada language by means of tasks—by which more than one concurrently executing task can be executing in a subprogram simultaneously. Again, it is the block structure features of the language that provide this characteristic.

3.11 VISIBILITY RULES AND COMPILATION ISSUES

It is not possible to complete a discussion of the basic concepts of the Ada language without some consideration of the scope and visibility rules of the language. The discussion here will be cursory and applicable only to subprograms and block statements. Extension of the principles introduced here to other program units, and to the communication among program units, will be presented as other program units are discussed.

The scope and visibility rules of the Ada language result from the block structure of the language, but they are quite functional in enhancing the use of abstraction for reducing the complexity of programs. A key property of block-structured languages is that the elaboration of a declaration, for all practical purposes, brings into existence the declared entity. Thus, the order of elaboration is extremely important because an entity cannot be referenced before it is elaborated. A second property of such languages is that the effect of the elaboration of a declaration is limited—that is, it does not necessarily extend to the end of the program. This fact leads to the concept of the scope of a declaration.

3.11.1 The Scope of a Declaration

The scope and visibility rules of the Ada language are defined in terms of what is called a *declarative region,* which is a portion of the program text. A declarative region is formed by

- a subprogram declaration and the corresponding body
- a record declaration
- a block statement
- a loop statement

There are also other kinds of declarative regions associated with certain Ada features that have not yet been discussed.

The scope of a declaration is the region of the program text in which the declaration is in effect. The scope of the declaration is also referred to as the scope of the entity declared by the declaration. Thus, one can speak of the scope of a type or the scope of an object, for example. The scope of a declaration—or, equivalently, of the entity created by the elaboration of the declaration—extends from the declaration itself to the end of the innermost declarative region in which it occurs. This rule implies, for example, that objects declared within the declarative part of a subprogram have a scope that extends from the point of declaration to the end of the subprogram body. In essence, they come into existence at the time of elaboration and then cease to exist once the subprogram is exited. A declaration such as this is said to be *local* to its innermost declarative region. If one declarative region encloses another declarative region—as occurs, for example, when a block statement appears within a subprogram—declarations in the outer region are said to be *global* to the inner region.

In some instances, the scope of a declaration extends beyond the innermost declarative region in which the declaration appears. For this reason, the part of the scope that extends to the end of the innermost declarative region is termed the *immediate scope* of the declaration. This concept is significant to the visibility rules of the Ada language discussed in the following section. An example of a declaration whose scope extends beyond its immediate scope is the declaration of a record component. Since a record declaration forms a declarative region, the immediate scope of a component declaration extends only to the end of the record declaration. The *extended scope,* on the other hand, extends to the end of the scope of the enclosing declarative region. The discussion of selected components in Section 3.7.1.2 reflects this fact. Other examples of extended scope are represented by discriminant specifications and parameter specifications.

The important concept here is that, outside of the scope of a declared entity, the entity simply does not exist. Any reference to the name of the entity will result either in an unresolved reference or in access to some other entity with the same name that happens to be in scope in the region in which reference is made.

Several examples of scope rules are given below for several kinds of declarative regions.

```
procedure SWAP_BITS(BIT_1, BIT_2 : in out BOOLEAN) is
    TEMP  : BOOLEAN;
begin
    TEMP  := BIT_1;
    BIT_1 := BIT_2;
    BIT_2 := TEMP;
end SWAP_BITS;
--here, the scope of the declaration of TEMP extends
  from the declaration itself to the reserved word
  end.
```

In this example, the object TEMP is local to the procedure SWAP_BITS. Outside the procedure, TEMP does not exist.

```
ROUND:
   declare
        INT : INTEGER;
   begin
        INT     := INTEGER(VALUE);
        RESULT  := FLOAT(INT);
   end ROUND;
--this is a block statement with the declaration of
  local object INT. The scope of INT extends from the
  point of declaration to the reserved word end.
```

In this example the object INT is local to the block statement and cannot be referenced outside the block itself. The object RESULT, on the other hand, must be declared in the enclosing code and is global to block ROUND. The declaration of RESULT must occur prior to its use in the block statement.

```
for INDEX in reverse 1..50 loop
   TOT_WEIGHT := TOT_WEIGHT + WEIGHTS(INDEX);
end loop;
--in this for loop, the loop index INDEX is
  implicitly declared. The scope of INDEX extends from
  the point of implicit declaration in the loop
  parameter specification to the reserved words
  end loop.
```

The implicit declaration of the loop parameter in a for loop is the only permitted instance of a declaration in a loop.

Since the Ada language supports almost any kind of encapsulation and nesting, it is quite common to find subprograms nested wtihin other subprograms, subprograms within block statements and vice versa, subprograms within loops and vice versa, or any combination thereof. The rules of scope permit the programmer to declare entities—principally types and objects, but the concept applies equally well to subprograms and other program units—locally within various subprograms and block statements, without concern for name conflicts with objects declared elsewhere. This feature is extremely useful in large-scale programs, since it frees the programmer from having to devise a large number of meaningful names. Also, the program design is less error prone because the set of names that are accessible at any one point in the program is limited, thus tending to reduce the complexity of the resulting program text.

3.11.2 The Visibility of an Identifier

The scope rules of the Ada language provide some freedom in the selection of identifiers for the names of declared entities. Such freedom does present ambiguities in some cases; that is, a particular identifier may have more than one meaning at some particular point in the program text because more than one entity denoted by the identifier is in scope. A simple example serves to illustrate the concept.

```
procedure MAIN is
   .....
   TEMP : BOOLEAN;
   .....
   procedure SWAP_BITS(BIT_1, BIT_2 : in out BOOLEAN) is
        TEMP  :  BOOLEAN;
   begin
        TEMP  := BIT _1;
        BIT_1 := BIT_2;
        BIT_2 := TEMP;
   end SWAP_BITS;
   .....
end MAIN;
```

Here, procedure SWAP_BITS is declared within the declarative part of another procedure, which in turn contains the declaration of a boolean object named TEMP. Within the declarative part of procedure SWAP_BITS, a second boolean object with the name TEMP is declared. According to the discussion to this point, this program text will cause the elaboration of two separate declarations and will result in two objects with the same name. The scope rules say that the object TEMP declared in procedure SWAP_BITS is local to the procedure itself, so there is no ambiguity outside the procedure. The potential ambiguity arises within the procedure, because the object TEMP declared in the enclosing program text is global to procedure SWAP_BITS and is therefore in scope within the procedure. Thus, two separate objects, both with the same name, are in scope within procedure SWAP_BITS.

In order to resolve ambiguities caused by overlapping scopes such as this, the Ada language has a separate concept called the *visibility* of a declaration. Visibility is determined by a specific set of rules that ensure than an identifier either denotes only a single entity at any point within the program text or represents an unresolved reference. The exception to these rules occurs in *overloading,* which is discussed in Section 8.2.1.

Within its scope, a declaration is either directly visible or visible by selection. *Direct visibility* refers to the situation in which the declaration can be referenced by its simple name—that is, by the identifier specified in the declaration. A declaration is directly visible only within its immediate scope and only at those locations in the immediate scope where it is not hidden by a local declaration, as described below.

Hiding of declarations is the way in which Ada resolves ambiguities resulting from the declaration of different entities with the same name, and it occurs when the inner declarative region of one declaration encloses that of another declaration. The example of this section—the body of procedure SWAP_BITS—illustrates this situation. The inner declarative region of the first TEMP declaration encloses that of the second TEMP declaration. Thus, the immediate scope of the first TEMP declaration extends from the declaration itself to the end of the declarative region containing the declaration. This declarative region, of course, includes the body of procedure SWAP_BITS. Thus, both declarations are in scope within procedure SWAP_BITS, but the first declaration is *hidden.* That is, it can no longer be referenced by its simple name, but rather must be referenced by use of an *expanded name* expressed in the selected component notation of Statement (3.33). In this situation, the selector is limited to be a simple name, a character literal, or an operator symbol, and the prefix can only be a name.

In the example of procedure SWAP_BITS, then, the first declaration of TEMP is hidden within the procedure SWAP_BITS, but it may be referenced by the expanded name MAIN.TEMP. Any occurrence of the simple name TEMP within procedure SWAP_BITS will reference the local object TEMP. Any occurrence of the simple name TEMP within procedure MAIN, but external to procedure SWAP_BITS, will reference the first declaration of TEMP. Any occurrence of the expanded name SWAP_BITS.TEMP within procedure MAIN, but external to procedure SWAP_BITS, will result in an unresolved reference because the scope of SWAP_BITS.TEMP is limited to procedure SWAP_BITS.

Expanded names can always be used to reference an object, whether or not they are required because of hiding. In many instances, such use is good programming practice since it enhances the understandability of the code.

The scope and visibility rules of the Ada language have ramifications extending much further than indicated by the discussion here. For this reason, the concepts of scope and visibility are an integral part of the consideration of packages, tasks, and generic units presented in the sequel.

3.11.3 Compilation Issues

There has been considerable focus on the separate compilation facilities of the Ada language. While an Ada program consists of a collection of program units—subprograms, packages, tasks, and generic units—the compilation of a program is achieved by the separate compilation of one or more *compilation units*. Even though more than one compilation unit may be submitted in a single compilation, the result is as if each were submitted separately. Thus, separate compilation is forced in the Ada language. Ada's compilation units are

- subprogram declaration (specification)
- subprogram body
- package declaration (specification)
- package body
- generic declaration (specification)
- generic body
- generic instantiation
- subunit

At this point, only those compilation issues relating to the subprogram specifications and bodies, and to subunits, will be considered. Issues relating to the remaining compilation units will be discussed at appropriate places in the sequel.

Formally, a compilation can be described by a syntax statement:

```
compilation ::= {compilation_unit}          (3.59)
```

where

```
          compilation_unit ::=
              context_clause library_unit |
                   context_clause secondary_unit   (3.59.1)

      library_unit ::=
          subprogram_declaration | package_declaration
        | generic_declaration     | generic_instantiation
        | subprogram_body                             (3.59.2)

       secondary_unit ::= library_unit_body | sub_unit
                                                      (3.59.3)

    library_unit_body ::= subprogram_body | package_body
                                                      (3.59.4)
```

The declaration of a subprogram, package, or generic unit consists simply of the specification of the unit. See Statement (3.55), for example. While some of the terms in these syntax statements have not yet been fully discussed, the applications of the statements to subprograms can be explored. First, some terms must be defined. These terms are *program library, library unit,* and *secondary unit.*

The Ada language was designed to function in a host-target environment, in which the host computer contains the programming support environment. Of course, the host computer and target computer can actually be the same machine, but the host must provide the support environment. When a program unit is successfully compiled, the resulting compiled unit becomes part of a program library residing on a mass storage device of the host computer. As implied by Statement (3.59.2), these units are called *library units* if they are the compiled version of a specification, of a subprogram body that has no associated specification, or of a generic instantiation, as indicated by Statement (3.59.2). A *secondary unit* is the body associated with a library unit, or it is a *subunit,* which is discussed later in this section. With respect to subprograms, then, a separately compiled declaration (specification) produces a library unit residing in the program library. When the associated body is compiled, either in a separate submission to the compiler or in the same submission, a secondary unit is produced. On the other hand, if a subprogram has no separate specification, then the body is compiled as a library unit. These relationships are illustrated in Figure 3.10. The rules of compilation require a subprogram specification, if it is present, to be compiled prior to compilation of the body. Otherwise, the body would be compiled as a library unit rather

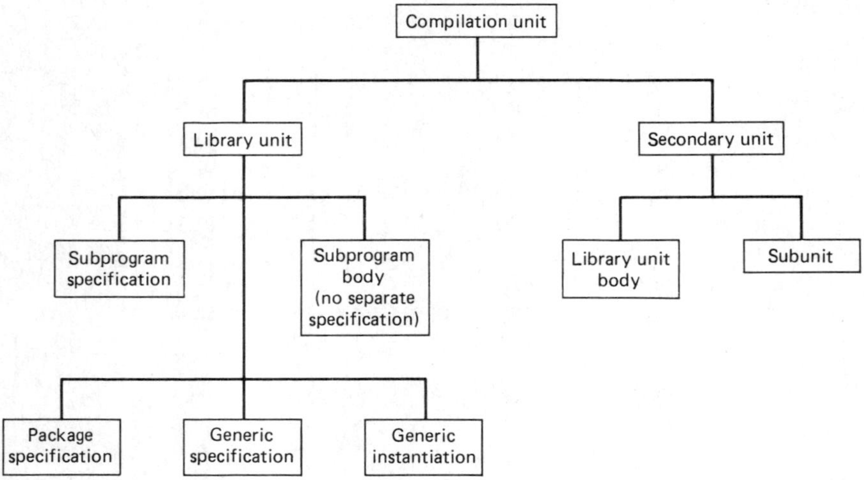

Figure 3.10. Units residing in a program library.

than as a secondary unit. The same requirement applies to packages and generic units as well.

A library unit that is a subprogram can be used as a *main program,* in the usual context of the use of the phrase in other languages. That is, the basic executable unit in the Ada language is the subprogram. In most cases, the main program is a parameterless procedure, but the language rules do not prohibit other forms of subprograms from being used as main programs. The precise use of parameters and/or results in such cases must be specified in the documentation provided by the implementation.

3.11.3.1 The Context Clause. A subprogram may contain, as part of its declarative part, other program units—as implied by Statements (3.50) and (3.56). A subprogram body containing any number of other subprograms in its declarative part constitutes only a single compilation unit and will compile into a single secondary unit or library unit, depending upon whether or not a corresponding declaration (specification) has been previously compiled. The scope and visibility rules discussed in the previous section then apply. As an altenative, it is possible to remove a subprogram from the declarative part of the enclosing subprogram, and then to submit it as a separate compilation unit—or units, if both declaration and body are present. The result is the production of a library unit—together with an associated secondary unit if the declaration is present—completely independent of that produced by compilation of the original subprogram.

The scope and visibility rules are different in these two cases, as is discussed below.

When a compilation unit consisting of a subprogram declaration or body is submitted for compilation, library units or secondary units resulting from previous compilations are not visible to the compilation unit unless such visibility is explicitly requested by the use of a context clause, in accordance with the syntax of Statement (3.59.1). The syntax of a context clause is

```
context_clause ::= {with_clause { use_clause }}    (3.60)
```

where

```
with_clause ::= with unit_simple_name
                    {, unit_simple_name};      (3.60.1)
```

and

```
use_clause ::= use package_name {, package_name };
                                                (3.60.2)
```

Consideration of the use clause will be deferred until packages are discussed in Chapter 4. The names appearing in the with clause are the names of library units. When used in a compilation unit, the effect of a with clause is to make all library units whose names appear in the with clause directly visible within the compilation unit, except, of course, where they are hidden by other declarations in accordance with the discussion of Section 3.11.2. A with clause applied to the compilation of a library unit need not be repeated when the secondary unit is compiled, although such inclusion is permitted. In the case of a subprogram library unit, the use of the name of the subprogram within a with clause makes the subprogram directly visible, and thus callable, within the compilation unit. Local declarations within the declarative part of the library unit, however, are not visible, even if expanded names are used. Thus, the integrity of the library unit is protected.

If a compilation unit uses a with clause to gain visibility of a program unit, and that program unit in turn gained visibility of a second program unit through use of a with clause, the compilation unit should not reference the second unit in its own with clause—unless, of course, the compilation unit also requires visibility of the second program unit. The general rule is that the with clauses of a compilation unit should contain only the names of library units whose visibility is actually necessary within the unit. Although the discussion here relates to subprograms, equivalent features exist with reference to packages and generic units. Specific applications will be developed when these program units are considered.

An example of the use of a with clause is given below, in the case of the example procedure MAIN of Section 3.11.2. This procedure contains, in its declarative part, the body of subprogram SWAP_BITS. The code segment is repeated here for convenience:

```
procedure MAIN is
   .....
   TEMP : BOOLEAN;
   .....
   procedure SWAP_BITS(BIT_1, BIT_2 : in out BOOLEAN) is
      TEMP  :  BOOLEAN;
   begin
      TEMP  := BIT_1;
      BIT_1 := BIT_2;
      BIT_2 :- TEMP;
   end SWAP_BITS:
   .....
end MAIN;
```

When submitted as a compilation unit, this procedure body will compile into a named library unit. The name could be MAIN, but most implementations will permit a different name.

If, instead, the procedure SWAP_BITS were compiled first, in the form

```
procedure SWAP_BITS(BIT_1, BIT_2 : in out BOOLEAN) is
   TEMP : BOOLEAN;
begin
   TEMP  := BIT_1;
   BIT_1 := BIT_2;
   BIT_2 := TEMP;
end SWAP_BITS:
```

then it would compile into a named program unit. Suppose the name of the program unit is also SWAP_BITS. Then, program unit SWAP_BITS will reside within the mass storage of the host computer on which it was compiled. If it is now desired to compile procedure MAIN, and in that compilation to use the library unit SWAP_BITS, the compilation unit should be submitted as

```
with SWAP_BITS;
procedure MAIN is
   TEMP : BOOLEAN;
begin
   .....
end MAIN;
```

Procedure SWAP_BITS need no longer be declared within procedure MAIN, since it is now a library unit and, as such, is available for use in any compilaton unit requesting visibility through a with clause. Furthermore, when procedure MAIN is compiled, the result is another program unit that, in turn, can be available for use by any other compilation unit.

The full impact of Ada's separate compilation features is not evident until their use with the package concept of the Ada language is considered. Yet, even with the limited use discussed here, it is easy to see how these features can be an appreciable help in the development of large-scale programs.

3.11.3.2 Subunits. The separate compilation facilities of the Ada language, coupled with use of the context clause, are a notable feature of the language. There may be instances, however, in which it is desired to have the convenience—from a program development perspective—of separate compilation, but to retain the visibility limitation produced by the nesting of one subprogram declaration within another. The Ada language provides this feature through the use of a *body stub* and an associated *subunit*. The syntax of a body stub is

```
body_stub ::=
   subprogram_specification is separate;
| package body package_simple_name is separate;
| task body task_simple_name is separate;          (3.61)
```

As indicated, body stubs can be applied to subprograms, packages, and tasks. Only the use of body stubs as they apply to subprograms will be considered here. Discussion of their uses with packages and with tasks will be deferred until those program units are discussed.

The use of a subunit entails the substitution of the body stub for the full declaration of the subprogram body as it would normally appear in the declarative part of an enclosing program unit. The enclosing program unit can then be compiled normally. The missing subprogram body must then be separately compiled as a subunit, whose syntax is given as

```
subunit ::=
   separate (parent_unit_name) proper_body   (3.62)
```

The parent unit is the program unit in which the associated body stub appears, and the proper body is the subprogram body as it would normally appear if declared within the declarative part of the *parent unit*. Note that a subunit must mention the name of the parent unit. This fact, together with the use of the reserved word **separate,** indicates to the compiler that the result of the compilation is to be a secondary unit, and that it is to be visible only to the parent unit. That is, the parent unit has visibility of the subunit without a with clause, and no other compilation unit can obtain visibility even through the use of a with clause. The net effect is the same as would occur if the proper body were actually compiled as part of the parent unit.

An example is provided by examining the application of the subunit concept to the subprograms of the previous section, in which two versions of the same program were presented—one with procedure SWAP_BITS declared within the declarative part of procedure MAIN, and the other with procedure SWAP_BITS separately compiled. A third alternative is presented here—that of compiling procedure SWAP_BITS as a subunit. The modification to procedure MAIN is shown below:

```
procedure MAIN is
   .....
   TEMP : BOOLEAN
   .....
   procedure SWAP_BITS(BIT_1, BIT_2 : in out
                          BOOLEAN) is separate;
   .....
   end MAIN;
```

The net effect is the replacement of the proper body of procedure SWAP_BITS with the body stub as shown. Once procedure MAIN is compiled and exists in the program library, as a library unit, the corresponding subunit can be compiled. The compilation unit used for compiling the subunit is

```
separate (MAIN)
procedure SWAP_BITS(BIT_1, BIT_2 : in out BOOLEAN) is
   TEMP  :  BOOLEAN;
```

```
begin
   TEMP  := BIT_1;
   BIT_1 := BIT_2;
   BIT_2 := TEMP;
end SWAP_BITS;
```

The use of subunits, as opposed to separate compilation into library units, will be dictated by the specific desires of the program designer. The use of a subunit, as opposed to including the proper body within the parent unit, has two advantages. The first, of course, is the flexibility it provides in program design. The second advantage is more related to the understandability of software—it produces code that is less cluttered and thus is easier to understand.

3.11.4 Order of Compilation

The order of compilation or of recompilation is very important in Ada program development because of the linkages formed between program units. In general, the rules defining the order of compilation are a direct consequence of the visibility rules. The following rules apply to subprograms as well as to other compilation units.

- A compilation unit may not be compiled before all library units named in its context clause are compiled.
- A secondary unit that is a subunit must be compiled after the parent unit is compiled.
- A secondary unit that is the body of a subprogram must be compiled after the corresponding library unit (specification) is compiled.

Similar rules apply to recompilation because of the potential effect that any change in one library unit may have on others that name it in their context clause. On the other hand, some recompilations do not require further action. For example:

- A subunit can be recompiled without affecting the parent unit.
- A subprogram body can be recompiled without affecting other units, so long as the specification is not changed.

These two characteristics result from the scope and visibility rules of the Ada language. They enhance the modifiability of software by making it possible to change the implementation of an algorithm represented by a subprogram without complete recompilation of the entire program. It is the responsibility of the programming support environment to maintain the recompilation requirements for all program units.

REFERENCES

1. Reference Manual for the Ada Programming Language, ANS1/MIL-STD-1815A-1983, United States Department of Defense, 1983.
2. Olsen, E. W. and Whitehill, S. B. *Ada for Programmers*. Reston, Va: Reston Publishing Company, 1983.
3. Fisher, Gerry, "Universal Arithmetic Packages," *Ada Letters,* a Bimonthly Publication of SIGAda, the ACM Special Interest Group on Ada, **III**(6) (May–June 1984).
4. Bohm, C., and Jacopini, "Flow Diagrams, Turing Machines, and Languages with Only Two Formation Rules," *Communication of the ACM,* **9**(5): 366 (May 1966).
5. Wulf, W. A., "A Case Against the GOTO," *Proceedings of the 25th National ACM Conference:* 791–797 (August 1972).
6. Hopkins, M. E., "A Case For the GOTO," *Proceedings of the 25th National ACM Conference:* 787–790 (August 1972).

EXERCISES

1. Determine which of the following are not valid Ada identifiers, and in each case indicate the reason.

a. ADD_TO_LIST
b. Print_list
c. :RIGHT_PARAMETER
d. STANDARD_RATE_TURN_
e. 7_TEST
f. is_prime
g. ISPRIME
h. IS_PRIME
i. QUEUETYPE_
j. L_7221_B
k. A_a_B_b_C_c
l. 737_200
m. TEST_OF_ALL_CASES
n. A
o. 2
p. A1
q. 1A
r. A:1
s. A_1
t. 6_ALPHA

2. Determine which of the following are not valid numeric literals, and in each case indicate the reason.

a. 1,372
b. 16_372_475
c. 16372475
d. .3672
e. 0.3672
f. 16_37_24_75
g. 16#FC36#
h. 2#3297#
i. 8#6_742#
j. 16#32.97#
k. 374E10
l. 0.374E10
m. 374e10
n. 374E-10
o. 374 E10
p. 0.36_74
q. 24#3A62#
r. 374E+10
s. 374E 10
t. 2#1_001.001#

3. Give the equivalent decimal values of the following numeric literals.

a. 10#3692.74#
b. 2#1011_0110_0111#
c. 2#1011.0110_0111#
d. 16#C3.2F#
e. 8#7.77#E-2
f. 16#EE.E#E2
g. 8#1_011#E1
h. 2#1101#E11
i. 9#11.1#
j. 2#101_101_100_111#

4. Compare the reserved words of Table 3.1 with those of Pascal. Which Ada reserved words are not found in Pascal?

5. Examine the declarations of type CHARACTER and package ASCII in package STANDARD. How can ASCII control characters be represented in an Ada program? How can lowercase letters be represented in an Ada program when the implementation does not support lowercase? Package STANDARD is listed in Appendix A.

6. Ada's reserved words, listed in Table 3.1, cannot be used as identifiers. Can they be used in string literals? Can they be used in comments?

7. Discuss the meaning of the term *elaboration*.

8. What is meant by the statement that "Ada is a strongly typed language"?

9. Differentiate between a subtype and a derived type in Ada. How do the declarations differ?

10. All data types in an Ada program can be considered to be subtypes. Why is this true?

11. What are the two kinds of Ada objects? How do they differ?

12. How do number declarations differ from constant declarations?

13. What is an attribute?

14. Distinguish between an integer data type and type INTEGER.

15. Distinguish between a floating-point data type and type FLOAT.

16. What is meant by the term *scalar data type?*

17. What is meant by the term *discrete data type?*

18. What is meant by the term *numeric data type?*

19. Discuss the term *representational accuracy* as it is applied to the representation of real numbers in a computer. Relate this term to the concept of round-off errors in computation.

20. Distinguish between the two real data types—floating-point types and fixed-point types.

21. Give five meaningful examples of declarations of enumeration types.

22. Give the values of the attributes FIRST and LAST for the types declared in Exercise 21.

23. List the enumeration types declared in package STANDARD.

24. Describe the properties of the predefined types NATURAL and POSITIVE.

25. Give declarations for the following:

a. An integer type.
b. An integer type with bounds −1000 and 1000.
c. A subtype of the integer type of part (a) with bounds −1000 and 1000.
d. A subtype of type INTEGER with bounds −1000 and 1000. Discuss how the typing rules of the Ada language affect the mixing of objects of these data types in expression.

26. Give declarations for the following:
  a. A real data type with a representational error bound implied by eight digits of precision.
  b. A real data type with an absolute representational error bound no larger than 0.001.

27. For the real data types of Exercise 26, give the largest and smallest positive (nonzero) model numbers.

28. Determine the model numbers associated with the declaration

```
type VALUE is digits 3;
```

29. For the declaration of Exercise 28, find the values of the following attributes:

• EMAX	• FIRST
• LARGE	• MANTISSA

30. Determine the model numbers associated with the declaration

```
type VALUE is delta 0.01 range 0.0..10.0;
```

31. For the declaration of Exercise 30, find the values of the following attributes:

• FIRST	• LAST
• LARGE	• AFT

32. Distinguish between a constrained array type and an unconstrained array type.

33. Give an example of a constrained array type declaration. Also give three examples of declarations of objects of the type.

34. Give an example of an unconstrained array type declaration. Also give three examples of declarations of objects of the type.

35. Give three examples of declarations of arrays of anonymous types. Are such declarations limited to constrained arrays?

36. Distinguish between an array slice and an array aggregate.

37. Distinguish between positional association and named association in array aggregates.

38. Give an aggregate which is the value of a 3 × 4 integer array, in which the four components in the first row have the value 1; in the second row, the value 2; and in the third row, the value 3.

39. Distinguish between a variant record and a discriminated record.

40. Compare Ada's variant record with that of Pascal.

41. What four characteristics of a record declaration can depend upon a discriminant value?

42. Give a declaration for a 100-component, one-dimensional array whose components are records. Each record constituting an array component is to have three record components, each of which is a 20 × 20 floating-point array, and each of which is of a distinctly different type.

43. Repeat Exercise 42, only in this case the square arrays comprising the components of the records are of a dimension that is determined by a record discriminant.

44. Give a record aggregate that will assign the value 0.0 to all component values of the type declared in Exercise 42.

45. Compare Ada's access data type to Pascal's type POINTER.

46. Give the declarations necessary to produce an access object designating a 10 × 10 array of records, each of which has two integer components and one component that is a one-dimensional, 1024-component array of type CHARACTER.

47. Give an expression, using an aggregate, that assigns zero values to all components of the designated object of Exercise 46.

48. Repeat the declaration of Exercise 46, but now initialize the values to zero.

49. Give declarations for the following types:

a. an enumeration type with name ACC_TYPE with values SEQ, DIR, ISAM, VSAM

b. a record type named FILE_REC with integer components PRIOR_1, PRIOR_2, PRIOR_3, and PRIOR_4

c. an access type named FILE_PTR that designates objects of type FILE ARRAY

d. a one-dimensional unconstrained array type named PTR_ARRAY with an integer index and components of type FILE_PTR.

Explain the kind of data structure represented by objects of type PTR_ARRAY.

50. Give a declaration of a three-component array object of type PTR_ARRAY from Exercise 49. How many scalar objects are represented by this object? Give expanded names for these scalar objects.

51. Distinguish between an expression and a simple expression.

52. Distinguish between a term and a factor.

53. Ada's strong typing feature is relaxed with respect to fixed-point multiplication operations. Discuss the reason and ramifications of this fact.

54. What is meant by the term *static expression?*

55. Discuss the rationale behind explicit type conversion. How must two data types be related in order for explicit conversion between them to be permitted?

56. Describe the implicit type conversion that can take place in an Ada program.

57. Discuss the concept of the universal_real and universal_integer data types. In particular, what is the effect of arithmetic operations on these types?

58. Compare Ada's if statement to that of Pascal. Consider both syntax and semantics.

59. Compare Ada's case statement to that of Pascal. Consider both syntax and semantics.

60. Discuss the use of the **others** choice in a case statement.

61. Compare Ada's loop statements with those of Pascal.

62. Give an example of an application for an endless loop.
63. The Ada language has an exit statement for use in exiting loops. Is there a comparable statement in Pascal?
64. What is the primary purpose of the block statement?
65. Compare Ada's user-defined exceptions to a comparable feature in any other language.
66. Describe how the exception-handling feature of the Ada language can be used to enhance run-time reliability.
67. Distinguish between user-defined exceptions and predefined exceptions. Consider both the raising and the handling of exceptions.
68. List the locations within an Ada program where exception handlers can occur.
69. Where must an exception be raised in order to be handled by an exception handler in a block statement?
70. What Ada statements may be included within an exception handler?
71. Describe the sequence of events that take place when an exception is raised within the sequence of statements of a block statement. Consider the case in which the block statement contains an appropriate exception handler, and the case in which it does not.
72. Describe the sequence of events that take place when an exception is raised during the elaboration of declarations in a block statement.
73. Compare Ada's subprograms to those of Pascal.
74. Discuss the information-hiding features of Ada's subprograms.
75. Discuss the significance of the return statement to both the function and the procedure.
76. Discuss the separate compilation of subprogram specifications and subprogram bodies. Relate this feature to the programming of large projects by teams of programmers.
77. Distinguish among in, out, and in out subprogram parameters.
78. Distinguish between formal and actual subprogram parameters.
79. In the text, a procedure call is classified as a statement, while a function call is classified as an expression. Justify these statements.
80. Describe the sequence of events that take place when an exception is raised within the sequence of statements of a subprogram. Consider the case in which the subprogram body contains an appropriate exception handler, and the case in which it does not.
81. Describe the sequence of events that take place when an exception is raised during the elaboration of declarations in a subprogram body.
82. Describe the sequence of events that occur when an exception is raised during the execution of the sequence of statements in an exception handler.
83. What is meant by the statement that Ada's subprograms support recursion? What characteristics make subprograms recursive?
84. What is meant by the statement that Ada's subprograms are reentrant? What features make subprograms reentrant?
85. Distinguish between the scope and visibility of an Ada declaration.
86. Describe the immediate scope of an Ada declaration.

87. Describe the extended scope of an Ada declaration.
88. Explain the effect of one declaration hiding another.
89. How do the scope and visibility rules of the Ada language help in reducing the complexity of large programs?
90. Distinguish between the terms *directly visible* and *visible by selection* as applied to Ada declarations.
91. Explain what is meant by the term *separate compilation.*
92. List those Ada program units that can be separately compiled.
93. Distinguish between a library unit and a secondary unit.
94. Distinguish among a context clause, a with clause, and a use clause.
95. Why is it not necessary to name package STANDARD in either a with clause or a use clause?
96. How does a subprogram body compiled as a subunit differ from that declared within the parent unit?
97. How does a subprogram compiled as a compilation unit differ from that whose body is compiled as a subunit?
98. What is a body stub?
99. Explain why the order of compilation or recompilation is important in an Ada program.
100. What information relating to recompilation should a support environment provide?

PROGRAMMING EXERCISES

These programming exercises may require use of input-output support from package TEXT_IO. The reader is referred to Section 6.2.2 for details.

1. Write and compile a function that implements the series evaluation of the natural logarithm, as contained in the block statement example of Section 3.8.5. Then write and compile a main program (procedure) that calls this function. Verify your results by comparing them with a table or with calculator results.
2. Repeat Exercise 1, but now declare an exception that is raised when an improper argument is provided. Also provide an exception handler in the calling environment.
3. Compile procedure SWAP_BITS of Section 3.10.3. Then write and compile a main program (procedure) that exercises this procedure.
4. Repeat Exercise 3, but now declare SWAP_BITS in the delcarative part of the main program.
5. Repeat Exercise 3, but now compile the body of SWAP_BITS as a subunit.
6. Write and compile a function that calculates the factorial of an integer, using the loop statement example of Section 3.8.4. Then write and compile a main program (procedure) that exercises this function.
7. Repeat Exercise 6, but now declare the function in the declarative part of the main program.

8. Repeat Exercise 6, but now compile the body of the function as a subunit.
9. Repeat Exercises 6, 7, and 8, but now implement the factorial function using recursion.
10. Write and compile a function that computes the trace of a matrix with components of type FLOAT. Write and compile a main program (procedure) that exercises this function.
11. Write and compile functions to compute the sine, cosine, and tangent of an angle expressed in degrees.
12. Write and compile subprograms to form the sum, difference, and product of two matrices. Use unconstrained arrays to represent the matrices.

Chapter 4
PACKAGES

4.1 MODULARIZATION, ABSTRACTION, AND INFORMATION HIDING

The development of small programs presents no particular problem. Software exhibiting the characteristics of modifiability, reliability, efficiency, and understandability can be written in practically any language, so long as the complexity of the program is not too great. Complexity is, in great part, determined by the size of a program because, as the size of a program grows, so also does the number of concepts that the programmer must consider simultaneously as he designs, writes, modifies, or maintains the program. Research has indicated a definite limit to the capacity of the human mind for processing information,[1] and this limit is very quickly exceeded as program size grows to thousands of lines or even hundreds of thousands of lines of code. This kind of situation is not new to the human experience, however, since mankind has for some time had the capability of solving very complex problems. The most impressive examples of complex solutions have been in the field of engineering. Large-scale engineering problems are much too complex for one individual to comprehend all the details of the solution. Instead, the problem is divided into modules, and those modules into other modules, and so on until a module of manageable complexity is reached. The details of implementation at this lowest level are important only to the person responsible for the implementation. Those involved with the next level are concerned only with what the lower-level modules do, not how they do it. This process is repeated upward through the various levels until the project management level is reached. By modularizing the task in this way, and by permitting developers at each level to concern themselves only with an abstraction of the next lower level, the complexity of even large-scale problems can be efficiently managed.

And so it is with software. The modern software engineering techniques of abstraction, modularization, and information hiding provide the means for decomposing a complex program into manageable parts. At the same time, this decomposition makes it practical for teams of programmers to simultaneously work on individual modules—a situtation found in all large-scale software development projects.

4.1.1 Modularization

As the name implies, modularization refers to the decomposition of a large, complex program into smaller, manageable modules. Obviously, such modularization must be purposeful. In the well-known *top-down* design methodology,[2,3,4,5] for example, the modularization is by function. Those code statements implementing some particular function are grouped into a module. In the *object-oriented* design methodology,[6] the modules encapsulate abstractions of real-world objects.

Modularization is certainly not new in terms of programming language capability. The concept of a subprogram has been incorporated into virtually every programming language, starting with FORTRAN. But modularization without some sort of control over what the individual modules can do is also dangerous in large-scale systems. In fact, history has shown that large-scale programs developed by teams of programmers, each responsible for particular modules, often do not function as expected when the individual modules are finally integrated to form the complete system. The problems encountered in these systems most often can be traced to one or both of two general causes:

1. Modules interfere with one another during execution, even though the modules themselves are correctly coded and function properly. This interference is usually in the form of data contamination.
2. The interfaces beween modules are not properly defined, in which case the interaction among modules is sometimes erroneous.

While good programming practice, combined with a thorough knowledge of the language being used, can reduce the chances of software malfunction due to these causes, a language that provides well-defined functional interfaces between modules, together with a degree of control over just what access one module has to the implementation details of another, can ensure that proper interaction between modules is maintained. The Ada language does just this, by providing features that permit the use of abstraction to stress the function of a module while suppressing the details of its implementation, and by the use of information hiding to make the implementation detail inaccessible to a user of the module. Ada's subprograms—procedures and functions—support data abstraction and information hiding, but they are somewhat limited in their ability to provide the necessary control over communications among modules. The language unit provided to support the kind of modularization discussed here is the package.

4.1.2 Abstraction

In software engineering terms, abstraction is the representation of an entity by its purpose, while omitting the details of the implementation.[7] Abstraction in the development of software can be applied either to the data with which a program works or to the process of the program itself, or to both. Ada's package concept will support both *data abstraction* and *process abstraction*. It is the combination of modularity and abstraction that provides for two characteristics very important to large-scale program development of any kind. These characteristics are

1. Reduction of complexity—provided by the abstraction itself, since the functions of various modules can be easily understood without the necessity of understanding the detailed implementation
2. Separate module development—enhanced by the fact that the developer of a module need not be concerned with the implementation detail of lower-level modules

In addition to improving the understandability of software, as discussed above, the combination of modularity and abstraction also play an important role in enhancing the modifiability of software. The implementation of an algorithm can be modified without affecting the way in which the abstraction of the algorithm behaves, thus providing the controlled change necessary for effective modifiability.

Software designed with effective modifiability not only provides for efficiency of program maintenance; it also aids in producing efficient code, in that module modification designed to increase the efficiency of an algorithm can be incorporated into a system without affecting other modules. The feature of Ada's package concept that provides the necessary abstraction is the distinction between the visible part of the package, included within the package specification, and the hidden part represented by the package body. Data abstraction is provided by combining the package concept with that of a *private data type*—a data type whose actual implementation is hidden from the user. Private data types are discussed in Section 4.2.3.

4.1.3 Information Hiding

The ability of Ada's program units—and in particular, the package—to provide for both process abstraction and data abstraction permits the language to support the general design goals of modifiability and understandability. But the Ada language goes one step further—it enforces abstraction by use of information hiding. For example, no entity declared within a package body, or within other program units contained within a package body, can be accessed from outside the package. Such entities are actually local to the package body—their scope extends only to the end of the package. These entities are said to be *hidden* from outside users of the package. Thus, information hiding does not imply hiding in the sense that implementation details are not known to the user, since anyone can examine the program text and determine this information. Instead, the term information hiding refers to the situation in which knowledge of the implementation details cannot possibly influence the manner in which a particular module is accessed or used. Thus, a user ignorant of the implementation detail can employ a module just as effectively as one who is thoroughly familiar with the way in which the algorithm is implemented.

Data abstraction, obtained through use of Ada's private data type, also provides forced abstraction through the use of information hiding. The declarations of private types have a two-part structure—a visible part and a hidden part. The actual structure of the data type is hidden from the user by defining the structure in the hidden part. All operations associated with the type, except for certain very limited basic operations, also have their implementation details hidden from the user.

The remainder of this chapter will detail the structure and properties of Ada's package unit, together with the use of private data types as a method of achieving data abstraction.

4.2 ADA PACKAGES

The package concept is unique to the Ada language; it provides the language with an information hiding and encapsulation mechanism. Packages are used to group, by means of encapsulation, other entities of an Ada program. To be effective in terms of good software design, of course, these entities must share some common logical relationship with respect to the context in which they are used within the program. Packages may be declared in two parts—the specification and the body—and these parts may be compiled separately. The specification part is visible to other program units and itemizes the facilities provided by the package. The body of the package is hidden from other program units and contains the implementation details in terms of executable code and, perhaps, in terms of data structure.

As discussed in the previous section, this two-part structure serves to provide the information-hiding facility necessary to prevent a user of the package from exploiting any knowledge he may have of implementation detail, which in turn prevents a user from developing code that depends on the particular implementation of package facilities. Thus, once the question of the package specification has been resolved, the package body may be implemented in any way consistent with the specification. Furthermore, the implementation can be modified at any time and in any manner that preserves this consistency.

4.2.1 Package Specifications

The entities encapsulated within a package can be virtually any entity that can be declared in the language. This includes types, objects, subprograms, tasks, and even other packages. In order to be accessible outside of the package, the declaration of an entity must appear in the package specification. The syntax for a package declaration is

```
package_declaration ::= package_specification;  (4.1)
```

where

```
package_specification ::=
     package identifier is
          {basic_declarative_item}
     [private
          {basic_declarative_item}]
     end [package_simple_name]                (4.1.1)
```

and the syntax for a basic declarative item is given by Statement (3.50.1). The *visible part* of the specification lies between the reserved words **is** and **private,** while the hidden part—called the *private part*—lies between the reserved words **private** and **end**. If the reserved word **private** does not appear, then there is no private part, and the visible part extends to the reserved word **end**. As is the case with subprograms, the declaration of a package consists of the package specification. In contrast to the case of subprograms, which may have a declaration but must have a body, a package must have a declaration and may have a body.

An entity declared in the private part of the specification is not visible outside the package itself. Thus, users of the package may not reference these entities, even by use of expanded names. On the other hand, those entities declared in the visible part are visible to outside users by the use of expanded names in which the prefix is the package name. As will be discussed later, direct visibility—reference by use of the simple name rather than the expanded name—can be achieved by means of the use clause.

A package can have a specification and no body. Such a situation occurs when the package encapsulates only a group of type declarations, object declarations, or a combination thereof. These declarations must be visible to other program units, so they appear in the package specification. Since no subprograms, tasks, packages, or generic units appear in the specification, there is no requirement for a package body. An example of a package containing only object declarations can be found in package STANDARD, the specification of which is contained in Appendix A, where package ASCII contains only constant declarations. A second example can be found in Appendix C, where the predefined package IO_EXCEPTIONS contains only exception declarations. Other examples of package specifications are given below.

EXAMPLE 1: A more general case is represented by the following example:

```
package TRIG_FUNCTIONS is
   type DEGREES is digits 8;
   type VALUE is digits 8;
   function SIN(ANGLE: in DEGREES) return VALUE;
   function COS(ANGLE: in DEGREES) return VALUE;
   function TAN(ANGLE: in DEGREES) return VALUE;
   function ARCSIN(ARG: in VALUE) return DEGREES;
   function ARCCOS(ARG: in VALUE) return DEGREES;
   function ARCTAN(ARG: in VALUE) return DEGREES;
end TRIG_FUNCTIONS;
```

Here, the types DEGREES and VALUE are visible outside the package and can be referenced by the expanded names

```
TRIG_FUNCTIONS.DEGREES
TRIG_FUNCTION.VALUE
```

Similarly, the six functions are visible outside the package and can be referenced by the expanded names

```
TRIG_FUNCTIONS.SIN
TRIG_FUNCTIONS.COS
TRIG_FUNCTIONS.TAN
TRIG_FUNCTIONS.ARCSIN
TRIG_FUNCTIONS.ARCCOS
TRIG_FUNCTIONS.ARCTAN
```

Any particular program unit may obtain direct visibility of these types and functions by means of the use clause, to be discussed later in Section

4.3.3.1. Certainly, the entities declared here are logically related; the types are the parameter and return value types of the functions, and the functions themselves—assuming that they return the values of the functions as implied by the names—are related by a common characteristic. The package is said to *export* the two types and the six functions because, since they are declared in the package specification, they are accessible by other program units.

The above example illustrates a second important concept in the use of packages. The information contained in the specification provides a user with all he needs to know in order to use any of the six functions exported by the package. The user must declare objects of types DEGREES and VALUE, which he may then use to access the various functions. Note that no mention is made of the actual implementation of the six functions. The implementation is hidden from the user, in the sense discussed in the previous section. Furthermore, the specification may be compiled separately from the body. Thus, once the specification is compiled, other program units that issue calls to one of these six functions can themselves be compiled. While the resulting code cannot be executed, of course, the logical compatibility between the package and the calling unit—including type checking—is confirmed by successful compilation. All of this can be accomplished before the body of the package is compiled—or, for that matter, even before the algorithm for implementation is selected.

EXAMPLE 2: A second example—and a more comprehensive one—is provided by the package specification given below:

```
package QUEUE_OF_CHAR is
    type QUEUE_TYPE is limited private;
    procedure RESET(QUEUE_NAME : in out QUEUE_TYPE);
    procedure PUT(ELEM : in CHARACTER; QUEUE_NAME
                       : in out QUEUE_TYPE);
    procedure TAKE(ELEM : out CHARACTER; QUEUE_NAME
                        : in out QUEUE_TYPE);
    function IS_EMPTY(QUEUE_NAME : in QUEUE_TYPE)
                           return BOOLEAN;
    UNDERFLOW : exception;
private
    type POSITION;
    type LINK is access POSITION;
    type POSITION is
        record
            VALUE : CHARACTER;
            POINTER : LINK;
        end record;
```

```
        type QUEUE_TYPE is
            record
                FRONT : LINK:
                BACK : LINK;
            end record;
    end QUEUE_OF_CHAR;
```

This package specification contains both a visible part and a private part. In the visible part the limited private type QUEUE_TYPE is declared. The operations available for objects of this type are also declared in the visible part. They are RESET, PUT, TAKE, and IS_EMPTY. Declared there also is the exception UNDERFLOW. This package provides a type which is a first in–first out (FIFO) queue into which objects of type CHARACTER can be placed. More precisely, objects of this type are FIFO queues. Such objects are commonly found in programs dealing with communication or with the spooling of character data to a printer or some other device. A queue can be purged by procedure RESET; a character can be placed in the queue by procedure PUT; a character can be obtained from the queue by procedure TAKE; the queue can be tested to see if it is empty by function IS_EMPTY; and any attempt to TAKE from an empty queue will raise exception UNDERFLOW. The visible part of the specification, together with statements such as those above giving an abstract description of the effect of the various operations, serve as the interface between the user of a package and the implementer of the package. There are several ways in which a FIFO queue can be implemented, but the user need not be concerned with the implementation details.

The way in which the queue is implemented can be determined from examination of the private part. In this case, the mechanism is a linked list of records of type POSITION. The actual structure of the type QUEUE_TYPE is that of a record with two components, both of which are access objects. One of these components designates the front of the queue; the other designates the back of the queue. In the package body—the declarative part of which must contain the bodies of procedures RESET, PUT, and TAKE, and that of function IS_EMPTY—objects of type QUEUE_TYPE can be treated as record objects, but to the user of the package they are of a type that simply has the properties of a FIFO queue. This example illustrates the use of a private type to create what is termed an *abstract data type*.

Before leaving this example, it should be noted that the body of the package is not shown. This fact would in no way hinder a user of the package, since any declaration contained in the body is not visible outside the package body. All that is required of a user is confidence that the implementation will function correctly. It should also be pointed out that the implementation algorithm could be changed without affecting the user, so long as the effect of each operation remained unchanged. Such a change might well require modification of the private part of the specification, but since the private part is also hidden from the user, no change in user access would be produced.

4.2.2 Package Bodies

While the visible part of the specification of a package establishes the interface between the package and outside users, thus describing the abstraction afforded by the package, the body contains the actual implementation of those facilities provided by the package. The syntax for a package body is

```
package_body ::=
    package body package_simple_name is
        [declarative_part]
   [begin
        sequence_of_statements
   [exception
        exception_handler
       {exception_handler}]]
end [package_simple_name];                              (4.2)
```

where the syntax for a declarative part is given by Statement (3.50). The syntax for an exception handler is given by Statement (3.54).

A basic declarative item appearing in a package specification, as outlined in Statement (4.1.1), may be a basic declaration, a representation clause, or a use clause. The latter two terms will be defined later; a basic declaration is defined by Statement (3.6) and may contain the declaration of virtually any Ada entity. If the specification of a package contains the declaration—in this case, the specification—of a subprogram, of another package, of a task, or of a generic unit, then the body of the package must contain within its declarative part the corresponding subprogram, package, task, or generic unit body. There are exceptions to this requirement; specifically, some packages may have a declaration but no body, and some subprograms may be written in another language. The fact that these bodies are contained in the declarative part of the package body, rather than in the sequence of statements, is significant to the effect of the elaboration of a package.

When a package body is elaborated, its declarative part is first elaborated. Since the declarative part must contain the body of any subprogram, package, task, or generic unit, whose specification is contained in the package specification, these bodies—if present—are also elaborated, in the order in which they appear. The reader should recall that the elaboration of a subprogram body has no other effect than to establish the fact that the subprogram can be invoked by a subprogram call. When the declarative part of the package body has been elaborated, then the sequence of statements, if present, is executed. The optional exception part, if present, services exceptions raised during the execution of the sequence of statements. The net result is that the sequence of statements of a package body is executed only once for each elaboration of the package body, and it is executed at the time of elaboration. The sequence of statements of a subprogram body contained in the declarative part of a package body, on the other hand, is not executed when the package body is elaborated, but rather is executed each time a call to the subprogram is made. As a result, the sequence of statements in a package body is used primarily for implementing initializing operations required by the package. Often, the sequence of statements is omitted. Some examples will serve to clarify this issue.

EXAMPLE 1: In the previous section, the declaration—or equivalently, the specification—of package TRIG_FUNCTIONS was presented, containing the declarations of six functions. The purpose of package TRIG_FUNCTIONS is to provide to outside users the trigonometric functions SIN, COS, TAN, ARCSIN, ARCCOS, and ARCTAN. The package body must provide the implementation of these functions. In skeletal form, the body might be:

```
package body TRIG_FUNCTIONS is
      ..... declaration of local entities common to
            various of the subprogram bodies, if any
      .....

   function SIN(ANGLE : in DEGREES) return VALUE is
      ..... body of function SIN
      .....
   end SIN;

   function COS(ANGLE : in DEGREES) return VALUE is
      ..... body of function COS
      .....
   end COS;

   function TAN(ANGLE : in DEGREES) return VALUE is
      ..... body of function TAN
      .....
   end TAN;
```

```
        function ARCSIN(ARG : in VALUE) return DEGREES is
            ..... body of function ARCSIN
            .....
        end ARCSIN;

        function ARCCOS(ARG : in VALUE) return DEGREES is
            ..... body of function ARCCOS
            .....
        end ARCCOS;

        function ARCTAN(ARG : in VALUE) return DEGREES is
            ..... body of function ARCCOS
            .....
        end ARCTAN;
    end TRIG_FUNCTIONS;
```

In this example, the body of package TRIG_FUNCTIONS consists only of a declarative part; there is no sequence of statements, nor is there an exception part. Elaboration of this body does nothing more than establish the fact that each of six functions can be called. Execution of the sequence of statements in each function body can be effected only by a call to that function. Each of the function bodies may have its own declarative part, as well as its own exception handlers, as implied by Statement (3.56).

EXAMPLE 2: As a smaller but more complete example, consider a package that provides two functions—the natural logarithm and the logarithm to the base 10. In this example the predefined type FLOAT will be used, rather than a user-defined floating-point type. Use of type FLOAT will ensure that the package will compile in any implementation, although the accuracy bounds may vary from one implementation to another. The package specification is

```
        package LOGARITHM is
            function LN(ARG : in FLOAT) return FLOAT;
            function LOG(ARG : in FLOAT) return FLOAT;
        end LOGARITHM;
```

Again, this specification serves as the interface between the package and its user. The functions LN and LOG are visible outside the package; the implementation of these functions, contained in the body of package LOGARITHM, is hidden. A possible implementation of the package body is

```
package body LOGARITHM is
    VALUE_ERROR : exception;
```

```
function LN(ARG : in FLOAT) return FLOAT is
    SERIES_LIMIT  : INTEGER  := 10;
    RESULT        : FLOAT    := 0.0;
    POWER         : INTEGER  := 1;
    TERM          : FLOAT;
begin
    if ARG > 0.0 then
        while POWER < SERIES_LIMIT
            loop
                TERM    := ((ARG - 1.0)/(ARG + 1.0))
                           ** POWER;
                RESULT  := RESULT + (1.0/FLOAT(POWER))
                           * TERM;
                POWER   := POWER + 2;
            end loop;
        RESULT := 2.0 * RESULT;
        return RESULT;
    else
        raise VALUE_ERROR;
    end if;
exception
    when VALUE_ERROR =>
        PUT_LINE("*** INVALID INPUT TO LN ***");
        PUT("  INPUT VALUE =  ");
        PUT(ARG);
        RESULT := 0.0;
        PUT_LINE("  ZERO DEFAULT VALUE ASSIGNED");
        return RESULT;
    when others =>
        PUT_LINE("***UNKNOWN PROBLEM IN FUNCTION
                 LN***");
        raise;
    end LN;

function LOG(ARG : in FLOAT) return FLOAT is
    RESULT   :  FLOAT     := 0.0;
    CONVERT  :  constant  := 0.43429_44819_03251_82765;
begin
    if ARG > 0.0 then
        RESULT := CONVERT * LN(ARG);
        return RESULT;
    else
        raise VALUE_ERROR;
    end if;
    exception
        when VALUE_ERROR =>
```

```
                    PUT_LINE("***INVALID INPUT TO LOG***");
                    PUT("  INPUT_VALUE =  ");
                    PUT(ARG);
                    RESULT := 0.0;
                    PUT_LINE("  ZERO DEFAULT VALUE ASSIGNED
                    return RESULT;
                when others =>
                    PUT_LINE("***UNKNOWN PROBLEM IN FUNCTION
                             LOG***");
                    raise;
    end LOG;
end LOGARITHM;
```

The algorithm used here for determination of the natural logarithm is the series expansion

$$\ln x = 2\,[((x - 1)/(x + 1)) + (1/3)((x - 1)/(x + 1))^3 + (1/5)((x - 1)/(x + 1))^5 + \cdots]$$

as implemented in the sequence of statements in the body of function LN. The base ten logarithm, provided by function LOG, is determined from the relationship

$$\log x = \ln x/\ln 10$$

where

$$1/\ln 10 = 0.4342944819032518276 5\ldots$$

This example illustrates many features of the Ada language, not just those necessarily related to the use of packages. Some interesting aspects of this example are listed below:

- Entities declared in the package specification are visible outside the package. These are the functions LN and LOG.
- Entities declared in the declarative part of the package body are not visible outside the package. These are the exception VALUE_ERROR, and the objects SERIES_LIMIT, RESULT, POWER, TERM, and CONVERT.
- The scope of the exception VALUE_ERROR extends from the point of declaration to the end of package LOGARITHM. The declaration is global to functions LN and LOG.
- The objects SERIES_LIMIT, RESULT, POWER, and TERM are

declared in the declarative part of function LN. Their scope extends from the point of declaration to the end of function LN. These declarations are local to function LN and thus are not visible within function LOG.

- The objects RESULT and CONVERT declared in the declarative part of function LOG are local to function LOG. The identifier RESULT denotes a different object than the same identifier used in function LN.
- The value of the constant object CONVERT is of type universal_real. Implicit type conversion to type FLOAT is effected when it is used in the expression of type float.
- The same exception—VALUE_ERROR—can be raised in both functions, since its declaration is global. It is the exception handlers that distinguish between the two possible situations that may raise the exceptions.
- Any exception other than VALUE_ERROR—for example, a predefined exception such as NUMERIC_ERROR—will be handled by the **others** choice in the exception parts of the two functions. This exception handler simply prints a message and then reraises the exception at the point of the function call.
- Both the declaration of the exception VALUE_ERROR and those of the two function bodies occur in the declarative part of the package body. The package body has no sequence of statements and no exception handler. The exception handlers present are local to the function bodies.
- There are several PUT and PUT_LINE procedure calls in this package. The procedures are predefined in package TEXT_IO, which will be discussed in greater detail in Section 6.2.2.

If guaranteed minimum error bounds on the representation of the real numbers in this example is desired, then the variables should be declared as floating-point types with the desired number of digits of precision, as was done in the example package TRIG_FUNCTIONS in Section 4.2.1.

None of the examples so far has involved a sequence of statements in the package body. This situation is not uncommon; in fact, packages will most often be found without a sequence of statements as part of their body. This characteristic is due to the way in which packages are used and to the nature of a package body. The developments of this section have indicated that the sequence of statements of a package body is executed only once for each elaboration of the package body, as opposed, for example, to the bodies of subprograms declared within the package, which are executed each time the subprogram is called. The principal use of the sequence of statements in a package body is for producing some initial action whose effect need not be modified until the package is again elaborated. Two examples are given below.

EXAMPLE 3: A sequence of pseudo-random, uniformly distributed integers can be generated by use of what is termed a *linear congruential sequence*. Such a sequence is recursively formed by the relationship

$$x(n) = a * x(n - 1) \bmod b$$

where $x(n)$ is the nth value generated by the sequence, and a and b are constants chosen to give the sequence certain desirable characteristics.[8] Usually, each integer generated by this sequence is divided by the value $(b - 1)$ to yield a sequence of pseudo-random numbers, that is, real numbers uniformly distributed between zero and one. In order to start the recursively generated sequence, an initial value called a *seed* is used. The following package implements a random number generator. The package specification is

```
package RANDOM is
     function NUMBER return FLOAT;
end RANDOM;
```

Thus, the only entity from this package visible to outside users is function NUMBER, whose expanded name is RANDOM.NUMBER. The implementation is hidden from the user. The package body might be declared as follows:

```
package body RANDOM is
     RAND_INT : INTEGER range 0..32_767;
     function NUMBER return FLOAT is
          RAND_NO : FLOAT range 0.0 ..1.0;
     begin
          RAND_INT := (181 * RAND_INT) mod 32_768;
          RAND_NO  := FLOAT(RAND_INT)/FLOAT(32_768);
          return RAND_NO;
     end NUMBER;
begin
     RAND_INT := 573;
end RANDOM;
```

Notable features of this example are

- The object RAND_INT is declared in the declarative part of the package body. It is global to function NUMBER. Thus, its value can be used and modified within the body of function NUMBER.

- When the body of package RANDOM is elaborated, the body of function NUMBER, which is in the declarative part of the package body, is elaborated but not executed. Execution is effected by calls to the function from outside the package.
- Package RANDOM has a sequence of statements—in this case, the single assignment statement

```
RAND_INT := 573;
```

  This statement is executed during the elaboration of package RANDOM, immediately after the declarative part—containing the declaration of object RAND_INT and of the body of function NUMBER—is elaborated.
- Since the declaration of RAND_INT is not visible outside the package, the value of RAND_INT cannot be changed except by calls to function NUMBER from outside the package. In this manner the recursive nature of the algorithm is achieved.
- The object RAND_NO is declared within the declarative part of the body of function NUMBER. Its declaration is elaborated each time a call to function NUMBER is effected. The object simply goes out of existence—that is, it is out of scope—when a return from function NUMBER is executed. The object RAND_INT, on the other hand, is declared in the declarative part of the body of package RANDOM and is in scope so long as RANDOM is in scope, although it is not visible outside the package.

The distinction between the elaboration of a package body and that of a subprogram body is illustrated by the above example. In the case of a subprogram, the elaboration of the body has no other effect than to establish the fact that the subprogram can be invoked by a subprogram call. At the time of elaboration of the subprogram body, the declarative part is not elaborated, nor is the sequence of statements executed. These actions occur when the subprogram is called. In the case of a package, elaboration of the body results in immediate elaboration of the declarative part, followed by execution of the sequence of statements.

EXAMPLE 4: The example above illustrates the use of the sequence of statements in a package body to provide initial values. This approach may not be the best, however, since initialization can be provided in object declarations. Thus, the following declaration is equivalent to that of the package body above:

```
package body RANDOM is
    RAND_INT : INTEGER range 0..32_767 := 573;
```

```
        function NUMBER return FLOAT;
            .....
        end NUMBER;
    end RANDOM;
```

Here, the initial value of RAND_INT is provided by the object declaration, and no sequence of statements in the package body is required.

EXAMPLE 5: Yet a third version of the random-number package will return both the random integer and the random number. The package specification is:

```
package RANDOM is
    type PAIR is
        record
            RAND_INT : INTEGER range 0..32_767;
            RAND_NO  : FLOAT range 0.0..1.0;
        end record;
    function NUMBER return PAIR;
end RANDOM;
```

In this case the package exports both the record type PAIR and the function NUMBER. Now the function NUMBER returns a record with scalar components named RAND_INT and RAND_NO. Thus, a calling program might have a declaration such as

```
VALUE : RANDOM.PAIR;
```

and after a function call such as

```
VALUE := RANDOM.NUMBER;
```

the components are accessible as

```
VALUE.RAND_INT
VALUE.RAND_NO.
```

The package body might be implemented as follows:

```
package body RANDOM is
    RAND_PAIR : PAIR;
    function NUMBER return PAIR is
    begin
        RAND_PAIR.RAND_INT := (181 * RAND_PAIR.RAND_INT)
                                    mod 32_768;
```

```
        RAND_PAIR.RAND_NO  := FLOAT(RAND_PAIR.RAND_INT)
                              /FLOAT(32_768);
        return RAND_PAIR;
    end NUMBER;
begin
    RAND_PAIR.RAND_INT := 537;
end RANDOM;
```

Since the record object RAND_PAIR is declared in the declarative part of package random, both components RAND_PAIR.RAND_INT and RAND_PAIR.RAND_NO are global to function NUMBER. Thus, between calls to the function, both values are in scope and remain unchanged. The initialization of the record component RAND_PAIR.RAND_INT is accomplished here by execution of the sequence of statements of the package—in this case a single statement—as in Example 3. This initialization could also be achieved in the object declaration, using an aggregate:

```
RAND_PAIR : PAIR := (537,0.0);
```

Alternatively, initialization could have been implemented in the type declaration in the specification part of the package as follows:

```
type PAIR is
    record
        RAND_INT : INTEGER range 0..32_767 := 573;
        RAND_NO  : FLOAT range 0.0..1.0;
end record;
```

In this event, not only would the record object RAND_PAIR have the component RAND_INT initialized, but so would any record object declared in program units importing the type PAIR.

This example illustrates the use of the sequence of statements in a package body in a rather trivial way. There are instances in which the initialization process is complicated, or perhaps involves some detailed computation, so that the initialization of object or type declarations is not a reasonable alternative. In such instances, the execution of the sequence of statements provides a much-needed capability.

4.2.3 Private Data Types

In Section 1.1.4, the four classes of data types were discussed. They are repeated here for reference: (1) scalar, (2) composite, (3) access, and (4) private. The properties of scalar, composite, and access types were discussed in Sections 3.4 through 3.6. Discussion of the private data type was deferred until this point because private type declarations are limited to two instances: (1) as a declarative item in the visible part of a package specification and (2) as a generic parameter specification. The first instance will be considered here; a discussion of the latter instance will be deferred until generic units are introduced in Chapter 5.

In a package specification, the declaration of a private type occurs as a basic declarative item in the visible part, as represented in Statement (4.1.1). The visible part appears between the reserved words **is** and **private**. If the reserved word **private** is not present, then the visible part extends to the reserved word **end** and the entire specification is visible. The syntax for a private type declaration is

```
private_type_declaration ::=
    type identifier [discriminant_part] is
    [limited]private;                              (4.3)
```

where the syntax for a discriminant part is given by Statement (3.25.5). An example of a private type declaration was given in Section 4.2.1, in the declaration of package QUEUE_OF_CHAR:

```
type QUEUE_TYPE is limited private;
```

There is no discriminant part in this declaration. The effect of the optional reserved word **limited** will be discussed shortly.

When a private type is declared in the visible part of a package specification, then a corresponding full type declaration—using the same identifier—must appear in the private part of the specification. The syntax for a full type declaration is given by Statement (3.7.1), indicating that virtually any data type except another private type can be used. The discriminant part in Statement (4.3) is present only if the full type declaration is that of a discriminated record. This combination of a private type declaration in the visible part, and a corresponding full type declaration in the private part, serves to define a single data type of what might be called a dual nature. There are two views of private data types—one from outside the package that exports the type and the other from inside the package. These views are outlined below:

1. From outside the package, the type is abstract in that it is described in a black-box sense; that is, the user of the type is aware of the set of operations associated with the type, but the actual implementation is hidden. The operations associated with the type are

limited to assignment, tests for equality and inequality, membership tests, qualification, explicit conversion, selected components as applied to discriminant selection, and other operations as implied by the set of subprogram declarations accompanying the private type declaration in the visible part of the package specification. These additional operations are implemented by subprograms that have a parameter or a result of the private type. No other operations are permitted for objects of the private type by users of the package.

2. From inside the package, the type is no longer an abstraction. The structure of the type is visible—that is, knowledge of the structure can be exploited—from the corresponding full type declaration contained in the private part of the specification. Moreover, the complete set of predefined operations applicable to the full type declaration can be used for manipulating objects of the type within the package body. Even those additional operations defined by subprograms declared in the visible part of the package specification are available.

If the optional reserved word **limited** is used in the private type declaration, then the predefined operations of assignment and tests for equality and inequality are not available outside the package. Within the package, of course, these operations are part of the predefined operations available.

EXAMPLE 1: In Example 2 of Section 4.2.1, the visible part of the specification contains the declaration of QUEUE_TYPE as a limited private type. The private part of the specification contains the corresponding full type declaration

```
type QUEUE_TYPE is
   record
        FRONT  :  LINK;
        BACK   :  LINK;
   end record;
```

indicating that the view of objects of type QUEUE_TYPE from within the package is that of a record with two access type components designating the front and back of a simple linked list of nameless record objects of type POSITION. Thus, any operation predefined for record types can be used to manipulate objects of type QUEUE_TYPE within the package body, and any operation predefined for access types can be used in manipulating the two components of the record object.

To the outside user, the type QUEUE_TYPE is an abstraction of a FIFO queue—he can RESET, PUT, TAKE, and check to determine if it IS_EMPTY. Assignment and tests for equality or inequality are not permitted. Neither is the actual structure—as a record of two access components—visible to the outside user. Any attempt to use selected component notation to access these components will result in an unresolved reference. However, the user may declare as many FIFO queue objects as he desires, each of which can be individually manipulated by the operations RESET, PUT, and TAKE. For example, he may declare an array as

```
SET_OF_QUEUES : array(1..100) of QUEUE_TYPE;
```

which declares 100 different queue objects.

The body of package QUEUE_OF_CHAR might be implemented as indicated below. For convenience, the specification is repeated here.

```
package QUEUE_OF_CHAR is
    type QUEUE_TYPE is limited private;
    procedure RESET(QUEUE_NAME : in out QUEUE_TYPE);
    procedure PUT(ELEM : in CHARACTER;
                  QUEUE_NAME : in out QUEUE_TYPE);
    procedure TAKE(ELEM: out CHARACTER;
                   QUEUE_NAME : in out QUEUE_TYPE);
    function IS_EMPTY(QUEUE_NAME: in QUEUE_TYPE)
                      return BOOLEAN;
    UNDERFLOW : exception;
private
    type POSITION;
    type LINK is access POSITION;
    type POSITION is
        record
            VALUE    :  CHARACTER;
            POINTER  :  LINK;
        end record;
    type QUEUE_TYPE is
        record
            FRONT  :  LINK;
            BACK   :  LINK;
        end record
end QUEUE_OF_CHAR;

package body QUEUE_OF_CHAR is
    procedure RESET(QUEUE_NAME: in out QUEUE_TYPE) is
    begin
        QUEUE_NAME.FRONT  := null;
        QUEUE_NAME.BACK   := null;
    end RESET;
```

```
    procedure PUT(ELEM: in CHARACTER; QUEUE_NAME:
                  in out QUEUE_TYPE) is
        TEMP_POSIT : LINK;
    begin
        TEMP_POSIT := new POSITION;
        TEMP_POSIT.VALUE := ELEM;
        if QUEUE_NAME.FRONT /= null then
            QUEUE_NAME.BACK.POINTER := TEMP_POSIT;
            QUEUE_NAME.BACK := TEMP_POSIT;
        else
            QUEUE_NAME.FRONT := TEMP_POSIT;
            QUEUE_NAME.BACK := TEMP_POSIT;
        end if;
    end PUT;

    procedure TAKE(ELEM: out CHARACTER;
                   QUEUE_NAME: in out QUEUE_TYPE) is
        TEMP_POSIT : LINK;
    begin
        if IS_EMPTY(QUEUE_NAME) then
            raise UNDERFLOW;
        end if;
        ELEM                := QUEUE_NAME.FRONT.VALUE;
        TEMP_POSIT          := QUEUE_NAME.FRONT.POINTER;
        QUEUE_NAME.FRONT    := TEMP_POSIT;
    exception
        when UNDERFLOW =>
        ELEM := '*';
        raise;
    end TAKE;

    function IS_EMPTY(QUEUE_NAME: in QUEUE_TYPE)
                      return BOOLEAN is
    begin
        return QUEUE_NAME.FRONT = null and
               QUEUE_NAME.BACK = null;
    end IS_EMPTY;
end QUEUE_OF_CHAR;
```

The implementation here is a linked list of objects of type POSITION. The type QUEUE_TYPE is merely a record type whose components point to the front and back of the list, as indicated in Figure 4.1. The PUT procedure creates a new access object, stores the character in the VALUE component, and then adjusts the linkages. The sequence is

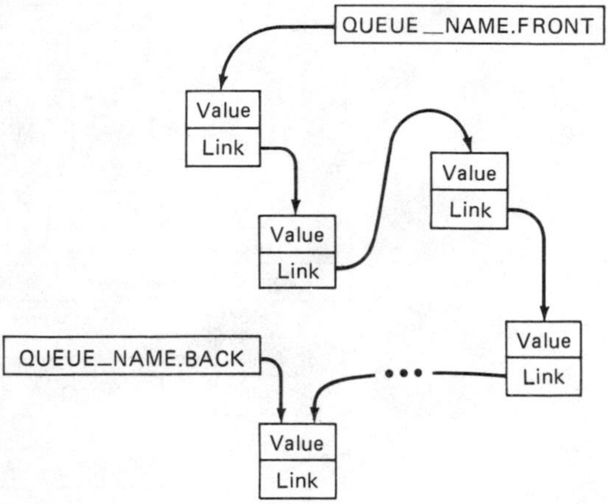

Figure 4.1. FIFO queue as a linked list.

shown in Figure 4.2. If a PUT is performed on an empty queue, both the FRONT and BACK components denote the newly created record.

The TAKE procedure returns the value of the VALUE component of the record object designated by the FRONT component, and then adjusts the linkages. The sequence is shown in Figure 4.3. If an attempt is made to TAKE from an empty queue, the exception UNDERFLOW is raised. This exception is handled by the exception handler in procedure TAKE and is then raised again and passed on to the point of call in accordance with the discussion of Section 3.10.5. When the last entry is taken from the queue, both components FRONT and BACK have the value **null,** which is in turn used to indicate an empty queue when function IS_EMPTY is called.

When the link between an access object and its designated object is severed, such as occurs when the access object is assigned a different value, the designated object does not go out of existence. Rather, the object simply can no longer be referenced. In a situation such as that implied by the implementation of package QUEUE_OF_CHAR above, new designated objects are created each time the PUT procedure is executed. But deallocation does not occur when the TAKE procedure is executed. Instead, the access values are reassigned so that designated objects in the front of the queue can no longer be referenced. After a number of PUT and TAKE operations, the memory allocated to objects that can no longer be accessed can become excessive. There are several ways around this problem. The most convenient solution is to use a

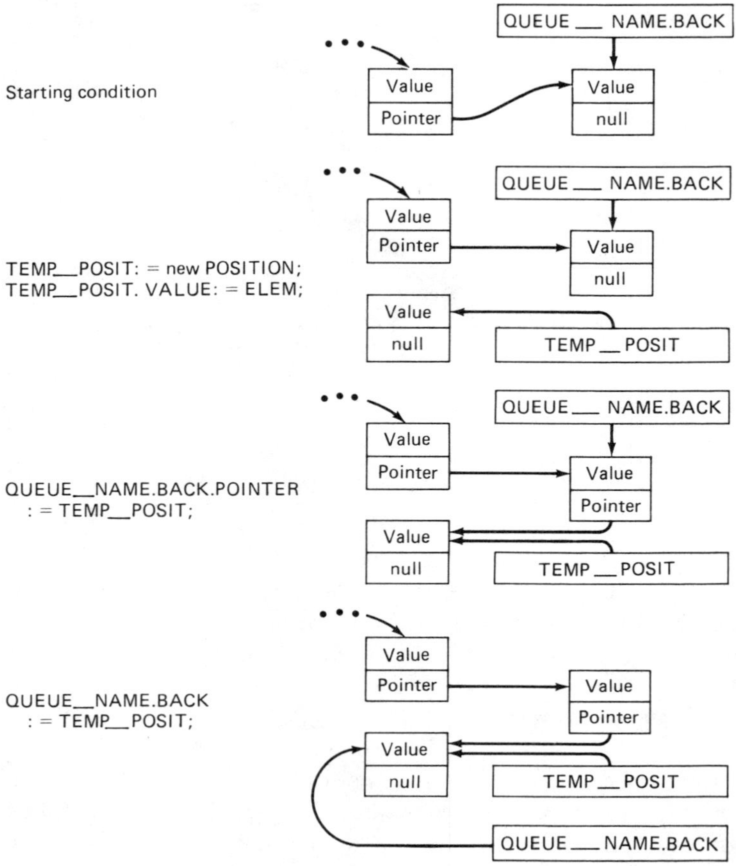

Figure 4.2. Sequence produced by procedure PUT.

compiler implementation that automatically deallocates any designated object that can no longer be accessed. Such a procedure is termed *garbage collection*. If garbage collection is not provided, the generic procedure UNCHECKED_DEALLOCATION can be used, in a manner to be discussed in Section 8.7.2.

EXAMPLE 2: Implementation by means of a linked list is not the only way in which a FIFO queue can be produced. As a matter of fact, the implementation can be completely changed without affecting the visible part of the package specification. For example, another way to implement a FIFO queue is by means of an array, with two associated integer objects used to indicate the front and back of the queue. This concept is shown in Figure 4.4 for an array with 4096 components. The specification

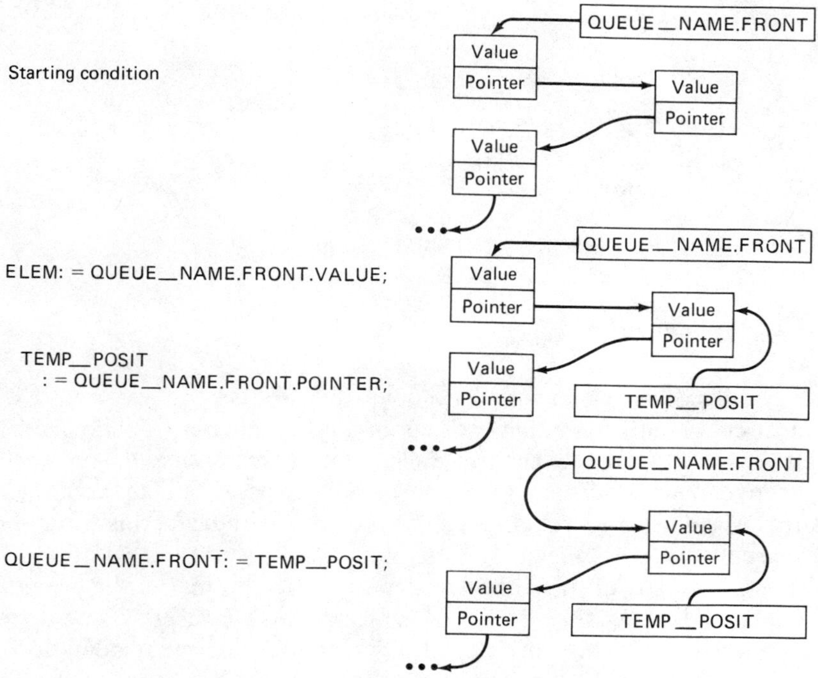

Figure 4.3. Sequence produced by procedure TAKE.

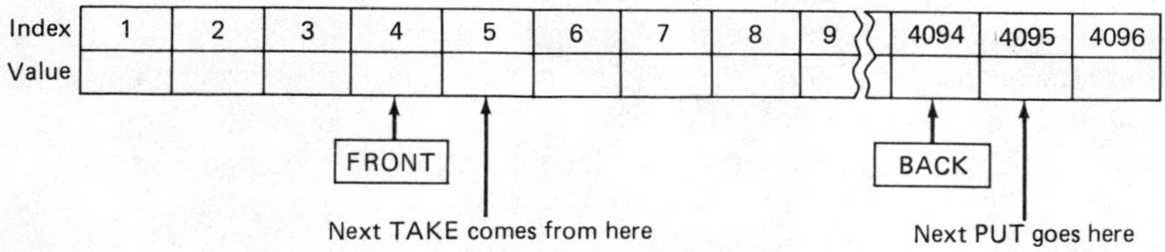

Figure 4.4. FIFO queue implemented as an array.

of the package QUEUE_OF_CHAR is now given as

```
package QUEUE_OF_CHAR is
    type QUEUE_TYPE is limited private;
    procedure RESET(QUEUE_NAME: in out QUEUE_TYPE);
    procedure PUT(ELEM: in CHARACTER;
                  QUEUE_NAME: in out QUEUE_TYPE);
    procedure TAKE(ELEM: out CHARACTER;
                   QUEUE_NAME: in out QUEUE_TYPE);
```

```
    function IS_EMPTY(QUEUE_NAME: in QUEUE_TYPE)
                              return BOOLEAN;
    UNDERFLOW : exception;
private
    type QUEUE_ARRAY is array(1..4096) of CHARACTER;
    type QUEUE_TYPE is
        record
            VALUE : QUEUE_ARRAY;
            FRONT : INTEGER range 1..4096;
            BACK  : INTEGER range 1..4096;
        end record;
end QUEUE_OF_CHAR;
```

The body of this package can be developed to use the array VALUE as a circular buffer, so that a fixed amount of memory is allocated to each object of type QUEUE_TYPE. This arrangement raises the possibility of an overflow condition, in which data is overwritten in the circular buffer. An additional exception can be provided to indicate this condition, if desired.

The visible part of this specification is identical to that of the previous example, indicating that the interface, and thus the user's view of the queue and its use, are unchanged, even though the implementation is completely different. Thus, the implementation can be changed from one form to the other without affecting the user's program. This fact frees the user from considering the details of how objects of type QUEUE_TYPE are actually manipulated, allowing him to concentrate only on the detail of the next higher level of abstraction. It also enhances the modifiability of the code, since subsequent modification of the implementation does not affect the user.

To illustrate this concept, consider the following package body:

```
package body QUEUE_OF_CHAR is
    procedure RESET(QUEUE_NAME : in out QUEUE_TYPE) is
    begin
        QUEUE_NAME.FRONT := 4096;
        QUEUE_NAME.BACK  := 4096;
    end RESET;

    procedure PUT(ELEM : in CHARACTER;
                  QUEUE_NAME : in out QUEUE_TYPE) is
        OVERFLOW : exception;
    begin
        if QUEUE_NAME.BACK = 4096 then
           QUEUE_NAME.BACK := 1;
```

```
        else
            QUEUE_NAME.BACK := QUEUE_NAME.BACK + 1;
        end if;
        if QUEUE_NAME.FRONT = QUEUE_NAME.BACK then
           raise OVERFLOW;
        else
           QUEUE_NAME.VALUE(QUEUE_NAME.BACK) := ELEM;
        end if;
        exception
            when OVERFLOW =>
                 QUEUE_NAME.BACK := QUEUE_NAME.BACK -1;
    end PUT;

    procedure TAKE(ELEM : out CHARACTER;
                   QUEUE_NAME : in out QUEUE_TYPE is
    begin
        if QUEUE_NAME.FRONT = QUEUE_NAME.BACK then
            raise UNDERFLOW;
        elsif QUEUE_NAME.FRONT = 4096 then
            QUEUE_NAME.FRONT := 1;
        else
            QUEUE_NAME.FRONT := QUEUE_NAME.FRONT +1;
        end if;
        ELEM := QUEUE_NAME.VALUE(QUEUE_NAME.FRONT);
        exception
            when UNDERFLOW =>
                 ELEM := '*';
                 raise;
    end TAKE;

    function IS_EMPTY(QUEUE_NAME : in QUEUE_TYPE)
             return BOOLEAN is
    begin
        return QUEUE_NAME.FRONT = QUEUE_NAME.BACK;
    end IS_EMPTY;
end QUEUE_OF_CHAR;
```

There is one critical difference between the behavior of this implementation using an array and that of the previous example, in which the queue was implemented by means of a linked list. Because elements of a linked list are created dynamically as they are needed at run time, there is no fixed limit to the number of characters that the queue may contain. On the other hand, in the current example the queue length is limited by the index range of the array—in this case, the limit is 4096. Thus, the possibility of overflow occurs; that is, an attempt may be made to PUT a character into a full queue. The exception OVERFLOW, declared in procedure PUT, is raised if such a situation exists. This exception is handled locally within procedure PUT by restoring the queue to the condition that existed when procedure PUT was called. That is, the character that was to be placed into the queue is lost. This result is in marked contrast to the handling of the exception UNDERFLOW, which is raised when an attempt is made to TAKE a character from an empty queue. Specifically, the following comments apply:

- Exception UNDERFLOW is declared within the visible part of the specification of package QUEUE_OF_CHAR. It is therefore visible to users of the package. The exception handler in procedure TAKE responds to this exception by returning the value '*' and reraising the exception, thus returning it to the calling environment. In this manner, the fact that an attempt has been made to TAKE a character from an empty queue is known by the calling environment. Note that this response is common to both the implementations of Example 1 and of Example 2.
- Exception OVERFLOW is local to procedure PUT. Therefore, it is not visible to users of the package. The exception is handled locally within procedure PUT, so that the calling environment is not notified that a problem exists with its attempt to PUT a character into the queue. Obviously, this situation would represent poor programming practice in most instances.

In actual practice, the amount of memory that can be allocated to objects designated by access objects is not completely unlimited. A program may actually limit the storage that can be allocated to objects designated by objects of a particular access type. Such limitation is effected by means of a length clause, which is discussed in Section 8.3.2.

4.2.3.1 Operations. The predefined operations associated with private types are given in Table 4.1. In addition to these operations, those

TABLE 4.1 Predefined Operations Associated with Private Types

OPERATION	SYMBOL	
explicit conversion		
membership	**in**	**not in**
qualification		
selection of discriminants		
If the type is not **limited private** then also		
assignment	:=	
relational	=	/=

subprograms declared in the visible part of the package specification in which the private type declaration appears, and which have a parameter or a result of the private type, can be applied to objects of the private type. These limitations, of course, apply outside the package. Within the package, any operation defined for the corresponding full type declaration can be used.

The no assignment limitation applied to limited private types has some subtle implications. Specifically:

- A declaration of an object of a limited private type cannot include an initial value.
- An allocator cannot contain an initial value if the designated object is a limited private type.
- A default expression is not permitted in the declaration of a record component if the component is of a limited private type.

Furthermore, these restrictions apply not only to limited private types themselves, but also to any composite types that have a component of a limited private type.

4.2.3.2 Attributes. The predefined attributes associated with private types are

- BASE
- CONSTRAINED
- SIZE

Objects of a private type have the attributes:

- ADDRESS
- SIZE

The reader is referred to Appendix B for details of these attributes.

4.2.3.3 Restrictions. When a private type is declared in the visible part of a package specification, there is a region within the specification between the private type declaration and the full type declaration in which certain restrictions apply. These restrictions apply to the private type itself, to any subtype of the private type, and to any composite type with a component of the private type. These types can be used only in the following contexts:

- a deferred-constant declaration
- a type or subtype declaration
- a subprogram specification

These restrictions imply that the following uses are not permitted:

- declarations of derived types of the private type
- use in a simple expression
- the declaration of an object of the private type, other than by a deferred-constant declaration
- the use of an allocator designating an object of the private type

The deferred-constant declaration represents the only object declaration permitted in this region of code; it is the subject of the following section.

4.2.4 Deferred-Constant Declarations

It is possible to declare constants of a private type in the visible part of the package specification containing the private type declaration. In this manner, the constant can be exported by the package. This kind of declaration is termed a deferred-constant declaration and is obtained by omitting the actual value of the constant in the visible part and then repeating the constant declaration in full in the private part, subsequent to the full type declaration of the private type. The syntax of a deferred-constant declaration is

```
deferred_constant_declaration ::=
    identifier_list : constant type_mark;        (4.4)
```

where the syntax for an identifier list and that for a type mark are given by Statements (3.10.1) and (3.8.2), respectively. The type mark must be a private type whose declaration appears in the visible part of the same package declaration as does the deferred-constant declaration.

If a deferred-constant declaration appears in the visible part of a package specification, then a corresponding constant declaration using the same identifier must be included as a declarative item in the private part of the package, subsequent to the full declaration of the private type specified by the type mark of Statement (4.4). In the region of the package specification between the deferred-constant declaration and the corresponding constant declaration in the private part, only two uses of a deferred constant are permitted: (1) as a default expression for a record component and (2) as a formal parameter. A deferred-constant declaration in the visible part of a package does make the constant visible to users of the package, although its structure is hidden.

A deferred-constant declaration may be used to eliminate the requirements for the procedure RESET in the FIFO queue implemented by package QUEUE_OF_CHAR in Section 4.2.3. The limited private type must be changed to a private type, in order to permit the use of the predefined assignment operation. The revised package specification is given below:

```
package QUEUE_OF_CHAR is
    type QUEUE_TYPE is private;
    RESET_VALUE : constant QUEUE_TYPE;
    procedure PUT(ELEM : in CHARACTER;
                  QUEUE_NAME: in out QUEUE_TYPE);
    procedure TAKE(ELEM : out CHARACTER;
                   QUEUE_NAME: in out QUEUE_TYPE);
    function IS_EMPTY(QUEUE_NAME : in QUEUE_TYPE)
                      return BOOLEAN;
    UNDERFLOW : exception;
private
    type POSITION;
    type LINK is access POSITION;
    type POSITION is
        record
            VALUE    : CHARACTER;
            POINTER  : LINK;
        end record;
    type QUEUE_TYPE is
        record
            FRONT : LINK;
            BACK  : LINK;
        end record;
    RESET_VALUE : constant QUEUE_TYPE := (null, null);
end QUEUE_OF_CHAR;
```

The body of the package is unchanged, except that the body of procedure RESET is no longer required. The constant RESET_VALUE is exported by the package and, since QUEUE_TYPE is now a private type—as opposed to a limited private type in the previous example—objects of type QUEUE_TYPE can be assigned the value of RESET_VALUE. Since both components of RESET_VALUE have the value **null,** this assignment resets the queue. Changing QUEUE_TYPE from a limited private type to a private type also makes possible the assignment of the value of one object of the type to another object of the type. The possibility of such assignments could be dangerous, since an entire queue could be irretrievably lost by accidental assignment.

4.3 VISIBILITY RULES AND COMPILATION ISSUES

The scope and visibility of entities declared within packages follow the same general rules of scope and visibility that were discussed in Section 3.11 when their application to subprograms was considered. Because a package specification can itself contain declarations of virtually any Ada entity, as implied by Statements (4.1.1) and (3.50.1), some additional comments are necessary here.

4.3.1 The Scope of a Declaration

As indicated in Section 3.11.1, the scope of a declaration, which is also the scope of the entity declared by the declaration, is the region of the program text in which the entity can be referenced by name—either by its simple name or by an expanded name. In general, the scope of a declaration extends from the point of the declaration to the end of the declarative region in which the declaration occurs. As discussed in Section 3.11.1, this region of program text is called the immediate scope of the declaration. In the case of a declaration that occurs in the visible part of a package specification, the scope of the declaration extends to the end of the declarative region containing the specification. This region of program text is called the *extended scope* of the declaration. For example, if a package specification is contained within the declarative part of a subprogram, the scope of a declaration appearing in the visible part of the package specification extends to the end of the subprogram, spanning both the immediate scope and the extended scope of the declaration. On the other hand, those declarations appearing within the private part of the specification—if there is a private part—and those declarations appearing in the declarative part of the package body are local to the package. That is, their scope is limited to the immediate scope of the declaration and therefore extends only to the end of the package.

EXAMPLE 1: To illustrate these concepts, consider the following skeletal form of procedure MAIN, in which package BIT_DIDDLE is declared:

```
procedure MAIN is
    type MATRIX is array(1..10,1..10) of BOOLEAN;
    .....
    package BIT_DIDDLE is
        type BIT_VECTOR is array(1..10) of BOOLEAN;
        procedure SWAP_ROWS(ROW_A, ROW_B :
                                   in out BIT_VECTOR);
        procedure SWAP_COLS(COL_A, COL_B :
                                   in out BIT_VECTOR);
```

```
    end BIT_DIDDLE;
    package body BIT_DIDDLE is
        TEMP_BIT : BIT_VECTOR;
        procedure SWAP_ROWS(ROW_A, ROW_B : in out
                                BIT_VECTOR) is
        begin
            ..... sequence of statements
        end SWAP_ROWS;
        procedure SWAP_COLS(COL_A, COL_B : in out
                                BIT_VECTOR) is
        begin
            ..... sequence of statements
        end SWAP_COLS;
    end BIT_DIDDLE;
begin
    ..... sequence of statements
end MAIN;
```

Some comments on scope in this example are presented below:

- The scope of type MATRIX extends to the end of MAIN. Type MATRIX is therefore global to package BIT_DIDDLE and to subprograms declared within BIT_DIDDLE. Unless the declaration is hidden by the declaration of a local data type within one of the subprograms, it is directly visible everywhere within procedure MAIN. Type MATRIX has only an immediate scope.
- The scope of package BIT_DIDDLE extends from its point of declaration to the end of procedure MAIN. Package BIT_DIDDLE has only an immediate scope.
- Type BIT_VECTOR and procedures SWAP_ROWS and SWAP_COLS are declared in the visible part of the specification of package BIT_DIDDLE, and therefore their scope extends from the point of declaration to the end of procedure MAIN. This result follows from the fact that package BIT_DIDDLE is declared within the declarative part of procedure MAIN, and therefore these declarations have both an immediate scope and an extended scope.
- Object TEMP_BIT is declared within the declarative part of package BIT_DIDDLE. Its scope extends only to the end of package BIT_DIDDLE. Thus, while TEMP_BIT can be referenced within the bodies of procedures SWAP_ROWS and SWAP_COLS, it cannot be referenced in the sequence of statements of procedure MAIN. The object TEMP_BIT has only an immediate scope.

Note that package BIT_DIDDLE is local to procedure MAIN; it cannot be referenced outside of MAIN, either by its simple name or by an expanded name, because it has only an immediate scope.

EXAMPLE 2: If package BIT_DIDDLE were declared within the visible part of the specification of another package, then its scope would extend to the end of the declarative region of the enclosing package, since it would then have an extended scope. For example, if the specification of package MATRIX_OPS is

```
package MATRIX_OPS is
    .....
    package BIT_DIDDLE is
        type BIT_VECTOR is array(1..10) of BOOLEAN;
        procedure SWAP_ROWS(ROW_A, ROW_B :
                                    in out BIT_VECTOR);
        procedure SWAP_COLS(COL_A, COL_B :
                                    in out BIT_VECTOR);
    end BIT_DIDDLE;
          .....
end MATRIX_OPS;
```

then the scope of package BIT_DIDDLE extends to the end of the declarative region containing package MATRIX_OPS. So also do the scopes of procedures SWAP_ROWS and SWAP_COLS, and that of type BIT_VECTOR.

4.3.2 The Visibility of Declarations

A declaration—or equivalently, the entity declared by a declaration—is said to be *visible* at a point in the program text if it can be referenced by a name there. An entity obviously cannot be visible if it is not in scope, since the entity simply does not exist if it is not in scope. But within the scope of an entity, there may be regions of program text where the entity is not visible. As discussed in Section 3.11.2, a visible entity is either *directly visible,* in which case it can be referenced by its simple name, or *visible by selection,* in which case an expanded name must be used. The declaration of a package, in particular, leads to situations in which visibility by selection exists for those declarations appearing in the visible part of a package specification. Specifically, these declarations have direct visibility within their immediate scope—except, of course, where they are hidden by other declarations—but have visibility by selection within their extended scope. This result implies that expanded names must be used when referencing an entity within its extended scope.

For instance, in relation to the procedure MAIN of Example 1 of the previous section, the following comments on visibility are offered:

- Type MATRIX has only an immediate scope and is therefore directly visible within its scope.
- Package BIT_DIDDLE has only an immediate scope and is therefore directly visible within its scope.
- Type BIT_VECTOR and procedures SWAP_ROWS and SWAP_COLS have both an immediate scope and an extended scope. Within their immediate scope, which extends from the point of declaration to the end of package BIT_DIDDLE, they can be referenced by their simple name. In their extended scope, which extends from the end of package BIT_DIDDLE to the end of procedure MAIN, they must be referenced by the expanded names

```
BIT_DIDDLE.BIT_VECTOR
BIT_DIDDLE.SWAP_ROWS
BIT_DIDDLE.SWAP_COLS
```

- Object TEMP_BIT is declared in the declarative part of package BIT_DIDDLE and therefore has only an immediate scope. Within this immediate scope it can be referenced by its simple name. Attempts to reference this object from outside package BIT_DIDDLE will result in an unresolved reference, even if the expanded name

```
BIT_DIDDLE.TEMP_BIT
```

  is used.

On the other hand, if package BIT_DIDDLE is declared in the specification of package MATRIX_OPS, as in Example 2 of the previous section, then the immediate scope of package BIT_DIDDLE extends from its point of declaration to the end of package MATRIX_OPS—that is, to the end of the body of package MATRIX_OPS. In this region, it may be referenced by the simple name BIT_DIDDLE. But package BIT_DIDDLE now also has an extended scope extending from the end of package MATRIX_OPS to the end of the declarative region that encloses the declaration of package MATRIX_OPS. In this region, it must be referenced by the expanded name

```
MATRIX_OPS.BIT_DIDDLE.
```

Furthermore, within the immediate scope of package BIT_DIDDLE procedure SWAP_ROWS, for example, must be referenced by the expanded name

```
BIT_DIDDLE.SWAP_ROWS
```

and in the extended scope of package BIT_DIDDLE it must be referenced by the expanded name

```
MATRIX_OPS.BIT_DIDDLE.SWAP_ROWS
```

Any of these declarations, either as simple names or as expanded names, could be hidden by local declarations of the same name. In such a situation, the next level prefix can be added to form an expanded version of the name, making the declaration again visible.

4.3.3 Compilation Issues

As indicated by Statements (3.59) through (3.59.4), package specifications and package bodies are *compilation units*. That is, they can be compiled separately into library units and secondary units, respectively, as implied by the discussion of Section 3.11.3. Since the specification and body of a package are both compilation units, they can be compiled separately—meaning that they can be compiled at different times—so long as the specification is compiled before the body is compiled. In fact, unless the specification and body are enclosed within another compilation unit, their compilations are treated as separate compilations even though they both may be contained in the same submission.

Once compiled, the package specification becomes a library unit, and the package body becomes the associated secondary unit. These units belong to the program library and can be accessed by other program units.

4.3.3.1 The Context Clause. The context clause was introduced in Section 3.11.3.1, in which the syntax for a context clause is given by Statements (3.60), (3.60.1), and (3.60.2). These statements are repeated here for convenience:

```
context_clause ::= {with_clause {use_clause}}
                                                    (3.60)

with_clause ::= with unit_simple_name {,unit_simple_name};
                                                    (3.60.1)

use_clause ::= use package_name {,package_name};
                                                    (3.60.2)
```

The use of a context clause in a compilation unit is specified by Statement (3.54.1).

The effect of a with clause that names a package is the same as that obtained by naming a subprogram. That is, the package name is made directly visible to the unit being compiled. Therefore, the package can be referenced within the compilation unit by its simple name. In the case of subprograms, direct visibility makes the subprogram callable by its simple name from within the compilation unit. In the case of packages, however, the effect is wider reaching, because those declarations appearing in the visible part of the package specification are also visible—but they are visible by selection rather than directly visible—within the compilation unit. Furthermore, these declarations can also be made directly visible by use of the use clause, as specified by Statement (3.60.2). The reader should note that a use clause can only be used with package names, since it would have no meaning if applied to a library unit that is a subprogram. Furthermore, the use clause can only name packages that have been named by previous with clauses within the context clause.

As a final note, it should be mentioned that use clauses can appear at places in the program text other than within context clauses, and that each use clause has a scope similar to the scope of declarations. Specifically, a use clause may appear either in a context clause or within the declarative part of a block statement, subprogram, package, task, or generic unit. If the use clause appears in a context clause, then its scope extends to the end of the compilation unit to which the context clause applies. If the use clause appears in a declarative part, its scope extends to the end of the declarative region containing the declarative part. That is, the scope of the use clause extends to the end of the block statement, subprogram, package, task, or generic unit in which it appears.

Examples are again provided by the sample packages of Section 4.3.1. If package BIT_DIDDLE of Example 1 were to be separately compiled, it would represent two compilations. First, the specification would be compiled by the submission:

```
package BIT_DIDDLE is
    type BIT_VECTOR is array(1..10) of BOOLEAN;
    procedure SWAP_ROWS(ROW_A, ROW_B : in out BIT_VECTOR);
    procedure SWAP_COLS(COL_A, COL_B : in out BIT_VECTOR);
end BIT_DIDDLE;
```

This specification would be compiled into a *library unit*, as discussed in Section 3.11.3. The package body could then be compiled by the submission

```
package body BIT_DIDDLE is
    TEMP_BIT : BIT_VECTOR;
    procedure SWAP_ROWS(ROW_A, ROW_B : in out
                                  BIT_VECTOR) is
```

```
        begin
            ..... sequence of statements
        end SWAP_ROWS;

        procedure SWAP_COLS(COL_A, COL_B : in out
                                 BIT_VECTOR) is
        begin
            ..... sequence of statements
        end SWAP_COLS;
    end BIT_DIDDLE;
```

This body would be compiled into a *secondary unit,* as discussed in Section 3.11.3. These compilations could be submitted together, but the specification must be compiled first.

With the library unit SWAP_BITS residing in the program library, and even before the body of package SWAP_BITS is compiled into the secondary unit, a compilation unit consisting of procedure MAIN can be compiled. The submission would be

```
with BIT_DIDDLE;
procedure MAIN is
    type MATRIX is array(1..10, 1..10) of BOOLEAN;
    .....
begin
    ..... sequence of statements
end MAIN;
```

Within the sequence of statements of procedure MAIN, the type BIT_VECTOR and the procedures SWAP_ROWS and SWAP_COLS are visible by selection. That is, they can be referenced by the expanded names

```
BIT_DIDDLE.BIT_VECTOR
BIT_DIDDLE.SWAP_ROWS
BIT_DIDDLE.SWAP_COLS
```

respectively. Furthermore, if the context clause also contains a use clause,

```
with BIT_DIDDLE; use BIT_DIDDLE;
```

then type BIT_VECTOR and procedures SWAP_ROWS and SWAP_COLS are directly visible within procedure MAIN and may be referenced by their simple names.

The use of context clauses naming predefined packages is quite common in Ada programs, because these packages provide service facilities such as input-output procedures and timing features. Since many of the predefined packages are actually generic units, detailed discussion will be deferred until generic units are considered.

4.3.3.2 Subunits. The syntax for a *body stub* and the corresponding *subunit* given in Statements (3.61) and (3.62) imply that this feature of the Ada language is applicable to packages as well as to subprograms and tasks. The syntax for a body stub applied to a package is

```
body_stub ::=
    package body package_simple_name is separate;
                                                  (4.5)
```

while that for a subunit is repeated here for convenience:

```
subunit ::=
    separate (parent_unit_name) proper body.   (3.62)
```

The use of a body stub and the associated subunit is equivalent in every way to a package body declaration, as is discussed in Section 3.11.3.2. The body of a package declaration that appears in the declarative part of a subprogram, of another package, or of a task, can be replaced by a body stub as implied by Statement (4.5). When this replacement occurs, a separately compiled subunit, formed in accordance with Statement (3.62), is required as a secondary unit in the program library. The subunit must mention the name of the parent unit—the compilation unit in which the corresponding body stub appears.

The visibility of various declarations from within the subunit is identical to the visibility that would be obtained if the proper body were to replace the body stub, and if the context clause of the subunit—if any—were appended to that of the parent unit.

An example of the use of a subunit can be obtained by again examining procedure MAIN and the enclosed package BIT_DIDDLE of Section 4.3.1. In Section 4.3.3.1, package BIT_DIDDLE was made a library unit and was separately compiled. It was then made visible to procedure MAIN by use of a context clause. Here, package BIT_DIDDLE will be separately compiled, but now as a subunit. Procedure MAIN is modified as follows:

```
procedure MAIN is
      type MATRIX is array(1..10, 1..10) of BOOLEAN;
      .....
      package BIT_DIDDLE is
          type BIT_VECTOR is array(1..10) of BOOLEAN;
```

```
            procedure SWAP_ROWS(ROW_A, ROW_B : in out
                                BIT_VECTOR);
            procedure SWAP_COLS(COL_A, COL_B : in out
                                BIT_VECTOR);
        end BIT_DIDDLE;
        package body BIT_DIDDLE is separate;
begin
    ..... sequence of statements
end MAIN;
```

This procedure can be submitted as a compilation unit, with no context clause. When it is compiled and exists in the program library as a library unit, then the subunit can be compiled. The form of the subunit is

```
separate (MAIN)
    package body BIT_DIDDLE is
        TEMP_BIT : BIT_VECTOR;
        procedure SWAP_ROWS(ROW_A, ROW_B : in out
                            BIT_VECTOR) is
        begin
            ..... sequence of statements
        end SWAP_ROWS;

        procedure SWAP_COLS(ROW_A, ROW_B : in out
                            BIT_VECTOR) is
        begin
            ..... sequence of statements
        end SWAP_COLS;
    end BIT_DIDDLE;
```

This subunit will compile into a secondary unit in the program library. The visibility of declarations within the subunit is the same as that which would prevail if the proper body were actually compiled within the parent unit at the location occupied by the body stub. For example, type MATRIX is visible within the subunit. If procedure MAIN were compiled with a context clause, then that context clause would also apply to the subunit. Additionally, the subunit itself could have a context clause.

4.3.4 Order of Compilation

As was the case with subprograms, the rules regarding the order of compilation and recompilation of packages are dictated by the visibility rules of the Ada language. Since packages are the more likely means of providing modularity in an Ada program, many of the library units associated with an Ada program are likely to be packages. Most of the predefined library units are packages.

For any package mentioned in the context clause of a compilation unit, the package specification must be previously compiled and must exist in the program library as a library unit. Similarly, before a package body can be compiled, the corresponding package specification must have been previously compiled and must exist in the program library as a library unit.

The rules above imply that the recompilation of a package specification will require subsequent recompilation of the body, although the reverse is not true. It also follows that package bodies implemented as subunits can be recompiled without requiring recompilation of the parent unit, so long as the package specification remains intact.

4.3.5 The Role of Package STANDARD

The predefined package STANDARD has been discussed previously in terms of the predefined data types and in terms of the operations applicable to these predefined types. There is a more fundamental conceptual role played by package STANDARD with respect to the visibility of library units. There may have been some concern on the part of the reader for the validity of visibility rules when library units were made visible to compilation units by the simple inclusion of a context clause. After all, entities can only be visible within their scope, and there has been no indication that the scope of a library unit extends beyond the library unit itself. The explanation lies in the fact that package STANDARD, in addition to providing for the declaration of predefined data types, also forms a conceptual declarative region that encloses the declaration of every library unit. Furthermore, these declarations are assumed to be ordered in such a manner that the scopes of these library units are precisely those implied by the with clauses of any given compilation unit. While this argument may seem specious, serving only to justify the visibility rules implied by use of the with clause, it amounts to more than just that. For example, library units can be referenced by expanded names starting with STANDARD, implying that program units conceptually reside within the predefined package STANDARD.

4.4 THE USE OF PACKAGES

In general, the package capability of the Ada language is used in one of three ways:

1. To encapsulate the declarations of closely related data types, data objects and constants. The package containing such declarations contains no subprograms or other program units, so there need not be a package body. However, a package body can be used to initialize the values of data objects through the exectuion of the optional sequence of statements contained within the body. See Statement (4.2) and Section 4.2.2 for details. Package ASCII, contained within package STANDARD, is an example—it contains only constant declarations.
2. To encapsulate related subprograms, and perhaps other related program units, in order to provide some sort of common service. An example is package TRIG_FUNCTIONS of Section 4.2.1, in which six commonly used trigonometric functions are encapsulated by the package. When the function specifications are included within the package specification, the functions are made available to users of the package. Normally, this kind of package must also export certain data types as well, as is the case with the types DEGREES and VALUE in the example cited.
3. To create abstract data types by coupling the package concept with that of a private data type. The private type and all applicable operations associated with the type are declared within the package specification—and are therefore visible to the user of the package—but the details of structure, representation, and implementation are hidden. The example package QUEUE_OF_CHAR in Section 4.2.3 is an example.

Each of these uses is important in the application of software engineering principles for the purpose of enhancing the reliability, modifiability, and understandability of software. They aid in the reduction of complexity of large software systems, and—as with the generic units to be discussed in Chapter 5—hold promise for the development of an industry of reusable software.

The remainder of this section is devoted to the presentation of examples of the three general uses of packages.

4.4.1 Encapsulation of Declarations

It is not uncommon in large-scale system development to have many different subprograms use a common set of constant values, a common set of data structures, a common set of variables, or some combination thereof. To ensure compatibility among the various subprograms—and, in the case of Ada software, among subprograms, packages, and tasks—

the declarations of commonly used entities can be encapsulated within a package. The package can then be compiled and the resulting library unit accessed by the other program units. In this manner, one can be assured that each program unit is using the same set of declarations—something that cannot be assured if each program unit provides its own declarations. Some examples of this particular use of Ada's package concept are given below, together with the context in which they might occur.

EXAMPLE 1: A program may require conversion of values from one system of units to another. A package specification that contains the conversion constants can be written and compiled. Two examples are shown below.

```
package VOLUME_CONSTANTS is
    CU_FT_TO_CU_METER       : constant := 0.028_3177;
    CU_YD_TO_CU_METER       : constant := 0.764_559;
    CU_IN_TO_CU_METER       : constant := 1.638_716E-5;
    BUSHEL_TO_CU_METER      : constant := 0.035_239;
    BARREL_TO_CU_METER      : constant := 0.119_240;
    GAL_TO_CU_METER         : constant := 0.003_7854;
end VOLUME_CONSTANTS;

package LENGTH_CONSTANTS is
    IN_TO_METER             : constant := 0.025_400_05;
    FT_TO_METER             : constant := 0.304_800_6;
    YD_TO_METER             : constant := 0.914_401_83;
    FATHOM_TO_METER         : constant := 1.828_804;
    MILE_TO_METER           : constant := 1_609.35;
    NAUT_MILE_TO_METER      : constant := 1_853.25;
end LENGTH_CONSTANTS;
```

These packages have no body; the specification may be compiled as shown. Once compiled, they become library units that export the constants indicated.

EXAMPLE 2: In many instances, programs may require physical constants for use in certain computations. These constants may be subject to revision as better data becomes available. Declaring these constants within a package, and then having program units using the constants import them from the package, ensures that the same values are being used by all program units. A simple example is given below:

```
package EARTH_CONSTANTS is
    EARTH_RADIUS_EQUAT      : constant := 6_378_388.0;
    EARTH_RADIUS_POLAR      : constant := 6_356_912.0;
```

```
    EARTH_RADIUS_EQUIV      : constant := 6_371_221.0;
    MEAN_DENSITY            : constant := 5.552;
    MASS                    : constant := 5.983E24;
    MEAN_LIN_VELOCITY       : constant := 465.0;
    GRAV_CONSTANT           : constant := 978.039;
end EARTH_CONSTANTS;
```

If better data becomes available, then modification of this package and subsequent recompilation will ensure distribution of the changes to all user program units. In accordance with the recompilation rules discussed in Section 3.11.4, all units using the package must also be recompiled.

EXAMPLE 3: When several different program units use data of a certain kind, good programming practice normally requires that a common data structure be used. The declaration of the data structure can be encapsulated within a package specification, compiled to produce a library unit, and then imported by the appropriate program units. While the examples above contain only constant declarations, the current example contains only type declarations. The example is provided below.

```
package TARGET_DATA_STRUCTURE is
    MAX_TARGETS : constant := 100;
    type SHIP_NAME is STRING(1..20);
    type FEET is digits 6;
    type YARDS is digits 6;
    type N_MILES is digits 6;
    type DEGREES is digits 6;
    type CLASS_TYPE is (FRIENDLY, ENEMY, UNKNOWN);
    type THREAT_TYPE is (HIGH, MODERATE, MID, LOW, NONE);
    type SHIP_DATA is
        record
            NAME    : SHIP_NAME;
            BEARING : DEGREES;
            RANGE   : YARDS;
        end record;
    type TARGET_DATA is
        record
            BEARING         : DEGREES;
            DISTANCE        : YARDS;
            ALTITUDE        : FEET;
            CLASSIFICATION  : CLASS_TYPE;
            THREAT          : THREAT_TYPE;
            COMMENT         : STRING(1..50);
        end record;
    type TARGET_ARRAY is array(1..MAX_TARGETS)
                                of TARGET_DATA;
```

```
    type SHIP_TARG_REC is
        record
            SHIP_INFO    : SHIP_DATA;
            SHIP_TARG    : TARGET_ARRAY;
        end record;
end TARGET_DATA_STRUCTURE;
```

This package specification need not have a corresponding body, since it does not contain the declaration of other program units. The specification may be compiled to produce a library unit that exports the data types as indicated. The principal data structure provided by the package is the data type SHIP_TARG_REC, which is a record with two components. One component is another record, SHIP_INFO, while the other is an array of records.

EXAMPLE 4: The data structure provided by the package of the previous example provides the form in which information is to be stored in a data base of some kind. The data base itself can be maintained within a package that exports an object that contains the information stored in the data base. For example, consider the package specification:

```
with TARGET_DATA_STRUCTURE;
use TARGET_DATA_STRUCTURE;
package TACTICAL_DATA_PACKAGE is
    MAX_SHIPS : constant := 50;
    type SHIP_INDEX is range 1..MAX_SHIPS;
    type DATA_ARRAY is array(SHIP_INDEX) of SHIP_TARG_REC;
    ACTIVE_SHIPS  : SHIP_INDEX;
    TACTICAL_DATA : DATA_ARRAY;
end TACTICAL_DATA_PACKAGE;
```

This package exports data types as well as the data objects ACTIVE_SHIPS and TACTICAL_DATA. The data object TACTICAL_DATA is the data base itself—it is an array, each of whose components is another array of type SHIP_TARG_REC. While this package need not have a corresponding body, because no other program units are declared, it may have a body consisting of a declarative part and a sequence of statements, as indicated by Statement (4.2). The declarative part is elaborated and the sequence of statements is executed when the package body itself is elaborated. Thus, the sequence of statements can be used to initialize the data base when the package body is elaborated. The package body, in skeletal form, might be

```
with SEQUENTIAL_IO;
package body TACTICAL_DATA_PACKAGE is
```

```
     .....
     declarations and statements to load data base from a
     sequential storage device.
     .....
end TACTICAL_DATA_PACKAGE;
```

Although this example illustrates some of the features of the Ada language, it may not be indicative of the best approach to problems of this sort. Certainly features such as unconstrained arrays, discriminated and variant records, and access types—because of their dynamic character—should be considered for use in situations such as this.

4.4.2 Encapsulation of Program Units

Certain procedures, functions, and perhaps even tasks, often have a relationship that binds them together in a logical fashion, even though they may not be dependent upon one another. An obvious example is provided by Example 1 of Section 4.2.1, in which trigonometric functions are grouped together to form a package. In fact, packages of this sort are among the first to be developed or acquired by new Ada users, because they are required by many embedded-system program development projects. The package structure provides an excellent vehicle for the provision of program units such as these. Further examples of this use of Ada's package concept are given below.

EXAMPLE 1: Matrix operations are often required in embedded-system programs. Operations such as matrix addition, subtraction, and multiplication, together with matrix inversion and solutions to the eigenvalue problem, may be needed. A package implementing these operations can be written and then compiled to produce a library unit that can be imported by any other program unit. For example, the three operations of matrix addition, subtraction, and multiplication might be packaged as follows:

```
package MATRIX_ARITH is
    type MATRIX is array(INTEGER range <>,
                         INTEGER range <>) of FLOAT;
    procedure MATRIX_ADD(LEFT,RIGHT : in MATRIX;
                         RESULT : out MATRIX);
    procedure MATRIX_SUB(LEFT,RIGHT : in MATRIX;
                         RESULT : out MATRIX);
    procedure MATRIX_MUL(LEFT,RIGHT : in MATRIX;
                         RESULT : out MATRIX);
    MATRIX_ERROR : exception;
end MATRIX_ARITH:
```

This package exports the single data type MATRIX, a two-dimensional unconstrained array type, and the three operations MATRIX_ADD, MATRIX_SUB, and MATRIX_MULT. It also exports the exception MATRIX_ERROR, which is intended to be raised in the calling environment if the matrix dimensions are not proper. The package body must contain, within its declarative region, either the proper bodies of these three procedures or body stubs indicating their separate compilation as subunits, in accordance with the discussion of Section 3.11.3.2. The proper body might be implemented as follows:

```
package body MATRIX_ARITH is
    procedure MATRIX_ADD(LEFT, RIGHT : in MATRIX;
                         RESULT : out MATRIX) is
    begin
        if LEFT'RANGE(1) /= RIGHT'RANGE(1) or
           LEFT'RANGE(1) /= RESULT'RANGE(1) or
           LEFT'RANGE(1) /= RIGHT'RANGE(2) or
           LEFT'RANGE(1) /= RESULT'RANGE(2) then
           raise MATRIX_ERROR;
        end if;
        for ROW in LEFT'RANGE(1) loop
            for COL in LEFT'RANGE(2) loop
                RESULT(ROW,COL) := LEFT(ROW, COL)
                                   + RIGHT(ROW, COL);
            end loop;
        end loop;
    end MATRIX_ADD;

    procedure MATRIX_SUB(LEFT, RIGHT : in MATRIX;
                         RESULT : out MATRIX) is
    begin
        if LEFT'RANGE(1) /= RIGHT'RANGE(1) or
           LEFT'RANGE(1) /= RESULT'RANGE(1) or
           LEFT'RANGE(2) /= RIGHT'RANGE(2) or
           LEFT'RANGE(2) /= RESULT'RANGE(2) then
           raise MATRIX_ERROR;
        end if;
        for ROW in LEFT'RANGE(1) loop
            for COL in LEFT'RANGE(2) loop
                RESULT(ROW, COL) := LEFT(ROW, COL)
                                    - RIGHT(ROW, COL);
            end loop;
        end loop;
    end MATRIX_SUB;

    procedure MATRIX_MUL(LEFT, RIGHT : in MATRIX;
                         RESULT : out MATRIX) is
```

```
    begin
        if LEFT'RANGE(1) /= RESULT'RANGE(1) or
           LEFT'RANGE(2) /= RIGHT'RANGE(1) or
           RIGHT'RANGE(2) /= RESULT'RANGE(2) then
           raise MATRIX_ERROR;
        end if;
        for ROW in LEFT'RANGE(1) loop
            for COL in RIGHT'RANGE(2) loop
                  RESULT(ROW, COLUMN) := 0.0;
                  for INDEX in LEFT'RANGE(2) loop
                      RESULT(ROW, COL) := RESULT(ROW, COL)
                      + LEFT(ROW, INDEX)
                      * RIGHT(INDEX, COL);
                  end loop;
            end loop;
        end loop;
    end MATRIX_MUL;
end MATRIX_ARITH;
```

Each of the three subprograms makes a check of the matrix index values and raises the exception MATRIX_ERROR if they do not match. Since no exception handler is provided within the procedures, the exception, when raised, will be propagated to the calling environment. The index range check is necessary because type MATRIX is an unconstrained array type, and therefore objects of this type can have any range of indices. This fact permits the three procedures to be applicable to any three arrays—the actual parameters associated with the three formal parameters LEFT, RIGHT, and RESULT—so long as the index ranges match properly. The range attributes provide this capability very nicely.

EXAMPLE 2: Complex numbers are used in certain kinds of analysis and in signal processing. A package that provides the structure and the operations associated with complex numbers is given below.

```
package COMPLEX is
    type NUMBER is
        record
            REAL : FLOAT  := 0.0;
            IMAG : FLOAT  := 0.0;
        end record;
    I  : constant NUMBER := (0.0,1.0);
    function ADD_COMPLEX(LEFT, RIGHT : NUMBER)
                        return NUMBER;
    function SUB_COMPLEX(LEFT, RIGHT : NUMBER)
                        return NUMBER;
```

```
        function MUL_COMPLEX(LEFT, RIGHT : NUMBER)
                                return NUMBER;
        function DIV_COMPLEX(LEFT, RIGHT : NUMBER)
                                return NUMBER;
    end COMPLEX;
```

This is the package specification, and it implies that complex numbers are implemented as a two-component record and that the data type COMPLEX.NUMBER is exported by the package. The operations of add, subtract, multiply, and divide are exported in the form of the appropriate function. The constant complex number I is also exported. The add, subtract, multiply, and divide operations have very definite meanings as applied to complex numbers; these operations are implemented in the package body shown below:

```
package body COMPLEX is
    function ADD_COMPLEX(LEFT, RIGHT : NUMBER)
                        return number is
    begin
        return (LEFT.REAL + RIGHT.REAL,
                LEFT.IMAG + RIGHT.IMAG);
    end ADD_COMPLEX;

    function SUB_COMPLEX(LEFT, RIGHT : NUMBER)
                        return NUMBER is
    begin
        return (LEFT.REAL - RIGHT.REAL,
                LEFT.IMAG - RIGHT.IMAG);
    end SUB_COMPLEX;
    function MUL_COMPLEX(LEFT, RIGHT : NUMBER)
                        return NUMBER is
    begin
        return (LEFT.REAL * RIGHT.REAL - LEFT.IMAGE
                * RIGHT.IMAG,
                LEFT.REAL * RIGHT.IMAG + LEFT.IMAG
                * RIGHT.REAL);
    end MUL_COMPLEX;

    function DIV_COMPLEX(LEFT, RIGHT : NUMBER)
                        return NUMBER is
    SUM_OF_SQ : FLOAT;
    begin
        SUM_OF_SQ := RIGHT.REAL ** 2 + RIGHT.IMAG ** 2;
        return ((LEFT.REAL * RIGHT.REAL + LEFT.IMAG
                 * RIGHT.IMAG)/SUM_OF_SQ,(LEFT.IMAG
```

```
                  * RIGHT.REAL - LEFT.REAL * RIGHT.IMAG)/
                  SUM_OF_SQ);
    end DIV_COMPLEX;
end COMPLEX;
```

This example makes use of record aggregates in all the return statements. The syntax for a record aggregate is given by Statement (3.2.4). Record aggregates are discussed in Section 3.6.2.3.

The user of this package would include in his program unit declaration the context clause

```
with COMPLEX;
```

in which case he can then declare objects such as

```
EL_GAIN   : COMPLEX.NUMBER;
FREQ_COMP : COMPLEX.NUMBER;
```

for which the components

```
EL_GAIN.REAL
EL_GAIN.IMAG
```

are scalar objects of type FLOAT.

It will be shown in Chapter 8 that the operator symbols "+", "−", "*", and "/", among others, can be overloaded. That is, the symbol can be given more than one meaning. In this case, the symbols can denote more than one subprogram, with the compiler distinguishing among several possible meanings by examination of the parameter list. Thus, it would be possible to replace the function specifications contained within the specification of package COMPLEX with

```
function "+" (LEFT, RIGHT : NUMBER) return NUMBER;
function "-" (LEFT, RIGHT : NUMBER) return NUMBER;
function "*" (LEFT, RIGHT : NUMBER) return NUMBER;
function "/" (LEFT, RIGHT : NUMBER) return NUMBER;
```

Similar changes must, of course, be made within the body of package COMPLEX. Function calls can then be made in the normal manner, such as

```
"*" (EL_GAIN, FREQ_COMP)
```

or, using named association,

```
"*" (LEFT => EL_GAIN, RIGHT => FREQ_COMP)
```

However, as outlined in Section 8.2.1.1, when overloaded operator symbols are used as function names the infix notation can also be used. Thus, the same function call can be effected by the expression

```
EL_GAIN * FREQ_COMP
```

so long as the overloading of the operator symbol "*" can be resolved by the compiler through examination of the parameter list and the result type.

This same concept could be applied to the matrix arithmetic package of Example 1 by implementing the operations as functions rather than procedures. Or, alternatively, each of the procedures may be encapsulated within a function; for example:

```
function "*" (LEFT, RIGHT : MATRIX) return MATRIX is
     PRODUCT : MATRIX (LEFT'RANGE(1)..RIGHT'RANGE(2));
begin
     MATRIX_MUL(LEFT, RIGHT, PRODUCT);
     return PRODUCT;
end "*";
```

Two matrix objects declared as

```
MEAS_MATRIX : MATRIX(1..6,1..3);
COV_MATRIX  : MATRIX(1..6,1..6);
```

can be multiplied by use of the function call

```
"*"(COV_MATRIX, MEAS_MATRIX)
```

or by use of infix notation in the expression

```
COV_MATRIX * MEAS_MATRIX
```

so long as the overloading of the operator symbol "*" can be resolved by the compiler.

4.4.3 Abstract Data Types

One of the major causes of problems in embedded-system software—or in any other large programs, for that matter—is the sheer complexity of the algorithm implemented by the software. Many of the features of the Ada language permit, and even encourage, the use of *abstraction* as a technique for handling the complexity of large programs. Subprograms, for example, provide for abstraction of program control, so that the programmer need only consider the input-output relationship implied by the subprogram specification rather than being concerned with the implementation details. In Ada programs, data can also be abstracted by use of packages and private data types. In fact, making a type private has the immediate consequence of making it abstract, at least from the point of view of a user of the package. That is, the structural details of the type are hidden, and there are no literals that can be assigned to objects of the type. All that is visible to the user is the name of the type and the operations that are associated with the type. While this concept may seem overrestrictive, there is benefit to be obtained from the abstraction provided. That is, objects of an abstract data type are declared and manipulated in the same manner as any other objects. The user need not concern himself with the details of manipulating objects of the type, and he is thus more able to concentrate on the higher level of design. Abstract data types can be provided as abstractions of the real-world entities with which the program itself is concerned, helping further to manage the complexity of the software by making it more understandable.

An example is provided by the FIFO queue implemented by the example of Section 4.2.3, in which the private type QUEUE_TYPE clearly is an abstraction of an object in which data in the form of characters can be stored. While the structure of the type entails the use of access types and records, and while the implementation requires manipulation of a linked list, the user of objects of the type is spared concern over these implementation details. Instead, he simply declares an object of type QUEUE_TYPE and proceeds to use it by application of the visible operations of RESET, PUT, TAKE, and IS_EMPTY, as indicated by Figure 4.5. The use of the abstraction is identical to the use of a hardware buffer. The independence of the user from the implementation is illustrated by the second part of this example, in which the implementation is changed from a linked list to an array. Such a change is undetectable by the user of the package.

Further examples of abstract data types are given below.

EXAMPLE 1: The complex number package of Example 2 of the previous section exported the data type COMPLEX.NUMBER as a record with two components of type FLOAT. Users of the type have access to the actual structure and can manipulate the components individually as objects of type FLOAT. While this situation represents a certain flexibility that may be advantageous, it also permits violation of the integrity of the type in that operations other than ADD_COMPLEX, SUB_COMPLEX, MUL_COMPLEX, and DIV_COMPLEX can be applied to objects of the type. That is, any record operation can be applied to an object of the type, and any FLOAT operation can be applied to the components of an object. If the integrity of the type is to be preserved, then NUMBER

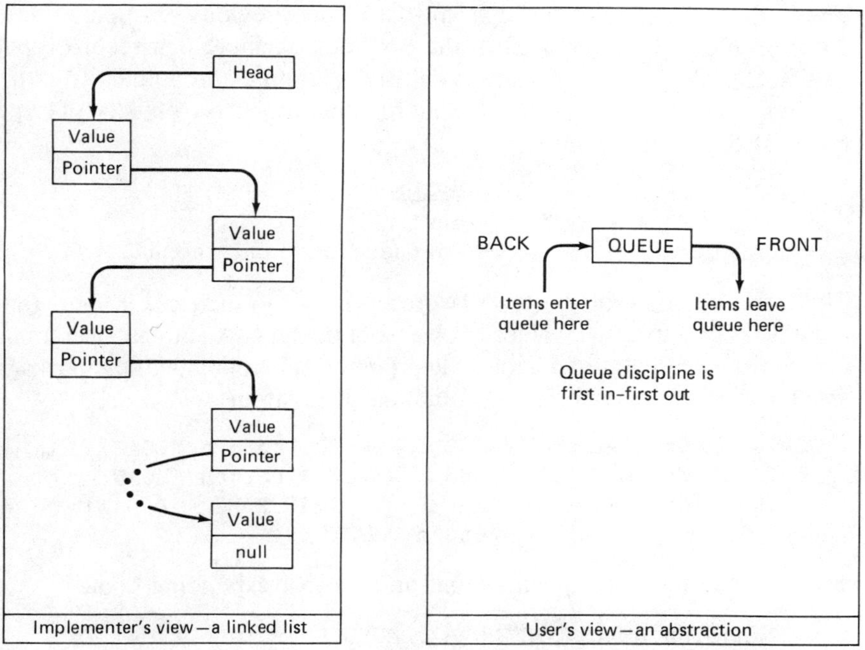

Figure 4.5. User's view vs. implementer's view of FIFO queue.

can be made into a private type, in which case the package specification is modified to the following:

```
package COMPLEX is
    type NUMBER is private;
    I : constant NUMBER;
    function ADD_COMPLEX(LEFT, RIGHT : NUMBER)
                         return NUMBER;
    function SUB_COMPLEX(LEFT, RIGHT : NUMBER)
                         return NUMBER;
    function MUL_COMPLEX(LEFT, RIGHT : NUMBER)
                         return NUMBER;
    function DIV_COMPLEX(LEFT, RIGHT : NUMBER)
                         return NUMBER;
private
    type NUMBER is
        record
            REAL : FLOAT := 0.0;
            IMAG : FLOAT := 0.0;
        end record;
        I : constant NUMBER := (0.0,1.0);
end COMPLEX;
```

The body remains unchanged from that in the previous example. While the type NUMBER declared in the previous example is a record type, that declared here is a private type, and therefore the actual structure is hidden from the user. Furthermore, operations on objects of type NUMBER are now limited to:

- ADD_COMPLEX
- SUB_COMPLEX
- MUL_COMPLEX
- DIV_COMPLEX
- assignment
- tests for equality and inequality

Thus, the integrity of the type is preserved—so much so, in fact, that there is no way to assign values to objects of the type. Additional operations can be provided by the addition of appropriate subprograms to the package specification. For example, the function declaration

```
function REAL_PART(NUMB : NUMBER) return FLOAT;
function IMAG_PART(NUMB : NUMBER) return FLOAT;
function FORM_COMP(REAL_PART, IMAG_PART : FLOAT)
                    return COMPLEX;
```

added to the package specification, and the corresponding bodies

```
function REAL_PART(NUMB : NUMBER) return FLOAT is
begin
    return NUMB.REAL;
end REAL_PART;

function IMAG_PART(NUMB : NUMBER) return FLOAT is
begin
    return NUMB.IMAG;
end IMAGE_PART;

function FORM_COMP(REAL_PART, IMAG_PART : FLOAT)
                    return NUMBER is
    return (REAL_PART, IMAG_PART);
end FORM_COMP;
```

added to the package body, would provide means for assigning values as well as means for extracting the real and imaginary parts of an object of type NUMBER. The individual components of an object of the type could not be manipulated, however, since operations associated with the type are limited to those seven functions declared in the visible part of the package declaration, plus those of assignment and tests for equality and inequality. Thus, the integrity of the data is protected against accidental or purposeful violation.

The reader should note that the actual implementation of a complex number can be changed without affecting the visible part of the package specification or, as a result, the user's perception of the data type NUMBER. For example, instead of a complex number being represented in cartesian form, it may be implemented in polar form—consisting of an angle and a magnitude. The only change to the package specification is in the private part:

```
private
    PI : constant := 3.141_159_265;
    type NUMBER is
        record
            MAG : NATURAL;
            ANG : FLOAT range 0.0..2.0 * PI;
        end record;
    I : constant NUMBER := (1.0, PI/2.0);
end COMPLEX;
```

The implementation of the operations, as provided in the package body, would be drastically changed to reflect the new structure. The user of the package, however, would see no difference. The function REAL_PART, for example, would still return the real part of the cartesian representation of the complex number.

EXAMPLE 2: The package of Example 1 of Section 4.2.3 implements a first in–first out (FIFO) queue using a private data type. In this example, a last in–first out (LIFO) queue—normally termed a stack—will be implemented for character objects. Two approaches will be used; the first might be termed an implementation of an abstract data object, while the second, given as Example 3 of this section, implements an abstract data type.

In the first instance, the package declaration is

```
package CHAR_STACK is
    procedure PUSH(ELEM : in CHARACTER);
    procedure PULL(ELEM : out CHARACTER);
end CHAR_STACK;
```

The corresponding package body is

```
package body CHAR_STACK is
    SIZE          : constant := 1024;
    STACK_ARRAY   : array(1..SIZE) of CHARACTER;
    POINTER       : NATURAL range 0..SIZE := 0;
    procedure PUSH(ELEM : in CHARACTER) is
    begin
        POINTER := POINTER + 1;
        STACK_ARRAY(POINTER) := ELEM;
    end PUSH;
```

```
        procedure PULL(ELEM : out CHARACTER) is
        begin
            ELEM := STACK_ARRAY(POINTER);
            POINTER := POINTER -1;
        end PULL
    end CHAR_STACK;
```

This package implements a data abstraction—a LIFO queue, or stack. The user of the package may PUSH characters onto the stack and may PULL them from the stack in LIFO sequence. Since only these two operations are declared in the package specification, only they are permitted. The structure of the stack itself—a one-dimensional array with 1024 components and a pointer—is hidden from the user. Thus, the integrity of the stack is protected—it is not possible for a user to directly access any component of the stack or to affect the value of the pointer. The reader should note that the actual storage of characters is maintained within the package by means of the array object STACK_ARRAY.

EXAMPLE 3: If more than one stack is required, then two options are available. First, additional packages can be declared with different names. The additional packages could be declared in the usual manner, or they could be quite easily declared by instantiating a generic package, as discussed in Chapter 5. Alternatively, an abstract data type can be implemented by use of a limited private type. In this case, the package exports the abstract data type and the user can declare objects of the type that themselves are stacks—and he can declare any number of them. The latter approach is used here. The package specification containing the declaration of the private data type is shown below:

```
package CHAR_STACK_TYPE is
    type CHAR_STACK is limited private;
    procedure PUSH(STACK_NAME: in out CHAR_STACK;
                   ELEM : in CHARACTER);
    procedure PULL(STACK_NAME: in out CHAR_STACK;
                   ELEM : out CHARACTER);
    private
        SIZE : constant := 1024;
        type CHAR_ARRAY is array(1..SIZE) of CHARACTER;
        type CHAR_STACK is
            record
                STACK_ARRAY : CHAR_ARRAY;
                POINTER     : NATURAL range 0..SIZE :=0;
            end record;
end CHAR_STACK_TYPE;
```

Here, the package exports the type CHAR_STACK as well as the operations PUSH and PULL. The user of the package may declare any number of objects of type CHAR_STACK, and the operations PUSH and PULL can be used to manipulate the objects. These procedures now have two parameters—the first specifies the stack object on which the operation is to take place, and the second contains the character to be PUSHed or PULLed. In addition, the structure of the stack is now a record, containing as components both the array and the pointer.

The package body is somewhat modified to reflect these changes, as indicated below:

```
package body CHAR_STACK_TYPE is
    procedure PUSH(STACK_NAME; in out CHAR_STACK;
                   ELEM : in CHARACTER) is
    begin
        STACK_NAME.POINTER := STACK_NAME.POINTER + 1;
        STACK_NAME.STACK_ARRAY(STACK_NAME.POINTER) := ELEM;
    end PUSH;

    procedure PULL(STACK_NAME: in out CHAR_STACK;
                   ELEM : in CHARACTER) is
    begin
        ELEM := STACK_NAME.STACK_ARRAY(STACK_NAME.POINTER);
        STACK_NAME.POINTER := STACK_NAME.POINTER -1;
    end PULL;
end CHAR_STACK_TYPE;
```

The reader should note that the formal parameter STACK_NAME has an **in out** mode, since it is modified by the procedure. Also of interest is the fact that the storage of characters on the stack is no longer accomplished within the package as is the case in the previous example. Instead, the stacks are maintained in the calling environment where the stack objects are declared.

The user of this package can declare any number of objects of the type, such as

```
ROUTINE_STACK   : CHAR_STACK;
PRIORITY_STACK  : CHAR_STACK;
EMERGENCY_STACK : CHAR_STACK;
```

and then make procedure calls that access any of the objects. For example, if the declaration

```
PACKET : array(1..128) of CHARACTER;
```

is in effect, the following procedure calls are valid

```
PUSH(STACK_NAME => ROUTINE_STACK, ELEM => PACKET(1));
PUSH(PRIORITY_STACK, PACKET(100));
PULL(EMERGENCY_STACK, PACKET(50));
```

The reader will recognize the use of named association in the first instance.

REFERENCES

1. Miller, G. A., "The Magic Number Seven, Plus or Minus Two: Some Limits on Our Capacity for Processing Information," *The Psychological Review,* **63**(2):81–97 (March 1956).
2. McCracken, D., "Revolution in Programming: An Overview," *Datamation,* **19**(12):50–52 (December 1973).
3. Wirth, N., "On the Composition of Well Structured Programs," *Computing Surveys,* **6**(4):247–259 (December 1974).
4. Donaldson, J. R., "Structured Programming," *Datamation,* **19**(12):52–54 (December 1973).
5. Stevens, W., Myers, G., and Constantine, L., "Structured Design," *IBM Systems Journal,* **13**(2):115–139 (May 1974).
6. Booch, G., *Software Engineering with Ada* (Menlo Park, Calif.: The Benjamin/Cummins Publishing Company, 1983).
7. Gardner, M. R., "When to Use Private Types," *Ada Letters,* A Bimonthly Publication of SIGAda, the ACM Special Interest Group on Ada, III(6) (May–June 1984).
8. Elbert, T. F., "Simulation, Games, and Random Variables," *68 Micro Journal,* **3**:II (November 1981).

EXERCISES

1. How does the package concept provide the Ada language with capability for encapsulation and information hiding?
2. Is a package specification always necessary? Is a package body always necessary?
3. What is the significance of placing a declaration within the visible part of a package specification rather than in the declarative part of the package body?
4. What is the significance of placing a declaration within the visible part of a package declaration rather than within the private part?
5. Must a package specification have both a visible and a private part?
6. What is the scope of declarations occurring in the declarative part of a package body?
7. When is the sequence of statements of a package body executed?
8. Where may a private data type be declared?
9. What is the relationship between the declaration of a private data type in the visible part of a package specification and the full type declaration contained in the private part?

10. Distinguish between the private type and the limited private type.
11. Describe the different ways an object of a private type can be treated outside the package.
12. Describe how the separate compilation of package specifications and package bodies can enhance the modifiability of Ada software.
13. Where is an exception handled if it is raised during the execution of the sequence of statements of a subprogram body declared within the declarative part of a package body?
14. Why is the deferred-constant declaration provided by the Ada language?
15. What is the scope of a declaration occurring in the declarative part of a subprogram body whose declaration occurs in the declarative part of a package body?
16. What is the effect of naming a package in a with clause within the context clause of a program unit? What is the additional effect of naming the package in a use clause?
17. Where may a use clause appear?
18. Differentiate between the concept of an abstract data object (sometimes called an abstract state machine) and an abstract data type. In particular, discuss their implementation by use of Ada packages.
19. Explain why a reasonable use for a package is to encapsulate type declarations.
20. Explain why a reasonable use for a package is to encapsulate constant declarations.
21. What is meant by the term *logically related entities* as it applies to encapsulation within a package?
22. Discuss the effect of compiling the body of an Ada package as a subunit. Compare this effect with that of separately compiling the specification and the body.
23. Explain how the combination of a private data type and a package serve to implement an abstract data type.
24. When would a private type, as opposed to a limited private type, be used to implement an abstract data type?
25. Discuss the manner in which abstraction is effected by the use of an abstract data type.

PROGRAMMING EXERCISES

These programming exercises may require use of input-output support from package TEXT_IO. The reader is referred to Section 6.2.2 for details.

1. Complete and compile the package TRIG_FUNCTION of Example 1, Section 4.2.2. Write a main program (procedure) that names this package in a with clause and that exercises the functions provided by the package.
2. Compile package LOGARITHM of Example 2, Section 4.2.2. Write a main program (procedure) that names this package in a with clause and that exercises the functions provided by the package.
3. Package RANDOM of Example 3, Section 4.2.2, will not compile using a

compiler in which type INTEGER is implemented using 16 bits. Modify this package so that it will compile under that situation.

4. Perform the modifications to the result of Exercise 3 to reflect the changes in Examples 4 and 5 of Section 4.2.2.

5. Compile package QUEUE_OF_CHAR of Example 1, Section 4.2.3. Write and compile a program (procedure) that names QUEUE_OF_CHAR in a with clause and that declares at least three objects of type QUEUE_TYPE. The main program should manipulate the objects in order to demonstrate the abstraction.

6. Recompile the body of package QUEUE_OF_CHAR using the private part and body given in Example 2, Section 4.2.3. Verify that the main program remains unchanged.

7. Repeat Exercise 5, only now use the deferred-constant implementation of Section 4.2.4. Verify that the main program remains unchanged.

8. Implement and compile the package BIT_DIDDLE of Example 1, Section 4.3.1. Write and compile a main program (procedure) that exercises the procedures supported by the package.

9. Repeat Exercise 8, but now declare package BIT_DIDDLE within the declarative part of the main program, as discussed in Example 2, Section 4.3.1.

10. Repeat Exercise 9, but now compile the body of package BIT_DIDDLE as a subunit.

11. Compile the package specifications of Examples 1, 2, and 3, Section 4.4.1.

12. Compile package MATRIX_ARITH of Example 1, Section 4.4.2. Write and compile a main program (procedure) that names MATRIX_ARITH in a with clause and that exercises the procedures supported by the package. Where should exception MATRIX_ERROR be handled?

13. Compile package COMPLEX of Example 2, Section 4.4.2. Use overloaded operator symbols for the function names. Write and compile a main program (procedure) that names COMPLEX in a with clause and that exercises the functions exported by the package.

14. Compile package CHAR_STACK of Example 2, Section 4.4.3. Write and compile a main program (procedure) that names CHAR_STACK in a with clause, and that exercises the stack.

15. Compile package CHAR_STACK_TYPE of Example 3, Section 4.4.3. Write and compile a main program (procedure) that declares three objects of type CHAR_STACK and that manipulates these objects.

16. Encapsulate the declarations of Exercise 49, Chapter 3, in a package called FILE_DECLAR. Write a program named TEST_FILE_DECLARE that imports the data type PTR_ARRAY from package FILE_DECLAR, declares an object of type PTR_ARRAY with three components, and assigns values to all data elements.

Chapter 5
GENERIC UNITS

5.1 THE GENERAL CONCEPT OF GENERIC UNITS

The strong typing property of the Ada language enhances its support of the software engineering goals of reliability and modifiability. But it also has potential for requiring tedious repetition of software modules within a given program. For example, suppose that three distinct integer data types are declared within a program:

```
type HIT_COUNT       is range 0..1000;
type NEAR_MISS_COUNT is range 0..1000;
type MISS_COUNT      is range 0..1000;
```

Further assume that three array types are declared as

```
type HIT_ARRAY  is array(1..100) of HIT_COUNT;
type NEAR_ARRAY is array(1..100) of NEAR_MISS_COUNT;
type MISS_ARRAY is array(1..100) of MISS_COUNT;
```

Clearly, these arrays are of distinctly different types. If it is now desired to develop a procedure that will sort the elements of an array object of type HIT_ARRAY, then the specification part of this procedure might be

```
procedure HIT_SORT(SORT_ARRAY : in out HIT_ARRAY);
```

The implementation of the sort algorithm would be contained in the procedure body, in which there would be declared one or more local variables of type HIT_COUNT to be used by the sort algorithm:

```
procedure HIT_SORT(SORT_ARRAY : in out HIT_ARRAY)is
   TEMP : HIT_COUNT;
begin
   .....sequence of statements
end HIT_SORT;
```

If it is also desired to provide a sort capability for array objects of type NEAR_ARRAY, it would not be possible to use procedure HIT_SORT, because the strong typing rules would not permit the association of formal parameter SORT_ARRAY—which is of type HIT_ARRAY—with an actual parameter of type NEAR_ARRAY. The same situation holds with respect to array objects of type MISS_ARRAY. This type conflict exists even though all three array types are 100-component integer arrays with identical range constraints and identical constraints on the components, because the types are distinct. In fact, even if the three array types were declared as

```
type HIT_ARRAY  is array(1..100) of INTEGER;
type NEAR_ARRAY is array(1..100) of INTEGER;
type MISS_ARRAY is array(1..100) of INTEGER;
```

they would still be distinct types and the conclusions above would hold.

So, if array objects of types NEAR_ARRAY and MISS_ARRAY are to be sorted, two additional procedures must be provided. The specifications of these procedures would be

```
procedure NEAR_SORT(SORT_ARRAY : in out NEAR_ARRAY);
procedure MISS_SORT(SORT_ARRAY : in out MISS_ARRAY);
```

The associated procedure bodies would be identical to that of procedure HIT_SORT, with the exception of the local declaration of object TEMP. It would be declared as type NEAR_MISS_COUNT and MISS_COUNT, respectively. Although the declaration of distinct named types by the programmer is encouraged for purposes of enhancing the reliability and modifiabilty of software, the practice could also lead to an unreasonable proliferation of subprograms as situations such as that described above are encountered. Even in input-output operations, separate procedures are required for each data type.

In order to provide a convenient means of dealing with a situation such as this, and for other reasons as well, the Ada language contains a feature called a *generic program unit*. A generic unit is either a generic subprogram or a generic package, and it permits the programmer to declare and compile a subprogram or package with some essential detail, such as a data type, missing from the declaration. The result of the compilation of a generic unit is not executable, because of the missing detail, but an executable subprogram or package can be obtained from the generic unit by supplying the missing detail through a process known as *instantiation*—the creation of an instance of the generic unit. Furthermore, the generic unit can be instantiated any number of times, creating any number of distinct subprograms or packages with their own particular provision for the missing detail. This process of deleting some detail, and then providing it at instantiation, is called *parametrization* of the subprogram or package. In the particular situation considered above, a generic sort procedure could be declared, with the missing parameter being the type of the array to be sorted. After this generic procedure is compiled, it can be instantiated three times, providing as the parameters the types HIT_ARRAY, NEAR_ARRAY, and MISS_ARRAY. The results of the three instantiations would, in essence, be identical to procedures HIT_SORT, NEAR_SORT, and MISS_SORT, respectively.

Generic units provide great flexibility in writing general-purpose library subprograms and packages, which can then be instantiated by the user as needed. Excellent examples are found in the package TEXT_IO, contained in Appendix C. Package TEXT_IO is not a generic unit, but it contains four generic packages:

1. INTEGER_IO
2. FLOAT_IO
3. FIXED_IO
4. ENUMERATION_IO

These input-output packages are provided so that they can be instantiated for each integer type, floating-point type, fixed-point type, or enumeration type decared within a program and requiring input-output services. This feature is discussed further in Section 6.2.2.

Generic units, like normal subprograms and packages, have a two-part structure consisting of a specification and a body. The specification and the body may be separately compiled. The specification of a generic unit differs from the normal subprogram or package specification by the addition of a generic part. The body of a generic unit is syntactically identical to that of a normal subprogram or package body.

5.1.1 Generic Unit Specifications

A generic unit is either a generic subprogram or a generic package, as implied by Figure 5.1. The declaration of a generic unit must contain a description of the parameter or parameters that are to be provided upon instantiation. These concepts will be developed in full in the discussion to follow. The general syntax for a generic unit declaration is

```
generic_declaration ::= generic_specification;  (5.1)
```

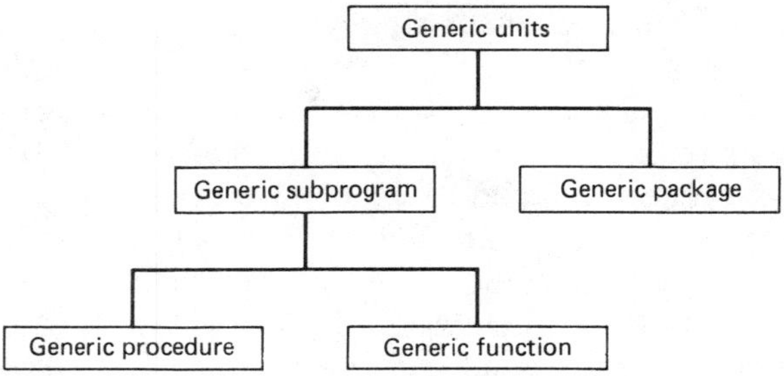

Figure 5.1. Ada's generic units.

where

```
generic_specification ::=
     generic_formal_part subprogram_specification
   | generic_formal_part package_specification     (5.1.1)

     generic_formal_part ::=
       generic {generic_parameter_declaration}     (5.1.2)

generic_parameter_declaration ::=
    identifier_list : [in[out]] type_mark [:=expression];
 | type identifier is generic_type_definition;
 | private_type_declaration
 | with subprogram_specification [is name];
 | with subprogram_specification [is <>];          (5.1.3)

   generic_type_definition ::=
      (<>) | range <> | digits <> | delta <> |
    | array_type_definition | access_type_definition
                                                   (5.1.4)
```

The syntax statements for a subprogram specification and that for a package specification are given by statements (3.55.1) and (4.1.1), respectively. Those for an identifier list, for a type mark, and for a private type declaration are given by statements (3.10.1), (3.8.2), and (4.3), respectively, while array type and access type definitions are given by statements (3.22.1) and (3.26.1), respectively. If a generic formal parameter is a constrained array type, the only form of discrete range permitted in the generic formal declaration is a type mark.

Statement (5.1.1) gives the general syntax for the specification of a generic unit—a generic formal part followed by the normal subprogram or package specification. The generic part contains the declaration of *generic formal parameters* which, by association with actual parameters at the time of instantiation, provide the missing details to the generic unit. As the syntax of Statement (5.1.2) indicates, generic formal parameters are not necessary to the declaration. That is, a generic unit can be declared without missing details, in which case the generic formal parameters are not required. The provision of information to the generic unit at instantiation time by an association of formal and actual parameters is analogous to the use of parameters in subprogram calls. Whereas subprogram parameters must be objects, generic formal parameters can be objects, types, or subprograms. Thus, the missing detail in a generic unit declaration, which is then supplied at the time of instantiation, can be the name of an object, the name of a type, the name of a subprogram, or any combination thereof. As implied by Statement (5.1.3) and by Figure 5.2, a formal object parameter of mode **out** is not permitted. The default mode is **in,** which is the only mode permitted for formal type and subprogram parameters. The particulars of the use of generic formal parameters will be discussed when each of the classes of parameters—object, type, and subprogram parameters—is considered.

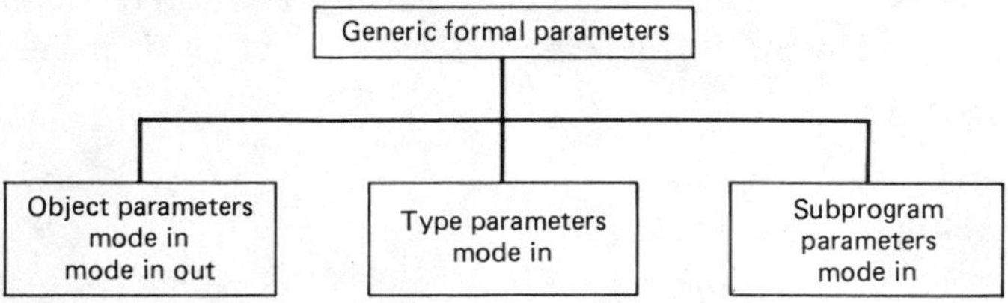

Figure 5.2. Generic formal parameters.

In the example of the sort procedures discussed previously, a generic procedure could be declared using the type of the array to be sorted as a generic formal parameter. Then, three instantiations—with actual parameters HIT_ARRAY, NEAR_ARRAY, and MISS_ARRAY—could be used to produce sort procedures applicable to each of these array types. The specifics of this example will be considered after the details of generic formal parameters are discussed and after the concept of instantiation has been introduced.

5.1.2 Generic Unit Bodies

The body of a generic subprogram or of a generic package is syntactically identical to that of a normal subprogram or package body. In direct analogy to the use of formal parameters by subprograms, the generic formal parameters are used within the generic unit body as data objects, data types, or subprograms, as the case may be. The body of a generic unit is the template from which are derived the bodies of those program units, either subprograms or packages, obtained by instantiation of the generic unit. The difference between the body of the generic unit and that of a program unit obtained by instantiation of the generic unit is the implicit substitution of actual generic parameters for formal generic parameters in the body of the program unit obtained by instantiation.

5.1.3 Generic Instantiation

When a generic program unit is compiled, the resulting library unit is not usable in the same sense that a normal subprogram or package can be referenced by other program units. Instead, *instances* of the generic unit must be declared, providing the actual parameters to be associated with the generic formal parameters, if any, declared in the generic part of the specification. A generic instantiation is itself a declaration, and therefore it can only appear in those regions of program text where declarations are permitted. A generic instantiation can also be a compilation unit, as indicated by Statement (3.59.2). The syntax of a generic instantiation is

```
generic_instantiation ::=
   package identifier is
      new generic_package_name[generic_actual_part];
  | procedure identifier is
     new generic_procedure_name[generic_actual_part];
  | function designator is
     new generic_function_name[generic_actual_part];
                                                    (5.2)
```

where

```
generic_actual_part ::=
   (generic_association {, generic_association})
                                                  (5.2.1)
```

and

```
generic_association ::=
   [generic_formal_parameter =>] generic_actual_parameter
                                                  (5.2.2)
```

```
generic_formal_parameter ::= parameter_simple_name
     | operator_symbol
                                                  (5.2.3)

generic_actual_parameter ::= expression | variable_name
   | subprogram_name | entry_name | type_mark        (5.2.4)
```

The syntax for an expression and that for a type mark are given by Statements (3.34) and (3.10.1), respectively. It can be seen from this syntax that a generic instantiation uses the reserved word **new,** as do subtype declarations and allocators, and that the association of actual parameters with formal parameters can be either positional or named.

At instantiation, a generic actual parameter must be provided, in accordance with Statement (5.2.2), for each generic formal parameter, unless the generic unit specification contains a default value as provided by Statement (5.1.3). The actual parameter must match the formal parameter, in a manner to be discussed thoroughly in the following sections. The general matching requirements are given below:

- A formal object parameter of mode **in** can only be matched by an expression.
- A formal object parameter of mode **in out** can only be matched by a variable name.
- A formal type parameter can only be matched by a type mark.
- A formal subprogram parameter can only be matched by a subprogram name or by an entry name.

Entry names are associated with tasks and will be discussed in Chapter 7. The matching of generic parameters, beyond these general matching requirements, is necessary for rather obvious reasons. It would not be possible, for example, for an array type to be used as an actual parameter to be associated with a formal parameter that is treated as a scalar type within the body of the generic unit. At the same time, it is desirable to permit the widest range of data types to match the generic formal parameter.

5.2 GENERIC FORMAL PARAMETERS

Generic formal parameters are declared in the generic formal part of a generic subprogram specification or of a generic package specification. These formal parameters may be either object, type, or subprogram parameters, as discussed in the previous section. In each of these cases, there is a specific set of characteristics and a set of matching rules.

5.2.1 Object Parameters

A formal generic *object parameter* is analogous to the parameter of a subprogram. The syntax is obtained from the first choice in Statement (5.1.3):

```
generic_object_parameter_declaration ::=
    identifier_list : [in[out]]type_mark[:= expression];
                                                        (5.3)
```

This kind of parameter has a mode that is either **in** or **in out;** the **out** mode is not permitted. Default is to the **in** mode, which implies that if no mode is specified, the mode will be considered to be **in.** The default expression is only permitted if the mode of the parameter is **in.**

The mode **in,** as applied to generic formal parameters, implies that the value of the actual parameter, which is an expression, is assigned to the formal parameter. Furthermore, the value cannot be changed within the generic unit—it is, in essence, a constant. Neither an object whose type is limited private, nor an object whose type is derived from a limited private type, nor a composite object with components of a type that is limited private can be used with the mode **in.**

The mode **in out** requires that the parameter be a variable, and the effect of parameter association is to rename the formal parameter to the name of the actual parameter. That is, every appearance of the formal parameter name within the generic unit is replaced by the actual parameter name. The use of the **in out** mode can produce a result known as a *side effect*—having a program unit change the value of a global variable. Such a situation is normally considered undesirable, because it makes the effect of a subprogram more difficult to understand. One rather subtle aspect of **in out** formal parameters is that the constraints that apply to the formal parameter, with respect to its use in the instantiated subprogram or package, are those that apply to the actual parameter rather than those implied by the type mark that appears in the declaration of the generic parameter, which occurs in the generic part of the subprogram or package specification.

Some examples of generic unit specifications with formal object parameters are given below, together with possible instantiations. Because the context of the use of a generic unit and its instantiations is important to understanding the generic unit and its parameter associations, these examples are given in the context of an application.

EXAMPLE 1: This example involves a data communication system that has a requirement for establishing circular buffers of various lengths by instantiation of a generic package named BUFFER. The package specification is

```
generic
   BUFFER_LENGTH : in POSITIVE;
package BUFFER is
   BUFFER_ARRAY : array(1..BUFFER LENGTH) of CHARACTER;
   FRONT, BACK : POSITIVE range 1..BUFFER_LENGTH;
   procedure PLACE(ELEMENT : in CHARACTER);
   procedure CLEAR;
   procedure TAKE(ELEMENT : out CHARACTER);
end BUFFER;
```

In this case, the circular buffer is implemented as an anonymous array with elements of type CHARACTER. The range constraint is supplied by the generic formal object parameter BUFFER_LENGTH. The front and back of the buffer are maintained by the values of the objects FRONT and BACK, as indicated in Figure 5.3 for BUFFER_LENGTH equal to 128. The operations provided for the circular buffer are PLACE, TAKE, and CLEAR, which would be implemented in the body of the generic package. An instantiation of this generic package might appear as

```
package PRIORITY_BUFFER is new BUFFER(128);
```

using positional association, or

```
package PRIORITY_BUFFER is new BUFFER(BUFFER_LENGTH
                                       => 128);
```

using named association. The procedures are then visible to user programs as

```
PRIORITY_BUFFER.PLACE
PRIORITY_BUFFER.CLEAR
PRIORITY_BUFFER.TAKE.
```

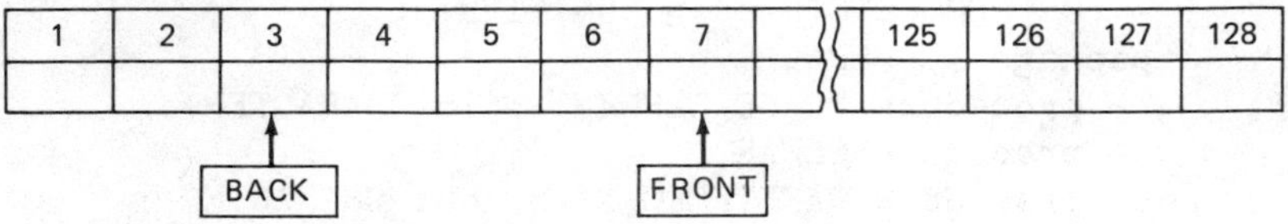

Figure 5.3. Circular buffer implemented as an array.

If a use clause appears,

```
use PRIORITY_BUFFER;
```

then, within the scope of the use statement, the simple names PLACE, CLEAR, and TAKE may be used. The generic package BUFFER may be instantiated any number of times to create packages supporting circular buffers of different lengths:

```
package EMERGENCY_BUFFER is new BUFFER(512);
package ROUTINE_BUFFER   is new BUFFER(1024);
```

The procedures would be visible as

```
EMERGENCY_BUFFER.PLACE
```

and

```
ROUTINE_BUFFER.PLACE
```

and so on. This implementation of circular buffers is not indicative of good software design, because the objects BUFFER_ARRAY, FRONT, and BACK are visible within the program unit using the instantiated package. For example, the objects

```
PRIORITY_BUFFER.BUFFER_ARRAY
PRIORITY_BUFFER.FRONT
PRIORITY_BUFFER.BACK
```

can be manipulated by the user of the package, thus endangering the integrity of the buffer itself.

A more reasonable approach would be to make the objects BUFFER_ARRAY, FRONT, and BACK local to the package by declaring them in the declarative part of the body of the generic package BUFFER. In this case, the generic package specification would be

```
generic
   BUFFER_LENGTH : in POSITIVE;
package BUFFER is
   procedure PLACE(ELEMENT : in CHARACTER);
   procedure CLEAR;
   procedure TAKE(ELEMENT  : out CHARACTER);
end BUFFER;
```

The form of an instantiation of package BUFFER remains unchanged. Here, since the objects BUFFER_ARRAY, FRONT, and BACK are local to the package body—because they are declared in the declarative part of the body rather than in the specification—they are not visible outside the package. Thus, they cannot be modified, either intentionally or unintentionally, by the user. This example illustates the use of information hiding to enhance the reliability of software.

A third approach to this problem is to implement the circular buffer as an abstract data type, as was done with the first in–first out queue example of Section 4.2.3. This concept will be explored further in Section 5.4.2.

EXAMPLE 2: This example concerns a process control environment in which several sensors are to be monitored. The sensors are of two types, pressure sensors and temperature sensors, and the number of each type varies among several different processes. A procedure that reads the sensors and returns the values of the minimum, the maximum, and the average reading for the two types of sensors is to be obtained by instantiation of the generic procedure READ_SENSORS. The procedure specification is

```
generic
   NO_PRESS_SENSORS : in POSITIVE;
   NO_TEMP_SENSORS  : in POSITIVE;
procedure READ_SENSORS(P_MIN,P_MAX,P_AV, T_MIN,
                       T_MAX,T_AV : out FLOAT);
```

An instantiation might be

```
procedure PASS_1_SENSOR_READ is new
          READ_SENSORS(NO_PRESS_SENSORS => 10,
                       NO_TEMP_SENSORS => 12);
```

using named association. Of course, positional association could also be used.

EXAMPLE 3: The third example concerns the use of the generic package whose specification is given below:

```
generic
package COUNT is
   procedure INCREMENT;
   function READING return NATURAL;
   procedure RESET;
end COUNT;
```

In this case, there is no generic parameter. Instantiations of this generic package implement simple counters, with the value of the count maintained as a local object within the package body. The body of this generic package might be as follows:

```
package body COUNT is
   VAL : NATURAL := 0;
   procedure INCREMENT is
   begin
      VAL := VAL +1;
   end INCREMENT;

   function READING return NATURAL is
   begin
      return VAL;
   end READING;

   procedure RESET is
   begin
      VAL := 0;
   end RESET;
end COUNT;
```

The actual count is maintained as the value of the local object VAL and is therefore protected from any modification from outside the package, except for those changes effected by calls to procedures INCREMENT and RESET. Instantiations might be

```
package FOE_COUNT is new COUNT;
package FRIEND_COUNT is new COUNT;
package UNKNOWN_COUNT is new COUNT;
```

in which case procedure calls such as

```
FOE_COUNT.INCREMENT
FRIEND_COUNT.RESET
UNKNOWN_COUNT.INCREMENT
```

can be used to alter the values of the three counters, and the function calls

```
FOE_COUNT.READING
FRIEND_COUNT.READING
UNKNOWN_COUNT.READING
```

can be used to obtain the counter readings. The local variable VAL in each of the three instantiated packages is not visible outside the package body, even if an expanded name such as

```
FOE_COUNT.VAL
```

is used. Thus, the integrity of the three counters is protected against either intentional or unintentional modification from outside the package.

5.2.2 Type Parameters

Probably the most widely used kind of generic parameter is the *type parameter,* because the strong typing characteristic of the Ada language makes it almost imperative that some means be provided for adapting common algorithms to specific types. The sort procedure of Section 5.1 is an example of the use of a generic type parameter. A second example is provided by the input-output packages contained in Appendix C, one of which can be instantiated to provide text input-output facilities for any scalar data type declared within a program. The syntax for the declaration of a generic formal type parameter is obtained from the second and third choices of Statement (5.1.3):

```
generic_type_parameter_declaration ::=
   type identifier is generic_type_definition
| private_type_declaration;                              (5.4)
```

where the syntax for a generic type definition is given by Statement (5.1.4) and that for a private type declaration is given by Statement (4.3). The form of a generic type definition must now be discussed in some detail.

When a generic unit has a generic formal type parameter, there will be objects of that type declared within the generic unit. These objects, in turn, will be involved in certain operations within the body of the generic unit, and these operations place particular limitations upon the actual parameter that can be associated with the formal parameter at instantiation. For example, if a generic unit declares objects of the generic formal parameter type, and the operations on these objects within the body of the generic unit are clearly limited to objects of a scalar type, then only actual parameters that are scalar data types can be associated with the generic formal parameter at instantiation. This limiting of formal and actual parameter association is effected by the generic formal type parameter declaration in the generic part of the generic unit specification.

The syntax is provided by Statement (5.4) and by Statement (5.1.4), which is repeated here for convenience.

```
generic_type_definition ::=
   (<>) | range <> | digits <> | delta <> |
| array_type_definition | access_type_definition
                                                  (5.1.4)
```

The array and access type definitions are given by Statements (3.22.1) and (3.26.1), respectively. Thus, there are nine possible forms of a generic formal type parameter declaration. Each of these nine declarations has two effects. First, it limits the operations on objects of the generic formal type that are declared within the generic unit. Second, it limits the types that can be used as the actual parameter to be associated with the formal parameter at instantiation. Each of the nine declarations is listed below, together with the limitations imposed by the declaration and with the rules for matching formal and actual parameters.

```
   type identifier is (<>);
operations permitted--those operations common to
                      enumeration and integer types
actual parameter    --can be any enumeration or
                      integer type              (5.4.1)
```

```
   type identifier is range <>;
operations permitted--those operations associated
                      with integer types
actual parameter    --can be any integer type   (5.4.2)
```

```
   type identifier is digits <>;
operations permitted--those operations associated with
                      floating-point types
actual parameters   --can be any floating-point type
                                                 (5.4.3)
```

```
   type identifier is delta <>;
operations permitted--those operations associated with
                      fixed-point types
actual parameter    --can be any fixed-point type
                                                 (5.4.4)
```

```
type identifier is array (index_subtype_definition
     {,index_subtype_definition} of
     component_subtype_indication;
```

```
   where the syntax for an index subtype definition is
   given by Statement (3.22.4)
operations permitted--any operation associated with
                      array types
actual parameter    --any unconstrained array type of the
                      same dimension, index type, and
                      component type                (5.4.5)

   type identifier is array index_constraint of
        component_subtype_indication;
   where the syntax for an index constraint is given by
   Statement (3.22.5)
operations permitted--any operation associated with
                      array types
actual parameter    --any constrained array type of the
                      same dimension, index constraint,
                      index type, and component type
                                                    (5.4.6)

       type identifier is access subtype_indication;
  operations permitted--any operation associated
                          with access types
  actual parameters    --any access type designating
                          same type object          (5.4.7)

   type identifier is private;
operations permitted--any operation associated with private
                      types. Specifically, assignment,
                      tests for equality and inequality,
                      membership, and explicit conversion
                      are permitted.
actual parameter    --any type that permits assignment
                      and tests for equality
                      and inequality.
                      This includes nearly all
                      data types.                   (5.4.8)

     type identifier is limited private;
  operations permitted--membership and explicit conversion
  actual parameter    --any data type               (5.4.9)
```

In addition to the operations specified above, in each case any operation declared as a generic formal subprogram parameter (to be considered in the following section) is also permitted.

The general concept should be clear from the discussion above. The operations permitted within the generic unit are limited to operations that are compatible with those data types allowed as actual parameters. Some examples of the use of generic formal type parameters are given below. As in the previous section, the examples are given in the context of an application.

EXAMPLE 1: This example further elucidates the details of the generic sort procedure discussed in Section 5.1, in which three integer data types were declared:

```
type HIT_COUNT        is range 0..1000;
type NEAR_MISS_COUNT is range 0..1000;
type MISS_COUNT       is range 0..1000;
```

These are three distinct types, even though they all belong to the general class of integer data types. There were also three array declarations:

```
type HIT_ARRAY  is array(1..100) of HIT_COUNT;
type NEAR_ARRAY is array(1..100) of NEAR_MISS_COUNT;
type MISS_ARRAY is array(1..100) of MISS_COUNT;
```

which, also, are three distinct types. The object is to provide a generic sort procedure that can be instantiated for each of the three array types above. The generic procedure declaration is, in accordance with Statement (5.1),

```
generic
   type COUNT is range <>;
   type COUNT_ARRAY is array(1..100) of COUNT;
procedure SORT_COUNT(LIST : in out COUNT_ARRAY);
```

In this case, the generic formal type declarations of Statements (5.4.2) and (5.4.6) have been used, which in turn imply limitations on the operations that can be applied to objects of types COUNT and COUNT_ARRAY within the body of the generic procedure, as indicated below:

- Operations on objects of type COUNT are limited to those operations permitted for integer objects. The components of an array of type COUNT_ARRAY are of type COUNT.
- Operations on objects of type COUNT_ARRAY are limited to those operations permitted for one-dimensional array objects.

A further implication of the declarations relates to actual parameters that can be associated with the generic parameters at instantiation:

- Actual parameters to be associated with formal parameters COUNT must be of an integer type. HIT_COUNT, NEAR_MISS_COUNT, and MISS_COUNT are integer types.
- Actual parameters to be associated with formal parameter COUNT_ARRAY must be one-dimensional, 100-component arrays with an integer index and integer components.

The body of generic procedure SORT would be implemented to sort the elements of array object LIST, the formal parameter of the procedure, under the condition that LIST is a 100-component integer array with elements of type COUNT. The instantiation of the generic procedure SORT to produce a sort procedure applicable to arrays of type HIT_ARRAY would be, in accordance with Statement (5.2),

```
procedure HIT_SORT is new SORT_COUNT(HIT_COUNT, HIT_ARRAY);
```

using positional association, or

```
procedure HIT_SORT is new SORT_COUNT(COUNT => HIT_COUNT,
                                     COUNT_ARRAY => HIT_ARRAY);
```

using named association. The elaboration of this single statement has the effect of declaring the entire body of procedure SORT_COUNT, with actual parameters HIT_COUNT and HIT_ARRAY replacing the formal parameters COUNT and COUNT_ARRAY in every occurrence.

In a similar manner, instantiations to provide sort procedures for arrays of types NEAR_ARRAY and MISS_ARRAY would be:

```
procedure NEAR_SORT is new
                SORT_COUNT(NEAR_MISS_COUNT, NEAR_ARRAY);
```

and

```
procedure MISS_SORT is new
                SORT_COUNT (MISS_COUNT, MISS_ARRAY);
```

It should again be noted that the strong typing feature of the Ada language would preclude the use of procedure HIT_SORT, for example, to sort an array of type MISS_ARRAY, even though both are integer arrays of 100 elements.

EXAMPLE 2: One of the most practical uses of generic units is to provide input-output capability for user-defined data types. Because of the strong typing features of the Ada language, it is not possible to provide individual input-output procedures and functions for all possible data types that a user may declare. For example, the three integer types of the previous example,

```
HIT_COUNT, NEAR_MISS_COUNT, MISS_COUNT
```

are distinct types. To provide input-output support for objects of these types would require three separate input-output packages, because the strong typing characteristics of the language would not permit an input procedure whose parameter is of type HIT_COUNT, for example, to be used for input of objects of type MISS_COUNT. In fact, separate procedures are indeed required, but the generic facilities of the Ada language make the provision of these input-output facilities an easy matter.

Within the predefined package TEXT_IO, which is contained in Appendix C, there are four generic packages:

1. INTEGER_IO
2. FLOAT_IO
3. FIXED_IO
4. ENUMERATION_IO

Particular interest here is in the generic package INTEGER_IO. The generic package specification, in skeletal form, is

```
generic
   type NUM is range <>;
package INTEGER_IO is
     . . . . .
end INTEGER_IO;
```

Examination of Appendix C reveals that this declaration contains several procedures for input and output of data. The generic part of the declaration above is in the form of Statement (5.4.2), and thus the actual parameter to be associated with the formal parameter NUM at instantiation can be any integer data type. In the current situation, the three instantiations

```
package HIT_IO  is new INTEGER_IO(HIT_COUNT);
package NEAR_IO is new INTEGER_IO(NEAR_MISS_COUNT);
package MISS_IO is new INTEGER_IO(MISS_COUNT);
```

create three different copies of the generic package INTEGER_IO, each with a different actual generic parameter. Each package has its own GET and PUT procedures, which can be accessed as, for example,

```
HIT_IO.PUT(...)
```

or

```
MISS_IO.GET(...)
```

Even predefined types such as FLOAT and INTEGER do not have predefined input-output procedures. Rather, input-output packages must be instantiated as, for example,

```
PD_INTEGER_IO is new INTEGER_IO(INTEGER);
PD_FLOAT_IO   is new FLOAT_IO(FLOAT);
```

As an alternative in any of these examples, named association may be used, in which case the above declarations would be

```
PD_INTEGER_IO is new INTEGER_IO(NUM => INTEGER);
PD_FLOAT_IO   is new FLOAT_IO(NUM   => FLOAT);
```

Even enumeration types can have input-output packages instantiated for them using the generic package ENUMERATION_IO. The generic package declaration from Appendix C, in skeletal form, is

```
generic
   type ENUM is (<>);
package ENUMERATION_IO is
   . . . . .
end ENUMERATION_IO;
```

The generic formal type parameter declaration above is of the general form given by Statement (5.4.1). Then, for example, if the enumeration type STATUS is declared as

```
type STATUS is (SAFE, READY, ARMED);
```

then an input-output package can be instantiated as

```
package STATUS_IO is new ENUMERATION_IO(STATUS);
```

This feature of the Ada language is distinctly different from those of Pascal, in which enumeration types can be declared and used but have no input-output facilities. In an Ada program, enumeration type values have the same general input-output facilities, through instantiation of the generic package ENUMERATION_IO, as do any other scalar data types. That is, a PUT procedure will actually cause the appropriate enumeration literal—in this case, either SAFE, READY, or ARMED—to appear on the output device. Similarly, in response to the call of a GET procedure, the actual enumeration literal SAFE, for example, would be entered on the input device.

5.2.3 Subprogram Parameters

The third kind of generic formal parameter is the *subprogram parameter*. In this case, the generic unit contains a formal parameter declaration that is a subprogram specification for which no corresponding body exists within the body of the generic unit. The identifier given in this subprogram specification is the generic formal parameter; at instantiation it must be associated with an actual parameter that is the name of a matching subprogram. Matching, in this context, means that the actual subprogram—that is, the subprogram whose name is associated with the formal parameter name at instantiation—has the same number of formal parameters of the same type and mode as are contained in the generic formal subprogram parameter specification. The syntax for a generic subprogram parameter declaration is obtained from the last two choices of Statement (5.1.3):

```
generic_subprogram_parameter_declaration::=
  with subprogram_specification [is name];
| with subprogram_specification [is <>];          (5.5)
```

The syntax for a subprogram specification is given by Statement (3.55.1). The use of the reserved word **with** has no connection to its use in a context clause, which is discussed in Section 4.3.3.1. It is used here solely to resolve a syntactic ambiguity that would otherwise arise.

The two optional parts in Statement (5.5) provide two methods by which subprogram names may be provided as default values, in much the same manner in which default values are provided for subprogram parameters. If the default subprogram is specified by a name, then that name is provided as an actual parameter if the instantiation fails to provide a value. If the default name is specified by the box symbol <>, then there must be a unique matching subprogram, with the same name as the generic formal subprogram parameter, visible at the point of instantiation. This subprogram becomes the actual parameter. Some examples will serve to clarify these concepts.

EXAMPLE 1: In a process control environment it is necessary to read various numbers of various types of sensors. These sensors may be thermocouples, pressure sensors, flow-rate sensors, or any other device that senses a physical quantity. Each type of sensor has a unique compensation that must be applied to the sensor output before it is used. The compensated outputs are then to be processed in groups to form a smoothed output. A generic procedure PROCESS_SENSOR_READING is to perform this processing, part of which is the sensor compensation mentioned above. The specification of the generic procedure PROCESS_SENSOR_READING is given below:

```
generic
   type UNITS is digits <>;
   type UNIT_ARRAY is array(INTEGER range <>) of UNITS;
   with procedure COMPENSATE(READING : in out UNIT_ARRAY);
procedure PROCESS_SENSOR_READING(RAW_DATA : in UNIT_ARRAY;
                                 SMOOTHED_DATA : out UNIT_ARRAY);
```

The two generic formal type parameters UNITS and UNIT_ARRAY conform with Statements (5.4.3) and (5.4.5), respectively. Thus, the formal parameter UNITS can match any actual parameter that is a floating-point type. Similarly, the formal parameter UNIT_ARRAY can match any actual parameter that is a one-dimensional unconstrained array type with an integer index and components of the type associated—as an actual parameter—with formal parameter UNITS. The generic formal subprogram parameter COMPENSATE is declared in accordance with Statement (5.5), and it can match any actual parameter that is the name of a procedure that has an **in out** parameter of the type that is associated with formal type parameter UNIT_ARRAY. The body of the generic procedure PROCESS_SENSOR_READING, which is not shown here, would contain the actual implementation of the sensor processing. Within this body, a call to procedure COMPENSATE will be effected in order to compensate the array of sensor readings.

An instantiation of generic procedure PROCESS_SENSOR_READING must provide three actual parameters:

1. One to match formal parameter UNITS—it must be the name of a floating-point type.
2. One to match formal parameter UNIT_ARRAY—it must be the name of a one-dimensional unconstrained array type with index of type INTEGER; the component type must be the same floating-point type matched with parameter UNITS.
3. One to match formal parameter COMPENSATE—it must be the name of a procedure with an **in out** parameter of the same type as that matched with formal parameter UNIT_ARRAY.

For example, the instantiation

```
procedure PROCESS_VOLTAGE_READINGS is new
   PROCESS_SENSOR_READING(VOLTS, VOLTAGE_ARRAY,
                          VOLT_COMPENSATE);
```

will create a procedure named PROCESS_VOLTAGE, the body of which is obtained from the body of the generic procedure PROCESS_SENSOR_READING by replacing all references to data types UNITS and UNIT_ARRAY by the actual type parameters VOLTS and VOLTAGE_ARRAY, respectively, and by replacing all calls to procedure COMPENSATE with calls to the actual subprogram parameter VOLT_COMPENSATE. Of course, named association could be used in the instantiation, yielding

```
procedure PROCESS_VOLTAGE_READINGS is new
   PROCESS_SENSOR_READING(UNITS => VOLTS, UNIT_ARRAY =>
   VOLTAGE_ARRAY, COMPENSATE => VOLT_COMPENSATE);
```

Default values for any of the formal parameters could be declared, in accordance with the general syntax of Statement (5.1.3). In particular, a default value for the formal subprogram parameter COMPENSATE can be declared using the first choice of Statement (5.5), in which case the specification of generic procedure PROCESS_SENSOR_READINGS is modified as follows:

```
generic
   type UNITS is digits <>;
   type UNIT_ARRAY is array(INTEGER range <>) of UNITS;
   with procedure COMPENSATE(READING : in out
                               UNIT_ARRAY) is IDENTITY;
procedure PROCESS_SENSOR_READING(RAW_DATA : in UNIT_ARRAY;
                          SMOOTHED_DATA : out UNIT_ARRAY);
```

In this case, procedure name IDENTITY will be associated with the formal subprogram parameter COMPENSATE at instantiation, unless some other procedure name is provided as the appropriate actual parameter. Thus, the following two instantiations are equivalent:

```
procedure PROCESS_VOLTAGE_READINGS is new
   PROCESS_SENSOR_READING(VOLTS, VOLTAGE_ARRAY, IDENTITY);

      procedure PROCESS_VOLTAGE_READINGS is new
         PROCESS_SENSOR_READING(VOLTS, VOLTAGE_ARRAY);
```

since the actual parameter IDENTITY is provided as a default value in the second case.

If there is a subprogram named COMPENSATE visible at the point of instantiation, and if this subprogram can be matched to the formal subprogram parameter COMPENSATE, then subprogram COMPENSATE can be used as a default value by use of the second choice of Statement (5.5). The generic formal subprogram parameter declaration is then

```
with procedure COMPENSATE(READING : in out
                          UNIT_ARRAY) is <>;
```

In this event, the following two instantiations are equivalent:

```
procedure PROCESS_VOLTAGE_READINGS is new
   PROCESS_SENSOR_READING(VOLTS, VOLTAGE_ARRAY,
                          COMPENSATE);

procedure PROCESS_VOLTAGE_READINGS is new
   PROCESS_SENSOR_READING(VOLTS, VOLTAGE_ARRAY);
```

since procedure name COMPENSATE is provided as the default value.

Whenever default values are provided, by either of the two methods exemplified above, they are overridden if the corresponding actual parameter is provided at instantiation. It should also be noted that default values can be provided for formal object parameters of mode **in** as well, as implied by Statement (5.1.3).

As a final note, the reader should recognize the difference between the parameter list of the instantiation that produces the instance PROCESS_VOLTAGE_READINGS—which has the three formal parameters UNITS, UNIT_ARRAY, and COMPENSATE—and the parameter list of a call to procedure PROCESS_VOLTAGE_READINGS—which has two formal parameters RAW_DATA and SMOOTHED_DATA. That is, in contrast to the instantiations considered above, a call to procedure PROCESS_VOLTAGE_READINGS would take the form

```
PROCESS_VOLTAGE_READINGS(RAW_VOLTS, SMOOTHED_VOLTS);
```

using positional association, or

```
PROCESS_VOLTAGE_READINGS(RAW_DATA => RAW_VOLTS,
                         SMOOTHED_DATA => SMOOTHED_VOLTS);
```

using named association. The actual parameters RAW_VOLTS and SMOOTHED_VOLTS, of course, must be previously declared objects of type VOLTAGE_ARRAY.

EXAMPLE 2: The second example is an extension of the generic sort procedure discussed in Example 1 of Section 5.2.2. In that example, only integer arrays were required to be sorted. It is possible to sort arrays whose components are of any data type—even array types, record types, or access types—if the concept of ordering is defined. A generic sort subprogram that can be instantiated to sort arrays of any data type can be declared as

```
generic
   type COMP is private;
   type COMP_ARRAY is array(INTEGER range <>) of COMP;
   with function GTR_THN(LEFT, RIGHT : COMP)
                              return BOOLEAN;
procedure SORT(LIST : in out COMP_ARRAY);
```

Here, the generic formal type parameter COMP is declared in accordance with Statement (5.4.8), and it can therefore be matched with virtually any data type as the actual type parameter at instantiation. The generic formal type parameter COMP_ARRAY is declared in accordance with Statement (5.4.5) and can be matched with any one-dimensional unconstrained array type whose components are of the type associated, as an actual parameter, with formal parameter COMP, and whose index type is INTEGER. The generic formal subprogram parameter GTR_THN is a function that defines the order of the values of the type associated with formal parameter COMP. An instantiation of the generic procedure SORT that will provide a sort procedure for objects of integer array type HIT_ARRAY, from Section 5.2.2, would be

```
procedure HIT_SORT is new SORT(HIT_COUNT, HIT_ARRAY, ">");
```

In this case, the operator symbol ">" is actually the name of a predefined function that defines the ordering of values of an integer data type. The reader is referred to package STANDARD for examples of functions with this name. If named association were to be used, the instantiation would be

```
procedure HIT_SORT is new SORT(COMP => HIT_COUNT,
                 COMP_ARRAY => HIT_ARRAY, GTR_THN => ">");
```

Again, the reader should note the distinction between the parameter list of the instantiation—which contains the three generic formal parameters COMP, COMP_ARRAY, and GTR_THN—and that of the instantiated procedure HIT_SORT, which contains the single formal parameter LIST.

Because the generic formal type parameter COMP is declared as **private,** the associated actual parameter can be virtually any data type. Thus, if a user defines an ordering procedure for record objects of a certain type, for example, and implements a function that determines this defined order, he may then instantiate the generic procedure SORT to provide a procedure for sorting arrays with components of the record type. For example, if the following declarations are effected,

```
type REC_TYPE is
   record
      . . . . .
   end record;
REC_ARRAY is array(INTEGER range <>) of REC_TYPE;
function REC_ORDER(LEFT, RIGHT : REC_TYPE)
                         return BOOLEAN is
begin
      . . . . .
end REC_ORDER;
```

and function REC_ORDER contains the implementation for the ordering of records objects of type REC_TYPE, then the instantiation

```
procedure REC_SORT is new SORT(COMP => REC_TYPE,
   COMP_ARRAY => REC_ARRAY, GTR_THN => REC_ORDER);
```

will produce procedure REC_SORT, which will sort arrays of type REC_ARRAY, the components of which are records of type REC_TYPE. The sorting will be in the order defined by the implementation of function REC_ORDER. A call to this procedure might be

```
REC_SORT(REC_LIST);
```

where REC_LIST is a previously declared array object of type REC_ARRAY.

5.3 GENERIC SUBPROGRAMS

The previous discussion has considered the general concepts of generic units—generic subprograms and generic packages. The specification, body, and instantiation of a generic unit, in terms of those characteristics common to both generic subprograms and generic packages, were presented in Section 5.1. Several examples of specification and instantiation were presented in Section 5.2 as part of the discussion of generic formal parameters. In this section, specific attention is focused on the generic subprogram as a complete unit, consisting of both specification and body.

The presentation is centered around several complete examples, some of which are extensions of previous examples.

5.3.1 General Characteristics

There are certain general characteristics of generic subprograms that should be considered at this point in order to complete the formal discussion.

5.3.1.1 Generic Specification. Whereas subprograms in general need not have a specification part—because the specification is also contained within the body—but must have a body, generic subprograms must have both a specification and a body. The principal reason for this requirement is that the generic formal part of the declaration, as implied by Statement (5.1.1), is contained only in the generic specification. Since both the generic specification and the generic body are compilation units, they may be compiled separately from one another. In fact, as implied by the discussion of Section 3.11.2, they are separate compilation units even if submitted together for compilation. The specification must be compiled prior to compilation of the body. The specification and body of a generic subprogram may occur within the declarative part of the body of another program unit, in which case the specification must be elaborated prior to elaboration of the body.

The specification of a generic subprogram, including the formal generic part, usually contains occurrences of the generic formal parameters. Within instances of the generic subprogram—those subprograms created by instantiation of the generic subprogram—these occurrences denote the actual parameter associated with the formal parameter at instantiation.

5.3.1.2 Generic Body. The body of a generic subprogram forms the template from which the bodies of instantiated subprograms are obtained. Usually, these bodies contain occurrences of the generic formal parameters, and perhaps of the generic subprogram name itself. Within instances of the generic subprogram—that is, within those subprograms created by instantiation of the generic subprogram—these occurrences denote specific entities, as defined below:

- Generic formal object parameter—occurrence denotes the corresponding actual parameter. If the mode of the parameter is **in,** a copy of the actual parameter is made at instantiation and is constant within the instance. If the mode is **in out,** the actual parameter is denoted by the formal parameter.

- Generic formal type parameter—occurrence denotes the type specified by the actual parameter.
- Discriminant of a generic formal type parameter—occurrence denotes the corresponding discriminant of the type specified by the actual parameter.
- Generic formal subprogram parameter—occurrence denotes the subprogram specified by the actual parameter.
- Formal parameter of a generic formal subprogram parameter—occurrence denotes the corresponding formal parameter of the subprogram specified by the actual parameter.

In addition, the following interpretations apply:

- A local entity declared within the generic subprogram—occurrence denotes the entity declared by the local declaration.
- The generic subprogram itself—occurrence denotes the subprogram produced by the current instantiation; that is, the instance itself. Thus, the generic subprogram name can be used in recursive calls of the instance. By the same token, it cannot be used in a recursive instantiation.

The elaboration of a generic subprogram body has no effect other than to establish that the generic subprogram name can be used in an instantiation.

A generic subprogram body occurring within the declarative part of another program unit may be replaced with a body stub and then separately compiled as a subunit. The syntax for a body stub applied to a generic subprogram is

```
generic_subprogram_body_stub ::=
    generic_subprogram_specification is separate;     (5.6)
```

while that for a subunit is repeated here for convenience:

```
subunit ::=
    separate (parent_unit_name) proper_body.     (3.62)
```

The use of a body stub and the associated subunit is equivalent in every way to the use of a generic subprogram body declaration, as is discussed in Section 3.11.3.2.

5.3.1.3 Instantiation. The instantiation of a generic subprogram is a specification. It can occur in any subprogram or package declaration, or within the declarative part of a subprogram, package, or task body, or of a block statement. The elaboration of an instantiation results in the creation of an instance of the generic subprogram. Within this instance, parameter associations are as outlined in the previous section. An instantiation can also be a compilation unit, as implied by Statement (3.59.2), in which case compilation produces an instance of the generic subprogram as a library unit.

5.3.2 The Use of Generic Subprograms

The use of generic subprograms—and, perhaps even more so, of generic packages—can be a major factor in managing the complexity of large-scale programs. In addition, the entire concept of generic units makes even more attractive the idea of a software library of useful packages and subprograms, some of which can be generic, thus broadening the general area of application of library units.

There can be no doubt that the strong typing characteristic of the Ada language makes the provision of a generic facility almost a necessity, for even the simplest of subprograms may not be reusable unless they are made generic. The examples in this section illustrate how subprograms can be made into generic units, thus making them applicable to a broad range of data types. The first example below illustrates how something as simple as it is useful, a procedure to interchange the values of two objects, must be implemented as a generic unit if it is to be applicable to more than one data type.

Example 1: This example illustrates a very simple use of a generic subprogram, but one that nevertheless provides an important service. Quite often the need arises to interchange the values of two objects. Although this interchange can be done in place, using some previously defined object for temporary storage, if it occurs often enough it should be implemented as a subprogram. In most other languages this is easily done, but in the Ada language, because of the strong typing characteristic of the language, a subprogram would be applicable to only one data type. Since the Ada language also promotes the use of many declared data types, the subprogram providing the interchange operation must be generic. While this application of the generic facility of the Ada language is a simple one, it is nevertheless one that fully demonstrates the use of generic formal type parameters. A generic procedure EXCHANGE is declared, which simply exchanges the values of two objects provided as actual parameters:

```
generic
   type EX_TYPE is private;
procedure EXCHANGE(LEFT, RIGHT : in out EX_TYPE);

procedure EXCHANGE(LEFT, RIGHT : in out EX_TYPE) is
   TEMP : EX_TYPE;
begin
   TEMP  := LEFT;
   LEFT  := RIGHT;
   RIGHT := TEMP;
end EXCHANGE;
```

It should be noted that both the specification and the body are required, and that they are separately compiled if submitted as compilation units. Alternatively, the specification and body may appear in the declarative part of another program unit. Since the general formal type parameter EX_TYPE is declared as **private,** it can be associated with virtually any data type at instantiation. For example, if a program contains the following declarations

```
type PAGE_COUNT is INTEGER range 1..500;
type LINE_COUNT is INTEGER range 1..66;
type WEIGHT is new FLOAT;
type LOCATION is
   record
      PAGE : PAGE_COUNT;
      LINE : LINE_COUNT;
   end record;
type LOC_POINTER is access LOCATION;
type LOC_ARRAY is array(INTEGER range <>) of LOC_POINTER;
```

then instances of procedure EXCHANGE can be produced using each of these data types as the actual parameter. The instantiations are

```
procedure PAGE_EXCHANGE is new EXCHANGE(PAGE_COUNT);
--produces an instance with formal parameters LEFT and
  RIGHT of the integer type PAGE_COUNT. Positional
  association is used here.

procedure LINE_EXCHANGE is new EXCHANGE(EX_TYPE =>
                                        LINE_COUNT);
--produces an instance with formal parameters LEFT and
  RIGHT of the integer type LINE_COUNT. Named
  association is used.
```

```
procedure WT_EXCHANGE is new EXCHANGE(WEIGHT);
--produces an instance with formal parameters LEFT and
  RIGHT of the floating-point type WEIGHT.
  Positional association is used.

procedure LOC_EXCHANGE is new EXCHANGE(EX_TYPE =>
                              LOCATION);
--produces an instance with formal parameters LEFT and
  RIGHT of the record type LOCATION. Named
  association is used.

procedure PTR_EXCHANGE is new EXCHANGE(LOC_POINTER);
--produces an instance with formal parameters LEFT and
  RIGHT which are access types designating record objects
  of type LOCATION. Positional association is used.

procedure ARRAY_EXCHANGE is new EXCHANGE(LOC_ARRAY);
--produces an instance with formal parameters that are one-
  dimensional, unconstrained array types. The component
  type of the array is LOC_POINTER, an access type
  designating record objects of type LOCATION.
```

The purpose here is to illustrate the use of a generic formal type parameter that is declared as **private.** As indicated in Statement (5.4.8), this type of formal parameter can be associated at instantiation with virtually any data type.

EXAMPLE 2: In this example, a generic function is developed that can be instantiated to sum the elements of any one-dimensional array with components of a floating-point type. The specification is

```
generic
   type INDEX_TYPE is (<>);
   type COMP_TYPE is digits <>;
   type COMP_ARRAY is (INDEX_TYPE range <> )of COMP_TYPE;
function ARRAY_SUM(LIST : COMP_ARRAY) return COMP_TYPE;
```

In this case, the generic formal type parameter INDEX_TYPE can match any discrete type—integer or enumeration—while COMP_TYPE can match any floating-point type. These conclusions follow from Statements (5.4.1) and (5.4.3). Furthermore, operations on objects of type INDEX_TYPE are limited to those operations common to both integer and enumeration types. Type COMP_ARRAY can match any one-dimensional unconstrained array type that has elements of the type that is associated—

as an actual parameter—with formal parameter COMP_TYPE, and an index type that is the same as that associated with formal parameter INDEX_TYPE. The conclusions follow from Statement (5.4.5).

The generic body, which implements the operation implied by the specification, is given below:

```
function ARRAY_SUM(LIST : COMP_ARRAY) return COMP_TYPE is
   SUM : COMP_TYPE := 0.0;
begin
   for INDEX in LIST'RANGE loop
      SUM := SUM + LIST(INDEX);
   end loop;
   return SUM;
end ARRAY_SUM;
```

The attribute RANGE is used here because the generic formal type parameter COMP_ARRAY is an unconstrained array, and therefore the number of components may vary even from one call to another of the same instance. If a program has the declarations

```
type MASS_ARRAY is array (INTEGER range <>) of FLOAT:
type DELTA_TIME is array (INTEGER range <>) of FLOAT;
type DELTA_VEL  is array (INTEGER range <>) of FLOAT;
```

then the generic function ARRAY_SUM can be instantiated three times to produce instances—in this case, functions—that will sum elements of array objects of these three types. The instantiations are

```
function MASS_SUM is new ARRAY_SUM(INDEX_TYPE=>INTEGER,
           COMP_TYPE => FLOAT,COMP_ARRAY => MASS_ARRAY);
--uses named association

function TIME_SUM is new ARRAY_SUM(INTEGER, FLOAT,
                                   DELTA_TIME);
--uses positional association

function VEL_SUM is new ARRAY_SUM(INTEGER, FLOAT,
                                  DELTA_VEL);
--uses positional association
```

Once the functions MASS_SUM, TIME_SUM, and VEL_SUM have been produced—as instances of the generic function ARRAY_SUM—through the process of instantiation, they can be called in the same manner as can any function. For example, if a program has the object declaration

```
TIME_TO_GO_ARRAY : DELTA_TIME(1..20);
```

then the function call

```
TIME_SUM(TIME_TO_GO_ARRAY)
```

will return the value of the sum of the 20 array elements. It will be a result of type FLOAT.

Because of the flexibility of the declaration of the generic function ARRAY_SUM, it is not necessary to use the predefined type INTEGER as the array index, nor is it necessary to use the predefined type FLOAT as the type of the array component. For example, if a program contains the following declarations

```
type ACCEL_TYPE is (THRUST, DRAG, LIFT, CORIOLIS);
type ACCEL_VALUE is digits 8;
type ACCEL_ARRAY is array (ACCEL_TYPE range <>)
                          of ACCEL_VALUE;
```

then an instantiation of the generic function ARRAY_SUM might be

```
function ACCEL_SUM is new ARRAY_SUM(INDEX_TYPE =>
         ACCEL_TYPE, COMP_TYPE => ACCEL_VALUE,
         COMP_ARRAY => ACCEL_ARRAY);
```

The instance created by this instantiation—the function ACCEL_SUM—will return a value of type ACCEL_VALUE. This value will be the sum of the elements of the array object of type ACCEL_ARRAY that is provided as the actual parameter of the function call. For example, if the following array is declared

```
ATMOS_ACCEL : ACCEL_ARRAY(DRAG..LIFT);
```

then the function call

```
ACCEL_SUM(ATMOS_ACCEL)
```

will return a value of type ACCEL_VALUE that is obtained as the sum of the two components of array object ATMOS_ACCEL. Similarly, if the object declaration

```
TOTAL_ACCEL : ACCEL_ARRAY(THRUST..CORIOLIS);
```

is in effect, then the function call

```
ACCEL_SUM(TOTAL_ACCEL)
```

will return the sum of the component values of the four-component array object TOTAL_ACCEL.

EXAMPLE 3: This example expands on Example 1 of Section 5.2.2, in which three types were declared, together with the specification of a generic sort subprogram. The declarations are repeated below:

```
type HIT_COUNT        is range 0..1000;
type NEAR_MISS_COUNT is range 0..1000;
type MISS_COUNT       is range 0..1000;
type HIT_ARRAY  is array(1..100) of HIT_COUNT;
type NEAR_ARRAY is array(1..100) of NEAR_MISS_COUNT;
type MISS_ARRAY is array(1..100) of MISS_COUNT;
generic
   type COUNT is range <>
   type COUNT_ARRAY is array(1..100) of COUNT;
procedure SORT_COUNT(LIST : in out COUNT_ARRAY);
```

It should be noted here that the generic procedure specification can be compiled to produce the associated library unit, even before the generic body is written. In fact, the body of this generic sort procedure can be implemented using one of several sort algorithms. Because of the information-hiding features of the language, the specification, as well as its compilation into a library unit, is in no way affected by the particular algorithm used in the implementation. The simplest algorithm is the insertion sort, implemented by the following body:

```
procedure SORT_COUNT(LIST : in out COUNT_ARRAY) is
   procedure EX_COUNT is new EXCHANGE(EX_TYPE => COUNT);
begin
   for INDEX_1 in 1..100 loop
      for INDEX_2 in INDEX_1 + 1..100 loop
         if LIST(INDEX_1) > LIST(INDEX_2) then
                  EX_COUNT(LIST(INDEX_1), LIST(INDEX_2));
         end if;
      end loop;
   end loop;
end SORT_COUNT;
```

Here, procedure EX_COUNT is obtained by instantiation of the generic procedure EXCHANGE of the previous example and is called within the statement part of the procedure body. A context clause may be necessary to provide direct visibility of the generic procedure EXCHANGE, as explained in Section 3.11.3.1. Instantiation follows the examples given in Section 5.2.2. For example, the instantiation

```
procedure HIT_SORT is new SORT_COUNT(HIT_COUNT, HIT_ARRAY);
```

produces a procedure that will sort arrays of type HIT_ARRAY.

EXAMPLE 4: The flexibility of the generic sort procedure can be increased by changing the generic type parameter declaration of the array component to **private,** by using an unconstrained array parameter, and by using a subprogram parameter to define the ordering of components. Example 2 of Section 5.2.3 considered this case, with the following specification:

```
generic
   type COMP is private;
   type COMP_ARRAY is array (INTEGER range <>) of COMP;
   with function GTR_THN(LEFT, RIGHT : COMP) return BOOLEAN;
procedure SORT(LIST : in out COMP_ARRAY);
```

The corresponding body is given below.

```
   procedure SORT(LIST : in out COMP_ARRAY) is
      procedure EX_COMP is new EXCHANGE(EX_TYPE => COMP);
   begin
      for INDEX_1 in LIST'RANGE loop
         for INDEX_2 in INDEX_1 + 1..LIST'LAST loop
            if GTR_THN(LIST(INDEX_1), LIST(INDEX_2)then
                  EX_COMP(LIST(INDEX_1),LIST(INDEX_2);
            end if;
         end loop;
      end loop;
   end SORT;
```

This body differs from that of the previous example in two ways. The first difference involves the use of the generic formal subprogram parameter GTR_THN in place of the ">" operator. This modification is required because of the private type declaration of the generic formal parameter COMP. The second difference is the use of attributes LIST'RANGE and LIST'LAST in the loop parameter specifications. Use of these attributes is necessary because the generic formal parameter COMP_ARRAY is an unconstrained array, and therefore the index constraint is not known until instantiation time.

Instantiation follows the examples given in Example 2 of Section 5.2.3. For instance, given the declarations

```
HIT_COUNT is range 0..1000;
HIT_ARRAY is array(INTEGER range <>) of HIT_COUNT;
```

then the instantiation

```
procedure HIT_SORT is new SORT(HIT_COUNT, HIT_ARRAY, ">");
```

would produce an instance—the procedure HIT_SORT—that will sort array objects of type HIT_ARRAY. Similarly, if the record type REC_TYPE is declared,

```
type REC_TYPE is
    record
      . . . . .
    end record;
```

together with a function REC_ORDER, defining the ordering of objects of type REC_TYPE,

```
function REC_ORDER(LEFT, RIGHT : REC_TYPE)
begin                    return BOOLEAN is
  . . . . . .
end REC_ORDER;
```

then the instantiation

```
procedure REC_SORT is new SORT(COMP => REC_TYPE,
     COMP_ARRAY => REC_ARRAY, GTR_THN => REC_ORDER);
```

will produce an instance—in this case the procedure REC_SORT—that will sort array objects of type REC_ARRAY. These arrays have components that are records of type REC_TYPE. They are sorted in the order implemented by the function REC_ORDER.

EXAMPLE 5: To illustrate the manner in which Ada's modularity and information-hiding features enhance the modifiability of software, the relatively inefficient insertion sort of the previous example will be replaced with the more efficient quicksort algorithm. This modification can be made to involve only changes in the generic body, leaving the interface features of the generic specification unaltered. The revised body is

```
procedure SORT(LIST : in out COMP_ARRAY) is
   INDEX_1 : INTEGER := LIST'FIRST;
   INDEX_2 : INTEGER := LIST'LAST;
   TEMP    : COMP    := LIST((INDEX_1 + INDEX_2) / 2);
   procedure EX_COMP is new EXCHANGE(EX_TYPE => COMP);
begin
    while INDEX_1 <= INDEX_2 loop
       while GTR_THN(TEMP, LIST(INDEX_1)) loop
           INDEX_1 := INDEX_1 + 1
       end loop;
       while GTR_THN(LIST(INDEX_2), TEMP) loop
            INDEX_2 := INDEX_2 - 1;
       end loop;
       if INDEX_1 <= INDEX_2 then
           EX_COMP(LIST(INDEX_1), LIST(INDEX_2));
           INDEX_1 := INDEX_1 + 1;
           INDEX_2 := INDEX_2 - 1;
       end if;
    end loop;
    if LIST'FIRST < INDEX_2 then
        SORT(LIST(LIST'FIRST..INDEX_2));
    end if;
    if INDEX_1 < LIST'LAST then
        SORT(LIST(INDEX_1 .. LIST'LAST);
    end if;
end SORT;
```

This generic procedure body can be compiled to replace that of the previous example. Since the specification has not been altered, the interface to user programs remains unchanged.

Several features of the Ada language used in this example deserve comment:

- The quicksort algorithm partitions the array into two parts and then recursively calls itself to sort the partitions. The recursive call to SORT denotes the instance produced by the instantiation and not the generic unit SORT, as explained in Section 5.3.1.2.
- As in the previous example, generic procedure EXCHANGE is instantiated to provide the ordering algorithm for elements of type COMP.
- Initializing values are provided for local objects INDEX_1, INDEX_2, and TEMP. Two of these initializing values are obtained from attributes.

- Array slices are used as the actual parameters in the recursive calls to procedure SORT—or, more precisely, in calls to the current instance of generic procedure SORT. Array slices are discussed in Section 3.6.1.3.

Instantiation of generic procedure SORT in this case is precisely the same as in Example 4, since the generic specification remains unchanged.

5.4 GENERIC PACKAGES

The concept of generic packages has been considered in Sections 5.1 and 5.2, in terms of the general characteristics of generic units and generic formal parameters. In this section, specific attention is focused on the generic package as a complete unit, consisting of both specification and body. The presentation is centered around several complete examples, some of which are extensions of previous examples.

5.4.1 General Characteristics

There are certain general characteristics of generic packages that should be considered at this point in order to complete the formal discussion.

5.4.1.1 Generic Specification. As with a package, a generic package must have a specification and may have a corresponding generic body. The package that results from instantiation of a generic package can export declarations in the same manner as can any package. Those declarations that are to be exported must appear in the generic package specification, exclusive of the generic formal part, as indicated in Statement (5.1.1). Both generic specifications and generic bodies are compilation units, so they may be compiled separately from one another. In fact, as implied by the discussion of Section 3.11.3, the specification and body are separate compilation units even if submitted together for compilation, and the specification must be compiled before the body, if any, can be compiled. The specification and body of a generic package may be contained within the declarative part of the body of another program unit, in which case the specification must be elaborated prior to the elaboration of the body.

The specification of a generic package, including the formal generic part, will usually contain occurrences of the generic formal parameters. Within the specification of instances of the generic package—those packages created by instantiation of the generic package—these occurrences denote specific entities, as defined below:

- Generic formal object parameter—occurrence denotes the corresponding actual parameter. If the mode of the parameter is **in,** a copy of the actual parameter is made at instantiation and is constant within the instance. If the mode is **in out,** the actual parameter is denoted.
- Generic formal type parameter—occurrence denotes the type specified by the actual parameter.
- Discriminant of a generic formal type parameter—occurrence denotes the corresponding discriminant of the type specified by the actual parameter.
- Generic formal subprogram parameter—occurrence denotes the subprogram specified by the actual parameter.
- Formal parameter of a generic formal subprogram parameter—occurrence denotes the corresponding formal parameter of the subprogram specified by the actual parameter.

In addition, the following interpretations apply:

- An entity declared within the package specification, exclusive of the formal generic part—occurrence denotes the entity declared by the declaration. This entity is exported by the instance.
- A global entity visible within the specification—occurrence denotes the global entity.

As an example of some of these definitions, consider the following generic package specification:

```
generic
   type COMP_TYPE is private;
   type VECTOR_TYPE is array(POSITIVE range <>)
                                 of COMP_TYPE;
   with function SUM(LEFT, RIGHT : COMP_TYPE)
                         return COMP_TYPE;
package VECTOR_SUMS is
   function VECTOR_ADD(VECT_1, VECT_2 : VECTOR_TYPE)
                           return VECTOR_TYPE;
   function SUM_OF_COMP(VECT : VECTOR_TYPE)
                            return COMP_TYPE;
   DIMENSION_EXCEPTION : exception;
end VECTOR_SUMS;
```

The bodies of functions VECTOR_ADD and SUM_OF_COMP must be contained within the declarative part of the body of the generic package VECTOR_SUMS. They presumably will contain calls to the formal subprogram parameter SUM.

Furthermore, assume that the following declarations are visible:

```
type SIGNAL_DELAY is digits 10;
type DEL_ARRAY is array(INTEGER range <>) of SIGNAL_DELAY;
function DELAY_SUM(LEFT, RIGHT: DEL_ARRAY)
                   return SIGNAL_DELAY;
```

Then, the instantiation

```
package SIG_DEL_SUMS is new VECTOR_SUMS(COMP_TYPE
        => SIGNAL_DELAY, VECTOR_TYPE =>
        DEL_ARRAY, SUM => DELAY_SUM);
```

will create an instance of the generic package VECTOR_SUMS. This instance is a package with name SIG_DEL_SUMS, and it exports the functions

```
SIG_DEL_SUMS.VECTOR_ADD
SIG_DEL_SUMS.SUM_OF_COMP
```

and the exception

```
SIG_DEL_SUMS.DIMENSION_EXCEPTION
```

Within the instance, the occurrences of various names are interpreted as follows:

- Occurrences of the name COMP_TYPE denote the type SIGNAL_DELAY.
- Occurrences of the name VECTOR_TYPE denote the type DEL_ARRAY.
- Occurrences of the name SUM, or of the expanded name SIG_DEL_SUMS.SUM as exported by the instance, denote the function DELAY_SUM.
- Occurrences of the name VECTOR_ADD, or of the expanded name SIG_DEL_SUMS.VECTOR_ADD as exported by the instance, denote the function VECTOR_ADD, whose body must occur within the declarative part of the body of generic package VECTOR_SUMS.

- Occurrences of the name SUM_OF_COMP, or of the expanded name SIG_DEL_SUMS.SUM_OF_COMP as exported by the instance, denote the function SUM_OF_COMP, whose body must occur within the declarative part of the body of generic package VECTOR_SUMS.
- Occurrences of the name DIMENSION_EXCEPTION, or the expanded name SIG_DEL_SUMS.DIMENSION_EXCEPTION as exported by the instance, denote the exception DIMENSION_EXCEPTION.

The reader should note the distinction between function SUM and the functions SUM_OF_COMP and VECTOR_ADD. The latter are actually implemented within the package body, while the former is a formal parameter that is associated with a specific function—in the form of an actual subprogram parameter—for each instantiation.

Finally, it should be noted that the specification of a generic package can contain, in addition to subprogram declarations, the declarations of any other program unit. That is, it may contain the specification of a package, of a task, or even of a generic subprogram or generic package. In such a case, the corresponding program unit body must be contained within the declarative part of the generic package body.

5.4.1.2 Generic Body. The body of a generic package forms the template from which the bodies of instantiated packages are obtained. As with package bodies, the body of a generic package may contain, within its declarative part, the declaration of local entities. Entities declared within the body of the generic package are not exported by instances created by instantiation of the package. Also, as is the case with packages, the declarative part of a generic package body must contain the bodies of any program units whose declaration—that is, whose specification—appears in the generic package specification, exlusive of the generic formal part.

As with a package body, the body of a generic package may contain a sequence of statements, for which the syntax is given by Statement (3.45.2). Whereas the sequence of statements of a package body, if present, is executed at the time of elaboration of the package body, that of a generic package body is executed each time the generic package is instantiated.

The bodies of generic packages usually contain occurrences of the generic formal parameters. Within instances of the generic package—those packages created by instantiation of the generic package—these occurrences denote specific entities. In particular, the occurrences of the following names denote the same entities as when they occur in the generic package specification, as delineated in the previous section:

- generic formal object parameters
- generic formal type parameters
- general formal subprogram parameters
- formal parameters of a generic formal subprogram parameter
- an entity declared within the package specification, exclusive of the formal generic part

In addition, the following occurrences denote entities as indicated:

- A global entity visible within the body—occurrence denotes the global entity.
- A local entity declared within the declarative part of the package body—occurrence denotes the local entity.

Finally, since the name of the generic package denotes the current instantiation of the package, recursive instantiation is not permitted.

A generic package body occurring within the declarative part of another program unit may be replaced with a body stub and then separately compiled as a subunit. The syntax for a body stub applied to a generic package is

```
generic_package_body_stub ::=
   package body generic_package_simple_name is separate;
                                                          (5.7)
```

while that for a subunit is repeated here for convenience:

```
        subunit ::=
            separate (parent_unit_name) proper body.    (3.62)
```

The use of a body stub and the associated subunit is equivalent in every way to a generic package body declaration, as is discussed in Section 3.11.2.1. Further discussion is contained in Section 4.3.3.2.

5.4.1.3 Instantiation. The instantiation of a generic package is a declaration. It can occur within any subprogram or package declaration, or within the declarative part of a subprogram or package body, or of a block statement. The elaboration of an instantiation results in the creation of an instance of the generic package. Within this instance, parameter association is as outlined in the previous section. Instantiation is equivalent to the elaboration of both the specification and the body, and if the body has a sequence of statements as described by Statement (4.2), the sequence of statements of the instance is executed at instantiation time—in much the same manner that the sequence of statements of a package body is executed when the body is elaborated, as described in Section 4.2.2.

An instantiation can also be a compilation unit, as implied by Statement (3.59.2), in which case compilation produces an instance of the generic package as a library unit.

5.4.2 The Use of Generic Packages

The generic package combines two of the most unique features of the Ada language—the package and the generic unit. It is no surprise, then, that the generic package provides some of the most useful features of the language. This fact is amply illustrated by the input-output provisions of the language, which are discussed in Chapter 6. Because of the strong typing characteristic of the Ada language, input-output procedures and functions must be provided for the specific data type of every object involved in input-output operations. These input-output procedures are provided by instantiation of one of several generic input-output packages, which are listed in Appendix C.

In general, generic packages have application in the same three situations in which packages are useful, and which are discussed in Section 4.4: (1) encapsulation of declarations, (2) encapsulation of related subprograms, and (3) the creation of abstract data types. The generic feature broadens the usefulness of the package concept in one or more of several ways, including:

- reduced complexity of source code, because instantiations are single statements
- increased abstraction, since an instantiation is an abstraction of a package or subprogram
- reduced programming effort
- increased usefulness of library units

In this section, several examples of the use of generic packages are presented. Several of these examples are generic versions of packages developed in Chapter 4.

EXAMPLE 1: In Section 4.4.2, the package of Example 1 provides certain matrix operations to users of the package. While generality is maintained with respect to the dimension of the matrices by use of an unconstrained array, the use of the package is limited to arrays with components of type FLOAT. A generic version of this package can be formed by adding a generic formal part containing a formal type parameter used as the type of the array component. The package specification then becomes:

```
generic
   COMP_TYPE is digits <>;
package MATRIX_ARITH is
   type MATRIX is array(INTEGER range <>,
                        INTEGER range <>) of COMP_TYPE;
   procedure MATRIX_ADD(LEFT, RIGHT : in MATRIX;
                        RESULT : out MATRIX);
   procedure MATRIX_SUB(LEFT, RIGHT : in MATRIX;
                        RESULT : out MATRIX);
   procedure MATRIX_MUL(LEFT, RIGHT : in MATRIX;
                        RESULT : out MATRIX);
   MATRIX_ERROR : exception;
end MATRIX_ARITH;
```

The package body of Example 1 in Section 4.4.2 contains no reference to data type FLOAT, and therefore it can be used here without modification. After this generic package is compiled and resides in the program library, it can be instantiated by user program units for use with two-dimensional arrays having any floating-point type as the component type and type INTEGER as the index type. The same package, except with the generic formal part given as

```
generic
   COMP_TYPE is range <>;
```

could be instantiated for use with any two-dimensional integer array. Similarly, the package with generic formal part

```
generic
   COMP_TYPE is delta <>;
```

could be instantiated for use with any two-dimensional fixed-point array. The reader should note the ease with which the nongeneric package can be converted to a generic package. He should also note that the selection of the generic formal type parameters—types **digit** <>, **range** <>, and **delta** <> in this example—is restricted to those types that permit the operations performed on objects of the formal type in the package body.

EXAMPLE 2: A FIFO queue implementation was developed in Section 4.2.3 as an example of the use of a private data type. That example provides an illustration of the creation and use of an abstract data type. Use is limited, however, to queues of type CHARACTER. The usefulness of the package can be increased by converting it to a generic package. This conversion is accomplished by adding a generic formal part to the package specification and by making minor changes in the package body. The specification is

```
generic
   ELEM_TYPE is private;
package GENERAL_QUEUE is
   type QUEUE_TYPE is limited private;
   procedure RESET(QUEUE_NAME : in out QUEUE_TYPE);
   procedure PUT(ELEM : in ELEM_TYPE; QUEUE_NAME :
                 in out QUEUE_TYPE);
   procedure TAKE(ELEM : out ELEM_TYPE; QUEUE_NAME :
                  in out QUEUE_TYPE);
   function IS_EMPTY(QUEUE_NAME : in QUEUE_TYPE)
                     return BOOLEAN;
   UNDERFLOW : exception;
private
   type POSITION;
   type LINK is access POSITION;
   type POSITION is
      record
         VALUE : ELEM_TYPE;
         POINTER : LINK;
      end record;
   type QUEUE_TYPE is
      record
         FRONT : LINK;
         BACK  : LINK;
      end record;
end GENERAL_QUEUE;
```

The only changes in the specification are the addition of the generic formal part and the substitution of the generic formal parameter ELEM_TYPE for the type CHARACTER. The selection of a private type for the generic formal parameter is possible because examination of the body shows that only the assignment operation is required for objects of type ELEM_TYPE. The body is only slightly different from that of the previous example:

```
package body GENERAL_QUEUE is
   procedure RESET(QUEUE_NAME : in out QUEUE_TYPE) is
```

```
      begin
         QUEUE_NAME.FRONT := null;
         QUEUE_NAME.BACK  := null;
      end RESET;

      procedure PUT(ELEM : in ELEM_TYPE; QUEUE_NAME:
                     in out QUEUE_TYPE) is
         TEMP_POSIT : LINK;
      begin
         TEMP_POSIT := new POSITION;
         TEMP_POSIT.VALUE := ELEM;
         if QUEUE_NAME.FRONT /= null then
            QUEUE_NAME.BACK.POINTER := TEMP_POSIT;
            QUEUE_NAME.BACK := TEMP_POSIT;
         else
            QUEUE_NAME.FRONT := TEMP_POSIT;
            QUEUE_NAME.BACK := TEMP_POSIT;
         end if;
      end PUT;

      procedure TAKE(ELEM : out ELEM_TYPE; QUEUE_NAME:
                      in out QUEUE_TYPE) is
         TEMP_POSIT : LINK;
      begin
         if IS_EMPTY(QUEUE_NAME) then
           raise UNDERFLOW;
         end if;
         ELEM             := QUEUE_NAME.FRONT.VALUE;
         TEMP_POSIT       := QUEUE_NAME.FRONT.POINTER;
         QUEUE_NAME.FRONT := TEMP_POSIT;
      exception
         when UNDERFLOW =>
             raise;
      end TAKE;

      function IS_EMPTY(QUEUE_NAME : in QUEUE_TYPE)
                         return BOOLEAN is
      begin
         return QUEUE_NAME = null;
      end IS_EMPTY;
   end GENERAL_QUEUE;
```

Examination of the body indicates that objects denoted by the identifier ELEM, which are the only object of type ELEM_TYPE, are used only in assignment statements, thus justifying the use of the private generic formal type parameter. The use of the private type implies that the general formal type parameter ELEM_TYPE can be matched with an actual parameter of virtually any data type. Thus, the package GENERAL_QUEUE can be instantiated using something as simple as a scalar type, or it may be instantiated to produce a FIFO queue type for a data structure of any complexity. For example, the instantiation

```
package QUEUE_OF_CHAR is new GENERAL_QUEUE(CHARACTER);
```

produces the same result as the elaboration of the original package QUEUE_OF_CHAR in Section 4.2.3. On the other hand, if the declarations

```
type WAY_POINT is
   record
      LATT : FLOAT;
      LONG : FLOAT;
   end record;
type WAY_POINT_ARRAY is array(1..20) of WAY_POINT;
```

are in effect, then the instantiation

```
package WAY_PT_QUEUE is new GENERAL_QUEUE(WAY_POINT_ARRAY);
```

will produce, upon elaboration, the implementation of a FIFO queue type named WAY_PT_QUEUE.QUEUE_TYPE. Objects of this type can store objects of type WAY_PT_ARRAY, which are arrays of records.

EXAMPLE 3: In Section 4.4.3, a LIFO queue, or stack, is implemented by a package in Example 2. In that example, the stack was limited to storage of values of type character. A generic stack package can be declared that can be instantiated for virtually any data type, in a manner completely analogous to that used in the previous example. Examination of the package body indicates that the only operation required is that of assignment, so that a private generic formal type parameter can be used. The generic package specification is then

```
generic
   ELEM_TYPE is private;
package GENERAL_STACK is
   procedure PUSH(ELEM : in ELEM_TYPE);
   procedure PULL(ELEM : out ELEM_TYPE);
end GENERAL_STACK;
```

The package body is obtained by simply replacing the data type CHARACTER by the generic formal type parameter ELEM_TYPE:

```
package body GENERAL_STACK is
      SIZE          : constant := 1024;
      STACK_ARRAY : is array(1..SIZE) of ELEM_TYPE;
      POINTER       :NATURAL range 0..SIZE := 0;
   procedure PUSH(ELEM : in ELEM_TYPE) is
   begin
      POINTER := POINTER + 1;
      STACK_ARRAY(POINTER) := ELEM;
   end PUSH;

   procedure PULL(ELEM : out ELEM_TYPE) is
   begin
      ELEM := STACK_ARRAY(POINTER);
      POINTER := POINTER -1;
   end PULL;
end GENERAL_STACK;
```

Since the private generic formal type parameter can match any data type for which assignment and tests for equality and inequality are permitted, this package can be instantiated for virtually any data type.

In this example, the stack size is fixed at 1024. If it is desired to provide the stack size at instantiation, the object SIZE can be made a generic formal object parameter. The generic formal part of the specification would be changed as follows:

```
generic
   SIZE : NATURAL;
   type ELEM_TYPE is private;
```

The declaration of SIZE as a constant would be removed from the declarative part of the package body. An instantiation of the package must then contain both the size of the stack and the type of values to be stored. For example, the instantiation

```
package CHAR_STACK is new GENERAL_STACK(1024, CHARACTER);
```

would create an instance equivalent in every way to the 1024-character stack of Example 2 in Section 4.4.3.

The reader is again cautioned that these stack implementations do not have overflow and underflow protection. User-defined exceptions OVERFLOW and UNDERFLOW can be declared and then raised when the value of POINTER lies outside the index range of STACK_ARRAY. The exceptions can be handled locally or passed to the calling environment.

EXAMPLE 4: The previous example is a generic package that can be instantiated to produce an instance that encapsulates what might be termed an *abstract data object*. If it is desired to have a generic package that can be instantiated to provide an *abstract data type* that is a stack, then a generic version of the package of Example 3 of Section 4.4.3 is required. The generic package specification is given below:

```
     generic
        type ELEM_TYPE is private;
     package GENERAL_STACK_TYPE is
        type GEN_STACK is limited private;
        procedure PUSH(STACK_NAME : in out GEN_STACK;
                       ELEM : in ELEM_TYPE);
        procedure PULL(STACK_NAME : in out GEN_STACK;
                       ELEM : out ELEM_TYPE);
        private
        SIZE : constant :=1024;
        type GEN_STACK is
           record
              STACK_ARRAY : array(1..SIZE) of ELEM_TYPE;
              POINTER : NATURAL range 0..SIZE := 0;
           end record;
  end GENERAL_STACK_TYPE;
```

The only change made, other than the name changes to GENERAL_STACK_TYPE and GEN_STACK and the addition of the generic part, is the substitution of the generic formal parameter ELEM_TYPE for the type name CHARACTER. The package body also reflects this change, as indicated below:

```
package body GENERAL_STACK_TYPE is
   procedure PUSH(STACK_NAME : in out GEN_STACK;
                  ELEM : in ELEM_TYPE)is
   begin
      STACK_NAME_POINTER := STACK_NAME.POINTER + 1;
      STACK_NAME.STACK_ARRAY(STACK_NAME.POINTER) := ELEM;
   end PUSH;
   procedure PULL(STACK_NAME : in out GEN_STACK;
                  ELEM : out ELEM_TYPE)is
   begin
      ELEM := STACK_NAME.STACK_ARRAY(STACK_NAME.POINTER);
      STACK_NAME.POINTER := STACK_NAME.POINTER - 1;
   end PULL;
end GENERAL_STACK_TYPE;
```

An instantiation of this generic package produces an instance that exports the abstract data type GEN_STACK. Any number of objects of this type may then be declared. For example, suppose the following declaration is in effect:

```
type RANGE_MARKER is digits 6;
```

Then, the instantiation

```
package RANGE is new GENERAL_STACK_TYPE(RANGE_MARKER);
```

will create an instance RANGE that exports the abstract data type RANGE.GEN_STACK and the operations RANGE.PUSH and RANGE.PULL. Thus, if a user program contains the following declarations

```
RADAR_RANGE   : RANGE.GEN_STACK;
LASER_RANGE   : RANGE.GEN_STACK;
OPTICAL_RANGE : RANGE.GEN_STACK;
```

then each of these objects is an abstract data object that is a stack for values of type RANGE_MARKER. Operations available for each of these objects are

```
RANGE.PUSH
RANGE.PULL.
```

Of course, a use clause could be declared in order to make the data type and the operations above directly visible, so that the expanded name notation would not be required.

Again here, as in the previous example, the object SIZE can be made a generic parameter, in which case the generic formal part can be modified as indicated below:

```
generic
   SIZE : NATURAL := 1024;
   type ELEM_TYPE is private;
```

In this case, a default value has been provided.

Yet another approach to providing the size of the stack is through the use of a discriminant. The package specification is modified as follows:

```
generic
   type ELEM_TYPE is private;
package GENERAL_STACK_TYPE is
   type GEN_STACK(SIZE : NATURAL) limited private;
   procedure PUSH(STACK_NAME : in out GEN_STACK;
                  ELEM : in ELEM_TYPE);
```

```
    procedure PULL(STACK_NAME : in out GEN_STACK;
                   ELEM : out ELEM_TYPE);
  private
     type GEN_STACK(SIZE : NATURAL) is
        record
           STACK_ARRAY : array(1..SIZE) of ELEM_TYPE;
           POINTER : NATURAL range 0..SIZE := 0:
        end record;
end GENERAL_STACK_TYPE.
```

The discriminant SIZE is provided a value when an object of the abstract data type GEN_STACK is declared. That is, if the instantiation

```
package RANGE is new GENERAL_STACK_TYPE(RANGE_MARKER);
```

is elaborated, then the abstract data type RANGE.GEN_STACK has a discriminant. Thus, the object declaration

```
RADAR_RANGE : RANGE.GEN_STACK(2048);
```

provides the discriminant value of 2048. Positional association is used in this example, but named association could just as well be used.

Perhaps the distinction among the three ways in which the size of the stack is provided in this example should be reviewed:

- In the first case, SIZE is declared as a constant within the private part of the specification. It is fixed at 1024 for all instantiations and therefore for all objects declared of type GEN_STACK.
- In the second case, SIZE is a generic formal object parameter. Its value is provided as an actual parameter at instantiation. Although it is fixed for all objects declared to be of a type resulting from any given instantiation, it can vary from instantiation to instantiation.
- In the third case, SIZE is a discriminant. Its value is not provided until an object is declared, so that it may vary among objects of a type resulting from a single instantiation.

The reader should note that, in the first case, the size of the stack is hidden from the user.

EXAMPLE 5: Perhaps one of the best ways to illustrate the concept of an abstract data type is to relate it to a familiar data type. In Pascal, there is a data type named SET. A programmer may declare objects of type SET by naming the elements of the set. There are also certain operations provided for the type SET by the language. One can then ask the question, just what is a SET type? Ordinarily, this question cannot be answered because the implementation is hidden from the user. Or, even if it can be answered, the information thus obtained is of no consequence to the user, since he need know only the applicable set of operations. The fact is, the type SET is an abstraction of the actual implementation, and it represents a considerable reduction in the detail with which the user must be concerned. The Ada language does not have a SET type, but a generic package can be written to provide such a feature. This package would export an abstract data type analogous to the type SET in Pascal. The specification of such a package might be as follows:

```
generic
   type ELEM_TYPE is (<>);
package SET_TYPE is
   type SET is private;
   type SET_LITERAL is array(NATURAL range <>)
                                  of ELEM_TYPE:
   function ASSIGN(LIST : SET_LITERAL) return SET;
   function ELEM_SET(ELEM : ELEM_TYPE) return SET:
   function UNION(LEFT, RIGHT : SET) return SET:
   function INTERS(LEFT, RIGHT : SET) return SET;
   function DIFF(LEFT, RIGHT : SET) return SET;
   function SUBSET(LEFT, RIGHT : SET) return BOOLEAN;
   function PROP_SUBSET(LEFT, RIGHT : SET) return BOOLEAN;
   function SUPERSET(LEFT, RIGHT : SET) return BOOLEAN;
   function PROP_SUPERSET(LEFT, RIGHT : SET)
                               return BOOLEAN;
   function IS_IN(LEFT : ELEM_TYPE, RIGHT : SET)
                       return BOOLEAN;
   EMPTY_SET : constant SET;
   UNIVERSE  : constant SET;
   private
      type SET is array(ELEM_TYPE) of BOOLEAN;
      EMPTY_SET : constant SET := (others => FALSE);
      UNIVERSE  : constant SET := (others => TRUE);
   end SET_TYPE;
```

Thus, type SET is an abstract data type. The operations permitted are tests for equality and inequality, and those operations defined in the package specification:

- ASSIGN
- ELEM_SET
- UNION
- INTERS
- DIFF

and

- SUBSET
- PROP_SUBSET
- SUPERSET
- PROP_SUPERSET
- IS_IN

The second group actually represents relational operators, since they return a value of type BOOLEAN. These operations are equivalent to those of Pascal's SET data type. It should be noted that the visible part of the package specification contains all information that a user need know about type SET—it corresponds to the information that a Pascal compiler provides to its users, who are not privy to the manner in which the data type SET is actually implemented. The actual implementation—as an array with components of type BOOLEAN—is declared in the private part of the specification, together with the full declaration of the deferred-constant declaration of constants EMPTY_SET and UNIVERSE. Within the package body, objects of type SET can be treated as boolean arrays. The index type of the array is the discrete type whose list of possible values constitute the universe of the set. The components have values of TRUE or FALSE depending upon whether or not a particular element is in the set. For example, if the declaration

```
type MICRO is (M68000, Z8000, I80286, MS1750A);
```

is used to define the universe of a set, then the set will be represented by a four-element boolean array, with index values M68000, Z8000, I80286, and MS1750A. A set object containing the values M68000 and I80286 would be represented by an array with component values of TRUE, FALSE, TRUE, FALSE, as shown in Figure 5.4. The body of the package must implement the operations contained in the visible part of the package specification, in terms of this boolean array representation.

Index	M68000	Z8000	I80286	MS1750A
Component	TRUE	FALSE	TRUE	FALSE

Figure 5.4. Boolean array representation of a set.

The package body might take the form shown below:

```
package body SET_TYPE is
   function ASSIGN(LIST : SET_LITERAL) return SET is
      VALUE : SET := EMPTY_SET;
```

```
begin
   for INDEX in LIST'RANGE loop
      VALUE(LIST(INDEX)):= TRUE;
   end loop;
   return VALUE;
end ASSIGN;

function ELEM_SET(ELEM : ELEM_TYPE) return SET is
begin
    return SET(ELEM => TRUE, others => FALSE);
end ELEM_SET;

function UNION(LEFT, RIGHT : SET) return SET is
begin
    return LEFT or RIGHT;
end UNION;

function INTERS(LEFT, RIGHT) return SET is
begin
    return LEFT and RIGHT;
end INTERS;

function DIFF(LEFT, RIGHT : SET) return SET is
begin
    return LEFT and (not RIGHT);
end DIFF;

function SUBSET(LEFT, RIGHT : SET) return BOOLEAN is
begin
    return (LEFT and RIGHT) = LEFT;
end SUBSET;

function PROP_SUBSET(LEFT, RIGHT : SET)
                        return BOOLEAN is
begin
    return ((LEFT and RIGHT ) = LEFT) and
             (LEFT /= RIGHT);
end PROP_SUBSET;

function SUPERSET(LEFT, RIGHT : SET) return BOOLEAN is
begin
    return (LEFT and RIGHT ) = RIGHT;
end SUPERSET;

function PROP_SUPERSET(LEFT, RIGHT : SET)
                          return BOOLEAN is
```

```
    begin
        return ((LEFT and RIGHT )= RIGHT)
                 and (LEFT /= RIGHT);
    end PROP_SUPERSET;

    function IS_IN(LEFT : ELEM_TYPE, RIGHT : SET)
        return BOOLEAN is
    begin
        return RIGHT(LEFT);
    end IS_IN;
end SET_TYPE;
```

This generic package permits the data type SET to be used in much the same manner as Pascal's type SET. The generic package must be instantiated using a discrete data type as the generic actual parameter. The set of values associated with the discrete type becomes the universe of the set. For example, using the type MICRO as previously declared, the instantiation

```
MICRO_SET is new SET_TYPE(ELEM_TYPE => MICRO);
```

creates the instance MICRO_SET of the generic package SET_TYPE. The package MICRO_SET implements an abstract data type MICRO_SET.SET, which, for all practical purposes, is a set with the universe

```
(M68000, Z8000, I80286, MS1750A)
```

Then, the operations contained in the package can be used to manipulate objects of this type. In particular, the ASSIGN function can be used to assign values to a set, and ELEM_SET can form a set with a single element. The remaining operations are equivalent to those provided by Pascal's SET type.

Even closer similarity to Pascal's SET type can be achieved by using overloaded operator symbols for the function names. Specifically, if the symbols are subsituted as indicated below, then they have the same meaning as in Pascal:

```
UNION   "+"     PROP_SUBSET    "<"
INTERS  "*"     SUPERSET       ">="
DIFF    "-"     PROP_SUPERSET  ">"
SUBSET  "<="
```

Since assignment and tests for equality and inequality are provided for private data types, the additional operators

```
:=, =, and /=
```

are also available for objects of type MICRO_SET.SET. The concept of overloading is discussed further in Chapter 8.

One could easily make the argument that the equivalent of a set type can be achieved in the Ada language without the use of an abstract data type. This is certainly true, since boolean arrays can be declared to represent the set objects. Operations on and among the arrays—similar to operations contained within generic package SET_TYPE above—could then be used to implement set operations. The difficulty with this approach is that the integrity of the arrays as set objects is not protected. That is, accidental or intentional modification of the boolean arrays, out of context of their character as set objects, is possible. With an abstract data type representation, the set character of the arrays is protected.

EXAMPLE 6: Linked lists represent a commonly used data structure. While the Ada language, like many other languages, permits the development of linked lists with rather complex structures, it also can provide a generic linked-list package that can be instantiated for virtually any data type. Since each node of a linked list contains a data item and a link to the next node, the generic package can be obtained by making the type of the data item a generic formal type parameter. The specification of such a package might be as follows:

```
generic
   type DATA_TYPE is private;
package LINKED_LIST_TYPE is
   type LINKED_LIST is private;
   type LIST_PTR is access LINKED_LIST;
   type DATA_ARRAY is array(NATURAL range <>)
                            of DATA_TYPE;
   function VALUE(LIST : LIST_PTR) return DATA_TYPE;
   function REMAINDER(LIST : LIST_PTR) return LIST_PTR;
   function APPEND(ELEM : DATA_TYPE; LIST : LIST_PTR)
                  return LIST_PTR;
   function FORM_LIST(DATA : DATA_ARRAY) return LIST_PTR;
private
   type LINKED_LIST is
      record
         DATA : DATA_TYPE;
         LINK : LIST_PTR;
      end record;
end LINKED_LIST_TYPE;
```

This package specification implies that type LINKED_LIST is an abstract data type—its structure is hidden from the user of the package. The operations declared in the visible part of the specification are those required for building and maintaining linked lists of objects of type LINKED_LIST, as indicated below:

- Function FORM_LIST will form a linked list from the data stored in the formal array parameter DATA. The returned value is of an access type, LIST_PTR, and it designates the first node of the resulting linked list.
- Function VALUE accepts an access type object, LIST, as a formal parameter, and then returns the value of the data stored in the object designated by the formal parameter. This is the data stored in the first node of a linked list designated by the formal parameter.
- Function REMAINDER accepts an access type object, LIST, as a formal parameter, and returns another access object that designates the second node in the linked list designated by the formal parameter.
- Function APPEND accepts a data object, ELEM, as a formal parameter, together with an access type designating a linked list. It returns an access object that designates a linked list formed by inserting the formal parameter ELEM at the top of the linked list designated by the second formal parameter.

Thus, the two functions VALUE and REMAINDER can be used to browse the list. Function APPEND can be used to add to the top of the list, and function FORM_LIST can be used to initialize a list. Other functions could be added; perhaps functions to delete or to insert nodes could be added, thus providing for list maintenance. Since the package is generic, it can be instantiated for virtually any data type. The only limitation on parameter association is that the data type of the actual parameter match the generic formal type parameter DATA_TYPE, which is a private type. Thus, the requirement is only that the operations of assignment and tests for equality and inequality be associated with the type.

The body of this generic package must contain the bodies of functions VALUE, REMAINDER, APPEND, and FORM_LIST. The only restriction is that no operations other than assignment and tests for equality and inequality be used on objects of type DATA_TYPE within the package. This restriction, of course, is imposed by the declaration of the generic formal type parameter DATA_TYPE as **private** in the formal generic part of the package specification. An implementation of the package body might be

```
package body LINKED_LIST_TYPE is
   function VALUE(LIST : LIST_PTR) return DATA_TYPE is
```

```
   begin
      return LIST.DATA;
   end VALUE;

   function REMAINDER(LIST : LIST_PTR) return LIST_PTR is
   begin
      return LIST.LINK;
   end REMAINDER;

   function APPEND(ELEM : DATA_TYPE; LIST : LIST_PTR)
                        return LIST_PTR is
   begin
      return new LINKED_LIST(ELEM, LIST);
   end APPEND;

   function FORM_LIST(DATA : DATA_ARRAY) return LIST_PTR is
      POINTER : LIST_PTR;
   begin
      for INDEX in reverse DATA'RANGE loop
          POINTER := APPEND(DATA(INDEX), POINTER);
      end loop;
      return POINTER;
   end FORM_LIST;
end LINKED_LIST_TYPE;
```

In function APPEND, the allocator assigns initial values to the designated objects, in accordance with the discussion of Section 3.6.3.1. In function FORM_LIST, the for loop simply starts a linked list from the last node and then builds the list using the components of the formal array parameter DATA. It returns an access value, under the function name FORM_LIST, that designates the first node in the resulting list.

To illustrate how this abstract data type functions, assume that the following declarations are in effect:

```
package CHAR_LIST is new LINKED_LIST_TYPE(CHARACTER);
POINTER : CHAR_LIST.NODE_PTR;
```

Then the statement

```
POINTER := CHAR_LIST.FORM_LIST(('A', 'B', 'C', 'D', 'E'));
```

will cause the building of a list of nodes whose DATA component is of type character. The value of the DATA component of the first node is ‘A’, the second, ‘B’, and so on. The access object POINTER designates the first node. The statement

```
POINTER := CHAR_LIST.APPEND('F', POINTER);
```

will append another node, with the DATA component value of 'F', to the first node. The access value POINTER will designate this new node, which now becomes the top node.

EXERCISES

1. Relate the strong typing feature of the Ada language to its generic facilities.
2. Describe what is meant by the "parameterization of a subprogram or package."
3. Must a generic subprogram always have both a specification and a body?
4. Must a generic package always have both a specification and a body?
5. Discuss the use of a generic type parameter.
6. Discuss the use of a generic object parameter.
7. Discuss the use of a generic subprogram parameter.
8. Distinguish between the generic formal parameters of a generic subprogram and the formal parameters of the subprogram.
9. Distinguish between the generic actual parameters of a generic subprogram and the actual parameters of a call to an instantiation of the subprogram.
10. What is meant by the "matching" of generic formal and actual type parameters?
11. What modes can generic formal parameters have?
12. Discuss the concept of a generic subprogram parameter. Does the formal subprogram parameter have a body?
13. What actual parameters can be matched to a formal generic type parameter that is private? What operations are permitted on objects of the formal parameter type?
14. What actual parameters an be matched to a formal generic type parameter that is (<>)? What operations are permitted on objects of the formal parameter type?
15. What actual parameters can be matched to a formal generic type parameter that is digits <>? What operations are permitted on objects of the formal parameter type?
16. Must a generic unit have generic formal parameters? Explain.
17. In what parts of an Ada program can an instantiation occur?
18. Are the specification and body of a generic unit separately compilable?
19. Can the body of a generic unit be replaced with a body stub, and then the proper body compiled as a subunit?
20. Can an instantiation of a generic unit be separately compiled? If so, what is the effect?
21. Discuss how Ada's generic units can provide the capability of generating reusable software.
22. List the generic units declared in the predefined environment.
23. Any number of instances of a generic unit can be created. What is the relationship among these instances?

24. A generic unit may reside in the program library as a library unit, or it may be declared in the declarative part of another program unit. Discuss the differences between these two cases.
25. What is the relationship between the context clause of a program unit and any instantiations of generic library units that may occur within the program unit?

PROGRAMMING EXERCISES

These programming exercises may require use of input-output support from package TEXT_IO. The reader is referred to Section 6.2.2 for details.

1. Compile the generic package COUNT of Example 3, Section 5.2.1. Write and compile a main program (procedure) that declares three instantiations of COUNT. The three counters thus produced should be exercised by the main program.
2. Compile the generic procedure EXCHANGE of Example 1, Section 5.3.2. Write and compile a main program (procedure) that instantiates EXCHANGE for an integer type, for an array type, and for a record type. The main program should exercise the instantiated procedures in each of the three cases.
3. Compile the generic function ARRAY_SUM of Example 2, Section 5.3.2. Write and compile a main program (procedure) that instantiates ARRAY_SUM for two integer and for two floating-point types. The main program should exercise the instantiated functions in each of the four cases.
4. Compile the generic procedure SORT_COUNT of Example 3, Section 5.3.2. Write and compile a main program (procedure) that instantiates SORT_COUNT for two different integer types, one of which is the predefined type INTEGER. The main program should call the instantiated procedures to sort an array of each type.
5. Compile the generic procedure SORT of Example 4, Section 5.3.2. Write and compile a main program (procedure) that instantiates SORT for a record type with the following declaration:

```
type TEST_RECORD is
   record
        REC_NO  : NATURAL;
        CONTENT : STRING (1..10);
   end record;
```

The records are to be sorted in ascending order of REC_NO components. Note that a function must also be declared that determines the ordering of records of type TEST_RECORD. The main program should call procedure SORT.

6. Repeat Exercise 5, only now substitute the body of Example 5, Section 5.3.2, for that of SORT in Example 4.
7. Compile the generic package GENERAL_QUEUE of Example 2, Section 5.4.2. Write and compile a main program (procedure) that instantiates GENERAL_QUEUE for three data types—a record, an array, and an array of records. The main program should declare two objects of each queue type exported by the instantiations, and it should exercise the resulting FIFO queue objects.
8. Compile the generic package GENERAL_STACK of Example 3, Section 5.4.2. Write and compile a main program (procedure) that instantiates GENERAL_STACK for three data types—a record, an array, and an array of records. The main program should exercise the three stacks implemented by the three instantiations.
9. Repeat Exercise 8, but now use the version of Example 3 that establishes the stack size at instantiation through the use of generic formal parameter SIZE.
10. Compile the generic package GENERAL_STACK_TYPE of Example 4, Section 5.4.2. Write and compile a main program (procedure) that instantiates GENERAL_STACK_TYPE for three data types—a record, an array, and an array of records. The main program should declare two objects of each stack type exported by the instantiations, and it should exercise the resulting stack objects.
11. Repeat Exercise 10, but now use the version of Example 4 that establishes the stack size at instantiation through the use of the generic formal parameter SIZE.
12. Repeat Exercise 10, but now use the version of Example 4 that establishes the stack size through the use of a discriminant.
13. Compile the generic package SET_TYPE of Example 5, Section 5.4.2. Write and compile a main program (procedure) that instantiates SET_TYPE for two enumeration types. The main program should declare at least two objects of each set type, and it should exercise the operations exported by the package.
14. Compile the package LINKED_LIST_TYPE of Example 6, Section 5.4.2. Write and compile a main program (procedure) that instantiates LINKED_LIST_TYPE for three data types—a record, an array, and an array of records. The main program should declare two objects of each linked-list type exported by the instantiations, and it should exercise the resulting linked-list objects.
15. Modify the package LINKED_LIST_TYPE by providing two functions—INSERT and DELETE—so that values can be inserted into the list or deleted from the list at arbitrary locations.

Chapter 6
INPUT-OUTPUT PROVISIONS

6.1 GENERAL CONCEPTS

The Ada language design considers input-output from two points of view. From the *host computer* viewpoint, a language must provide a set of facilities for using common devices such as terminals, printers, direct-access disk devices, and other peripherals commonly found in the software development environment. These devices are user-oriented, and the language facilities that support them should be hardware-independent. These are the so-called high-level input-output facilities, and the user orientation is often costly in terms of machine resources and/or execution time. From the *target computer* view point, however, the input-output requirement may be vastly different. Often, in the target environment input-output occurs at a primitive level, thus leading to the application of the term *low-level* input-output. In addition, the devices themselves are often devoted to some special-purpose activity, such as reading instruments or commanding actuator positions. Since the target environment may be critical with regard to machine resources and execution time, Ada target software usually cannot afford the added burden of high-level input-output support facilities that are not actually required in the target environment. Yet, these same high-level features are essential to host environment software.

To accommodate these diverse requirements for input-output facilities, the Ada language design uses a rather unique approach. The language itself is devoid of any input-output provisions; however, sufficient facilities are provided by two predefined packages

```
TEXT_IO
LOW_LEVEL_IO,
```

and two predefined generic packages

```
SEQUENTIAL_IO
DIRECT_IO
```

This arrangement permits the programmer to include only those input-output facilities needed for the particular application. In this manner, a wide-ranging capability can be provided in the host environment, while target system software can be limited to only those facilities necessary for functionality.

This particular kind of input-output support is rather functional from another aspect—the generic facilities permit instantiation of input-output packages for user-defined data types. With this feature, the Ada language can maintain its strict typing rules even in input-output subprogram calls. That is, the programmer can feel free to take advantage of the benefits of the use of user-defined data types, since he can usually instantiate predefined packages that will provide input-output facilities for objects of the user-defined types. This concept will become clear as some of the generic input-output facilities are discussed in detail.

The use of packages and generic packages to provide the input-output facilities of the language is one of the best examples of the abstraction afforded by the package concept. The package specifications given in Appendix C—SEQUENTIAL_IO, DIRECT_IO, TEXT_IO, and LOW_LEVEL_IO—are common to every Ada compiler. Since all interaction between an Ada program and these packages is through the package specifications, such interaction is standard from one Ada environment to another. This fact further enhances the portability of software. On the other hand, the actual implementation of the input-output functions and procedures are machine-dependent, and hence may vary from implementation to implementation. For this reason, the bodies of packages such as SEQUENTIAL_IO and DIRECT_IO are not specified in the standard language environment. The net result is that there is a single set of package specifications that is common to any implementation of the language. The bodies of these packages, however, will be implementation-dependent.

Input-output operations may produce exceptional conditions, in which case input-output exceptions are raised. These exceptions are declared in the predefined language environment as indicated in Appendix C. They are declared in package IO_EXCEPTIONS. Since this package consists only of a specification and no body, the entire package can be presented below:

```
package IO_EXCEPTIONS is
       NAME_ERROR   : exception;
       USE_ERROR    : exception;
       STATUS_ERROR : exception;
       MODE_ERROR   : exception;
       DEVICE_ERROR : exception;
```

```
            END_ERROR    : exception;
            DATA_ERROR   : exception;
            LAYOUT_ERROR : exception;
      end IO_EXCEPTIONS;
```

These exceptions will be discussed in the context of their use as various input-output operations are considered.

6.2 HIGH-LEVEL INPUT-OUTPUT

Input-output that is conducted at a high level of abstraction—and thus is user-oriented—is termed high-level input-output. The high-level facilities in Ada can be divided into two general areas: binary input-output and text input-output. The former refers to those input-output operations that involve data in binary form—the same form in which it is represented at the machine level. The latter concerns input-output of data in human readable form. All high-level input-output in an Ada program, whether in binary or text form, depends on the concept of a file—a sequence of data values of a common type. There are two file concepts in the Ada language: external file and internal file. All values that are read from the external environment, or are written to the external environment, are considered to occupy an external file. An external file may be a direct-access disk device, a magnetic tape, a keyboard, a terminal screen, a printer, or any other peripheral. It may also be an analog-to-digital converter, a digital-to-analog converter, a shaft encoder, or a myriad of other sensing or activating devices. Thus, an external file is a physical file, in the sense that it represents data in some physical form. External files are identified by a name, and they have a property called the *form* of the file. The form is a string that provides implementation-dependent characteristics that the file might have, such as access rights, file organization, and disposition features, among others.

An internal file, on the other hand, is a logical representation of a physical external file. It is an object that is declared to be of a specific file type. High-level input-output in the Ada language is always expressed as operations—that is, as functions or procedures—involving internal-file objects. An association between an internal-file object and an external file must be established; once this association is established, input-output operations involving the external file will be effected through this linking of internal- and external-file names.

In general, the steps necessary to provide input-output operations in an Ada program are as follows:

1. A file object must be declared of the appropriate file type. This is

the internal file, and it is denoted by an identifier called the internal-file name.

2. This file object is then associated with an external file. If the internal-file object is to be associated with a new external file—one that does not already exist, as, for example, on a direct-access disk device—then this process is called *creating* the file. If the internal-file object is to be associated with an existing external file—as, for example, with a printer or with an existing file on a direct-access disk device—then this process is called *opening* the file.
3. The input-output operations are performed on the internal-file object. The operations physically affect the associated external file. That is, writing to the internal-file object will cause data to be written to the external file. Likewise, reading from the internal-file object will cause data to be read from the external file.
4. When input-output operations are terminated, the association between the internal-file object and the external file is broken. This is called *closing* the file.

Once closed, the internal-file object may be opened again and associated with the same external file or with some other external file.

The details of high-level input-output operations vary slightly depending upon whether binary or text files are involved.

6.2.1 Input-Output of Binary Files

Binary files are those files that contain data in a binary representation, that is, in the same form as it is used by the hardware. Thus, a binary file is not in human readable form because it does not consist of character data. Binary files are used when the information need only be readable by the machine. In Ada's predefined environment, two kinds of binary files are supported:

1. sequential-access files, in which the data is represented by a sequence of values that can only be accessed in the order of their appearance
2. direct-access files, in which data is also represented by a sequence of values, but in which any data item can be accessed directly with no need for sequencing through preceding values

Sequential-access files are usually used for storing of programs or of textual material, or in any other situation in which an entire file is usually read or written in one operation. Sequential files are also used for data which is to be accessed in a sequential fashion but which is not necessarily to be read or written in a single operation. Support for sequential access files is provided by the predefined generic package SEQUENTIAL_IO, the specification of which appears in Appendix C.

Direct-access files are used when it is necessary to access components of the file in some order that is other than sequential, or perhaps in some order that is random. Support for direct-access files is provided by the generic package DIRECT_IO. The specification of the package DIRECT_IO is also given in Appendix C.

An open file has a characteristic known as the *mode* of the file. For sequential-access files, the mode is a value of an enumeration type declared in the generic package SEQUENTIAL_IO:

```
type FILE_MODE is (IN_FILE, OUT_FILE);
```

Direct-access file modes are of a type declared in the generic package DIRECT_IO:

```
type FILE_MODE is (IN_FILE, INOUT_FILE, OUT_FILE);
```

These file modes have the following interpretations:

```
IN_FILE     -- the file is a read-only file, it cannot be
               written to
OUT_FILE    -- the file is a write-only file, it cannot be
               read
INOUT_FILE  -- the file can be read and written to
```

The mode of a file is established when the file is created or opened. Thus, a file mode can be changed by closing the file and then opening it with a different mode, or by resetting the file and specifying a different mode.

6.2.1.1 Sequential-Access Files. All input-output operations involving sequential-access files are declared in the generic package SEQUENTIAL_IO. The generic formal part of SEQUENTIAL_IO is

```
generic
    type ELEMENT_TYPE is private;
```

implying that the generic formal parameter ELEMENT_TYPE can be matched to any actual parameter for which the operations of assignment and tests for equality and inequality are defined. Thus, it can be matched to virtually any Ada data type, no matter how complex the structure.

The only exception is that the effect of input-output of access types is implementation-dependent.

The specification of SEQUENTIAL_IO also contains the declarations

```
type FILE_TYPE is limited private;
type FILE_MODE is (IN_FILE, OUT_FILE);
```

FILE_TYPE and FILE_MODE are types exported by any instance of the generic package SEQUENTIAL_IO. Different instances, of course, declare different types FILE_TYPE and FILE_MODE. A program unit using an instance of SEQUENTIAL_IO will normally declare one or more internal-file objects of the type FILE_TYPE. These internal-file objects are then associated with external files when the internal-file objects are created or opened, as outlined in Section 6.2.

Input-output operations on sequential-access files are provided by those procedures and functions declared in the specification of generic package SEQUENTIAL_IO. They are given here together with some explanatory remarks.

```
procedure CREATE(FILE : in out FILE_TYPE;
                 MODE : in FILE_MODE := OUT_FILE;
                 NAME : in STRING := "";
                 FORM : in STRING := "");
--This procedure opens the internal-file object associated
  with the formal parameter FILE and associates it with a
  newly created external file with the name and form as
  given by the actual parameters associated with formal
  parameters NAME and FORM. A null string associated with
  the formal parameter NAME implies a temporary file--one
  that will not be retained on the external device when
  the file is closed. A null string associated with the
  formal parameter FORM permits the implementation to use
  its default value. The mode of the file is that value
  associated with the formal parameter MODE, which
  defaults to OUT_FILE. Exceptions that may be raised are

      STATUS_ERROR -- if the file is already open
      NAME_ERROR   -- if the external-file name is
                      not permitted
      USE_ERROR    -- if the implementation does not
                      support creation of an external
                      file with the specified
                      name and form
```

Before proceeding with a discussion of the remaining operations, it may be wise to pause and consider the relationship among the generic package SEQUENTIAL_IO, an instance of that generic package, and the data types and operations resulting from that instance. Since the package SEQUENTIAL_IO is a generic unit, an instance must be created by instantiation before any of its facilities can be used. For example, if the following declaration is in effect,

```
type HIT_COUNT is range 0..100;
```

and if it is desired to create an external sequential-access file named HIT_FILE into which objects of type HIT_COUNT can be stored, the following steps are required. These steps assume that the generic package SEQUENTIAL_IO is visible, through the use of a WITH clause.

1. An instance must be created by instantiation of the generic package SEQUENTIAL_IO with HIT_COUNT as the actual generic parameter:

   ```
   package HIT_IO is new SEQUENTIAL_IO(HIT_COUNT);
   ```

2. An internal-file object must be declared:

   ```
   HIT_LIST : HIT_IO.FILE_TYPE;
   ```

3. The internal-file object HIT_LIST must be associated with the external file name HIT_FILE. In this case, since HIT_FILE does not already exist on the external device, the create procedure is used.

   ```
   HIT_IO.CREATE(HIT_LIST, OUT_FILE, "HIT_FILE");
   ```

   In this case, the form defaults to the default option of the implementation. There are, of course, several different versions of this procedure call. For example,

   ```
   HIT_IO.CREATE(FILE => HIT_LIST, NAME => "HIT_FILE");
   ```

   uses named association and the default option OUT_FILE for the parameter MODE. The form defaults to the default option of the implementation.

At this point, the internal-file object is open and subject to any operations available for sequential-access files. Note that these operations are imported from the package HIT_IO, the instance of the generic package

SEQUENTIAL_IO. If the instantiation is followed by the use clause

```
use HIT_IO;
```

then the expanded names are not required.

Because the generic formal parameter ELEMENT_TYPE—declared in the generic formal part of the specification of SEQUENTIAL_IO—is declared as **private,** virtually any data type can be matched to ELEMENT_TYPE as the actual generic parameter. For example, if the following declarations are in effect,

```
type VECTOR is array(1..3) of FLOAT;
type STATE_VECTOR is
    record
        POSITION : VECTOR;
        VELOCITY : VECTOR;
    end record
type STATE_ARRAY is array (POSITIVE range <>)
                           of STATE_VECTOR;
```

then the instantiation

```
package STATE_IO is new SEQUENTIAL_IO(STATE_ARRAY);
```

creates an instance of SEQUENTIAL_IO that provides input-output capability for objects of type STATE_ARRAY. That is, the declaration

```
STATE_LIST : STATE_IO.FILE_TYPE;
```

and the procedure call

```
STATE_IO.CREATE(STATE_LIST, OUT_FILE, "STATE_FILE");
```

delare the internal-file object STATE_LIST, create the external file STATE_FILE, and associate the two. Each value written to the internal-file object STATE_LIST, and therefore stored in external file STATE_FILE, is of type STATE_ARRAY. That is, each value is a one-dimensional array of records; each record, in turn, has two array components. Since this is a binary file, the data is stored in machine-compatible format. The programmer need not be concerned with formatting.

The reader should keep the above concepts in mind as the remaining operations are presented.

```
procedure OPEN(FILE : in out FILE_TYPE;
               MODE : in FILE_MODE;
```

```
              NAME : in STRING;
              FORM : in STRING := "");
--This procedure opens the internal-file object associated
  with the formal parameter FILE. The mode is determined
  by the actual parameter associated with formal parameter
  MODE. The internal-file object is associated with an
  existing external file whose name is specified by the
  actual parameter associated with formal parameter NAME.
  An external-file name must be provided, because there is
  no default option. A form may be provided, or the
  default option can be used. Exceptions that may be
  raised are

      STATUS_ERROR -- if the file is already open
      NAME_ERROR   -- if the external-file name is not
                      found
      USE_ERROR    -- if the implementation does not
                      provide for opening an external file
                      with the specified name and form

procedure CLOSE(FILE : in out FILE_TYPE);
--This procedure closes the internal-file object specified
  by the actual parameter that is associated with the
  formal parameter FILE. That is, the association between
  the internal-file object and the external file is
  broken. The only exception that maybe raised is

      STATUS_ERROR -- if the file is not currently open

procedure DELETE(FILE: in out FILE_TYPE);
--This procedure deletes the external file currently
  associated with the internal-file object that is
  associated with the formal parameter FILE. The internal-
  file object is then closed. The internal-file object
  must currently be open, otherwise no association with an
  external file exists. Exceptions that may be raised are

      STATUS_ERROR -- if the file is not open
      USE_ERROR    -- if the implementation does not
                      provide for the deletion of the
                      external file

procedure RESET(FILE : in out FILE_TYPE;
                MODE : in FILE_MODE);
--This procedure resets the internal-file object that is
  associated with the formal parameter FILE. That is, the
```

```
  reading from or writing to the file restarts from the
  beginning of the file. The file mode is set to the value
  specified by the actual parameter associated with formal
  parameter MODE. Exceptions that may be raised are

      STATUS_ERROR -- if the file is not open
      USE_ERROR    -- if the implementation does not
                      support resetting to the specified
                      mode

procedure RESET(FILE : in out FILE_TYPE);
--This procedure is equivalent to procedure RESET above,
  except that there is no MODE parameter. The current mode
  remains unchanged.

function MODE(FILE : in FILE_TYPE) return FILE_MODE;
--This function returns a value that is the current mode
  of the internal-file object that is associated with the
  formal parameter FILE. Since a file has a mode only when
  it is open, the file object must be open. The only
  exception that may be raised is

      STATUS_ERROR -- if the file is not open

function NAME(FILE : in FILE_TYPE) return STRING;
--This function returns the name of the external file
  currently associated with the internal-file object that
  is associated with the formal parameter FILE. Since
  association implies an open file, the internal-file
  object must be open. The only exception that may be
  raised is

      STATUS_ERROR -- if the file is not open


function FORM(FILE : in FILE_TYPE) return STRING:
--This function returns the form of the external file
  currently associated with the internal-file object that
  is associated with the formal parameter FILE. Since
  association implies an open file, the internal-file
  object must be open. The only exception that may be
  raised is

      STATUS_ERROR -- if the file is not open

function IS_OPEN(FILE : in FILE_TYPE) return BOOLEAN;
--This function returns the value TRUE if the internal-
```

```
   file object that is associated with the formal parameter
   FILE is currently open. Otherwise, the value FALSE is
   returned. No input-output exceptions can be raised by
   this function.

procedure READ(FILE : in FILE_TYPE;
               ITEM : out ELEMENT_TYPE);
--This procedure reads an element from the external file
   currently associated with the internal-file object that
   is associated with formal parameter FILE. The value of
   the element is returned as the value of the actual
   parameter associated with the formal parameter ITEM.
   Notice that ITEM is of type ELEMENT_TYPE, which is the
   generic formal type parameter appearing in the generic
   formal part of the generic package SEQUENTIAL_IO. In
   accordance with the discussion of Section 5.4.1.1, the
   name ELEMENT_TYPE denotes the type specifed by the
   actual generic type parameter associated with formal
   parameter ELEMENT_TYPE at instantiation. In the two
   examples given previously in this section, the actual
   parameters are HIT_COUNT and STATE_ARRAY. The current
   mode of the file must be IN_FILE. Exceptions that
   may be raised are

       STATUS_ERROR -- if the file is not open
       MODE_ERROR   -- if mode is not IN_FILE
       END_ERROR    -- if the end of the external file has
                       been reached
       DATA_ERROR   -- if the element read is of the wrong
                       type

procedure WRITE(FILE : in FILE_TYPE;
                ITEM : out ELEMENT_TYPE);
--This procedure writes an element to the external file
   currently associated with the internal-file object that
   is associated with the formal parameter FILE. The value
   of the element must be provided as the actual parameter
   associated with the formal parameter ITEM. The type of
   ITEM is ELEMENT_TYPE, and the discussion related to
   procedure READ applies here as well. The current mode of
   the file must be OUT_FILE. Exceptions that may be raised
   are

       STATUS_ERROR -- if the file is not open
       MODE_ERROR   -- if the mode is not OUT_FILE
       USE_ERROR    -- if the capacity of the external file
                       is exceeded
```

```
function END_OF_FILE(FILE : in FILE_TYPE) return BOOLEAN;
--This function returns the value TRUE if the last element
  of the external file has been reached. The external file
  is that currenty associated with the internal-file
  object that is associated with the formal parameter
  FILE. The file must be open, and the current mode must
  be IN_FILE. Exceptions that may be raised are

      STATUS_ERROR -- if the file is not open
      MODE_ERROR   -- if the mode is not IN_FILE
```

The specification of each of these procedures and functions can be found in the specification of the generic package SEQUENTIAL_IO, which is contained in Appendix C.

A simple example illustrates the use of some of these operations. A generic procedure is desired that can be instantiated to copy files with elements of virtually any type. The following specification and body declarations provide such a procedure.

```
with SEQUENTIAL_IO;
generic
  type ELEM_TYPE is private;
procedure COPY(FROM, INTO : STRING);
procedure COPY(FROM, INTO : STRING) is
    package ELEM_IO is new SEQUENTIAL_IO(ELEM_TYPE);
    use ELEM_IO;
    SOURCE_FILE : FILE_TYPE;
    DEST_FILE   : FILE_TYPE;
    VALUE       : ELEM_TYPE;
begin
    OPEN(SOURCE_FILE, IN_FILE, FROM);
    begin
        OPEN(DEST_FILE, OUT_FILE, INTO);
    exception
        when NAME_ERROR =>
            CREATE(DEST_FILE, OUT_FILE, INTO);
    end;
    while not END_OF_FILE(SOURCE_FILE) loop
        READ(SOURCE_FILE, VALUE);
        WRITE(DEST_FILE, VALUE);
    end loop;
    CLOSE(SOURCE_FILE);
    CLOSE(DEST_FILE);
end COPY;
```

This procedure is fairly straightforward—the source file is opened and then an attempt is made to open the destination file as though the external file already exists. If the external file does not exist, then the exception NAME_ERROR is raised and subsequently handled within the block statement. The exception handler merely creates the external file if it does not already exist. In either case, the result is two open files. The while loop simply reads an element from the source file and writes it to the destination file, and then repeats this operation until the end of the source file has been reached. Both files are then closed.

The elements of the two files must be of the type ELEM_TYPE, which is the generic formal type parameter declared as a private type in the generic formal part of the specification of generic procedure COPY. Since ELEM_TYPE is private, it can be matched with virtually any data type as the generic actual parameter. For example, in the case of integer type HIT_COUNT, considered previously in this section, the instantiation

```
procedure HIT_COPY is new COPY(HIT_COUNT);
```

creates an instance—in this case, a procedure—named HIT_COPY that will copy files with elements of type HIT_COUNT. Similarly, the instantiation

```
procedure STATE_COPY is new COPY(STATE_ARRAY);
```

creates an instance that will copy files with elements of type STATE_ARRAY, also introduced previously in this section. The reader will note that, while HIT_ARRAY is a scalar type, STATE_ARRAY is an array type with components that are records, and that each record, in turn, has two array components.

6.2.1.2 Direct-Access Files. Direct-access files differ from sequential-access files in one very important way. Associated with each element in the file is a number called the *index* of the element. The index is of the type COUNT, which is declared in generic package DIRECT_IO as follows:

```
type COUNT is range 0.. implementation_defined;
subtype POSITIVE_COUNT is COUNT range 1..COUNT'LAST;
```

The first element in the file has index one; the second, index two; and so on to the last element. The index of the last element is called the *current size* of the file. The current size is a property of the external file with which the internal file object is currently associated.

Any direct-access internal-file object that is open, and is thus currently associated with an external file, has a current index, which is the index value that will be used by the next read or write operation. When a file is created or opened, the current index is set to one, but any read or write operation increments the current index. The current index may also be specifically set to any value in the range of type POSITIVE_COUNT by a read or write operation, or by a procedure that does nothing but set the current index value. The net effect is that any element of a direct-access file can be directly read from or written to by setting the current index to the index value of the desired element. If the current index is not specifically set by a read or write operation, then these operations are analogous to those of sequential-access files, since the current index is incremented with each operation.

The generic formal part of the generic package DIRECT_IO is

```
generic
    type ELEMENT_TYPE is private;
```

implying that the generic formal parameter ELEMENT_TYPE can be matched to any actual parameter for which the operations of assignment and tests for equality and inequality are permitted. Thus, it can be matched to virtually any Ada data type, no matter how complex the structure. The specification of DIRECT_IO also contains the declarations

```
type FILE_TYPE is limited private;
type FILE_MODE is (IN_FILE, INOUT_FILE, OUT_FILE);
```

These types, together with COUNT and POSITIVE_COUNT from above, are exported by any instance of the generic package DIRECT_IO. Different instances, of course, implicitly declare different types FILE_TYPE, FILE_MODE, COUNT, and POSITIVE_COUNT. A program unit using an instance of DIRECT_IO will normally declare one or more internal-file objects of the type FILE_TYPE, which is exported by the instance. These internal-file objects are then associated with external files when the internal-file objects are created or opened, as discussed in Section 6.2.

Input-output operations on direct-access files are provided by those procedures and functions declared in the specification of the generic package DIRECT_IO. They are given here with some explanatory remarks.

```
procedure CREATE(FILE : in out FILE_TYPE;
                 MODE : in FILE_MODE := INOUT_FILE;
                 NAME : in STRING := "";
                 FORM : in STRING := "");
--This procedure opens the internal-file object associated
```

```
  with the formal parameter FILE and associates it with a
  newly created external file with name and form as given
  by the actual parameters that are associated with formal
  parameters NAME and FORM. A null string associated with
  formal parameter NAME implies a temporary file—one that
  will not be retained on the external device when the
  file is closed. A null string associated with the formal
  parameter FORM permits the implementation to use its
  default value. The mode of the file is that value
  associated with the formal parameter MODE, which
  defaults to INOUT_FILE. The current index is set to one.
  Exceptions that may be raised are

      STATUS_ERROR -- if the file is already open
      NAME_ERROR   -- if the external-file name is not
                      permitted
      USE_ERROR    -- if the implementation does not
                      support creation of an external file
                      with specified name and mode

procedure OPEN(FILE : in out FILE_TYPE;
               MODE : in FILE_MODE;
               NAME : in STRING;
               FORM : in STRING := "");
--This procedure opens the internal-file object that is
  associated with formal parameter FILE. The mode is
  determined by the actual parameter associated with the
  formal parameter MODE. The internal-file object is
  associated with an existing external file whose name is
  specified by the actual parameter associated with formal
  parameter NAME. An external-file name must be provided,
  because there is no default option. The current index is
  set to one. A form may be provided, or the default may
  be used. Exceptions that may be raised are

      STATUS_ERROR -- if the file is already open
      NAME_ERROR   -- if the external-file name is not
                      found
      USE_ERROR    -- if the implementation does not
                      provide for opening an external file
                      with the given name and form

procedure CLOSE(FILE : in out FILE_TYPE);
--This procedure closes the internal-file object specified
  by the actual parameter that is associated with formal
  parameter FILE. The association between the internal-
```

```
  file object and external file is broken. The only
  exception that may be raised is

      STATUS_ERROR -- if the file is not currently open

procedure DELETE(FILE : in out FILE_TYPE);
--This procedure deletes the external file currently
  associated with the internal-file object that is
  associated with the formal parameter FILE. The internal-
  file object is then closed. The internal-file object
  must be currently open, otherwise no association with an
  external file exists. Exceptions that may be raised are

      STATUS_ERROR -- if the file is not open
      USE_ERROR    -- if the implementation does not
                      provide for the deletion of the
                      external file

procedure RESET(FILE : in out FILE_TYPE);
                MODE : in FILE_MODE);
--This procedure sets the current index to one, for the
  internal-file object that is associated with the formal
  parameter FILE. The file mode is set to the value
  specified by the actual parameter associated with the
  formal parameter MODE. Exceptions that may be raised are

      STATUS_ERROR -- if the file is not open
      USE_ERROR    -- if the implementation does not
                      support resetting to the specified
                      mode

procedure RESET(FILE : in out FILE_TYPE);
--Same as procedure RESET above, except that there is no
  mode parameter. The current mode remains unchanged.

function MODE(FILE : in FILE_TYPE) return FILE_MODE:
--This function returns a value that is the current mode
  of the internal-file object that is associated with the
  formal parameter FILE. Since a file has a current mode
  only when it is open, the file object must be open. The
  only exception that may be raised is

      STATUS_ERROR -- if the file is not open

function NAME(FILE : in FILE_TYPE) return STRING:
--This function returns the name of the external file
```

```
  currently associated with the internal-file object that
  is associated with the formal parameter FILE. Since
  association implies an open file, the internal-file
  object must be open. The only exception that may be
  raised is

      STATUS_ERROR -- if the file is not open

function FORM(FILE : in FILE_TYPE) return STRING;
--This function returns the form of the external file
  associated with the internal-file object that is
  associated with the formal parameter FILE. Since
  association implies an open file, the internal-file
  object must be open. The only exception that may be
  raised is

      STATUS_ERROR -- if the file is not open

function IS_OPEN(FILE : in FILE_TYPE) return BOOLEAN;
--This function returns the value TRUE if the internal-
  file object that is associated with the formal parameter
  FILE is currently open. Otherwise, the value FALSE is
  returned. No input-output exceptions are raised by this
  function.

procedure READ(FILE : in FILE_TYPE;
               ITEM : out ELEMENT_TYPE;
               FROM : in POSITIVE_COUNT);
--This procedure reads an element from the external file
  currently associated with the internal-file object that
  is associated with the formal parameter FILE. Before the
  element is read, the current index is set to the value
  of the actual parameter associated with formal parameter
  FROM. The value of the element is returned as the value
  of the actual parameter associated with the formal
  parameter ITEM. After the file is read, the current
  index is incremented. Notice that ITEM is of type
  ELEMENT_TYPE, which is the generic formal type parameter
  appearing in the generic formal part of the generic
  package DIRECT_IO. In accordance with the discussion of
  Section 5.4.1.1, the name ELEMENT_TYPE denotes the type
  specified by the generic actual parameter associated
  with generic formal parameter ELEMENT_TYPE at
  instantiation. Exceptions that may be raised are

      STATUS_ERROR -- if the file is not open
```

```
    MODE_ERROR   -- if the mode is not OUT_FILE
    END_ERROR    -- if the index exceeds the size of the
                    external file
    DATA_ERROR   -- if the element read is of the wrong
                    type

procedure READ(FILE : in FILE_TYPE;
               ITEM : out ELEMENT_TYPE);
--The effect is the same as that produced by procedure
  READ above, except that the current index is not changed
  before reading.

procedure WRITE(FILE : in FILE_TYPE;
                ITEM : in ELEMENT_TYPE;
                TO   : in POSITIVE_COUNT);
--This procedure writes an element to the external file
  currently associated with the internal-file object that
  is associated with the formal parameter FILE. Before the
  element is written, the current index is set to the
  value of the actual parameter associated with the formal
  parameter TO. The value of the element must be provided
  as the actual parameter associated with the formal
  parameter ITEM. After the element is written, the
  current index is incremented. The type of ITEM is
  ELEMENT_TYPE, and the discussion related to procedure
  READ applies here as well. The current mode of the file
  must be INOUT_FILE or OUT_FILE. Exceptions that may be
  raised are

    STATUS_ERROR -- if the file is not open
    MODE_ERROR   -- if the current mode is IN_FILE
    USE_ERROR    -- if the current index exceeds the
                    length of the file

procedure WRITE(FILE : in FILE_TYPE;
                ITEM : in ELEMENT_TYPE);
--The effect is the same as that produced by procedure
  WRITE above, except that the current index is not
  changed before writing.

procedure SET_INDEX(FILE : in FILE_TYPE;
                    TO   : in POSITIVE_COUNT);
--This procedure sets the current index of the internal-
  file object that is associated with formal parameter
  FILE to the value of the actual parameter associated
  with formal parameter TO. Since a current index exists
```

```
  only for an open file, the internal-file object must be
  open. The only exception that may be raised is

      STATUS_ERROR -- if the file is not open

function INDEX(FILE : in FILE_TYPE) return POSITIVE_COUNT;
--This function returns the current index of the internal-
  file object that is associated with the formal parameter
  FILE. The file must be open. The only exception that may
  be raised is

      STATUS_ERROR -- if the file is not open

function SIZE(FILE : in FILE_TYPE) return COUNT;
--This function returns the current size of the external
  file currently associated with the internal-file object
  that is associated with formal parameter FILE. Since
  association exists only for an open file, the file must
  be open. The only exception that may be raised is

      STATUS_ERROR -- if the file is not open

function END_OF_FILE(FILE : in FILE_TYPE) return BOOLEAN;
--This function returns the value TRUE if the current
  index of the internal-file object that is associated
  with formal parameter FILE exceeds the size of the
  currently associated external file. The file mode must
  be IN_FILE or INOUT_FILE. Exceptions that may be raised
  are

      STATUS_ERROR -- if the file is not open
      MODE_ERROR   -- if the file mode is OUT_FILE
```

The specification of each of these procedures and functions can be found in the specification of the generic package DIRECT_IO, contained in Appendix C.

A simple example illustrates the use of some of these concepts. Suppose that a file has been created with elements that are records of type FIGHTER_RECORD:

```
package FIGHTER_PACKAGE is
type AIRCRAFT is STRING (1..8);
type FIGHTER_RECORD is
    record
        AC_NO        : POSITIVE;
```

```
                    AC_TYPE     : AIRCRAFT;
                    SERV_DATE   : POSITIVE;
                    TOTAL_HOURS : POSITIVE;
                end record;
            end FIGHTER_PACKAGE;
```

Further suppose that the file exists on an external device under the name FIGHTER_FILE, and that the file is sorted in ascending order of component AC_NO. A procedure is to be developed to select from the file a record with a given value for the AC_NO component. If no record is found, a value with zeros in the numeric components and blanks in the component AC_TYPE is to be returned. A possible implementation is as follows:

```
with DIRECT_IO, FIGHTER_PACKAGE;
use FIGHTER_PACKAGE;
  function SEARCH(FNAME : STRING; NUMB: POSITIVE)
              return FIGHTER_RECORD is
        package FIGHTER_IO is new DIRECT_IO(FIGHTER_RECORD);
        use FIGHTER_IO;
        AFILE              : FILE_TYPE;
        VALUE              : FIGHTER_RECORD;
        LAST, MID, FIRST : POSITIVE_COUNT;
  begin
        OPEN(FILE => AFILE, MODE => IN_FILE, NAME => FNAME);
        FIRST := 1;
        LAST := SIZE(AFILE);
        while FIRST <= LAST loop
             MID := (LAST + FIRST)/2;
             READ (FILE => AFILE, ITEM => VALUE, FROM => MID);
             if VALUE.AC_NO = NUMB then
                return VALUE;
             elsif VALUE.AC_NO > NUMB then
                LAST := MID - 1;
             else
                FIRST := MID + 1;
             end if;
        end loop;
        return FIGHTER_RECORD'(0,"         ",0,0);
        CLOSE(AFILE);
  end SEARCH;
```

The algorithm is a simple binary search, which depends upon the file being sorted in ascending order of the record component AC_NO.

6.2.2 Input-Output of Text Files

Text files are those files whose elements are in human readable form. In general, the file itself consists of ASCII characters, but the particular grouping of the characters is made to conform to the actual information being read or written in a text format. For example, an integer number would be written into a text file as the proper grouping of ASCII numeric characters. There are six kinds of values that can be manipulated by the text input-output facilities of the Ada language. These are (1) character, (2) string, (3) integer, (4) floating-point, (5) fixed-point, and (6) enumeration. Moreover, in text input-output, it is necessary to merge values of all six of these types in a single file. This merging is accomplished by converting the values to an appropriate sequence of characters in an output operation, or by converting a sequence of characters to the appropriate value in an input operation. The conversion is basically from a machine representation to a text representation, and vice versa, as implied by Table 6.1. Such conversion is entirely transparent to the user.

Table 6.1 Machine Format/Text Format Equivalencies.

MACHINE FORM	HUMAN READABLE FORM
string	sequence of ASCII characters
integer	sequence of ASCII numeric characters
floating-point	sequence of ASCII numeric characters and one decimal point
fixed-point	sequence of ASCII numeric characters and one decimal point
enumeration	sequence of ASCII characters comprising the enumeration literal

The conversion facilities are provided, together with other input-output services for text files, by the predefined package TEXT_IO. This package is not a generic unit, but declared within TEXT_IO are four generic packages:

```
INTEGER_IO
FLOAT_IO
FIXED_IO
ENUMERATION_IO
```

This particular arrangement is used for text input-output because of the unique requirement to merge the character sequence representation of values of various types within the same file. This same consideration results in the fact that only one type FILE_TYPE and one type FILE_MODE is declared for TEXT_IO, and that their scope includes the four generic packages. That is, while each instantiation of the generic packages SEQUENTIAL_IO and DIRECT_IO declares different types FILE_TYPE and FILE_MODE, there are unique types FILE_TYPE and FILE_MODE for all TEXT_IO operations, including those produced by instantiation of the four generic packages. These and other features can be inferred from examination of the specification of the predefined package TEXT_IO in Appendix C.

The package TEXT_IO contains a number of subprograms applicable to text input-output in general. In addition, it contains specific input and output procedures for character data and string data. Thus, if only character and string data are to be manipulated, the user program unit need have included within its context clause only

```
with TEXT_IO;
```

In addition, the use clause

```
use TEXT_IO;
```

can be included to make the various operations directly visible, so that expanded names need not be used. An examination of package TEXT_IO in Appendix C reveals that there are several overloaded subprogram names occurring within the package.

If input-output operations are to involve integer values—that is, values of the predefined type INTEGER or values of any other integer data type—then an instance of the generic package INTEGER_IO must be instantiated for each integer data type requiring input-output services. For example, if input-output capability is required for type INTEGER and for the integer type HIT_COUNT, then two instantiations are required:

```
package INT_IO is new INTEGER_IO(INTEGER);
package HIT_IO is new INTEGER_IO(HIT_COUNT);
```

These instantiations may be followed by

```
use INT_IO, HIT_IO;
```

which makes the operations contained in the instances directly visible. Overloading the subprogram names occurs, of course, but any ambiguities can be resolved by the compiler because of the differing types in the parameter list. It should be noted that the context clause

```
with TEXT_IO;
```

suffices to make INTEGER_IO visible, since INTEGER_IO is declared within TEXT_IO.

If input-output operations for the predefined type FLOAT—or for any other floating-point type—is required, then the generic package FLOAT_IO must be instantiated for each floating-point type. Similarly, to provide input-output capability for fixed-point types or for enumeration types, the generic packages FIXED_IO and ENUMERATION_IO, respectively, must be instantiated for each unique data type for which such capability is required.

The package TEXT_IO contains seven type declarations that are germaine to many of the text input-output operations. These declarations are

```
type FILE_TYPE is limited private;
type FILE_MODE is (IN_FILE, OUT_FILE);
type COUNT is range 0..implementation_defined;
subtype POSITIVE_COUNT is COUNT range 1..COUNT'LAST;
subtype FIELD is INTEGER range 0..implementation_defined;
subtype NUMBER_BASE is INTEGER range 2..16;
type TYPE_SET is (LOWER_CASE, UPPER_CASE);
```

There is also one constant declared:

```
UNBOUNDED : constant COUNT := 0;
```

The significance of these type and constant declarations is as follows:

```
type FILE_TYPE           -- This is the file type for text
                            files. All internal text file
                            objects must be declared as
                            objects of this type.
type FILE_MODE           -- This is the file mode type.
                            Notice that the only values are IN
                            FILE and OUT_FILE.
type COUNT and
subtype POSITIVE_COUNT   -- Objects of these types are used
                            to signify the current column
                            number, line number, and page
                            number in text file operations.
```

```
subtype FIELD          -- Objects of this type are used as
                          format parameters to specify
                          field lengths in certain input-
                          output operations.
subtype NUMBER_BASE    -- Objects of this type are used to
                          specify the number base to be
                          used for certain integer input-
                          output operations.
type TYPE_SET          -- Objects of this type are used to
                          specify uppercase or lowercase
                          letters for use in certain
                          enumeration input-output
                          operations.
constant UNBOUNDED     -- This is used to indicate zero
                          values of maximum line length
                          and maximum page length. By
                          convention, this means that line
                          length and page length are
                          unbounded.
```

In addition to these type and constant declarations, the package TEXT_IO contains a number of subprograms which apply to all text input-output operations. Before these general operations are examined, however, some discussion of text files in general is in order.

6.2.2.1 General Characteristics of Text Files. Text files are read and written sequentially, and therefore their characteristics are similar to those of sequential-access file. The format of a text file, however, is a sequence of characters grouped into lines, with the lines, in turn, grouped into pages. The end of a line is marked by a line terminator; the end of a page is marked by a line terminator followed immediately by a page terminator; the end of a file is formed by the sequence of a line terminator, a page terminator, and a file terminator, in that order. The actual form of these terminators is implementation-dependent, but because the form is hidden from the user, this does not affect portability. Terminators are generated during output by one of two means:

1. Automatically and implicitly when some limit such as maximum line length or maximum page length is reached.
2. Explicitly, as a result of calling a procedure that specifically outputs a particular terminator. Procedure NEW_LINE, for example, generates a line terminator.

Terminators are recognized by certain input-output procedures, and they are generated by others.

In a text file, the columns in a line are numbered, starting with one, as are the lines in a page and the pages in a file. This fact leads to the following definitions:

current column number	— the column number of the next character to be read or written
current line number	— the number of the current line
current page number	— the number of the current page

These numbers have values of subtype POSITIVE_COUNT.

For an output file, one can specify a maximum line length and a maximum page length, which causes automatic output of line and page terminators during output. When a file is opened with mode OUT_FILE, both the maximum line length and maximum page length are set to zero. By convention, this value signifies unbounded line length and page length, so that line and page terminators are provided only in an explicit manner by calls to procedures that produce them. The maximum line number and maximum page number for any file of mode OUT_FILE can be set by procedures expressly provided for that purpose. Any file of mode OUT_FILE can also be queried to determine its current maximum line and page lengths, through calls to functions that return these values.

As indicated by the declaration of type FILE_MODE in package TEXT_IO, text files can only have the modes IN_FILE and OUT_FILE. File management of these files is similar to that for sequential-access files as discussed in Section 6.2.1.1. There are many more input-output procedures and functions relating to text files, however, because of the formatting required of these files. The procedures and functions, listed by use are

File Management:

```
procedure CREATE    function MODE
procedure OPEN      function NAME
procedure CLOSE     function FORM
procedure RESET     function IS_OPEN
procedure DELETE
```

Operations on standard input and output files:

```
procedure SET_INPUT    function STANDARD_OUTPUT
```

```
procedure SET_OUTPUT    function CURRENT_INPUT
                        function CURRENT_OUTPUT
                        function STANDARD_INPUT
```

Operations on columns, lines, and pages:

```
procedure NEW_LINE             function END_OF_FILE
procedure SKIP_LINE            function SET_COL
procedure END_OF_LINE          function COL
procedure NEW_PAGE             function LINE
procedure SKIP_PAGE            function PAGE
procedure END_OF_PAGE          function LINE_LENGTH
procedure SET_LINE_LENGTH      function PAGE_LENGTH
procedure SET_PAGE_LENGTH
procedure SET_LINE
procedure SET_COL
```

Input-output operations for characters:

```
procedure GET   procedure PUT
```

Input-output operations for strings:

```
procedure GET   procedure GET_LINE
procedure PUT   procedure PUT_LINE
```

Input-output for integer types:

```
procedure GET   procedure PUT
```

Input-output for floating-point types:

```
procedure GET   procedure PUT
```

Input-output for fixed-point types:

```
procedure GET   procedure PUT
```

Input-output for enumeration types:

```
procedure GET   procedure PUT
```

As discussed previously, the input-output procedures for integer, floating-point, fixed-point, and enumeration types are provided by generic packages that must be instantiated for each particular data type requiring input-output support. The next nine sections deal with specific text input-output operations.

6.2.2.2 Management of Text Files. Text files can be opened by calls to either procedure OPEN or procedure CREATE, depending upon whether or not the external file with which the internal-file object is to be associated is already in existence or not. These files can also be closed and reset. The precise effect of each of these operations is given below:

```
procedure CREATE(FILE : in out FILE_TYPE;
                 MODE : in FILE_MODE := OUT_FILE;
                 NAME : in STRING := "";
                 FORM : in STRING := "");
--This procedure opens the internal-file object that is
  associated with the formal parameter FILE and associates
  it with a newly created external file with the name and
  form as given by the actual parameters associated with
  formal parameters NAME and FORM. A null string
  associated with the formal parameter NAME implies a
  temporary file--one that will not be retained on the
  external device when the file is closed. A null string
  associated with the formal parameter FORM permits the
  implementation to use its default value. The mode of the
  file is either IN_FILE or OUT_FILE and is determined by
  the actual parameter associated with formal parameter
  MODE, which defaults to OUT_FILE. If the mode is OUT_
  FILE, the maximum line length and maximum page length
  are set to zero, implying that line and page terminators
  will not be automatically output. That is, the line
  length and page length are unbounded. The current column
  number, the current line number, and the current page
  number are set to one, regardless of the file mode.
  Exceptions that may be raised are

      STATUS_ERROR -- if the file is already open
      NAME_ERROR   -- if the external file name is not
                      permitted
      USE_ERROR    -- if the implementation does not
                      permit creation of an external file
                      with the specified name and form.

procedure OPEN(FILE : in out FILE_TYPE;
               MODE : in FILE_MODE;
               NAME : in STRING;
               FORM : in STRING := "");
```

```
--This procedure opens the internal-file object that is
  associated with the formal parameter FILE. The mode is
  determined by the actual parameter associated with the
  formal parameter MODE. The internal-file object is
  associated with an existing external file whose name is
  specified by the actual parameter associated with the
  formal parameter NAME. An external-file name must be
  provided, because there is no default option. A form may
  be provided, or the default value may be used. If the
  mode is OUT_FILE, the maximum line length and maximum
  page length are set to zero, implying that line and page
  terminators will not be automatically output. That is,
  the line length and page length are unbounded. The
  current column number, the current line number, and the
  current page number are set to one, regardless of the
  file mode.

      STATUS_ERROR -- if the file is already open
      NAME_ERROR   -- if the external-file name is not
                      found
      USE_ERROR    -- if the implementation does not
                      provide for opening an external file
                      with the specified name and mode

procedure CLOSE(FILE : in out FILE_TYPE);
--This procedure closes the internal-file object specified
  by the actual parameter that is associated with the
  formal parameter FILE. That is, the association between
  the internal-file object and the external file is
  broken. If the file mode is OUT_FILE, closing the file
  causes line, page, and file terminators to be output.
  The only exception that may be raised is

      STATUS_ERROR -- if the file is not open

procedure DELETE(FILE : in out FILE_TYPE);
--This procedure deletes the external file currently
  associated with the internal-file object that is
  associated with the formal parameter FILE. The internal-
  file object must currently be open, otherwise no
  association with an external file exists. The internal-
  file object is then closed. Exceptions that may be
  raised are

      STATUS_ERROR -- if the file is not open
```

```
     USE_ERROR      -- if the implementation does not
                       provide for the deletion of the
                       external file

procedure RESET(FILE : in out FILE_TYPE;
                MODE : in FILE_MODE);
--This procedure resets the internal-file object that is
  associated with the formal parameter FILE. That is,
  reading from or writing to the file restarts from the
  beginning of the file. The file mode is set to the value
  specified by the actual parameter associated with the
  formal parameter MODE. If the current mode is OUT_FILE,
  line and page terminators are output. If the new file
  mode is OUT_FILE, the page and line lengths are
  unbounded. The current column, line, and page numbers
  are set to one, regardless of the file mode. Exceptions
  that may be raised are

     STATUS_ERROR -- if the file is not open
     USE_ERROR    -- if the implementation does not
                     support resetting to the specified
                     mode
     MODE_ERROR   -- if an attempt is made to change the
                     mode of the current default input
                     and output files

procedure RESET(FILE : in out FILE_TYPE);
--Same as procedure RESET above, except that there is no
  MODE parameter. The current mode remains unchanged.

function MODE(FILE : in FILE_TYPE) return FILE_MODE;
--This function returns a value that is the current mode
  of the internal-file object that is associated with the
  formal parameter FILE. Since a file has a mode only when
  it is open, the file object must be open. The only
  exception that may be raised is

     STATUS_ERROR -- if the file is not open

function NAME(FILE : in FILE_TYPE) return STRING;
--This function returns the name of the external file
  currently associated with the internal-file object that
  is associated with the formal parameter FILE. Since
  association implies an open file, the internal-file
  object must be open. The only exception that may be
```

```
  raised is

      STATUS_ERROR -- if the file is not open

function FORM(FILE : in FILE_TYPE) return STRING;
--This function returns the form of the external file
  currently associated with the internal-file object that
  is associated with the formal parameter FILE. Since
  association implies an open file, the internal-file
  object must be open. The only exception that may be
  raised is

      STATUS_ERROR -- if the file is not open

function IS_OPEN(FILE : in FILE_TYPE) return BOOLEAN;
--This function returns the value TRUE if the internal-
  file object that is associated with the formal parameter
  FILE is currently open. Otherwise, the value FALSE is
  returned. No input-output exceptions can be raised by
  this function.
```

6.2.2.3 Operations on Standard Input and Standard Output Files. Because many text input-output operations are often directed to the same input or output file, such as a keyboard or terminal screen, several text input-output subprograms permit the actual parameter associated with formal parameter FILE to be omitted in calls to the subprogram. If the file parameter is omitted, then a specified file called the *default input* or *default output* file, as appropriate, is provided as the file parameter. In addition, there are two implementation-defined files called STANDARD_INPUT and STANDARD_OUTPUT. Ordinarily, these files are the keyboard and terminal screen, respectively. At the beginning of program execution, the default input and output files are set to STANDARD_INPUT and STANDARD_OUTPUT, but they may be changed and queried by the following subprograms:

```
procedure SET_INPUT(FILE: in FILE_TYPE);
--This procedure sets the current default input file to
  the internal-file object that is associated with the
  formal parameter FILE. The internal-file object must be
  currently open and must have mode IN_FILE. Exceptions
  that may be raised are

      STATUS_ERROR -- if the file is not open
      MODE_ERROR   -- if the mode is not IN_FILE
```

```
procedure SET_OUTPUT(FILE : in FILE_TYPE);
--This procedure sets the current default output file to
  the internal-file object that is associated with the
  formal parameter FILE. The internal-file object must be
  currently open and must have mode OUT_FILE. Exceptions
  that may be raised are

      STATUS_ERROR -- if the file is not open
      MODE_ERROR   -- if the mode is not OUT_FILE

function STANDARD_INPUT return FILE_TYPE;
--This function returns the standard input file. No input-
  output exceptions can be raised by this function.

function STANDARD_OUTPUT return FILE_TYPE;
--This function returns the standard output file. No
  input-output exceptions can be raised by this function.

function CURRENT_INPUT return FILE_TYPE;
--This function returns the current default input file. No
  input-output exceptions can be raised by this function.

function CURRENT_OUTPUT return FILE_TYPE;
--This function returns the current default output file.
  No input-output exceptions can be raised by this
  function.
```

6.2.2.4 Operations on Columns, Lines, and Pages. The formatting of text files, for both input and output, is provided by a number of procedures and functions that affect the line and page structure of a file. Some of these subprograms apply only to files of mode IN_FILE, some apply only to files of mode OUT_FILE, and others apply to files of either mode. In any case, the formats of read and write operations are controlled by calls to these subprograms.

The following group of four subprograms concern the line and page structure of files of mode OUT_FILE. They provide control over the maximum line length and maximum page length.

```
procedure SET_LINE_LENGTH(FILE : in FILE_TYPE;
                          TO   : in COUNT);
--This procedure sets the maximum line length of the
  internal-file object that is associated with the formal
  parameter FILE to the value associated with the formal
  parameter TO. A value of zero specifies an unbounded
```

```
  length. The file mode must be OUT_FILE and the file must
  be open. If no file parameter is provided, the parameter
  defaults to the current default output file. Exceptions
  that may be raised are

      STATUS_ERROR -- if the file is not open
      MODE_ERROR   -- if the file mode is not OUT_FILE
      USE_ERROR    -- if the specified line length is not
                      appropriate for the associated
                      external file

procedure SET_PAGE_LENGTH(FILE : in FILE_TYPE;
                          TO   : in COUNT);
--This procedure sets the maximum page length of the
  internal-file object that is associated with the formal
  parameter FILE to the value associated with the formal
  parameter TO. A value of zero specifies an unbounded
  page length. If no file parameter is provided, the
  parameter defaults to the current default output file.
  Exceptions that may be raised are

      STATUS_ERROR -- if the file is not open
      MODE_ERROR   -- if the file mode is not OUT_FILE
      USE_ERROR    -- if the specified page length is not
                      appropriate for the associated
                      external file

function LINE_LENGTH(FILE : in FILE_TYPE) return COUNT;
--This function returns the current maximum line length of
  the internal-file object that is associated with the
  formal parameter FILE. A value of zero implies an
  unbounded line length. If no file parameter is provided,
  the parameter defaults to the current default output
  file. Exceptions that may be raised are

      STATUS_ERROR -- if the file is not open
      MODE_ERROR   -- if the file mode is not OUT_FILE

function PAGE_LENGTH(FILE : in FILE_TYPE) return COUNT;
--This function returns the current maximum page length of
  the internal-file object that is associated with the
  formal parameter FILE. A value of zero implies an
  unbounded page length. If no file parameter is provided,
  the parameter defaults to the current default output
  file. Exceptions that may be raised are
```

```
STATUS_ERROR -- if the file is not open
MODE_ERROR   -- if the file mode is not OUT_FILE
```

The following group of seven subprograms provides for explicit control of the line and page formatting of a file. Two of these subprograms, NEW_LINE and NEW_PAGE, relate to formatting of output files. The remaining five subprograms control the reading of input files. When any of these subprograms is called, the actual parameter associated with the formal parameter FILE may be omitted, in which case the parameter defaults to the default input file or to the default output file, as appropriate.

```
procedure NEW_LINE(FILE : in FILE_TYPE;
                   SPACING : POSITIVE_COUNT := 1);
--This procedure causes a line terminator to be sent to
  the external file currently associated with the
  internal-file object that is associated with the formal
  parameter FILE. The current line number is then
  incremented a number of times equal to the value of the
  actual parameter associated with the formal parameter
  SPACING. If no file parameter is provided, the parameter
  defaults to the current default output file. The file
  must be open and the file mode must be OUT_FILE.
  Exceptions that may be raised are

      STATUS_ERROR -- if the file is not open
      MODE_ERROR   -- if the file mode is not OUT_FILE

procedure SKIP_LINE(FILE : in FILE_TYPE;
                    SPACING : in POSITIVE_COUNT := 1);
--This procedure reads the internal-file object that is
  associated with the formal parameter FILE until a line
  terminator is encountered, discarding the characters
  that have been read. It then sets the current column
  number to one and increments the current line number a
  number of times equal to the value of the actual
  parameter associated with the formal parameter SPACING.
  If no file parameter is provided, the parameter defaults
  to the current default input file. The file must be open
  and the file mode must be IN_FILE. Exceptions that may
  be raised are

      STATUS_ERROR -- if the file is not open
      MODE_ERROR   -- if the file mode is not IN_FILE
      END_ERROR    -- if an attempt is made to read a file
                      terminator
```

```
function END_OF_LINE(FILE : in FILE_TYPE) return BOOLEAN;
--This function returns the value TRUE if a line
  terminator or a file terminator is to be read next on
  the internal-file object that is associated with the
  formal parameter FILE. Otherwise, the value FALSE is
  returned. If no file parameter is provided, the
  parameter defaults to the default input file. Exceptions
  that may be raised are

      STATUS_ERROR -- if the file is not open
      MODE_ERROR   -- if the file mode is not IN_FILE

procedure NEW_PAGE(FILE : in FILE_TYPE);
--This procedure causes a line terminator and a page
  terminator to be sent to the external file currently
  associated with the internal-file object that is
  associated with the formal parameter FILE. The current
  page number is incremented, and the current line number
  and current column number are set to one. If no file
  parameter is provided, the parameter defaults to the
  default output file. The file must be open and the file
  mode must be OUT_FILE. Exceptions that may be raised are

      STATUS_ERROR -- if the file is not open
      MODE_ERROR   -- if the file mode is not OUT_FILE

procedure SKIP_PAGE(FILE : in FILE_TYPE);
--This procedure reads the internal-file object that is
  associated with the formal parameter FILE until a page
  terminator is encountered, discarding the characters
  that have been read. It then sets the current line
  number and current column number to one, and increments
  the current page number. The file must be open and the
  file mode must be IN_FILE. If no file parameter is
  provided, the parameter defaults to the default input
  file. Exceptions that may be raised are

      STATUS_ERROR -- if the file is not open
      MODE_ERROR   -- if the file mode is not IN_FILE
      END_ERROR    -- if an attempt is made to read a file
                      terminator

function END_OF_PAGE(FILE : in FILE_TYPE) return BOOLEAN;
--This function returns the value TRUE if a line
  terminator followed by a page terminator, or a file
  terminator, is to be read next on the internal-file
```

```
  object that is associated with the formal parameter
  FILE. The file must be open and the file mode must be IN_
  FILE. If no file parameter is provided, the parameter
  defaults to the default input file. Exceptions that may
  be raised are

      STATUS_ERROR -- if the file is not open
      MODE_ERROR   -- if the file mode is not IN_FILE
```

```
function END_OF_FILE(FILE : in FILE_TYPE) return BOOLEAN;
--This function returns the value TRUE if a line
  terminator followed by a page terminator and a file
  terminator, or a file terminator, is to be read next on
  the internal-file object that is associated with the
  formal parameter FILE. The file must be open and the
  file mode must be IN_FILE. If no file parameter is
  provided, the parameter defaults to the default input
  file. Exceptions that may be raised are

      STATUS_ERROR -- if the file is not open
      MODE_ERROR   -- if the file mode is not IN_FILE
```

Two procedures and three functions provide control of the current column number and current line number when reading from or writing to a text file. When any of these subprograms is called, the actual parameter associated with the formal parameter FILE may be omitted, in which case the parameter defaults to the default input file or to the default output file, as appropriate.

```
procedure SET_COL(FILE : in FILE_TYPE);
                  TO   : in POSITIVE_COUNT);
--This procedure sets the current column number in the
  internal-file object that is associated with the formal
  parameter FILE, in the following way:

      For a file with mode OUT_FILE: The procedure causes
      spaces to be sent to the associated external file,
      incrementing the current column number each time,
      until the column number equals the value of the
      actual parameter associated with the formal
      parameter TO. If the value associated with the
      formal parameter TO has the same value as the
      current column number, there is no effect. If it is
      less than the current column number, the current
      line number is incremented and the current column
```

number is set to one. Sufficient spaces are then sent to the external file in order to produce the specified current column number.

For a file with mode IN_FILE: The procedure causes reading of the file until the current column number is equal to the value of the actual parameter associated with the formal parameter TO. All characters and terminators read are discarded. Short lines will be skipped until a line is reached that has a character in the specified column.

The file must be open. If no file parameter is provided, the parameter defaults to the default input file or to the default output file, as appropriate. The only exception that may be raised is

STATUS_ERROR -- if the file is not open

```
procedure SET_LINE(FILE : in FILE_TYPE;
                   TO   : in POSITIVE_COUNT);
```

--This procedure sets the current line number in the internal-file object that is associated with the formal parameter FILE, in the following way:

For a file with mode OUT_FILE: The procedure causes successive line terminators to be sent to the associated external file, incrementing the current line number and setting the current column number to one each time, until the current line number equals the value of the actual parameter associated with the formal parameter TO. If the value associated with the formal parameter TO is equal to the current line number, then there is no effect. If it is less than the current line number, then a line terminator and a page terminator are sent, and the current page number is incremented. Sufficient line terminators are then sent to the external file to produce the specified current line number.

For a file with mode IN_FILE: The procedure causes reading of the file until the current line number is equal to the value of the actual parameter associated with the formal parameter TO. All characters and terminators read are discarded. If the value associated with the formal parameter TO is equal to the current line number, then there is no effect. Short pages will be skipped until a page is reached that has a line at the specified position.

The file must be open. If no file parameter is provided, then the parameter defaults to the default input file or to the default output file, as appropriate. Exceptions that may be raised are

```
STATUS_ERROR -- if the file is not open
LAYOUT_ERROR -- if the specified line value in an
                output file exceeds the maximum page
                length
END_ERROR    -- if an attempt is made, in an input
                file, to read a file terminator
```

function COL(FILE : **in** FILE_TYPE) **return** POSITIVE_COUNT;
--This function returns the value of the current column number of the internal-file object that is associated with the formal parameter FILE. The file must be open. If no file parameter is provided, the function defaults to the default output file. Exceptions that may be raised are

```
STATUS_ERROR -- if the file is not open
LAYOUT_ERROR -- if the current column number exceeds
                COUNT'LAST
```

function LINE(FILE : **in** FILE_TYPE) **return** POSITIVE_COUNT;
--This function returns the value of the current line number of the internal-file object that is associated with the formal parameter FILE. The file must be open. If no file parameter is provided, the function defaults to the default output file. Exceptions that may be raised are

```
STATUS_ERROR -- if the file is not open
LAYOUT_ERROR -- if the current line number exceeds
                COUNT'LAST
```

function PAGE(FILE : **in** FILE_TYPE) **return** POSITIVE_COUNT;
--This function returns the value of the current page number of the internal-file object that is associated with the formal parameter FILE. The file must be open. If no file parameter is provided, the function defaults

```
  to the default output file. Exceptions that may be
  raised are

      STATUS_ERROR -- if the file is not open
      LAYOUT_ERROR -- if the current page number exceeds
                      COUNT'LAST
```

6.2.2.5 Input-Output Operations for Characters. The input and output procedures for reading from and writing to text files are named GET and PUT, as compared to the names READ and WRITE used for binary files. Because of the strong typing of the Ada language, each distinct data type must have its own set of input-output procedures. For user-defined types, these procedures are obtained by instantiating one of the four generic packages contained within package TEXT_IO. For the predefined types CHARACTER and STRING, however, the input-output procedures are contained directly within the nongeneric part of TEXT_IO, and therefore they can be used without further concern at any point in a program in which TEXT_IO is visible. All text file input-output procedures use the overloaded names GET and PUT.

For character data, the following two procedures are provided:

```
procedure GET(FILE : in FILE_TYPE;
             ITEM : out CHARACTER);
--This procedure reads the next character from the
  external file currently associated with the internal-
  file object that is associated with the formal parameter
  FILE. Line and page terminators are skipped. The value
  is returned as the actual parameter associated with the
  formal parameter ITEM. The file must be open, and the
  file mode must be IN_FILE. If no file parameter is
  provided, the parameter defaults to the default input
  file. Exceptions that may be raised are

      STATUS_ERROR -- if the file is not open
      MODE_ERROR   -- if the file mode is not IN_FILE
      END_ERROR    -- if a file terminator is encountered
      DATA_ERROR   -- if data provided is not of type
                      CHARACTER

procedure PUT(FILE : in FILE_type;
             ITEM : in CHARACTER);
--This procedure writes the character value associated
  with the formal parameter ITEM to the external file
  currently associated with the internal-file object that
  is associated with the formal parameter FILE. If the
```

```
  maximum line length is exceeded, a line terminator is
  sent and the current column number is set to one prior
  to writing of the character. The file must be open. The
  file mode must be OUT_FILE. If no file parameter is
  provided, the parameter defaults to the default output
  file. Exceptions that may be raised are

      STATUS_ERROR -- if the file is not open
      MODE_ERROR   -- if the file mode is not OUT_FILE
```

6.2.2.6 Input-Output Operations for Strings. The input and output procedures for string objects are contained in the nongeneric part of TEXT_IO. Thus, they are available for use without further concern at any point in the program text where TEXT_IO is visible. There are four procedures, as detailed below:

```
procedure GET(FILE : in FILE_TYPE;
              ITEM : out STRING);
--This procedure reads a string value from the external
  file currently associated with the internal-file object
  that is associated with the formal parameter FILE. The
  value is returned as the value of the actual parameter
  associated with the formal parameter ITEM. Since type
  STRING is an unconstrained array of type CHARACTER, the
  procedure must determine the length of the string and
  then perform a number of GET operations for successive
  characters of the string. The file must be open, and the
  file mode must be IN_FILE. If no file parameter is
  provided, the parameter defaults to the default input
  file. Exceptions that may be raised are

      STATUS_ERROR -- if the file is not open
      MODE_ERROR   -- if the file mode is not IN_FILE
      DATA_ERROR   -- if data provided is not of type
                      CHARACTER

procedure PUT(FILE : in FILE_TYPE;
              ITEM : in STRING);
--This procedure writes the string value associated with
  the formal parameter ITEM to the external file currently
  associated with the internal-file object that is
  associated with the formal parameter FILE. The procedure
  must determine the length of the string and then perform
  a number of PUT operations for successive characters of
  the string. The file must be open, and the file mode
```

```
  must be OUT_FILE. If no file parameter is provided, the
  parameter defaults to the default output file.
  Exceptions that may be raised are

      STATUS_ERROR -- if the file is not open
      MODE_ERROR   -- if the file mode is not OUT_FILE
      LAYOUT ERROR -- if the length of the string provided
                      is not sufficient

procedure GET_LINE(FILE : in FILE_TYPE;
                   ITEM : out STRING;
                   LAST : out NATURAL);
--This procedure reads successive characters from the
  external file currently associated with the internal-
  file object that is associated with the formal parameter
  FILE. Reading continues until a line terminator is
  encountered, at which point the current line number is
  incremented and the current column number is set to one.
  The characters that are read replace successive
  characters in the string value associated with the
  formal parameter ITEM. Reading also stops if all the
  characters in the string have been replaced prior to
  encountering a line terminator. The value returned in
  the actual parameter associated with the formal
  parameter LAST is the index value of the last character
  replaced. If no characters are read, then the value
  returned is one less than the first index of the actual
  parameter associated with the formal parameter ITEM. The
  file must be open, and the file mode must be IN_FILE. If
  no file parameter is provided, the parameter defaults to
  the default input file. Exceptions that may be raised
  are

      STATUS_ERROR -- if the file is not open
      MODE_ERROR   -- if the file mode is not IN_FILE
      END_ERROR    -- if a file terminator is encountered
      DATA_ERROR   -- if data provided is not of type
                      CHARACTER

procedure PUT_LINE(FILE : in FILE_TYPE;
                   ITEM : in STRING);
--This procedure executes procedure PUT with the two
  parameters FILE and ITEM, after which a line terminator
  is sent, the current line number is incremented, and the
  current column number is set to one. The file must be
  open, and the file mode must be OUT_FILE. If no file
```

```
  parameter is provided, the parameter defaults to the
  default output file. Exceptions that may be raised are

      STATUS_ERROR -- if the file is not open
      MODE_ERROR   -- if the file mode is not OUT_FILE
      LAYOUT_ERROR -- if the length of the string provided
                      is not sufficient
```

As is implied by some of the comments above, it is possible for a string value to extend past a line terminator.

6.2.2.7 Input-Output Operations for Integer Types. The input-output operations for characters and strings, as well as those for file formatting, are contained within the nongeneric part of package TEXT_IO, and they are therefore available for use at any point at which TEXT_IO is visible. If the text information contains integer values, then the generic package INTEGER_IO—itself contained within package TEXT_IO—must be instantiated using, as the actual generic type parameter, the type of the integer value for which input-output operations are desired. Furthermore, the generic package INTEGER_IO must be instantiated for each distinct integer data type requiring input-output services, including the predefined type INTEGER. Within generic package INTEGER_IO, the following additional objects are declared:

```
DEFAULT_WIDTH : FIELD := NUM'WIDTH;
DEFAULT_BASE  : NUMBER_BASE := 10;
```

As indicated in Section 6.2.2., both FIELD and NUMBER_BASE are subtypes of type INTEGER. From Appendix C, it can be determined that NUM is the generic formal type parameter.

The generic package INTEGER_IO contains four procedures, using the overloaded names GET and PUT. These procedures are detailed below.

```
procedure GET(FILE  : in FILE_TYPE;
              ITEM  : out NUM;
              WIDTH : in FIELD := 0);
--This procedure reads an integer literal from the
  external file currently associated with the internal-
  file object that is associated with the formal parameter
  FILE. The value is returned as the value of the actual
  parameter associated with the formal parameter ITEM. The
  type of the returned value is NUM, the generic formal
  type parameter. In accordance with the principles
```

```
  outlined in Section 5.4.1.1, the identifier NUM denotes
  the type that is the actual parameter associated with
  the generic formal parameter NUM at instantiation. If
  the actual parameter associated with the formal
  parameter WIDTH is zero, which is the default value, any
  leading blanks, line terminators, or page terminators
  are skipped prior to the reading of the integer value.
  The value may have a sign and may be a based literal. If
  a nonzero value is associated with the formal parameter
  WIDTH, a number of characters equal to that value are
  read, including leading blanks, unless a line terminator
  is reached first, in which case reading ends at the
  terminator. The file must be open, and the file mode
  must be IN_FILE. If no file parameter is provided, the
  parameter defaults to the default input file. Exceptions
  that may be raised are

      STATUS_ERROR -- if the file is not open
      MODE_ERROR   -- if the file mode is not IN_FILE
      END_ERROR    -- if a file terminator is encountered
      DATA_ERROR   -- if the data provided is not of the
                      correct type

procedure PUT(FILE  : in FILE_TYPE;
              ITEM  : in NUM;
              WIDTH : in FIELD := DEFAULT_WIDTH;
              BASE  : in NUMBER_BASE := DEFAULT_BASE);
--This procedure writes the value of the actual parameter
  that is associated with the formal parameter ITEM, as an
  integer literal, to the external file currently
  associated with the internal-file object that is
  associated with the formal parameter FILE. A minus sign
  is included for negative values. The field width is
  determined by the value of the actual parameter
  associated with the formal parameter WIDTH. If this
  value is greater than that required for the sequence of
  characters representing the integer value to be written,
  leading blanks are used to fill the field. If the
  specified field is insufficiently wide for the data
  provided, it is increased to the minimum required size.
  The value of the actual parameter associated with the
  formal parameter BASE determines the number base in
  which the integer value is to be represented. The
  default, as indicated, is to the value of DEFAULT_BASE.
  The file must be open, and the file mode must be OUT_
  FILE. If no file parameter is provided, the parameter
```

```
   defaults to the default output file. Exceptions that may
   be raised are

       STATUS_ERROR -- if the file is not open
       MODE_ERROR   -- if the file mode is not OUT_FILE

procedure GET(FROM : in STRING;
              ITEM : out NUM;
              LAST : out POSITIVE);
--This procedure reads an integer literal from a string
   object rather than from a file, following the same rules
   as the GET procedure that reads an integer from a file.
   The end of the string is treated as a file terminator.
   The string is provided as the actual parameter that is
   associated with the formal parameter FROM, and the
   integer value is returned as the value of the actual
   parameter associated with the formal parameter ITEM. The
   index value of the last character read is returned as
   the value of the actual parameter associated with the
   formal parameter LAST. The only exception that may be
   raised is

       DATA_ERROR -- if the string does not have the proper
                     syntax, or if the data provided is not
                     of the proper type

procedure PUT(TO   : out STRING;
              ITEM : in NUM;
              BASE : in NUMBER_BASE := DEFAULT_BASE);
--This procedure writes the value associated with the
   formal parameter ITEM, as an integer literal, to the
   string associated with the formal parameter TO. The
   rules of the PUT procedure that writes to an output file
   apply. The length of the string serves the function of
   the parameter WIDTH. No input-output exceptions can be
   raised by this procedure. The value of the actual
   parameter associated with the formal parameter BASE
   determines the number base in which the data will be
   written. The default is to the value of DEFAULT_BASE.
```

The reader should note that the objects DEFAULT_WIDTH and DEFAULT_BASE can be modified by assignment, allowing a programmer to specify the default values for each instance created.

The PUT and GET procedures relating to strings rather than to files, coupled with Ada's capability to handle array slices, permit external data to be exchanged with a string at the input-output speed and then accessed by the program at memory speed.

6.2.2.8 Input-Output for Floating-Point Types. When floating-point values, including those of the predefined type FLOAT, are to be read from or written to text files, the generic package FLOAT_IO must be instantiated. The values are read as literals that may be in a base other than decimal. Output values are written as decimal literals consisting of three fields:

```
FORE field
AFT field
EXP field
```

The general form of the output literal is written as

```
FORE.AFT E EXP
```

with no spaces between the fields. The sizes of these three fields are provided as parameters in the PUT procedures. Within the generic package FLOAT_IO, three objects are declared that determine the default values for the widths of these fields:

```
DEFAULT_FORE : FIELD := 2;
DEFAULT_AFT  : FIELD : NUM'DIGITS - 1;
DEFAULT_EXP  : FIELD := 3;
```

The default values of these objects can be overridden by assignment, permitting the programmer to specify default values for each instance of the generic package FLOAT_IO.

There are four procedures provided for input-output of floating-point types. They use the overloaded names GET and PUT.

```
procedure GET(FILE  : in FILE_TYPE;
              ITEM  : out NUM;
              WIDTH : in FIELD := 0);
--This procedure reads a real literal from the external
  file currently associated with the internal-file object
  that is associated with the formal parameter FILE. The
  value is returned as the value of the actual parameter
  associated with the formal parameter ITEM. The type of
  the returned value is NUM, which is the generic formal
  type parameter. In accordance with the principles
  outlined in Section 5.4.1.1, the identifier NUM denotes
  the type that is the actual parameter associated with
```

the generic formal type parameter at instantiation. If the actual parameter associated with the formal parameter WIDTH is zero, which is the default value, any leading blanks, line terminators, or page terminators are skipped prior to the reading of the floating-point value. The value may have a sign and may be a based literal. If a nonzero value is associated with formal parameter WIDTH, a number of characters equal to that value are read, including leading blanks, unless a line terminator is reached first, in which case the reading ends at the terminator. The file must be open, and the file mode must be IN_FILE. If no file parameter is provided, the parameter defaults to the default input file. Exceptions that may be raised are

```
STATUS_ERROR -- if the file is not open
MODE_ERROR   -- if the file mode is not IN_FILE
END_ERROR    -- if a file terminator is encountered
DATA_ERROR   -- if the data provided is not of the
                correct type
```

```
procedure PUT(FILE : in FILE_TYPE;
              ITEM : in NUM;
              FORE : in FIELD := DEFAULT_FORE;
              AFT  : in FIELD := DEFAULT_AFT;
              EXP  : in FIELD := DEFAULT_EXP);
```

--This procedure writes the floating-point value of the actual parameter associated with the formal parameter ITEM to the external file currently associated with the internal-file object that is associated with the formal parameter FILE. The value is written as a decimal literal with format defined by the values of the actual parameters associated with formal parameters FORE, AFT, and EXP, in the following manner:

If EXP has the value zero, there is no EXP field. The FORE field is written with as many digits as are needed to represent the integer part of the value, overriding the FORE parameter if necessary.

If EXP has a nonzero value, then the FORE field has a single digit. The EXP field includes a plus or minus sign. Leading zeros are used, as necessary, to fill the field.

In either case above, leading blanks are used, as necessary, to fill the FORE field.

The number of digits in the AFT field is equal to the value of the AFT parameter, unless it is zero, in which case there is one digit in the AFT field. The value is rounded.

The file must be open, and the file mode must be OUT_FILE. If no file parameter is provided, the parameter defaults to the default output file. Exceptions that may be raised are

```
STATUS_ERROR -- if the file is not open
MODE_ERROR   -- if the file mode is not OUT_FILE
```

```
procedure GET(FROM : in STRING;
              ITEM : out NUM;
              LAST : out POSITIVE);
```

--This procedure reads a real literal from a string object rather than from a file, following the same rules as the GET procedure that reads a floating-point value from a file. The end of the string is treated as a file terminator. The string is provided as the actual parameter that is associated with the formal parameter FROM, and the floating-point value is returned as the value of the actual parameter associated with the formal parameter ITEM. The index value of the last character read is returned as the actual parameter associated with the formal parameter LAST. The only exception that may be raised is

```
DATA_ERROR -- if the string does not have the proper
              syntax, or if the data provided is not
              of the proper type
```

```
procedure PUT(TO   : out STRING;
              ITEM : in NUM;
              AFT  : in FIELD := DEFAULT_AFT;
              EXP  : in FIELD := DEFAULT_EXP);
```

--This procedure writes the value associated with the formal parameter ITEM, as a decimal literal, to the string associated with the formal parameter TO. The rules of the PUT procedure that writes to an output file apply. A value of FORE is used such that the sequence of output characters is precisely the same as the string length. That is, leading blanks are used to fill the string, if necessary. No input-output exceptions can be raised by this procedure.

6.2.2.9 Input-Output Operations for Fixed-Point Types. The generic package FIXED_IO, contained within package TEXT_IO, provides input-output support for fixed-point types. Analogously to integer and floating-point support, the generic package FIXED_IO must be instantiated for each distinct fixed-point data type for which input-output support is required. The values are read as literals that may be in a base other than decimal. Output values are written as decimal literals consisting of three fields:

```
FORE field
AFT field
EXP field
```

The general form of the output literal is

```
FORE.AFT E EXP
```

with no spaces between the fields. As with PUT operations for floating-point types, the sizes of these three fields are provided as parameters in the PUT procedures. Within the generic package FIXED_IO, three objects are declared that determine the default values for the widths of these fields:

```
DEFAULT_FORE  : FIELD := NUM'FORE;
DEFAULT_AFT   : FIELD := NUM'AFT;
DEFAULT_EXP   : FIELD := 0;
```

The attributes NUM'FORE and NUM'AFT, as outlined in Appendix C, yield, respectively:

- the minimum number of characters needed for the integer part of the decimal representation of any value of type NUM
- the number of decimal digits needed after the point to accommodate the precision of type NUM, unless the delta of the type is greater than 0.1, in which case the attribute yields the value one

In accordance with the principles outlined in Section 5.4.1.1, the identifier NUM denotes the type that is the actual parameter associated with the generic formal parameter NUM at instantiation. Thus, the default values in the object declaration above will vary from one instantiation to another, depending upon the particular type for which the generic package is instantiated. Furthermore, the default values in the object declarations can be overridden by assignment of values to the objects.

There are four procedures provided, using the overloaded names GET and PUT.

```
procedure GET(FILE  : in FILE_TYPE;
              ITEM  : out NUM;
              WIDTH : in FIELD := 0);
--This procedure reads a real literal value from the
  external file currently associated with the internal-
  file object that is associated with the formal parameter
  FILE. The rules of this GET procedure, and the
  exceptions that may be raised, are identical to those
  outlined in the previous section for the corresponding
  floating-point GET procedure.

procedure PUT(FILE : in FILE_TYPE;
              ITEM : in NUM;
              FORE : in FIELD := DEFAULT_FORE;
              AFT  : in FIELD := DEFAULT_AFT;
              EXP  : in FIELD := DEFAUT_EXP);
--This procedure writes the fixed-point value of the
  actual parameter associated with the formal parameter
  ITEM to the external file currently associated with the
  internal-file object that is associated with the formal
  parameter FILE. The rules of this PUT procedure, and the
  exceptions that may be raised, are identical to those
  outlined in the previous section for the corresponding
  floating-point PUT procedure.

procedure GET(FROM : in STRING;
              ITEM : out NUM;
              LAST : out POSITIVE);
--This procedure reads a real literal value from a string
  rather than from a file, following the same rules as the
  GET procedure that reads from a file. The rules of this
  GET procedure, and the exceptions that may be raised,
  are identical to those outlined in the previous section
  for the corresponding floating-point GET procedure.

procedure PUT(TO   : out STRING;
              ITEM : in NUM;
              AFT  : in FIELD := DEFAULT_AFT;
              EXP  : in FIELD := DEFAULT_EXP);
--This procedure writes the fixed-point value associated
  with the formal parameter ITEM, as a decimal literal, to
  the string that is associated with the formal parameter
```

```
  TO. The rules of this PUT procedure are identical to
  those outlined in the previous section for the
  corresponding floating-point PUT procedure.
```

6.2.2.10 Input-Output Operations for Enumeration Types. In the Ada language, the values of an enumeration object can be read from or written to a text file. That is, the enumeration literals themselves, in the form of a character sequence, can be manipulated in input-output operations. The generic package ENUMERATION_IO, contained within the package TEXT_IO, is provided for this purpose. Analogously with integer, floating-point, and fixed-point input-output, the generic package ENUMERATION_IO must be instantiated for each distinct enumeration data type for which input-output support is required. The values are read and written as enumeration literals, and in the case of output, either lowercase or uppercase letters are specified by the parameter SET in the PUT procedure. The format, which may include trailing blanks, is specified by the parameter WIDTH. Within the generic package ENUMERATION_IO, two objects are declared:

```
DEFAULT_WIDTH   : FIELD := 0;
DEFAULT_SETTING : TYPE_SET := UPPER CASE;
```

Both type FIELD and type TYPE_SET are declared in the nongeneric part of the package TEXT_IO, as discussed in Section 6.2.2. There are four procedures provided:

```
procedure GET(FILE : in FILE_TYPE;
              OUT  : out ENUM);
--This procedure reads an enumeration literal from the
  external file currently associated with the internal-
  file object that is associated with the formal parameter
  FILE. The value is returned as the value of the actual
  parameter associated with the formal parameter OUT. The
  type of the returned value is ENUM, which is the generic
  formal type parameter. In accordance with the principles
  outlined in Section 5.4.1.1, the identifier ENUM denotes
  the type that is the actual parameter associated with
  the generic formal parameter ENUM at instantiation. The
  reading skips any leading blanks, line terminators, or
  page terminators, and does not differentiate between
  lowercase and uppercase letters. If the enumeration
  literal is a character, it must be enclosed by
  apostrophes. The file must be open, and the file mode
```

```
  must be IN_FILE. If no file parameter is provided, the
  parameter defaults to the default input file. Exceptions
  that may be raised are

      STATUS_ERROR -- if the file is not open
      MODE_ERROR   -- if the file mode is not IN_FILE
      END_ERROR    -- if a file terminator is encountered
      DATA_ERROR   -- if the input sequence does not have
                      the required syntax, or if the
                      enumeration literal does not belong
                      to the required type

procedure PUT(FILE  : in FILE_TYPE;
              ITEM  : in ENUM;
              WIDTH : in FIELD := DEFAULT_WIDTH;
              SET   : in TYPE_SET := DEFAULT_SETTING);
--This procedure writes the value of the actual parameter
  associated with the formal parameter ITEM to the
  external file currently associated with the internal-
  file object that is associated with the formal parameter
  FILE. The value is written as an enumeration literal,
  either as an identifier or as a character literal. An
  identifier is written in uppercase or in lowercase
  letters, as specified by the value associated with the
  formal parameter SET. This parameter has no effect on
  character literals. Trailing blanks are provided to fill
  the field specified by the value associated with the
  formal parameter WIDTH. If the specified field is
  insufficiently wide for the data provided, it is
  increased to the minimum required size. The file must be
  open. The file mode must be OUT_FILE. If no file
  parameter is provided, the parameter defaults to the
  default output file. Exceptions that may be raised are

      STATUS_ERROR -- if the file is not open
      MODE_ERROR   -- if the file mode is not OUT_FILE

procedure GET(FROM : in STRING;
              ITEM : out ENUM;
              LAST : out POSITIVE);
--This procedure reads an enumeration value from a string
  object rather than from a file, following the same rules
  as the GET procedure that reads an enumeration value
  from a file. The end of the string is treated as a file
  terminator. The string is provided as the actual
```

```
  parameter that is associated with the formal parameter
  FROM, and the enumeration value is returned as the value
  of the actual parameter associated with the formal
  parameter ITEM. The index value of the last character
  read is returned as the actual parameter associated with
  the formal parameter LAST. The only exception that may
  be raised is

      DATA_ERROR -- if the string does not have the proper
                    syntax, or if the enumeration literal
                    does not belong to the required type

procedure PUT(TO   : out STRING;
              ITEM : in ENUM;
              SET  : in TYPE_SET := DEFAULT_SETTING);
--This procedure writes the value associated with the
  formal parameter ITEM, as an eumeration literal, to the
  string associated with the formal parameter TO. The
  rules of the PUT procedure that writes to an output file
  apply. The length of the string serves the function of
  the parameter WIDTH. No input-output exceptions can be
  raised by this procedure.
```

The predefined type BOOLEAN is an enumeration type. If input-output operations are required for boolean values, then the generic package ENUMERATION_IO must be instantiated using BOOLEAN as the actual parameter associated with the formal parameter ENUM.

6.3 LOW-LEVEL INPUT-OUTPUT

Embedded computer systems often interact with special devices such as sensors, actuators, displays, and other automated equipment. Communication with these devices is often effected directly at the hardware level and normally requires access to the status, control, or data registers of the device. There must also be some means of handling interrupts. While most languages require the programmer to resort to assembly language subprograms to effect this kind of communications, the Ada language provides means for low-level programming within the structure of the language itself. Some of the advanced features considered in Chapter 8, such as the interrupt handling and representation features, particularly serve to meet this need.

The predefined package LOW_LEVEL_IO contains the following highly implementation-dependent procedure declarations:

```
procedure SEND_CONTROL(DEVICE : device_type;
                        DATA : in out data_type);
procedure RECEIVE_CONTROL(DEVICE : device_type;
                           DATA : in out data_type);
```

The procedure SEND_CONTROL is used to send information to a physical device, while RECEIVE_CONTROL may request information from the physical device. Since the kind of data, and the format of that data, is highly dependent upon the physical characteristics of the underlying hardware and of the physical device, the types device_type and data_type must be implementation-dependent. Typically, the representation specification features of the language are used to declare these types in a manner consonant with the hardware configuration. The names SEND_CONTROL and RECEIVE_CONTROL will normally be overloaded to provide communications with all supported devices.

EXERCISES

1. Why is it usually desirable to have the target software include only that input-output support actually needed? Why is this not normally important in the host system?
2. What part do the generic facilities of the Ada language play in input-output support?
3. Why is it not necessary to name INTEGER_IO, FLOAT_IO, FIXED_IO, or ENUMERATION_IO in a with clause?
4. Differentiate between an external file and an internal-file object. What is meant by association of an internal-file object with an external file?
5. Why is it not necessary for a program unit to name the predefined package IO_EXCEPTIONS in a with clause?
6. Differentiate between the CREATE and the OPEN procedures.
7. How is an internal-file object associated with an external file?
8. Differentiate between a binary file and a text file.
9. Differentiate between a sequential-access file and a direct-access file.
10. What is a file mode?
11. What is a file form?
12. What is the significance of the fact that SEQUENTIAL_IO and DIRECT_IO are generic packages?
13. What is the significance of the fact that package TEXT_IO is not a generic unit?
14. Even though package TEXT_IO is not a generic unit, it contains the declarations of four generic packages. Name these packages and explain how their input-output services can be provided to a program unit.
15. Input-output operations for what data types are supported by the nongeneric parts of package TEXT_IO?

16. Why is the file mode of sequential files limited to IN_FILE and OUT_FILE, while direct files can have a mode of IN_FILE, OUT_FILE, or INOUT_FILE?
17. Why is special input-output support required—in the form of instantiations of the generic packages INTEGER_IO, FLOAT_IO, FIXED_IO, and ENUMERATION_IO—for the inclusion of numeric and enumeration types in text files?
18. Are text files sequential or direct files?
19. What is meant by the terms *standard input file* and *standard output file*?
20. What is meant by the terms *default input file* and *default output file*? In particular how are default files related to standard files?
21. Why is no instantiation necessary for input-output operations involving strings and characters?
22. Discuss the possible use of those text input-output operations that read from and write to strings, rather than reading from or writing to files.
23. Discuss the operator overloading used in package TEXT_IO.
24. What input-output package supports input-output operations for the predefined type BOOLEAN? Show the declarations required to obtain this support for a program unit.
25. Describe what an implementation would provide in the package LOW_LEVEL_IO.

PROGRAMMING EXERCISES

1. Compile the generic procedure COPY of the example in Section 6.2.1.1. Write and compile a program (procedure) that creates a file whose components are arrays of records, and use this program to create a file. Write a program (procedure) that instantiates COPY and then copies the file to a second file.
2. Compile the package FIGHTER_PACKAGE of the example in Section 6.2.1.2. Write and compile a program (procedure) that creates a direct file of records of type FIGHTER_RECORD. Compile the function SEARCH and write and compile a second program that uses function SEARCH to search the file of type FIGHTER_RECORD.

Chapter 7
TASKS

7.1 PARALLELISM AND CONCURRENT PROGRAMMING

Two of the usual requirements for Department of Defense embedded computer systems, as outlined in Chapter 1, are *real-time processing* and *concurrency*. These two concepts are related, with real-time requirements often being met by use of concurrent processing, or *parallelism*. In general, the term *concurrent processing* refers to those situations in which the execution of more than one sequential thread of code takes place in parallel—or at least it has the appearance of occurring in parallel. The term *concurrent programming* refers to those tools and techniques for dealing with concurrent processing. Concurrent programming is typical in the development of operating system and real-time system software, and it often distinguishes these kinds of systems from other software systems.

In general, concurrent processing is obtained in one of three ways:

1. multicomputing—in which different processes execute on totally different computers, but with detailed intercommunication requirements
2. multiprocessing—in which different tasks execute on different processors within the same computer, possibly sharing the same memory and other resources
3. multiprogramming—in which different processes are executed in an interleaved manner on a single processor

There is currently a trend toward *abstract concurrency* that is unrelated to the parallelism of the actual target computer.[1] The data flow diagrams found in certain software engineering techniques can be envisioned as networks of concurrent processes, even though eventual implementation has traditionally been in a sequential language. The Ada language supports the concept of abstract concurrency by the inclusion of concurrent programming features as an integral part of the language, regardless of the actual parallelism present in the target environment. Each thread of code in an Ada program is considered to be executing on a single *logical processor*. A program containing only a single thread of code—the main program, so to speak—executes on a single logical processor, even though the actual implementation may be obtained by multiprocessing or multicomputing. Ada programs executing more than one thread of code in parallel accomplish this concurrency by the use of the Ada task—one task for each additional thread of executing code. Each task also executes on a single logical processor, even though the actual implementation may be obtained through multicomputing, multiprocessing, interleaving on a single processor, or any combination of these techniques. That is, the language and its run-time support environment completely isolate the programmer from the implementation in such a way that concurrent programming can be developed as though each Ada task were to execute on its own logical processor. A very specific set of rules determines the task dependencies and the interactions and communications among tasks.

7.1.1 Traditional Approaches to Concurrent Programming

In general, embedded-system software applications fall into one of three categories:[2]

1. Synchronous, or purely cyclic: All tasks performed by the software are, by definition, periodic and execute in a synchronous, sequential pattern according to a fixed schedule. Some very simple control systems fit into this category.
2. Mostly cyclic, with some asynchronous events: Most tasks are cyclic in nature and can be scheduled deterministically, but some asynchronous events and burst computing loads must be handled without interfering with the cyclic processing. Many modern weapon control, flight control, and navigation systems fit into this category.
3. Asynchronous: Most tasks are asynchronous, rather than cyclic, in nature. These systems depend almost exclusively on asynchronous, interrupt-driven processing. Stimuli arrive at unpredictable times, and software responses must be delivered within rigid time constraints even under peak load conditions. These kinds of systems are said to be *event-driven*. Command, control, communications, and intelligence systems (C^3I) fall into this category.

The means of achieving the proper scheduling of tasks in embedded computer systems has typically been provided in one of two ways:

1. By use of a user-written supervisor program implemented in assembly code. This program would normally respond to timed interrupts in order to provide the scheduling process. Context switching—the saving and restoring of processor states—must be provided by this program.
2. By use of a *real-time operating system* or *real-time executive*. The program must then make operating system calls to access task control, memory management, and interrupt handling facilities of the operating system. Operating system services such as semaphores, mailboxes, and queues are used for synchronization of and communication among concurrently executing tasks. In essence, a real-time kernel provides a basis around which a special-purpose operating system is generated, with the concurrently executing tasks in the role of processes within the operating system.

The use of a real-time operating system to serve as an interface between the hardware and the applications program greatly simplifies the development of embedded-system software. In addition, because the operating system itself normally has had wide use, the reliability of the resulting software is usually enhanced.

In the first category of embedded-system software, for which synchronous features dominate, the traditional approach to real-time operating systems has been the cyclic executive approach, in which a scheduler allocates to tasks certain time intervals in which to execute. Because different tasks often must execute at different cyclic rates, elaborate methods for allocating processor time must often be developed. The smallest time interval allocated by the scheduler is called a *minor cycle*. Multiples of the minor cycle, usually powers of two multiples, are called *major cycles*. The various tasks execute within these cycles, and each task is run to completion and has access to all global data. Asynchronous events, if present, are usually signaled by interrupts. The interrupt service must be provided quickly enough so that it does not interfere with the cyclic portion of the program. Often, the cyclic and asynchronous functions are run as *foreground* processes, with *background* processing—that is, processing using whatever processor time is not required by the foreground tasks—performing low-priority functions that are not time-critical. A computer self-check program, for example, is often provided as a background task.

For the last two categories of embedded-system software, in which asynchronous features either are present to a significant degree or dominate the software requirements, the cyclic executive approach fails because of the complexity involved. Concurrent tasking is the best approach in this case, and the management of concurrent tasking is most easily obtained by the use of a real-time operating system.

7.1.2 Ada's Approach to Concurrent Programming

Ada's approach to concurrent programming makes the concurrently executing task a basic program unit. The synchronization of and communication among tasks are provided within the language itself by a process called *synchronization by rendezvous,* a variant of a method originally proposed by C. A. R. Hoare.[3] Ada programs, of course, cannot execute without a run-time support environment provided by the implementation. This run-time support environment may well be formed around the same real-time operating system used to provide services to traditional real-time languages. In an Ada program, however, no operating system calls are required—all synchronization of and communication among concurrently executing tasks are provided by features of the language itself. These high-order language constructs may cause invocation of operating system calls by the run-time environment, but such action is transparent to the programmer. When all task control facilities are provided within the high-order language, the portability of the resulting software is greatly enhanced.

Although the tasking features of the Ada language closely fit the requirements of event-driven software, the third category of embedded-system software in the previous section, they are diametrically opposed to those of the cyclic executive approach to task management. Ada's tasks are concurrent and asynchronous, whereas cyclic tasks are sequential and synchronous. Cyclic tasks have access to all global data, but Ada's tasks are subject to the rigid visibility rules of the language. If an Ada task requires periodic execution, explicit provisions for interaction with the system clock must be provided by the programmer, whereas cyclic tasks are periodic by definition. Nevertheless, it is possible to provide Ada compatibility with the cyclic executive approach to task scheduling while remaining within the structure of the high-order language.[4] As the language use matures, this compatibility should be further developed.

7.2 ADA TASKS

The Ada task, together with the subprogram, the package, and the generic unit, is one of the four primary program units of the language. Like subprograms and packages, tasks have a two-part form consisting of a specification and a body; both must be present. The specification part defines the interface of the task with other Ada program units, while the body contains the implementation of whatever action the task produces. Unlike the case with subprograms and packages, however, task specifications and task bodies may not be separately compiled, since they are not compilation units. They may be textually separated within a declarative part of a program unit, however, in order to provide desired visibility. In addition, the specification and body may appear in the separately compiled specification and body, respectively, of a package, in which case the task is exported by the package.

While subprogram and package specifications declare the associated entities—that is, they declare subprograms and packages—a task specification declares a task type. Task objects can then be declared in a manner analogous to any other object declaration. The value of an object of a task type designates a task, so that many different tasks of the same task type may be declared.

7.2.1 Task Specifications

The specification part of a task defines the interface between the task and other program units. This interface provides the synchronization and communication requirements of the rendezvous mechanism. A rendezvous is produced by the execution of an *entry call statement* in the calling program unit, coupled with the execution of a corresponding *accept statement* in the called task. The entry call and the accept statement are interfaced through an entry declaration in the specification part of the called task. An entry declaration may have a formal part that contains a list of formal parameters. Actual parameters in the entry call statement are associated with these formal parameters, thus providing the communication function of the rendezvous. The specific details of the rendezvous mechanism are covered thoroughly in subsequent sections.

The syntax for a task declaration is given below:

```
task_declaration ::= task_specification;      (7.1)
```

where

```
task_specification ::=
   task [type] identifier is
       {entry_declaration}
       {representation_clause}
   end [task_simple_name]                     (7.1.1)
```

and

```
entry_declaration ::=
    entry identifier [(discrete_range)][formal_part];
                                                    (7.1.2)
```

The syntax for a discrete range is given by Statement (3.22.6). The optional discrete range is used to declare a family of entries, as discussed in a later section. The syntax for the formal part is identical to that of a subprogram declaration, as given by Statement (3.55.4).

The optional representation clause in Statement (7.1.1) will be treated in Chapter 8. The task simple name, if used, must be the same as the task identifier. It should be noted that the only kind of declaration permitted in a task specification is an entry declaration. This limitation implies that the only interaction between a task and any other program unit is that obtained through an entry call. That is, since there can be no subprogram or package specifications within the task specification, any subprograms or packages declared within the task body are local to the task body and therefore cannot be accessed by any other program unit.

The entry declaration given by Statement (7.1.2) provides a name for the entry, and it declares the entry parameter list in the optional formal part. The parameter modes defined for these formal entry parameters are the same as those defined for subprogram parameters. Formal parameters may have **in, out,** or **in out** modes, and the rules relating to these modes are the same as those defined for subprogram formal parameters. If no parameter mode is given, the default is to mode **in.** The entry declaration, together with the corresponding accept statements, constitute a declarative region in the sense discussed in Section 3.11. Thus, the formal parameters declared in an entry specification have a scope that is limited to the corresponding accept statements within the package body. This concept is completely analogous to that applying to subprogram parameters, whose scope is limited to the subprogram body.

Finally, the reader should note that the reserve word **type** in Statement (7.1.1) is optional. A task specification that does not contain the reserved word **type** defines a single task rather than a task type. It is equivalent to two declarations: (1) the declaration of an anonymous task type and (2) the declaration of a task object, of the anonymous type, which is denoted by the identifier contained in the task specification. The distinction among the terms *task, task type,* and *task object* may need some clarification, since the concepts implied by these terms run counter to those applying to other Ada program units. The following comments are offered:

- A task is a program unit. It provides for the execution of the sequence of statements of the task body.
- A task type is an Ada data type. It is a limited type in that there are no predefined operations provided. Thus, not even assignment or tests for equality and inequality are predefined. Objects of a task type may be declared.
- A task object is an object whose type is a task type. It is not a task but rather is an object that designates a task in a manner somewhat analogous to the way in which an access object designates another object. The designated task has the entries of the corresponding task type, and its execution is specified by the corresponding task body.

It is clear, then, how one may declare, for example, an array of task objects, or how a task object may be declared as part of a record, or how task objects can be passed as parameters. These concepts will be discussed further in Section 7.2.4.

7.2.2 Task Bodies

The task body contains the implementation of whatever action is accomplished by the task. The syntax of a task body is

```
task_body ::=
    task body task_simple_name is
        [declarative_part]
    begin
        sequence_of_statements
    [exception
        exception_handler
       {exception_handler}]
    end [task_simple_name];                          (7.2)
```

where the syntax for a declarative part, that for a sequence of statements, and that for an exception handler are given by Statements (3.50), (3.45.2), and (3.54), respectively.

Since the only declarations permitted in the task specification are those of entries, the declarative part of the body must contain the declarations of all local entities referenced within the sequence of statements or within the exception handler. As is the case with the other Ada program units, this declarative part may contain the declarations of subprograms, of packages, or even of other tasks.

The sequence of statements can contain virtually any Ada statements.

For each entry declared in the specification, the sequence of statements should contain at least one accept statement. The syntax for an accept statement is

```
accept_statement ::=
   accept entry_simple_name [(entry_index)][formal_part][do
       sequence_of_statements
   end [entry_simple_name]];                              (7.2.1)
```

where the entry index is used with families of entries, to be discussed in Section 7.2.3, and for which the syntax is simply

```
                entry_index ::= expression          (7.2.2)
```

The sequence of statements in an accept statement, if present, specifies the action to be performed when a call to the corresponding entry—that is, the entry whose declaration contains an identifier that is the same as the entry simple name in the accept statement—is made. The formal part of the accept statement must conform to the formal part given in the declaration of the corresponding entry. The details of the role that the accept statement plays in the rendezvous mechanism will be discussed in Section 7.3.

Finally, the optional exception handlers contained in Statement (7.2), if present, handle exceptions raised during the execution of the sequence of statements, if any, contained within the task body.

The syntax of Statement (7.1.1) can be used to declare a task type or, by deletion of the reserved word **type,** to declare a task object. The task body, as given by Statement (7.2), is the same in either case. If a task object is declared by the specification, then, within the task body, the task name denotes the task object that is declared by the specification. If a task type is declared by the specification and task objects of the task type are declared, then the task name appearing within the body denotes the task object designating the task currently executing in the body. Examples of task declarations are given below.

EXAMPLE 1: This example involves a task that provides a form of buffer between two other program units. One of these program units, either the main program or another task, places a character into the buffer by a call to entry PUT, while another program unit retrieves the value by a call to entry TAKE. The precise mechanics of the rendezvous will be discussed in Section 7.3; only the syntax is of interest here. If a single task object is to be declared, the specification has the following form:

```
task BUFFER is
    entry PUT(ELEM : in CHARACTER);
    entry TAKE(ELEM : out CHARACTER);
end BUFFER;
--This is a task object specification with two
  entries, PUT and TAKE. The formal part of each entry
  contains a single parameter. In the case of entry
  PUT, the parameter has mode in, so that the
  parameter value is passed to this task from the
  calling task. The mode out specified for the
  parameter in entry TAKE implies that the value is
  passed from this task to the calling task.
```

The corresponding task body is

```
task body BUFFER is
    TEMP : CHARACTER;
begin
    loop
        accept PUT(ELEM : in CHARACTER) do
            TEMP := ELEM;
        end PUT;
        accept TAKE(ELEM : out CHARACTER) do
            ELEM := TEMP;
        end TAKE;
    end loop
end BUFFER;
--The task body consists of an endless loop containing
  only the two accept statements corresponding to the
  two entries PUT and TAKE.
```

If more than one task object is needed, a task type can be declared by use of the reserved word **type**:

```
task type BUFFER is
    entry PUT(ELEM : in CHARACTER);
    entry TAKE(ELEM : out CHARACTER);
end BUFFER;
--Here, a task type is declared. The body remains
  unchanged, but one or more task objects must be
  declared before any task is designated.
```

Task object declarations, in their simplest form, might be

```
BUFFER_1, BUFFER_2, BUFFER_3 : BUFFER;
```

in which case three task objects are declared. Each of these objects designates a separate task, and these tasks will execute concurrently. The task specification and task body are common to each of these tasks. For example, there are six entries now involved:

```
BUFFER_1.PUT     BUFFER_2.PUT     BUFFER_3.PUT
BUFFER_1.TAKE    BUFFER_2.TAKE    BUFFER_3.TAKE.
```

There are also the equivalent of three identical task bodies.

EXAMPLE 2: This example involves the use of two tasks, one to find the sum of two one-dimensional arrays and one to find the difference of the arrays. Both tasks are declared within a subprogram which receives the two arrays as **in** parameters and returns the sum and difference arrays as **out** parameters. The example assumes the following declaration to be in effect:

```
type VECTOR is array(INTEGER range <>) of FLOAT;
```

The procedure body contains the specifications and bodies of the two tasks ADD and SUBTRACT.

```
procedure ADD_SUB(LEFT, RIGHT : in VECTOR;
                  SUM, DIF : out VECTOR) is
    task ADD;
    task SUBTRACT;

    task body ADD is
    begin
        for INDEX in VECTOR'FIRST..VECTOR'LAST loop
            SUM(INDEX) := LEFT(INDEX) + RIGHT(INDEX);
        end loop;
    end ADD;

    task body SUBTRACT is
    begin
        for INDEX in VECTOR'FIRST..VECTOR'LAST loop
            DIF(INDEX) := LEFT(INDEX) - RIGHT(INDEX);
        end loop;
    end SUBTRACT;
begin
     --sequence of statements of ADD_SUB
end ADD_SUB;
--The two tasks, ADD and SUBTRACT, are declared in the
  declarative part of procedure ADD_SUB. The
```

```
specifications and bodies are textually separated.
The sequence of statements of procedure ADD_SUB are
executed concurrently with those of the two tasks.
These simple tasks have no entries, because no
synchronization is required.
```

The tasks ADD and SUBTRACT have no entries, and they pass no parameters. Hence, the task specifications have a very simple form. In accordance with the rules of task activation, to be discussed in Section 7.2.5, both tasks begin execution in parallel immediately upon elaboration of the subprogram. When both tasks have completed execution, their results are returned to the calling program unit through the two **out** parameters of the procedure ADD_SUB. Here, both ADD and SUBTRACT are task objects, because the reserved word **type** was not used in the specification. On a multiprocessor hardware system, the two tasks executing concurrently would terminate more quickly than a purely sequential version of the same procedure. However, if the concurrent processing is obtained by interleaving on a single processor, no such advantage is obtained.

Further tasking examples are given throughout the remainder of this chapter, as the rendezvous mechanism is examined in detail.

7.2.3 Families of Entries

When a number of entries into a single task are required, and when each of these entries has the same formal part, then it may be appropriate to declare a family of entries. The necessary syntax is given by Statements (7.1.1) and (7.1.2), using the optional discrete range provided in the entry declaration. The members of the family are denoted by indexed notation, in the same manner as are components of an array, and corresponding accept statements are provided for each member of the family. The example described below serves to illustrate the concept.

If a message handler deals with messages having four priority classes—flash, emergency, priority, and routine—the transmission of such messages may be effected by a task with four entries, one for each priority class. Given the declarations

```
type MESSAGE is ...;
type CLASS is (FLASH, EMERGENCY, PRIORITY, ROUTINE);
```

then the specification of the transmitting task might be

```
task XMIT is
    entry SEND(CLASS)(DATA : MESSAGE);
end XMIT;
```

There are actually four entries declared here:

- SEND(FLASH)
- SEND(PRIORITY)
- SEND(EMERGENCY)
- SEND(ROUTINE)

Hence, there should be at least one accept statement for each of these entries within the task body. The accept statements use the indexed notation specified by the optional entry index in Statement (7.2.1). For example, one accept statement might be

```
accept SEND(FLASH)(DATA : MESSAGE) do
   ... sequence of statements of the accept statement
end SEND:
```

The reader should note that the discrete range of Statement (7.1.2) can be of an integer type as well as of an enumeration type, and also that Statement (7.2.2) implies that the entry index can be an expression. Thus, the entry index can be computed at run time.

7.2.4 Declaration and Elaboration of Tasks

It has been previously noted that task specifications and task bodies are not separately compilable. The basic difference between the compilation features of tasks and those of other program units is implied by the discussion of compilation issues contained in Section 3.11.3, which indicates that a task does not constitute a compilation unit. That is, the only manner in which a task can be compiled is as a declarative item within another program unit—a subprogram, package, or generic unit. Both the task specification and task body must be declared within this program unit, although as indicated previously, their declarations may be textually separated so long as the specification is elaborated prior to the elaboration of the body. The effect of separate compilation of a task can be achieved by encapsulating the task within a package, and then treating the package as a compilation unit. If such an arrangement is used, then the task specification must appear as a declaration in the package specification, in order for the task entries to be accessible from outside the package, and the task body must appear in the declarative part of the package body, either as a proper body or as a body stub. If a body stub is used, the proper task body must reside in the program library as a subunit, as discussed in Section 3.11.3.2. The package specification and package body can, of course, be separately compiled.

A task specification may declare a task type or a task object, as indicated in Section 7.2.1. A task object may also be declared by an object declaration, in accordance with Statement (3.10), using the task type as a type indication. The value of a task object designates a task that has the entries contained in the task specification, and whose execution is specified by the task body. The task type is a limited type—there are no predefined operations associated with the type, not even those of assignment and tests for equality or inequality. Because the order of elaboration is important to the scope and visiblity rules of the Ada language, and because task objects can be treated as any other Ada object—subject to the restrictions of being a limited type—certain points should be made here relating to the declaration of task objects.

- Task objects essentially are constants, since no assignment or any other operation that could cause a task object to designate any task other than that initially designated is provided by the language.
- Task objects can be declared in a task declaration by deleting the reserved word **type,** in which case the value of the object is defined at the time that the task specification is elaborated.
- Task objects can be declared by object declarations. In this case, the value of the object is defined at the time of elaboration of the object declaration.
- Task objects may be components of records or components of arrays. In these cases, the value of the object is defined at the time of elaboration of the composite object.
- Task objects may be designated by access objects, in which case the value of the task object is defined at the time that the task object is created by the evaluation of an allocator. This same principle holds if the designated object is a composite object with components of task types. The assignment operation is available for access types, so that the effect of assignment of task objects can be obtained by use of access object designating task objects.
- Task objects may be used for subprogram parameters, in which case the formal parameter designates the same task as the associated actual parameter. This rule holds for all parameter modes—in, out, and in out.
- Task objects may be used as generic parameters. The rules above also hold in this case.

Finally, it should be noted that, since a task type is a limited type, it can be used in the declaration of a limited private type in the private part of a package specification. A task type can also be used as an actual parameter to be associated with a generic formal parameter of the type limited private.

All of the above features of tasks—features that are not exhibited by subprograms and packages—are due to the fact that a task name does not denote the task itself, but rather it denotes a task object which, in turn, designates the task. Once this concept is accepted, the features outlined above more or less fall into place.

If the values of task objects are defined at the time that their declarations are elaborated, then the question of just what effect is produced by the elaboration of a task body is raised. In this respect, task bodies are similar to the bodies of generic units. That is, the elaboration of a task body has no other effect than to establish the fact that the body can be used for the execution of tasks designated by task objects of the corresponding task type. The execution of a task body takes place whenever a task designated by a task object of the corresponding task type is activated. The activation of tasks is the subject of the following section.

7.2.5 Activation of Tasks

Tasks execute concurrently, with each task executing in accordance with the appropriate task body. As indicated by previous discussion, more than one task may be concurrently executing the same task body. The problems of synchronization of and communication among concurrently executing tasks will be considered in Section 7.3. Here, the concern is with the precise point in program execution at which a task is activated—or begins execution.

Every task has a master—a currently executing block statement or subprogram, a library package, or another task—upon which it depends in one of the following ways:

- A task designated by any task object, other than that created by the evaluation of an allocator, depends on the master whose execution created the task object.
- A task designated by a task object created by an allocator depends on the master in which the corresponding access type declaration was elaborated.

The dependence of a task on a master is manifested in several ways relating to task activation and task termination. Indirect dependencies also exist. For example, if a task has as its master a subprogram, and this subprogram is called by another subprogram, by a block statement, by a library package, or by another task, the calling unit is also a master. Similarly, block statements may be executed by another master, and a task that is a master will always have a master itself. Such indirect dependencies are important because of their effect on task termination.

The activation of a task takes place during the execution of its master.

Activation consists of the elaboration of the declarative part, if one is present, of the task body. The execution of the sequence of statements then proceeds in a manner partially determined by the rendezvous characteristics of the task. Because of the different ways in which task objects can be declared or created, several specific rules governing task activation apply:

- If the task object is declared in the declarative part of the master, then the task is activated after the elaboration of the declarative part of the master. Thus, activation occurs concurrently with the execution of the first statement following the reserved word **begin** in the body of the master. This rule holds as well for tasks that are designated by task objects that are components of composite objects.
- If the task object is declared in a package specification, the task is activated after elaboration of the declarative part of the package body. This rule holds as well for tasks that are designated by task objects that are components of composite objects.
- If the task object is created by an allocator, then activation occurs immediately upon the allocation. This rule holds as well for tasks that are components of a designated object. If several components of a composite object are task objects, they are activated simultaneously.

The concept here is one of simultaneous activation of related tasks. For example, if a subprogram declares a number of tasks within its declarative part, then all of the tasks are activated simultaneously at the time that the execution of the subprogram body begins. If a number of tasks are declared within a package, either in the specification or in the declarative part of the body, all tasks are activated simultaneously upon elaboration of the declarative part of the package body. There is no explicit action on the part of the programmer required to activate a task.

The concept of simultaneous activation of Ada tasks refers to the abstract notion that each Ada task runs on its own logical processor. In actual practice, of course, such is not usually the case. Execution of different tasks is normally interleaved on one or more physical processors in a manner that is implementation-dependent. Thus, the physical activation of tasks most likely occurs in a sequential fashion and in an order that is not specified by the language.

7.2.6 Completion and Termination of Tasks

The terms completion and termination refer to particular conditions with respect to tasks. These conditions are important because they effect the execution of Ada program units.

The term completion refers to the condition that exists when a program unit or block statement has no more statements to execute. Completion can occur in different ways, as indicated below:

- For a task, completion occurs when the end statement of the task body has been reached—either through normal execution of the sequence of statements or through the raising of an exception.
- For a procedure, completion occurs when the end statement of the procedure body has been reached—either through normal execution of the sequence of statements or through the raising of an exception—or when a return statement is executed.
- For a function, completion occurs after the evaluation of the result expression of a return statement. Completion also occurs when the end statement of the function body has been reached—either through normal execution of the sequence of statements or through the raising of an exception. In the former case, the exception PROGRAM_ERROR will be raised, as discussed in Section 3.10.2.1.
- For a block statement, completion occurs when the end statement of the block has been reached—either through normal execution of the sequence of statements or through the raising of an exception—or when an exit, return, or goto statement transfers control out of the block.

A task that is completed is also considered to be terminated if it has no dependent tasks or if all of its dependent tasks are terminated. This concept is important because of the following rule concerning task execution.

- A block statement or subprogram body that has been completed is not left until all of its dependent tasks are terminated.

Note that the dependent tasks must be terminated, not merely completed. This rule implies, for example, that a return from a subprogram cannot be effected until all tasks either directly or indirectly dependent on the subprogram are terminated, even though the subprogram may be completed—that is, execution of its sequence of statements has reached the end statement.

A task may also be terminated without completion, if certain conditions are met. This situation will be considered further in Section 7.3.3.1.

7.3 THE RENDEZVOUS

The interaction between two concurrently executing tasks is called a *rendezvous*. The rendezvous provides for both synchronization of and communication between the two tasks involved in the rendezvous. A rendezvous is produced when one task—the calling task—issues an entry call, and the second task—the called task—accepts the call. An entry call is issued by the calling task by the execution of an entry call statement, for which the syntax is

```
entry_call_statement ::= entry_name
                              [actual_parameter_part];
                                                  (7.3)
```

where the syntax for the actual parameter part is identical to that of a subprogram call given by Statement (3.58.1). Note that the entry call statement specifies the entry by name, and that it may include a parameter list by which information is exchanged with the called task. The entry name must be prefixed by the task name, using expanded name notation.

The called task accepts the entry call when an accept statement with the corresponding entry name is executed. The syntax for an accept statement is given by Statement (7.2.1). The synchronization of the two tasks is achieved through the specific rules of the rendezvous, which will be considered in detail in the following section, while the communication between the tasks, if any, is accomplished by the association of the actual parameters in the entry call statement with the formal parameters in the accept statement. The key point here is that the rendezvous is not effected until the calling task has executed the entry call statement and the called task has executed a corresponding accept statement.

7.3.1 The Simple Rendezvous

A rendezvous between two tasks occurs as a consequence of the calling task executing an entry call statement that names an entry in the called task. The actual synchronization is effected by the manner in which task execution responds to entry call statements and to accept statements. While a great deal of flexibility is provided by the use of the select statement in conjunction with both entry call statements and accept statements, it is best to begin discussion with the concept of a simple rendezvous—a rendezvous in which no select statements are used. The select statement and its use will be considered in Section 7.3.3.

In a simple rendezvous, task synchronization is produced by the response of the calling task to the entry call statement and by the response of the called task to the accept statement. These responses are as follows:

- When an executing task encounters an entry call statement, a check

is made to determine if the called task is waiting at a corresponding accept statement—that is, an accept statement containing the name of the entry—in which case the rendezvous is effected. If the called task is not waiting at a corresponding accept statement, the execution of the calling task is suspended until a rendezvous can be effected.
- When an executing task encounters an accept statement, a check is made to determine if any task has executed an entry call statement naming the entry associated with the accept statement and is therefore awaiting rendezvous. If there is a calling task awaiting rendezvous, then the rendezvous is effected. If no calling task is awaiting rendezvous, then the execution of the task is suspended until a rendezvous can be effected.

Thus, a rendezvous occurs under one of two conditions:

1. A calling task executes an entry call to a called task that is waiting at a corresponding accept statement.
2. A called task executes an accept statement for which a calling task is waiting at a corresponding entry call statement.

The simultaneous arrival of the calling task at an entry call, and of the called task at a corresponding accept statement, can be viewed as either case above. Such a situation cannot occur when the underlying hardware has a single processor, of course, because the parallel execution of the two tasks is only apparent. Even in multiprocessor systems, such simultaneity is very unlikely. The point is that the two tasks are synchronized when the rendezvous is effected. This synchronization is achieved by one of the tasks having its execution suspended until the other is ready for rendezvous.

When the rendezvous is effected, the following actions occur:

- If the calling task has been suspended, it remains suspended. If it has not been previously suspended, it is suspended at this time.
- Execution of the accept statement in the called task continues with the evaluation of the actual parameters, if any, and the association of formal and actual parameters. The sequence of statements, if any, of the accept statement is then executed, while the calling task remains suspended. When the end of the accept statement is reached, any required **out** and **in out** parameter association is made, and the rendezvous is completed.
- Upon completion of the rendezvous, the calling task resumes execution, and the called task continues execution, in a parallel and independent manner.

The rendezvous concept is illustrated in Figure 7.1 for the case in which the calling task is suspended awaiting rendezvous, and in Figure 7.2 for the case in which the called task is suspended awaiting rendezvous.

The simple rendezvous concepts above were developed under the premise of a single calling task. In general, any number of tasks may be

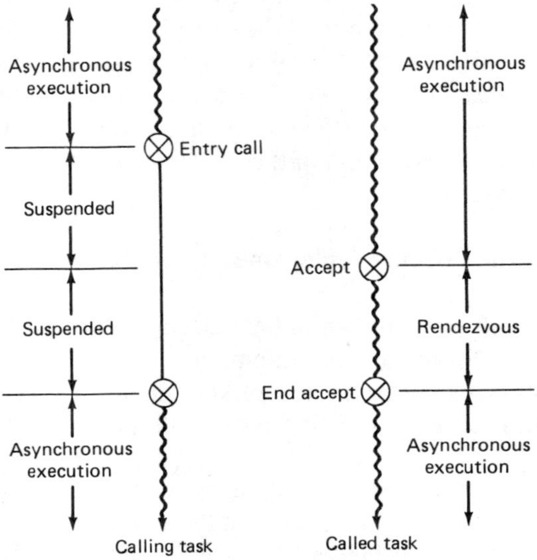

Figure 7.1. The rendezvous: calling task suspended.

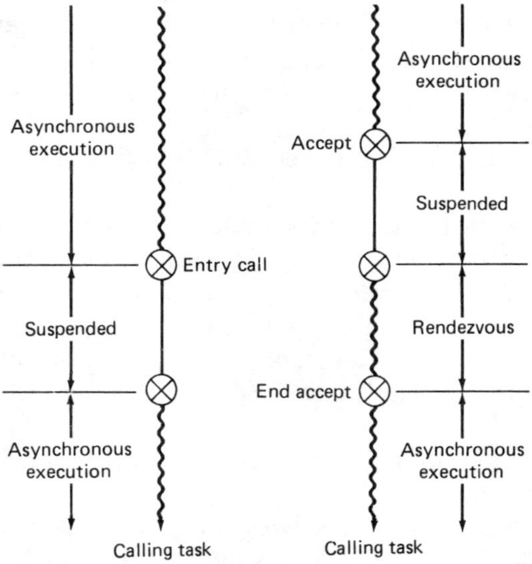

Figure 7.2. The rendezvous: called task suspended.

capable of calling a single entry, which raises the possibility that several entry calls may be made before a corresponding accept statement is reached in the execution of the called task. Ada's tasking features provide for this circumstance in the following way:

- With each entry there is associated a first in–first out queue. Entry calls are queued in the order of their occurrence. Each execution of a corresponding accept statement removes one entry call from the queue.

The order in which entry calls in an entry queue are serviced is always first in–first out. The priority associated with a task—a concept that will be discussed in Section 7.4.5—has no effect on this order.

Finally, there are several characteristics of accept statements and of the rendezvous that should be mentioned:

- An accept statement corresponding to an entry of a given task can appear only directly in the sequence of statements in the task body. It cannot occur within a subprogram contained within the sequence of statements, but it may occur within a block statement or within an accept statement corresponding to some other entry. It cannot occur within an accept statement for the same entry or, in the case of a family of entries, within the accept statement of any other entry of the same family.
- A task body can contain more than one accept statement for the same entry.
- There are no particular constraints on the kinds of statements that may be included in the sequence of statements of an accept statement. In general, the sequence of statements may include subprogram calls, entry calls, block statements, and accept statements corresponding to other entry calls.
- The sequence of statements of an accept statement may contain a return statement, the execution of which simply completes the rendezvous. The optional expression of the return statement, specified in Statement (3.57), is not permitted.
- A task can call its own entries. In the case of a simple rendezvous, such an occurrence will cause a deadlock.
- As implied by Statement (7.2.1), the sequence of statements in an accept statement is optional. This is true even if the corresponding entry has parameters.
- An attempt to call an entry of a task that is completed will raise the exception TASKING_ERROR upon execution of the entry call statement.

The suspension of task execution at an entry call or at an accept statement is an abstract notion based on the concept that each task executes on its own logical processor. Just how this concept maps to the underlying hardware depends upon the particular implementation, but it is typical in multitasking operating systems for a task to be in one of four states:

1. Executing—the task is currently assigned computational resources (memory and processor).
2. Ready—the task is eligible for execution, but has not yet been assigned computational resources.
3. Suspended—the task execution has been halted awaiting some event. It is not eligible for execution.
4. Inactive—the task either has not been activated or has completed.

The suspension of an Ada task in its logical processor may cause the run-time support system to place the task in the suspended state. When again eligible for execution in its logical processor, the task is moved to the ready state to await availability of computational resources. Thus, execution may not resume immediately upon the completion of the rendezvous. The Ada language itself does not specify how the logical processor concept maps to the underlying hardware and to the run-time support system, but the programmer has some control over scheduling through the assignment of priorities to various tasks. Task priority is discussed in Section 7.4.5.

Examples of communicating tasks are given below. Each example is accompanied by a description of the context in which it is considered.

EXAMPLE 1: The so-called producer-consumer problem is a classic instance of concurrent processing. The producer task generates some kind of data, which is then passed to the consumer task for processing. In this example, the producer is a task that reads characters from the standard input file, while the consumer task encrypts each character and writes it to the standard output file. Traditionally, real-time languages would approach this problem by the use of shared variables. An Ada implementation using a shared variable is shown below. A previous declaration of the form

```
SH_CHAR : CHARACTER;
```

is assumed. The object SH_CHAR is the shared variable. The producer task, GET_CHAR, is declared as

```
task GET_CHAR;
```

```
task body GET_CHAR is
    CHAR : CHARACTER;
begin
    while not END_OF_FILE(STANDARD_INPUT) loop
        GET(CHAR);
        SH_CHAR : = CHAR;
    end loop;
end GET_CHAR;
```

This task simply performs the loop statement, reading from the standard input file. The consumer task, CRYPT_CHAR, is declared as

```
task CRYPT_CHAR;
task body CRYPT_CHAR is
    CHAR : CHARACTER;
begin
    loop
        CHAR := SH_CHAR;
        CHAR := CRYPT(CHAR);
        PUT(CHAR);
    end loop;
end CRYPT_CHAR;
```

The function CRYPT provides the required encryption. The bodies of these tasks are written in a manner that emphasizes the use of the shared variable SH_CHAR. The producer task stores values in the shared variable, and the consumer task reads values from the shared variable.

The arrangement shown above is normally unsatisfactory for two reasons:

1. The loops in the two tasks will execute at different rates, so that one cannot guarantee that the consumer task reads the shared data at the same rate that the producer writes to it. This problem is one of *synchronization*.
2. The producer task may attempt to assign a value to the shared variable at the same time that the consumer task is attempting to read the value. This problem is one of *mutual exclusion*.

The problems of synchronization and mutual exclusion are classic in the practice of concurrent programming. Real-time, multitasking operating systems provide semaphores, queues, and mailboxes as means of solving these problems, and real-time languages normally make operating system calls in order to use these facilities. With concurrent processing in Ada, both synchronization and mutual exclusion are provided by the rendezvous mechanism. In this example, the use of shared data can be avoided by declaring an entry in the consumer task. The resulting program code is

```
task GET_CHAR;
task CRYPT_CHAR is
    entry IN_CHAR(ELEM : CHARACTER);
end CRYPT_CHAR;

task body GET_CHAR is
    CHAR : CHARACTER;
begin
    while not END_OF_FILE(STANDARD_INPUT) loop
         GET(CHAR);
         CRYPT_CHAR.IN_CHAR(CHAR);
    end loop;
end GET_CHAR;

task body CRYPT_CHAR is
    CHAR : CHARACTER;
begin
    loop
        accept IN_CHAR(ELEM : CHARACTER) do
            CHAR := ELEM;
        end IN_CHAR;
        CHAR := CRYPT(CHAR);
        PUT(CHAR);
    end loop;
end CRYPT_CHAR;
```

The basic concept is clear—the loop in the producer task is not completed until the rendezvous is completed, so that a new character cannot be obtained until the current character is read by the accept statement in the consumer task. Likewise, the loop in the consumer task cannot proceed past the accept statement until an entry call has been issued by the producer task. The data, which previously had been shared between the two tasks, is now passed as an **in** parameter in the entry call. There are two subtle features of task CRYPT_CHAR that should be noted:

1. The additional local object CHAR is needed because the scope of the formal parameter ELEM is limited to the accept statement.
2. The calls to function CRYPT and to procedure PUT have been placed outside the accept statement, thus permitting the rendezvous to be completed without waiting for these subprograms to complete. This feature allows the producer task to resume execution while the subprograms are being executed.

This example has been predicated upon a single producer task. If more than one task can make entry calls to task CRYPT_CHAR, then the possibility exists that one or more entry calls will be made before the task is ready to execute the accept statement. In such an event, the entry calls will be queued in a first in–first out fashion, as discussed earlier in this section.

EXAMPLE 2: An alternative approach to the problem of Example 1, and one that adds more parallelism to the solution, is to include a third task to buffer the transfer of data from the producer task to the consumer task. Both the producer and the consumer tasks then make entry calls to the buffer task. The program code is

```
task CHAR_BOX is
    entry IN_CHAR(CHAR : in CHARACTER);
    entry OUT_CHAR(CHAR : out CHARACTER);
end CHAR_BOX;
task GET_CHAR;
task CRYPT_CHAR;

task body CHAR_BOX is
    ELEM : CHARACTER;
begin
    loop
        accept IN_CHAR(CHAR : in CHARACTER) do
            ELEM := CHAR;
        end IN_CHAR;
        accept OUT_CHAR(CHAR : out CHARACTER) do
            CHAR := ELEM;
        end OUT_CHAR;
    end loop;
end CHAR_BOX;

task body GET_CHAR is
    CHAR : CHARACTER;
begin
    while not END_OF_FILE(STANDARD_INPUT)
        loop
            GET(CHAR);
            CHAR_BOX.IN_CHAR(CHAR);
        end loop;
end GET_CHAR;

task body CRYPT_CHAR is
    CHAR : CHARACTER;
begin
    loop
        CHAR_BOX.OUT_CHAR(CHAR);
        CHAR := CRYPT(CHAR);
    end loop;
end CRYPT_CHAR;
```

In this arrangement, the producer and consumer tasks alternate in effecting a rendezvous with the buffer task CHAR_BOX. The rules of rendezvous ensure that calls to entries IN_CHAR and OUT_CHAR are accepted in a mutually exclusive manner and that they occur in an alternating sequence.

7.3.2 The Delay Statement and Package CALENDAR

In some instances of concurrent processing, it may be necessary for a concurrently executing task—or perhaps for the main program—to suspend its execution for a specified period of time. As will be demonstrated in the following section, the ability to generate time delays is important to the inclusion of a timeout feature in an Ada rendezvous. A delay can be produced by the execution of a delay statement, for which the syntax is

```
delay_statement := delay simple_expression;     (7.4)
```

where the syntax for a simple expression is given by Statement (3.34.2). The simple expression must be of the predefined type DURATION, and its value is expressed in seconds. Type DURATION is declared in package STANDARD as

```
type DURATION is delta implementation_defined
        range implementation_defined;
```

Since type DURATION is a fixed-point type, the addition of values of type DURATION can be accomplished without loss of accuracy. That is, as implied by the discussion of Section 3.5.3, if two fixed-point model numbers are added, the result is another model number, unless the range constraint is violated. Because the operand of the delay statement is a simple expression, it can be computed at run time. The value of the delay can also be expressed more clearly by using a suitable number of constant declarations, such as:

```
SECONDS : constant := 1.0;
MINUTES : constant := 60.0;
HOURS   : constant := 3600.0;
```

so that the operand of a delay statement may be expressed as, for example,

```
3.0 * HOURS + 22.0 * MINUTES + 36 * SECONDS
```

While the delta and the range of the predefined type DURATION are implementation-dependent, the language rules require certain minimum characteristics:

- The range must be at least −86,400 to 86,400. Since the values represent seconds, a minimum range of one day is required.
- The smallest representable duration can be no greater than 20 milliseconds, with a value not greater than 50 microseconds recommended by the language standard.

A delay statement with a negative operand is equivalent to a delay statement with a zero operand. Even though the characteristics of type DURATION are implementation-defined, their fundamental values are available through the use of attributes. For example:

- DURATION'SMALL is the smallest representable delay.
- DURATION'LARGE is the largest representable delay.

If delays of more than DURATION'LARGE are required, they can be obtained by use of a loop.

The particular results of the execution of a delay statement may vary, depending upon just how concurrency is effected by the run-time support system. The language rules require that execution be suspended for at least the duration specified. Most likely, an implementation will place a task in the suspended state for the designated duration and then raise it to the ready state. When in the ready state, the task must await the availability of computational resources before execution can resume. Thus, the actual delay may be longer than that specified.

If timing operations more sophisticated than those obtainable by use of the delay statement are required, the facilities of the predefined package CALENDAR can be used. The specification of package CALENDAR is given in Appendix C; it is repeated here for convenience:

```
package CALENDAR is
    type TIME is private;
    subtype YEAR_NUMBER  is INTEGER range 1901..2099;
    subtype MONTH_NUMBER is INTEGER range 1..12;
    subtype DAY_NUMBER   is INTEGER range 1..31;
    subtype DAY_DURATION is DURATION range 0.0..86_400.0;
    function CLOCK return TIME;
    function YEAR    (DATE : TIME) return YEAR_NUMBER;
    function MONTH   (DATE : TIME) return MONTH_NUMBER;
    function DAY     (DATE : TIME) return DAY_NUMBER;
    function SECONDS (DATE : TIME) return DAY_DURATION;
```

```
    procedure SPLIT  (DATE : in TIME;
                      YEAR    : out YEAR_NUMBER;
                      MONTH   : out MONTH_NUMBER;
                      DAY     : out DAY_NUMBER;
                      SECONDS : out DAY_DURATION;
    function TIME_OF(YEAR     : YEAR_NUMBER;
                      MONTH   : MONTH_NUMBER;
                      DAY     : DAY_NUMBER;
                      SECONDS : DAY_DURATION := 0.0)
                      return TIME;
    function "+" (LEFT : TIME;     RIGHT : DURATION)
                 return TIME;
    function "+" (LEFT : DURATION; RIGHT : TIME)
                 return TIME;
    function "-" (LEFT : TIME;     RIGHT : DURATION)
                 return TIME;
    function "-" (LEFT : TIME;     RIGHT : TIME)
                 return DURATION;
    function "<"  (LEFT,RIGHT : TIME) return BOOLEAN;
    function "<=" (LEFT,RIGHT : TIME) return BOOLEAN;
    function ">"  (LEFT,RIGHT : TIME) return BOOLEAN;

    function ">=" (LEFT,RIGHT : TIME) return BOOLEAN;
    TIME_ERROR : exception; -- can be raised by TIME_OF,
                            -- "+", and "-"
private
    -- implementation_dependent
end;
```

Objects of the private type TIME contain year, month, day, and seconds information in some manner that is implementation-dependent and is hidden in the private part of the specification. Operations permitted on objects of type TIME are those of assignment, tests for equality and inequality, and those operations declared in the visible part of the package specification. These latter operations are

```
function CLOCK      -- returns the current value of the date
                       and time
function YEAR       -- extracts the year number from the
                       parameter DATE and returns it under
                       the function name
function MONTH      -- extracts the month name from the
                       parameter DATE and returns it under
                       the function name
function DAY        -- extracts the day name from the
                       parameter DATE and returns it under
                       the function name
```

```
function SECONDS        -- extracts the seconds number from the
                           parameter DATE and returns it under
                           the function name
procedure SPLIT         -- extracts the year number, month
                           name, day name, and seconds number
                           from the in parameter DATE
function TIME_OF        -- combines the year number, month
                           name, day name, and seconds number
                           into a value of the private type TIME
                           and returns this value under the
                           function name
functions "+"           -- provide for addition
and "-"                    and subtraction as indicated
functions "<", "<=",    -- provide for comparison
">", ">="                  as indicated
```

The type TIME declared within package CALENDAR is a classic example of an abstract data type; a general discussion of abstract data types is contained in Section 4.4.3. In this case, the implementation is hidden from the user in a literal sense—unless the user actually has intimate knowledge of the run-time support system, he cannot determine how type TIME is actually implemented. Lack of this knowledge, however, does not hamper or limit in any way his declaration and use of objects of type TIME.

To compare the use of a delay statement with that of an object of type TIME from package CALENDAR, consider first an example use of a delay statement:

```
loop
    delay 0.32;
    --sequence of statements
end loop;
--The time required for execution of this loop is 0.32
  seconds, plus whatever time is required to execute the
  sequence of statements. There are two unpredictable
  effects here. First, the delay statement may produce a
  delay longer than 0.32 seconds, because of the time
  required to acquire computational resources after
  expiration of the delay. Second, the sequence of
  statements may require different execution times for
  different iterations.
```

While the time variations above may not present a problem in some applications, they may be intolerable in those applications in which the loop must iterate at a regular cyclical rate. An alternative approach, using an object of type TIME from package CALENDAR, is given by the block statement below:

```
declare
    PERIOD     : constant DURATION := 0.32;
    START_TIME : CALENDAR.TIME := CALENDAR.CLOCK;
begin
    loop
        delay START_TIME - CALENDAR.CLOCK;
        --sequence of statements
        START_TIME := START_TIME + PERIOD;
    end loop;
end;
--The delay statement in this instance delays the amount
  of time necessary to make the loop iterate at a precise
  periodic rate. Any particular iteration of the sequence
  of statements may vary from this rate because of
  variations in the delay or because of differing
  execution times for the sequence of statements itself.
  The variable duration in the delay statement compensates
  for these effects. The net result is that the task
  completes the delay statement at a precise periodic
  rate.
```

There are some subtle features of this code sequence that deserve comment:

- The object START_TIME and the value returned by the function CALENDAR.CLOCK are of type CALENDAR.TIME.
- The delay statement requires an operand of type DURATION. The "–" operator has a left parameter of type CALENDAR.TIME and a right parameter of type CALENDAR.TIME, and it returns a value of DURATION.
- The "+" operator has a LEFT parameter of type CALENDAR.TIME and a RIGHT parameter of type DURATION, and it returns a value of type CALENDAR.TIME.
- The scope of the objects PERIOD and START_TIME extends only to the end of the block statement.

One other effect that must be considered is that type DURATION—and therefore subtype DAY_DURATION—is a fixed-point type. For the timing to be precise, the value of PERIOD must be a model number of the type.

Periodic execution of tasks, obtained through the use of a cyclic executive in traditional real-time systems, would probably be achieved through the use of interrupts in an Ada program. The task is the vehicle by which interrupts are served in an Ada program. Details of interrupt servicing will be presented in Section (8.4).

7.3.3 The Select Statement

For the concept of synchronization by rendezvous to have the flexibility required for effective concurrent programming, capability beyond that of the simple rendezvous is required. Often, it is necessary to select from a number of accept statements, depending upon which entry call occurs first. In other instances, some kind of timeout mechanism is necessary, so that a task does not wait an excessive amount of time either at an entry call statement or at an accept statement. Nor is the mutual exclusion problem completely solved by the simple rendezvous, since concurrent calls can be made to the same task if more than one entry is provided into the task.

The extension of task synchronization features beyond those provided by the simple rendezvous is obtained through the use of the select statement, which can be used in the calling task in conjunction with the entry call statement, in the called task in conjunction with one or more accept statements, or in both the calling and the called task. The syntax for a select statement is

```
select_statement ::= selective_wait
      | conditional_entry_call | timed_entry_call.    (7.5)
```

The selective wait is used in called tasks, in conjunction with one or more accept statements. The conditional entry call and the timed entry call are used in calling tasks and are associated with entry call statements.

7.3.3.1 The Called Task and the Selective Wait. The selective wait is obtained from the syntax of Statement (7.5) through the path

```
select_statement ::= selective_wait        (7.6)
```

where

```
selective_wait ::=
    select
        select_alternative
    {or
        select_alternative}                (7.6.1)
    [else
        sequence_of_statements]
    end select;
```

The syntax for a sequence of statements is given by Statement (3.45.2). Thus, the selective wait may have any number of select alternatives, but it must have at least one. The else part is optional. The syntax for a select alternative is

```
select_alternative ::=
    [when condition =>]
        selective_wait_alternative        (7.6.2)
```

where

```
selective_wait_alternative ::= accept_alternative
    | delay_alternative | terminate alternative    (7.6.3)
```

Each select alternative in Statement (7.5.1) is thus seen to consist of an optional when condition, followed by either an accept alternative, a delay alternative, or a terminate alternative. The syntax for each of these choices is given below:

```
accept_alternative ::= accept_statement [sequence_of_
                       statements]                (7.6.4)

 delay_alternative ::= delay_statement [sequence_of_
                       statements]                (7.6.5)

        terminate_alternative ::= terminate;      (7.6.6)
```

The syntax for an accept statement is given by Statement (7.2.1). It should be noted that the accept statement itself contains an optional sequence of statements, distinct from the optional sequence of statements contained in Statement (7.6.4).

The implication of the syntax contained in Statements (7.6) through (7.6.6), and of the syntax rules associated with these statements, can be summarized as follows:

- The selective wait consists of a select statement followed by one or more select alternatives, with an optional else part containing a sequence of statements.
- A select alternative may have an optional when condition. If the when condition evaluates as TRUE, or if the when condition is not present, the alternative is called an open alternative. If the when condition evaluates as FALSE, the alternative is said to be closed. Only open alternatives can be selected for execution.

- A select alternative may be either an accept alternative, containing an accept statement; a delay alternative, containing a delay statement; or a terminate alternative, containing only the reserved word **terminate.**
- A selective wait must have at least one accept alternative, but it may have more than one. In addition to accept alternatives, a selective wait may contain one, but only one, of the following:

  an else part
  one or more delay alternatives
  a terminate alternative

The execution of a selective wait occurs in accordance with the following rules:

- The when conditions, if any, are evaluated immediately upon execution of the select statement. These conditions are evaluated only *once for each execution of the select statement.* Thus, once an alternative is determined to be closed, that alternative cannot be selected for the current execution of the selective wait statement. Similarly, an alternative determined to be open is available for selection for the current execution of the selective wait statement, even though the when condition may be changed prior to the rendezvous.
- If there is an entry call waiting to be accepted at any of the open accept alternatives, that alternative is selected and the rendezvous is effected immediately. If more than one accept alternative is open and also has an entry call waiting, one of these alternatives is arbitrarily selected—and in a manner not specified by the language rules. When the resulting rendezvous is completed—that is, when the **end** in the accept statement, if present, is executed—the optional sequence of statements in the accept alternative, if present, is executed. Control then passes to the statement following the **end select.** Thus, only one alternative is selected for execution.
- If there are no open accept alternatives—or if there are no entry calls waiting at those accept alternatives that are open—and an else part is included, the sequence of statements in the else part is executed. Control then passes to the statement following **end select.** Recall that the presence of an else part precludes that of delay and terminate alternatives.
- If there is at least one open accept alternative—but there are no entry calls waiting at those accept alternatives that are open—and no else part, delay alternative, or terminate alternative is present, then the execution of the task is suspended awaiting the availability of an open accept alternative upon which an entry call has been

made. When an entry call is made to an open accept alternative, the rendezvous is effected immediately. Recall that the else part and the delay and terminate alternatives are optional, and that they are mutually exclusive.

- If there are no open accept alternatives—or if there are no entry calls waiting at those accept alternatives that are open—but there is an open delay alternative, the delay alternative will be selected if no rendezvous can be effected through an open accept alternative before the specified delay has elapsed. Selection of a delay alternative causes the associated sequence of statements, if any, to be executed. Control is then transferred to the statement following the **end select.** If, prior to the expiration of the specified delay, an entry call is made to an open accept alternative, then the accept alternative is selected immediately and the delay alternative is abandoned. Recall that the presence of delay alternatives precludes that of an else part and that of a terminate alternative.
- If there are no open accept alternatives, and a terminate alternative is present and is open, then the terminate alternative will be selected under the following conditions:

  The master upon which the task depends has completed, as discussed in Section 7.2.6.

  Each task that depends on the master has already terminated or is similarly able to select a terminate alternative in a selective wait.

  If the task itself has dependent tasks, each of these dependent tasks has terminated.

  There is no queued entry call for any entry of the task.

  If these conditions are not met, then the task is suspended awaiting an entry at an open accept alternative or the satisfaction of the four conditions above. If the terminate alternative is selected, then the task terminates. Recall that the presence of a terminate alternative precludes that of an else part and that of delay alternatives.
- Finally, if all alternatives are closed and there is no else part, then the predefined exception PROGRAM_ERROR is raised. Because of the mutual exclusion of delay alternatives, a terminate alternative, and an else part, this situation can arise only under the following select statement configurations:

  accept alternatives only with no else part
  accept alternatives with delay alternatives
  accept alternatives with a terminate alternative

  The exception PROGRAM_ERROR is raised if all alternatives—including delay alternatives and terminate alternatives, if present—

are closed. Obviously, a program should ensure that this condition does not arise.

In Section 7.2.6, the conditions of task termination through completion—that is, execution of the sequence of statements of the task body through the end statement—was discussed. The use of a terminate alternative represents another way that a task may be terminated. The rules outlined above for selection of a terminate alternative are reasonable, because if the four conditions specified for the selection of a terminate alternative are met, all of the tasks involved are of no further use. That is, the only tasks that can call entries in any of the tasks are other tasks in the group, all of which are either terminated, completed, or able to select a terminate alternative. Thus, the whole group of tasks, including the master, terminates simultaneously.

Several examples of selective waits are given below, in order to exemplify the various options discussed above.

EXAMPLE 1: Consider the declaration below:

```
task GET_DATA is
    entry INERTIAL(DATA : out STATE);
    entry DOPPLER(DATA  : out STATE);
    entry AIR_DATA(DATA : out STATE);
end GET_DATA;
--This is a task specification that declares three
  entries. The type STATE is presumed to be previously
  declared and visible to the task.
task body GET_DATA is
        .
        .
        .
begin
        .
        .
        .
    select
        accept INERTIAL(DATA : out STATE) do
            --sequence of statements of accept statement
        end INERTIAL;
            --sequence of statements of accept alternative
    or
        accept DOPPLER(DATA : out STATE) do
            --sequence of statements of accept statement
```

```
        end DOPPLER;
            --sequence of statements of accept alternative
    or
        accept AIR_DATA(DATA : out STATE) do
            --sequence of statements of accept statement
        end AIR_DATA;
            --sequence of statements of accept alternative
    end select;
        .
        .
        .
end GET_DATA;
--Shown in this body is a single accept statement with
  three accept alternatives. All alternatives are open.
```

The form of the select statement should be compared to Statements (7.6.1) through (7.6.4). The following points should be noted:

- None of the select alternatives have when conditions. See Statement (7.6.2). Therefore, they are all open.
- Each of the accept statements has the optional sequence of statements. See Statement (7.2.1).
- After the end statement of an accept statement is executed, the rendezvous is completed and the calling task can resume execution.
- Each of the accept alternatives has the optional sequence of statements. See Statement (7.6.4). This sequence of statements is executed after the rendezvous has been completed.

When the execution of the task reaches the reserved word **select,** a determination is made of which, if any, of the three accept statements have entry calls waiting. If there is an entry call waiting, the rendezvous is effected immediately by that accept statement and the sequence of statements of that accept statement is executed. Upon completion of this sequence of statements, the rendezvous is completed and the parameter DATA is passed to the calling task, which then resumes execution. At the same time, the sequence of statements of the accept alternative begins execution. When the execution of this sequence of statements reaches the reserved word **or,** control is transferred to the end of the select statement, indicated by the reserved words **end select.**

If more than one accept statement have entry calls waiting, then an immediate rendezvous is effected with one of them, but the language rules do not specify how this selection is made. On the other hand, if none of the accept statements has entry calls waiting, then the execution of the task is suspended awaiting an entry call to one of the accept statements. When such an entry call is made, the task resumes execution and an immediate rendezvous is effected. The reader should note, however, that when execution of a task is suspended, the computational resources assigned to the task may be returned to the run-time support system for further allocation. Thus, resumption of execution of a suspended task may imply merely raising the task from the suspended state to the ready state, where it must then await allocation of computational resources. Such effects are implementation-dependent.

EXAMPLE 2: The manner in which an implementation selects which of several open accept alternatives will be chosen is not specified by the language rules. The following program will test an implementation with regard to this selection:

```
with TEXT_IO;
use TEXT_IO, INTEGER_IO;
procedure SELECT_TEST is
    INT_IO is new INTEGER_IO(INTEGER);
    TEST_NUM : INTEGER;
    use INT_IO;
    task TEST is
       entry TEST_CALL (NUM : out INTEGER);
    end TEST;

    task body TEST is
    begin
        loop
            select
               accept TEXT_CALL(NUM : out INTEGER) do
                  NUM := 1;
               end TEST_CALL;
            or
               accept TEST_CALL(NUM : out INTEGER) do
                  NUM := 2;
               end TEST_CALL;
            or
               accept TEST_CALL(NUM : out INTEGER) do
                  NUM := 3;
               end TEST_CALL;
            or
               accept TEST_CALL(NUM : out INTEGER) do
                  NUM := 4;
               end TEST_CALL;
```

```
            or
               accept TEST_CALL(NUM : out INTEGER) do
                  NUM := 5;
               end TEST_CALL;
            or
               terminate;
            end select;
         end loop;
      end TEST;

   begin
      for INDEX in 1..40 loop
          TEST.TEST_CALL(TEST_NUM);
          PUT(TEST_NUM);
      end loop;
   end SELECT_TEST;
```

Here, the task is a declarative item in the declarative part of procedure SELECT_TEST. According to the rules of task activation presented in Section 7.2.5, task TEST will be activated and begin execution when the reserved word **begin** is encountered in the sequence of statements in the procedure body. The task executes to the select statement, where it awaits an entry call to one of the accept statements. Procedure SELECT_TEST meanwhile executes to the entry call statement, at which point all five accept statements are available for rendezvous. One will be selected arbitrarily each time around the loop, for 40 iterations.

In addition to providing an insight into how an implementation arbitrarily selects open accept alternatives, this example also exhibits the following characteristics:

- Each accept statement has a sequence of statements, but the accept alternatives do not include the optional sequence of statements. See Statements (7.2.1) and (7.6.4).
- The task contains more than one accept statement for the entry TEST_CALL.
- The terminate alternative avoids the deadlock that would occur as the procedure waited for the task to complete.

EXAMPLE 3: The semaphore is an elegant yet simple solution to the mutual exclusion problem. Real-time operating systems usually provide for the use of semaphores through operating system calls. The *general semaphore* is an integer variable that can assume only nonnegative integer values. The *binary semaphore* assumes only the values zero and one, and constitutes an indication of whether some resource is busy or is available for use. The resource is normally considered to be a critical resource of some kind for which mutual exclusion is required. While the rendezvous feature of the Ada language normally precludes the requirement for the use of semaphores, a simple binary semaphore can be implemented by means of an Ada task, as indicated below:

```
task BIN_SEMAPHORE is
    entry WAIT;
    entry SIGNAL;
end BIN_SEMAPHORE;

task body BIN_SEMAPHORE is
    BUSY : BOOLEAN := FALSE;
begin
    loop
        select
            when not BUSY =>
                accept WAIT do
                    BUSY := TRUE;
                end WAIT;
        or
            when BUSY =>
                accept SIGNAL do
                    BUSY := FALSE;
                end SIGNAL;
        end select;
    end loop;
end BIN_SEMAPHORE;
```

The purpose of the semaphore is to protect some critical resource from concurrent use by more than one task. For example, all Ada subprograms are reentrant; that is, more than one concurrently executing task may be executing the subprogram simultaneously. A semaphore may be used to protect a procedure from this kind of simultaneous execution if mutual exclusion is required. If the procedure name is CRITICAL, then all calls to procedure CRITICAL would be implemented as

```
BIN_SEMAPHORE.WAIT;
CRITICAL;
BIN_SEMAPHORE.SIGNAL;
```

In this manner, a call to CRITICAL can be effected only if the entry call WAIT results in a rendezvous which, in turn, sets the value of BUSY within the semaphore task to TRUE. With BUSY set to TRUE, the WAIT accept alternative is closed, and thus any other call to WAIT will cause both the calling task and the semaphore task to be suspended. Upon return from procedure CRITICAL, an entry call to SIGNAL results in an immediate rendezvous, since SIGNAL is an open accept alternative. This rendezvous assigns the value FALSE to BUSY, thus opening the WAIT select alternative. Therefore, if one task has completed a rendezvous with entry WAIT, other calling tasks queue in a first in–first out order at the WAIT entry until the first task completes the SIGNAL entry.

EXAMPLE 4: If there is more than one critical resource requiring that mutual exclusion be obtained by means of a semaphore task as described in Example 3, then a separate task can be provided for each resource. In this instance, a task type can be declared, providing for the declaration of any number of objects of the type. The specification for the task type declaration is

```
task type BIN_SEMAPHORE_TYPE is
    entry WAIT;
    entry SIGNAL;
end BIN_SEMAPHORE_TYPE;
```

The task body is identical to that of Example 3. Object declarations, such as

```
CRITICAL_SEMAPHORE : BIN_SEMAPHORE_TYPE;
```

then declare task objects. In this case, procedure CRITICAL would be provided mutual exclusion protection by implementing all procedure calls as

```
CRITICAL_SEMAPHORE.WAIT;
CRITICAL;
CRITICAL_SEMAPHORE.SIGNAL;
```

A different task object can be declared for each resource in need of mutual exclusion.

EXAMPLE 5: The first in–first out queue, implemented as an abstract data type in Chapter 4, can also be implemented as an Ada task. The following example implements a queue for objects of type character, but the reader should recognize that type CHARACTER could be replaced by virtually any Ada data type, no matter how complex the structure. The specification and body declarations are as given below:

```
task FIFO_TASK is
    entry PUT(ELEM  : in  CHARACTER);
    entry TAKE(ELEM : out CHARACTER);
```

```
    entry RESET;
    entry COUNT(NUM : out INTEGER);
end FIFO_TASK;

task body FIFO_TASK is
    MAX          : constant := 128;
    LIST         : array(1..MAX) of CHARACTER;
    FRONT, BACK  : INTEGER range 1..MAX := 1;
    LENGTH       : INTEGER range 0..MAX := 0;
begin
    loop
        select
            when LENGTH < MAX =>
                accept PUT(ELEM : in CHARACTER) do
                    LIST(FRONT) := ELEM;
                end PUT;
                FRONT  := (FRONT rem MAX) + 1;
                LENGTH := LENGTH + 1;
        or
            when LENGTH > 0 =>
                accept TAKE(ELEM : out CHARACTER) do
                    ELEM := LIST(BACK);
                end TAKE;
                BACK   := (BACK rem MAX) + 1;
                LENGTH := LENGTH - 1;
        or
            accept RESET do
                FRONT  := 1;
                BACK   := 1;
                LENGTH := 0;
            end RESET;
        or
            accept COUNT(NUM : out INTEGER) do
                NUM := LENGTH;
            end COUNT;
        or
            terminate;
        end select;
    end loop;
end FIFO_TASK;
```

The FIFO queue is implemented here as a circular buffer, represented by the array LIST and the integer valued pointers FRONT and BACK. The integer object LENGTH denotes the number of characters currently in the queue. When the queue is empty, the TAKE alternative is closed; when the queue is full, the PUT alternative is closed. A PUT entry call when the queue is full, or a TAKE entry call when the queue is empty, does not result in rejection of the entry call. Rather, such calls are queued in a first in–first out manner at the accept alternatives, as required by the rendezvous rules. Other notable features of this example are as follows:

- The PUT and TAKE accept alternatives have when conditions, while the RESET and COUNT accept alternatives do not.
- The PUT and TAKE accept alternatives have the optional sequence of statements following the accept statements. The RESET and COUNT accept alternatives do not.
- The terminate alternative is included to avoid the deadlock that would result if the select statement were left awaiting an entry call after all calling tasks have completed.
- The implementation of the queue is hidden from calling tasks, since the task specification contains only the entry declarations. Thus, the integrity of the queue, in terms of the values of the objects LIST, FRONT, BACK, and COUNT, is protected against interference from outside the task.

This task implements a single queue. If more than one queue is needed, a task type can be declared and then task objects of the type declared.

The Ada language does not support tasks as library units, nor does it support generic tasks. The effect of these features can be produced by encapsulating one or more tasks within a package. In this particular case, such encapsulation might be effected as follows:

```
package FIFO_PACKAGE is
   task FIFO_TASK is
        entry PUT(ELEM  : in CHARACTER);
        entry TAKE(ELEM : out CHARACTER);
        entry RESET;
        entry COUNT(NUM : out INTEGER);
   end FIFO_TASK;
end FIFO_PACKAGE;
```

This package specification contains the specification of the task FIFO_TASK, making the task visible to users of the package. Thus, any program unit that mentions package FIFO_PACKAGE in a with clause can call entries to task FIFO_TASK. Entry calls would appear as

```
FIFO_PACKAGE.FIFO_TASK.PUT
FIFO_PACKAGE.FIFO_TASK.TAKE
FIFO_PACKAGE.FIFO_TASK.RESET
FIFO_PACKAGE.FIFO_TASK.COUNT
```

If a use clause is also present, the entries are directly visible as:

```
FIFO_TASK.PUT
FIFO_TASK.TAKE
FIFO_TASK.RESET
FIFO_TASK.COUNT
```

The body of package FIFO_PACKAGE must contain the body of task FIFO_TASK. It would appear as

```
package body FIFO_PACKAGE is
   task body FIFO_TASK is
         --body of task FIFO_TASK as previously
           outlined
   end FIFO_TASK;
end FIFO_PACKAGE;
```

The body of task FIFO_TASK, as previously presented, applies here with no modification. The reader should note that other declarations could appear in the specification of package FIFO_PACKAGE, making the declared entities also visible to users of the package. These declarations could be type or object declarations, or they could be the specifications of other program units—that is, specifications of subprograms, other packages, or additional tasks.

Even more versatility can be obtained by making package FIFO_PACKAGE a generic unit that can be instantiated for virtually any data type and for any queue length. This modification is produced by including a formal generic part, as indicated below:

```
generic
   MAX : POSITIVE;
   type ELEM_TYPE is private;
package FIFO_PACKAGE is
   task FIFO_TASK is
        entry PUT(ELEM  : in ELEM_TYPE);
        entry TAKE(ELEM : out ELEM_TYPE);
        entry RESET;
        entry COUNT(NUM : out INTEGER):
   end FIFO_TASK;
end FIFO_PACKAGE;
```

The only two modifications necessary to the package body are

1. deletion of the declaration of the constant MAX in the declarative part of body of task FIFO_TASK

2. replacement of the type name CHARACTER with the type name ELEM_TYPE wherever it appears

The generic package can also be separately compiled as a library unit. Instantiations of the generic package must include actual parameters specifying the data type and the length of the queue. For example, if type COMPLEX_TYPE is some complex data type consisting of records and arrays, then the instantiation

```
package COMPLEX_FIFO is new FIFO_PACKAGE(MAX => 1024;
                              ELEM_TYPE => COMPLEX_TYPE);
```

will create a package implementing a FIFO queue for objects of type COMPLEX_TYPE containing a maximum length of 1024.

EXAMPLE 6: The else part of a selective wait provides an alternative when none of the accept alternatives are open or when no open accept alternative has an entry call waiting. In the select statement given below in skeletal form, two accept alternatives provide for rendezvous with tasks that supply data in a time-critical fashion. If an immediate rendezvous is not effected immediately upon execution of the select statement, the else part is executed. The else part contains routine self-diagnostic tests that the computer performs on the system.

```
select
   accept RADAR_INPUT(DATA : RADAR_TYPE) do
   --sequence of statements of accept statement
   end RADAR_INPUT;
or
   accept INERTIAL_INPUT(DATA : INERTIAL_TYPE) do
   --sequence of statements of accept statement
   end INERTIAL_INPUT;
else
   --sequence of statements of else part
end select;
```

The sequence of statements in the else part, in this example, contains the self-diagnostic program. When the select statement is executed, the two accept statements are checked to determine if entry calls are waiting. If there is at least one, then an immediate rendezvous is effected according to the rules outlined previously in this section. On the other hand, if no entry calls are waiting, the else part is executed. Execution of the else part is not interrupted by a subsequent entry call. If the select statement is in a loop, as might often be the case,

```
loop
    select
        --remainder of select statement
    end select;
end loop;
```

then one—and only one—of three things happens during each iteration of the loop:

1. rendezvous with RADAR_INPUT
2. rendezvous with INERTIAL_INPUT
3. execution of the sequence of statements of the else part

In this example the accept alternatives have no when conditions, so that both alternatives are always open. If when conditions are present, then entry calls may be waiting at a closed alternative. If an immediate rendezvous cannot be effected, for whatever reason, the else part is executed.

The else part may contain a null statement:

```
select
    accept REN1;
or
    accept REN2;
or
    accept REN3;
else
    null;
end select;
```

In this case, the else part is used to prevent the task from being suspended awaiting a call to one of the entries. Upon execution of the select statement, an immediate rendezvous is effected if at least one entry call is waiting. Otherwise, execution continues at the statement following **end select.**

EXAMPLE 7: In the absence of an else part, a select statement will cause suspension of a task whenever an immediate rendezvous cannot be effected. The task will remain suspended until an entry call is made to an open alternative. In many instances it is important to guard against abnormally long suspensions, or even against deadlock, by providing timeout protection within the select statement. Timeout protection is obtained through use of the delay statement. An example, in skeletal form, is given below:

```
select
    accept INERTIAL_INPUT(DATA : INERTIAL_TYPE) do
    --sequence of statements of accept statement
```

```
        end INERTIAL_INPUT;
         --sequence of statements of accept alternative
    or
        delay 0.005;
         --sequence of statements of delay alternative
    end select;
```

When the select statement is executed, an immediate rendezvous is effected if an entry call to INERTIAL_INPUT is waiting. If an entry call is not queued, then the task is suspended. If an entry call is made within five milliseconds, then the rendezvous is effected immediately upon execution of the entry call statement. On the other hand, if no entry call is made within five milliseconds, then the delay alternative is selected and the associated sequence of statements is executed. It should be noted that all three sequences of statements are optional.

In general, any number of accept alternatives, either containing or not containing when conditions, may be present. The first rendezvous that becomes possible prior to the expiration of the delay—through an entry call to an open accept alternative—is effected immediately. If no rendezvous can be effected prior to expiration of the delay, then the delay alternative is selected and the associated sequence of statements, if any, is executed.

Finally, it should be noted that there may be more than one delay alternative and that delay alternatives themselves may have when conditions. The reader should also recall that the presence of one or more delay alternatives precludes that of an else part or that of a terminate alternative.

These examples come nowhere near exhausting the possible forms that selective waits may take. The rich structure implied by the syntax of Statements (7.6.1) through (7.6.6) makes available a myriad of possible synchronization techniques.

7.3.3.2. The Calling Task and the Entry Call. A calling task effects an entry call through the execution of an entry call statement. The syntax for an entry call statement is given by Statement (7.3). When an entry call statement is executed, an immediate rendezvous is effected if the called task is waiting at a corresponding accept statement. An immediate rendezvous may be impossible for one of the following reasons:

- The called task is not waiting at a corresponding accept statement.
- The called task is waiting at a select statement containing a corresponding accept statement, but the accept alternative is closed.

In either case, the entry call is queued awaiting the availability of the called task at a corresponding accept statement, or at an open accept alternative containing a corresponding accept statement. Just as a timeout protection feature is needed for the selective wait, so also is this feature required to protect the entry call statement from excessive delays, or possibly from a deadlock condition. This timeout feature is provided by the select statement through the use of the timed entry call. The syntax is obtained from Statement (7.5) through the path

```
select_statement ::= timed_entry_call        (7.7)
```

where

```
timed_entry_call ::=
    select
        entry_call_statement                  (7.7.1)
      { sequence_of_statements }
    or
        delay_alternative
    end select;
```

The syntax for an entry call statement is given by Statement (7.3) and that for a delay alternative by Statement (7.6.5). The semantics of a timed entry call are analogous to those of a selective wait with a delay alternative. Specifically, the execution of a timed entry call occurs in accordance with the following rules:

- The expression specifying the delay is evaluated. Then, if the called task is waiting at a corresponding accept statement, an immediate rendezvous is effected. When the rendezvous is completed, the sequence of statements following the entry call, if any, is executed. Control then passes to the statement following **end select.**
- If an immediate rendezvous cannot be effected—either because the called task is not waiting at a corresponding accept statement, or because the called task is waiting at a selective wait with a corresponding accept alternative that is closed—and the duration of the delay is not zero or a negative value, the entry call is queued in the normal manner at the corresponding entry. If the duration is zero or negative, the entry call is abandoned immediately if no rendezvous can be effected, and the sequence of statements of the delay alternative, if any, is executed.
- If the entry call is queued awaiting a rendezvous, and no rendezvous is effected prior to expiration of the delay, the entry call is canceled and the sequence of statements of the delay alternative, if any, are executed. Control then passes to the statement following **end select.**

Examination of Statements (7.6.5) and (7.4) shows that the duration of the delay in a delay statement is a simple expression, implying that it is not static and can therefore be computed at run time. Thus, zero or negative values are possible, and the rules above specify that these values produce zero delay. That is, if an immediate rendezvous cannot be effected, the entry call is canceled and the optional sequence of statements of the delay alternative, if present, is executed. If the particular application requires a static value of zero for the delay, a more useful structure is the conditional entry call. The syntax for a conditional entry is obtained from Statement (7.5) through the path

```
        select_statement ::= conditional_entry_call    (7.8)
```

where

```
conditional_entry_call ::=
    select
        entry_call_statement
      { sequence_of_statements }
    else
        sequence_of_statements
    end select;                                        (7.8.1)
```

The syntax for an entry call statement is given by Statement (7.3). The execution of a conditional entry call is in accordance with the following rules:

- If the called task is waiting at a corresponding accept statement, then an immediate rendezvous is effected. When the rendezvous is completed, the sequence of statements following the entry call, if any, is executed. Control then passes to the statement following **end select.**
- If an immediate rendezvous cannot be effected, either because the called task is not waiting at a corresponding accept statement or because the called task is waiting at a selective wait with a corresponding accept alternative that is closed, the entry call is canceled and the sequence of statements is executed. Control then passes to the statement following **end select.**

Thus, the conditional entry call is similar to the timed entry call with zero or negative delay. The sequence of statements of the conditional entry call is required, even if it consists only of the null statement, while the sequence of statements of the delay alternative in a timed entry call is optional.

Examples of conditional and timed entry calls are given below to illustrate their use.

EXAMPLE 1: A conditional entry call may be used in a loop statement to avoid having execution of the calling task suspended awaiting rendezvous. Consider the following procedure:

```
procedure ADMIT is
begin
    loop
        select
            BIN_SEMAPHORE.WAIT;
            return;
        else
            null;
        end select;
    end loop;
end ADMIT;
--The entry call statement has no parameter. The return
  statement comprises the optional sequence of statements,
  and the null statement comprises the required sequence
  of statements of the else part.
```

When procedure ADMIT is called, the loop is iterated repeatedly until the rendezvous is effected. Thus, each iteration consists of the issuing and then the canceling of an entry call, followed by execution of the null statement, until the rendezvous is effected. Upon completion of the rendezvous, the return statement is executed and control passes to the calling environment. The reader should note the distinction between this method of making an entry call and the standard method represented by the entry call statement alone:

```
BIN_SEMAPHORE.WAIT;
```

A calling task executing this statement may be suspended awaiting the availability of the rendezvous. When a rendezvous can be effected, the task is moved from the suspended to the ready state, but it must await the allocation of computational resources before execution can resume. On the other hand, a call to procedure ADMIT causes no suspension of execution if an immediate rendezvous is not effected. This kind of result is termed a busy wait, as opposed to the suspended wait produced by the simple entry call statement. The reader should note, however, that the entry call in this example is never queued at a busy entry, which fact could produce rather long busy waits.

EXAMPLE 2: In Example 6 of the previous section, it was shown how a called task might be assigned some routine background function, such as self-diagnostic tests, if an immediate rendezvous cannot be effected. Similarly, a calling task can be directed to perform some routine function by use of the conditional entry call. For example, consider the following code segment:

```
select
    PRIMARY_LOOP.RADAR_INPUT(RADAR_DATA);
    --optional sequence of statements
else
    --sequence of statements of else part
end select;
```

The sequence of statements in the else part performs the routine background function if an immediate rendezvous cannot be effected.

A variation of this approach can be obtained using the timed entry call:

```
select
    PRIMARY_LOOP.RADAR_INPUT(RADAR_DATA);
    --optional sequence of statements
or
    delay 0.01;
    --optional sequence of statements of delay alternative
end select;
```

In this case, the optional sequence of statements of the delay alternative performs the routine background function, but it is executed only after a 10-millisecond delay, and only if a rendezvous is not effected during that 10 milliseconds.

If no background function is to be performed, then the conditional entry call

```
select
    PRIMARY_LOOP.RADAR_INPUT(RADAR_DATA);
    --optional sequence of statements
else
    null;
end select;
```

will simply continue execution after **end select** if an immediate rendezvous cannot be effected. On the other hand, the timed entry call

```
select
    PRIMARY_LOOP.RADAR_INPUT(RADAR_DATA);
    --optional sequence of statements
```

```
    or
        delay 0.01;
    end select;
```

will suspend the calling task for up to 10 milliseconds awaiting an available rendezvous, after which time the entry call will be canceled and control will be passed to the statement following **end select.**

7.4 CHARACTERISTICS AND PROPERTIES OF TASKS

Because the task is a relatively unique form of program unit, and because the basic declaration of a task is in terms of a task type and subsequent declaration of task objects, the characteristics and properties of tasks differ somewhat from those of other program units. This section discusses language features such as attributes, exceptions and exception handling, and compilation issues as they apply to tasks.

7.4.1 The Status of a Task

Previous discussion of task activation and task termination in Sections (7.2.5) and (7.2.6) implies that a task may be either *unactivated, activated, completed,* or *terminated.* A fifth status is now considered—that of being *abnormal.* A task is made abnormal by the execution of an abort statement, for which the syntax is:

```
abort_statement ::= abort task_name {, task_name};     (7.9)
```

The abort statement can be used anywhere that the task name or task names are visible. A task can even abort itself. The effect of the abort statement is to change the status of the named tasks to abnormal—unless the task is already terminated, in which case there is no effect. The abnormal status of a task has the following consequences:

- Any further rendezvous with the task is prevented.
- Any task that is dependent upon the abnormal task also becomes abnormal.
- If the task is currently suspended at an accept statement, a select statement, or a delay statement, it becomes completed.
- If the task is suspended at an entry call, it becomes completed and is removed from the entry queue.
- If the task is unactivated, it becomes completed and therefore becomes terminated.
- If the task has been activated and is not currently suspended, its

completion must take place no later than the time when one of the following points is reached in its execution:
the end of its activation
the point where it activates another task
an entry call
the beginning or end of an accept statement
a select statement
a delay statement
an exception handler
another abort statement
This rule prevents further rendezvous with an abnormal task that is still executing, that is, with an abnormal task that is not completed or terminated.
- If the task is a calling task involved in a rendezvous, its completion does not take place before the rendezvous is completed.

In summary, the status of a task is one of the following:

- Unactivated—The task has not yet been activated, even though the specification has been elaborated. See Section 7.2.1.
- Activated—The task is currently executing, or execution is awaiting the completion of the elaboration of the declarative part of the package body. See Section 7.2.5. Activated tasks may also be suspended awaiting rendezvous at an entry call statement or at an accept statement.
- Completed—Execution of the task has reached the end statement of the task body. See Section 7.2.6.
- Terminated—This is the condition under which a task relinquishes its allocated resources. Termination occurs when the task is completed and all its dependent tasks, if any, are terminated; or when the task has reached an open teminate alternative in a select statement, the task's master is completed, and all dependent tasks are either terminated or waiting at an open terminate alternative. See Section 7.2.6.
- Abnormal—No further rendezvous with the task is permitted, and the task is awaiting completion as discussed above.

The abort statement should be executed only in exceptional situations in which normal termination procedures have failed.

7.4.2 Attributes

Because a task is an object, it has attributes just as any other Ada object has attributes. Task types also have attributes applicable to every object of the type. Specifically, task types and task objects have the following attributes:

- STORAGE_SIZE
- ADDRESS
- SIZE

The reader is referred to Appendix B for a description of these attributes. In addition, a task object has the following attributes:

```
CALLABLE   -- This attribute has the value FALSE
              when the task object is either
              completed or terminated, or is
              abnormal. Otherwise, the value is
              TRUE.
TERMINATED -- This attribute has the value TRUE if
              the task is terminated. Otherwise, the
              value is FALSE.
```

In addition, every entry of a task has an attribute COUNT, with the following properties:

```
COUNT -- This attribute yields the number of entry
         calls currently queued for the entry. The
         value returned is of type universal_
         integer.
```

With the use of these attributes, a calling task can predict the result of an entry call.

7.4.3 Exceptions

The effects of exceptions raised within a task depend on the point at which the exception is raised. The general conditions under which an exception is raised and the resulting effects are summarized below:

- During elaboration of declarations in a task specification: The elaboration is abandoned. If the task is in a library package, the execution of the main program is abandoned. Otherwise, the exception is propagated to the enclosing declarative part or package specification.
- During elaboration of declarations in the task body: The task becomes completed, and the predefined exception TASKING_ERROR is raised after the reserved word **begin** of the body of the enclosing program unit. Thus, the exception TASKING_ERROR can be handled locally within the enclosing program unit.

- During activation of a task created by an allocator: The task becomes completed and the predefined exception TASKING_ERROR is raised at the point at which the allocator is evaluated.
- During execution of statements in a task body, but not within an accept statement: If the exception is raised within a frame enclosed by the task body, the exception may be handled locally within the frame. If it is not handled within the frame, or if there is no enclosing frame, the exception may be handled in the exception handler of the task body, after which the task becomes completed. If there is no exception handler, the task becomes completed. No propagation of the exception takes place. See Section 3.9.4 for the definition of a frame.
- During execution of statements within an accept statement: If the exception is raised within a frame enclosed by the accept statement, then the exception may be handled locally within the frame. If it is not handled within the frame, or if there is no enclosing frame, the execution of the accept statement is abandoned. The same exception is raised immediately after the accept statement, and it is also propagated to the calling task at the point of the entry call.

Thus, exceptions raised during execution of a task are propagated to other tasks only if a rendezvous is in progress, and then only if it is not handled within a local frame.

Other problems may arise during rendezvous or attempted rendezvous. In this event, the predefined exception TASKING_ERROR is raised in the calling task at the point of entry call. Such action occurs when

- An entry call is issued for an entry of a task that becomes completed before accepting the entry call. This situation can occur if the entry call is issued after the task is completed or if the entry call is queued at the time the called task becomes abnormal due to the execution of an abort statement.
- A task involved in a rendezvous becomes abnormal due to the execution of an abort statement. In this case, the task may complete the rendezvous before becoming completed. See Section 7.4.1.

The raising of TASKING_ERROR in the calling task is appropriate, since the calling task must be informed of trouble in the rendezvous. On the other hand, if the calling task becomes abnormal due to the execution of an abort statement, no exception is passed to the called task. If a rendezvous is in progress when the calling task becomes abnormal, the rendezvous is completed normally. If the entry call is queued awaiting rendezvous, then the entry call is canceled and removed from the queue.

7.4.4 Shared Variables

Although the normal means of task communications is through the rendezvous mechanism and the interchange of parameters in the rendezvous process, some applications may require the use of shared variables. A variable is said to be *shared* among two or more tasks if it is accessible to each of the tasks. Such accessibility requires that the variable be visible to each of the tasks, a fact that affects just where the declaration of the variable may occur with respect to the task declarations. The use of shared variables in any language requires extreme care to provide the synchronization and mutual exclusion characteristics that are implicit in the use of the rendezvous. Example 1 of Section 7.3.1 provides a simple example of the use of a shared variable and of some of the problems that may be encountered.

A basic premise of the Ada language design is that shared variables normally will not be used. Because of this fact, Ada programs using shared variables are subject to two rather severe limitations applying to shared variables that are of a scalar or access type:

1. If a shared variable is read by a task between two synchronization points, then no other task may assign a value to the variable while the first task is between the synchronization points.
2. If a task assigns a value to a shared variable between two synchronization points, then no other task may read or assign a value to the variable while the first task is between the synchronization points.

Synchronization points of a task are the beginning and end of a rendezvous, activation of the task, and completion of the task. These restrictions permit an implementation to use local copies of the shared variable between synchronization points. A program that violates these restrictions is said to be *erroneous*—that is, as discussed in Section 1.2.1, the effect of execution is unpredictable because there is no requirement for an implementation either to provide a compile-time or run-time detection of an erroneous program or to properly execute an erroneous program. The restriction apparently applies only to scalar or access types because composite types would not normally be copied locally.

It is possible to make every reading of and assignment to a shared variable a synchronization point for the variable. A compiler directive, or *pragma,* is used to accomplish this. The general concept of pragmas is discussed in Chapter 8. In this case, pragma SHARED is used, as indicated below:

```
pragma SHARED(variable_simple_name);        (7.10)
```

The pragma must appear after the object declaration that declares the variable, and both must appear in the same declarative part or package specification. If every reading of and assignment to a shared variable is a synchronization point for the variable, then the two restrictions outlined above are automatically satisfied. The reader should note, however, that this kind of synchronization only lifts the restrictions outlined above. It does not preclude the program logic from encountering synchronization or mutual interference problems.

7.4.5 Task Priorities

When the execution of a task is suspended at an entry call statement, an accept statement, or a select statement, the computational resources used by the task may be reallocated to other tasks. If such reallocation occurs, then the task, when it is ready to resume execution, must await the availability of resources before execution can resume. The Ada model of each task executing on its own logical processor does not consider the fact that some implementations may be subject to this effect, which is briefly discussed in Section 7.3.1. An implementation may support the concept of *priority* of tasks, in which case each task may—but need not—have a priority assigned to it by pragma PRIORITY, as indicated below:

```
pragma PRIORITY(static_expression);        (7.11)
```

The general concept of pragmas is discussed in Chapter 8. This particular pragma must appear in the specification of the task, or in the outermost declarative part of the main program, to which it assigns a priority. The priority of a task is an integer value of subtype PRIORITY, which is declared in the predefined package SYSTEM; package SYSTEM is also considered in Chapter 8. The range of type PRIORITY is implementation-dependent, but a higher value implies a higher priority. Priorities can be assigned only to the main program and to tasks.

Even if priorities are supported by the implementation, all tasks need not be assigned priority values, so that a program may have some tasks with priorities and some tasks without priorities. The rules of priority are listed below:

- If two tasks have the same priority, the scheduling order is not defined by the language rules.
- If two tasks engaged in a rendezvous have priorities, the rendezvous is executed with the higher of the two priorities.

- If only one of two tasks engaged in a rendezvous has a priority, then the rendezvous is executed with at least that priority.
- For tasks without explicit priorities, there is no defined scheduling rule.

For tasks with priorities, the scheduling rule is stated in the LRM in the following manner:

> If two tasks with different priorities are both eligible for execution and could sensibly be executed using the same physical processors and the same other processing resources, then it cannot be the case that the task with the lower priority is executing while the task with the higher priority is not.

Thus, the scheduling rules apply only to tasks with priorities. Tasks without priorities do not have low priorities, nor do they have high priorities. They simply have no priority, and tasks with no priority are subject to no defined scheduling rules. That is, the implementation is free to determine scheduling of these tasks in an arbitrary manner.

The priority of a task has no effect on how entry calls are queued at an entry of a task—this queue discipline is always first in–first out regardless of the priorities of the calling tasks. However, an implementation may permit task priorities to affect which of two eligible tasks will be selected for rendezvous if they are both waiting at open accept alternatives of a selective wait.

In general, task priorities should be used only to specify the degree or urgency of a task in time-critical applications. They should not be used for task synchronization. Finally, it should be noted that priorities are assigned at compile time and cannot be altered at run time, except as noted above for the special instance of a rendezvous.

7.4.6 Compilation Issues

Tasks are not separately compilable. That is, a task cannot be a compilation unit as described in Section 3.11.3. Rather, a task must be declared in the declarative part of a program unit that is a compilation unit or is contained within a compilation unit. The specification and body of a task may, however, be textually separated within a declarative part for visibility purposes, or they may appear in the separately compiled specification and body, respectively, of a package. The task body may be represented by a subunit. The general subunit rules of Section 3.11.3.2 apply in this case.

Finally, the effect of separate compilation of a task can be produced by encapsulating the task within a package, which can be separately compiled. Example 5 of Section 7.3.3.1 exemplifies this concept.

7.4.7 Concurrent Processing Concerns

The concepts presented in this chapter imply a very powerful and versatile capability within the Ada language for implementing programs with concurrently executing tasks. It should be noted, however, that the scheduling of tasks within a program is accomplished by the run-time support system, which may—and probably will—vary from implementation to implementation. For example, different run-time systems may support different numbers of processors, or a single processor system may provide different degrees of multiprogramming. There are other areas of concern that have been previously mentioned; these concerns are summarized below:

- The programmer cannot assume that the run-time system schedules tasks in any manner that tends to avoid deadlock.
- The pragma SHARED does not enforce mutually exclusive access to the shared variable.
- The scheduling of tasks with no priority, or of tasks with equal priorities, is implementation-dependent.
- A program cannot depend upon any particular task-scheduling discipline. Programs with such dependence are erroneous.

The net result is that the concurrent processing features of an Ada program may not be portable. The programmer can use some discretion to minimize these concerns by using the rich concurrent processing features of the language to explicitly avoid potential problems. For example, the use of shared data should be minimized. Deadlock prevention should be specifically designed into the program rather than having it depend upon implicit language features that may not be portable. Program correctness should not depend on the relative speed of execution of concurrent tasks. Circular dependency among tasks should be avoided. Finally, some care should be taken in selecting the run-time support system. They are not all the same.

REFERENCES

1. Ben-Ari, M., *Principles of Concurrent Programming* (Englewood Cliffs, N.J.: Prentice-Hall, 1982).
2. MacLaren, Lee, "Evolving Toward Ada in Real-Time Systems," in *Real-Time Software,* by Robert Glass (Englewood Cliffs, N.J.: Prentice-Hall, 1983).

3. Hoare, C. A. R., "Communicating Sequential Processes," *Communications of the ACM,* **21**:666–677 (1978).
4. Phillips, Stephen P., and Stevenson, Peter R., "The Role of Ada in Real Time Embedded Applications," *Ada Letters,* a Bimonthly Publication of SIGAda, the ACM Special Interest Group on Ada, **III**(4) (February 1984).

EXERCISES

1. How does the requirement for concurrent processing arise in embedded-system programming?
2. Distinguish between multiprogramming, multiprocessing, and multicomputing.
3. Discuss the meaning of the term *cyclic executive*.
4. What is a real-time operating system?
5. Describe the Ada rendezvous.
6. Tasks are not reentrant. Comment on this statement.
7. Describe a task specification.
8. Discuss the concept of a task type.
9. What is the scope of a formal parameter in an accept statement?
10. When is a task activated?
11. Distinguish between completion and termination of a task.
12. List the requirements for task termination.
13. Tasks cannot be separately compiled because neither a task specification nor a task body is a compilation unit. Explain how the effect of separate compilation may be obtained. Give an example.
14. Explain how deadlock occurs if a task calls its own entry.
15. When does a rendezvous begin? When does it end?
16. How do the beginning and end of a rendezvous affect the calling task? The called task?
17. Discuss the concept of a *logical processor,* and relate it to multiprogramming and multiprocessing.
18. Explain the terms *synchronization* and *mutual exclusion* as they relate to concurrent processing.
19. Explain the term *shared data* as it relates to concurrent processing.
20. List the predefined operations available for objects of type DURATION.
21. Discuss the use of package CALENDAR. In particular, discuss the purpose of the various functions exported by the package.
22. What is the purpose of the select statement?
23. Show how the select statement can be used to prevent deadlock.
24. Explain the effect of an else part in a selective wait.
25. Explain the effect of a delay alternative in a selective wait.
26. Explain the effect of a terminate alternative in a selective wait.
27. Does it make sense to have more than one delay alternative in a selective wait? Explain.
28. At what point is a when condition evaluated in a selective wait?
29. Distinguish between a timed entry call and a conditional entry call.
30. What is an abnormal task? How is a task made abnormal?

31. If an exception is raised in the execution of the sequence of statements in a task, where is it handled?
32. What is a synchronization point in a task?
33. Discuss the requirements of the Ada language relating to the synchronization of concurrently executing tasks.
34. Discuss pragma SHARED and its relation to concurrently executing tasks.
35. How is a task priority assigned? What is the effect of a task priority?

PROGRAMMING EXERCISES

1. Write a program (procedure) that contains both task BUFFER of Example 1, Section 7.2.2, and another task. The main program should get a character from the keyboard, and the other task should print the character to the screen. The character is to be transmitted from the main program to the printing task through task BUFFER.
2. Complete the body of procedure ADD_SUB of Example 2, Section 7.2.2, to calculate and print the inner product of the two parameters of type VECTOR. Declare procedure ADD_SUB within a main program (procedure) that calls ADD_SUB and prints out the sum and difference vectors.
3. Write a program (procedure) in which the two tasks GET_CHAR and CRYPT_CHAR of Example 1, Section 7.3.1, are declared. The function CRYPT must also be declared in the declarative part of the procedure. The procedure body may contain a null statement, or it may contain some other sequence of statements.
4. Modify the program of Exercise 3 to include the buffering represented by Example 2, Section 7.3.1.
5. Compile and execute procedure SELECT_TEST of Example 2, Section 7.3.3.1. Interpret the results.
6. Write and compile a program (procedure) that declares the task type BIN_SEMAPHORE_TYPE of Example 4, Section 7.3.3.1. This program should declare two task objects of the type, and the semaphores thus created should be used to protect two critical sections of code.
7. Write and compile a program (procedure) that declares the task FIFO_TASK of Example 5, Section 7.3.3.1. The program should exercise the FIFO queue thus established.
8. Compile FIFO_PACKAGE as given in Example 5, Section 7.3.3.1. Write and compile a program (procedure) that imports and exercises FIFO_TASK.
9. Convert FIFO_PACKAGE into a generic package, as indicated in Example 5, Section 7.3.3.1, and separately compile it as a library unit. Write and compile a main program that instantiates the package for two data types—one a scalar and one an array of records. The program should exercise the FIFO queue packages resulting from the instantiation.
10. Write and compile a program (procedure) that declares two tasks. Deliberately produce a deadlock situation, and then show how it can be broken by use of a select statement.

Chapter 8
REMAINING LANGUAGE FEATURES

8.1 GENERAL CONCEPTS

Chapters 3 through 7 have covered the major features of the Ada language. These features have dealt mainly with programming and with program design for reliable, maintainable, and modifiable software. In this chapter, the remaining aspects of the language will be considered. There are three principal areas of interest:

1. remaining programming features:
   - overloading
   - renaming
   - pragmas
   - derivable subprograms
2. relating programs to the underlying machine:
   - representation clauses
   - address clauses
   - interrupt handling
   - machine code insertions
3. implementation features:
   - package SYSTEM

The first area deals with topics that have been mentioned in previous discussion but which, for clarity of presentation, were not thoroughly explored at the time. The second area is a very important one for embedded-system programming; it relates to the primitive input-output package LOW_LEVEL_IO, to the manner in which vectored interrupts are handled within the high-order language, and to the manner in which machine code instructions can be executed from within the high-order language.

8.2 LANGUAGE FEATURES

One of the characteristics of embedded systems is that programs tend to be large. Large programs, and particularly large programs written in a strongly typed language, tend to have a large number of identifiers. Identifiers, of course, are used for names of types, objects, subprograms, tasks, exceptions, and enumeration literals. Management of names can be quite a problem, particularly if the software engineering practice of using meaningful names is embraced. In general, three kinds of naming problems are encountered: (1) difficulty in selecting meaningful names that have not already been used, (2) expanded names that can become quite lengthy, and (3) the necessity of simultaneously dealing with a very large number of names. To aid in the use of meaningful names, the Ada language has an *overloading* feature, by which the same name can be used for more than one entity—even if the entities are of the same kind. For example, the same name may be used for any number of subprograms, as long as any ambiguities can be resolved by the compiler from examination of the parameter list. Exceptionally long or confusing expanded names can be given a simple name by Ada's *renaming* facility, by which more than one name can denote a single entity. The following sections will deal with these two language features and with the concepts of pragmas and derivable subprograms.

8.2.1 Overloading of Identifiers

The scope and visibility rules considered in Sections 3.11.1 and 3.11.2 serve to define the visibility of identifiers within an Ada program. When an identifier occurs, one of two conditions will exist:

1. The visibility rules will serve to specify a unique meaning for the identifier at the point at which it occurs, or they will indicate that the identifier is not valid at the point at which it occurs.
2. The visibility rules will indicate that there is more than one possible meaning for the identifier at the point at which it occurs.

In the former case, the compiler will accept the occurrence of the identifier if a unique meaning is established, and it will otherwise reject the identifier as being undeclared. In the latter case, the compiler does not necessarily reject the identifier, because Ada does permit overloading—the use of the same identifier to denote more than one entity—in certain situations in which the context in which the identifier appears serves to resolve the resulting ambiguity. For example, if the two procedure declarations

```
procedure GET(ITEM : out CHARACTER);
procedure GET(ITEM : out STRING);
```

appear in the same declarative region, then the context in which the identifier GET appears serves to resolve the ambiguity produced by using the same name for the two procedures. That is, the use of the identifier GET with a parameter of type CHARACTER obviously refers to the first declaration above, while an occurrence of the identifier GET with a parameter of type STRING refers to the second declaration. These two declarations actually occur in the predefined package TEXT_IO, as indicated in Appendix C and by the developments of Section 6.2.2.

Thus, the overloading rules of Ada apply when the visibility rules imply more than one possible meaning for an identifier. If the overloading rules cannot resolve the ambiguity produced by the visibility rules, then the compiler will reject the occurrence of the identifier. Overloading in an Ada program is not a general concept applicable to all identifiers. It is instead limited to identifiers that denote subprogram names, enumeration literals, operator symbols, or single task entries. The resolution of an overloading ambiguity must be obtainable from the context in which the overloaded identifier appears. In this respect, the context is interpreted to include a declaration, a statement, or a representation clause. Representation clauses are considered in Section 8.3. Within the context, the following rules are used in the resolution of ambiguities: syntax rules, scope and visibility rules, and typing rules. The specific application of these rules to different instances of overloading are the subject of the remainder of this section.

8.2.1.1 Overloading of Subprogram Names. The same identifier can be used to denote more than one subprogram, even though the visibility rules do not suffice to resolve the resulting ambiguity. Such subprogram names are thus overloaded, and the resolution of any ambiguities must then be provided by the overloading rules. In the case of procedures, ambiguities are resolved by examination of the order and base type of the parameters. In the case of functions, ambiguities are resolved by the order and base type of the parameters and the result base type of the function. Specifically not considered in resolving overloading ambiguities are parameter names, parameter modes, and default expressions for parameters. Base types are specifically indicated above because it is the base type of the parameter, rather than the subtype, that is significant if a subtype name is contained in the parameter declaration.

Examples of subprogram overloading abound in the predefined input-output packages contained in Appendix C and described in Chapter 6.

8.2.1.2 Overloading of Enumeration Literals. Enumeration literals are the identifiers that appear in a type declaration as values of an enumeration type, as is implied by Statement (3.12). It would be quite common in a large program for a particular identifier to appear as an enumeration literal in more than one enumeration type declaration, thus overloading the identifier. Resolution of ambiguities involving an overloaded enumeration literal must be resolvable solely from the context in which the enumeration literal appears. For example, if the following declarations appear within the same declarative region,

```
type SYSTEM_STATUS is (OFF, NO_DATA, COMPUTING, READY,
                        FIRE);
type SENSOR_VALUE is (OFF, UNDER_TEMP, NORMAL, OVER_TEMP,
                       FIRE);
```

then the enumeration literals OFF and FIRE are obviously overloaded. Furthermore, if the object declarations

```
GUN_STATUS     : SYSTEM_STATUS;
SENSOR_READING : SENSOR_VALUE;
```

are visible at some point in a program, then assignments such as

```
GUN_STATUS     := OFF;
SENSOR_READING := OFF;
```

are permissible, because the ambiguity relating to which enumeration literal OFF is to be used is satisfactorily resolved by the context in which it apears in either case. On the other hand, a loop statement containing the iteration scheme

```
for STATUS in OFF..FIRE
```

is ambiguous, and furthermore, the ambiguity cannot be resolved from the context. In such situations in which the context does not suffice to resolve an ambiguity, a *qualified expression* may be used, as indicated by the developments of Section 3.7.6. In this case,

```
for STATUS in GUN_STATUS'(OFF)..GUN_STATUS'(FIRE)
```

or even

```
for STATUS in GUN_STATUS'(OFF)..FIRE
```

should suffice to resolve the ambiguity. In this particular case, an even better solution is to use the discrete subtype indication of Statements (3.22.6) and (3.8.1), in the form

```
for STATUS in GUN_STATUS
```

which more clearly indicates the specific action accomplished by the loop.

8.2.1.3 Overloading of Operator Symbols. In Section 3.7.2, the predefined operations of the Ada language are listed, together with the symbol used to denote each of these operations. These predefined operations can be considered to be implemented as functions that accept the operands as parameters and return the values implied by the symbols. The declarations, within package STANDARD, of functions using these operator symbols as names serve as appropriate examples. In particular, the predefined types INTEGER and FLOAT have associated with them the standard operations implemented as functions. In order to provide flexibility in the naming of certain kinds of user-defined subprograms, the Ada language permits most of these operator symbols to be overloaded. Specifically, the following symbols may be used to name user-defined functions:

```
and    or     xor
=      <      <=     >      >=
+      -      &
*      /      mod    rem
**     abs    not
```

In fact, package STANDARD itself contains overloading of most of these symbols. When overloaded symbols are used as function names, they are enclosed by double quotation marks in order to distinguish them from the associated characters, which are enclosed within single quotation marks.

From package STANDARD, the specification of which is contained in Appendix A, the following examples of function specifications are provided:

```
function "+"(LEFT, RIGHT : INTEGER) return INTEGER;
function "+"(LEFT, RIGHT : FLOAT)   return FLOAT;
```

The overloading ambiguity of calls to function "+" is resolved by examination of the parameter and return types. Further overloading of the symbol "+" may be produced by one or more user-defined functions. For example, if the declaration

```
type MATRIX is array(1..20, 1..20) of FLOAT;
```

is in effect, and if a user-defined function is to be provided that sums two arrays of type MATRIX, the function specification might be written as

```
function "+"(LEFT, RIGHT : MATRIX) return MATRIX;
```

Furthermore, if the following objects are declared

```
INT_1, INT_2, INT_SUM : INTEGER;
FL_1, FL_2, FL_SUM    : FLOAT;
MAT_1, MAT_2, MAT_SUM : MATRIX;
```

then the following uses of the overloaded functions are proper:

```
INT_SUM := "+"(INT_1, INT_2);
FL_SUM  := "+"(FL_1, FL_2);
MAT_SUM := "+"(MAT_1, MAT_2);
```

The ambiguities associated with the use of the symbol "+" are resolved by consideration of the parameter and result types. The particular form of the function used above is termed *out-fix* notation. The more meaningful *in-fix* notation is normally used for the predefined operations:

```
INT_SUM := INT_1 + INT_2;
FL_SUM  := FL_1  + FL_2;
```

Ada also permits in-fix notation to be used in calls to user-defined functions with names that are operator symbols. Thus, in the example above the matrix sum could be obtained as

```
MAT_SUM := MAT_1 + MAT_2;
```

in a manner completely analogous to the call to the predefined functions. The only requirement for use of in-fix notation is that the overloaded function must be directly visible—that is, it must be recognizable by the simple name "+", rather than requiring an expanded name such as MATRIX_PACKAGE. "+".

8.2.1.4 Overloading of Entry Names. Overloading of names associated with task entries is limited to single entries, as opposed to families of entries. As with subprogram calls, the resolution of overload ambiguities depends upon the context in which the overloaded name appears.

8.2.2 Renaming Facilities

The renaming facilities of the Ada language provide for the renaming of declared entities—that is, they provide alternate names that denote the entity. The following entities can be renamed: objects, exceptions, packages, subprograms, and task entries. Renaming is usually considered poor programming practice, because it provides alternative ways of accessing an object, but there are some instances in which renaming might be appropriate. For example, renaming can be used to resolve an otherwise unresolvable overloading ambiguity. Extremely long and cumbersome expanded names can be renamed to provide access to the entity by use of a simpler name. The syntax of a renaming declaration is

```
renaming_declaration ::=
   identifier : type_mark renames object_name
  | identifier : exception renames exception_name
  | package identifier     renames package_name
  | subprogram_specification   renames
              subprogram_or_entry_name;          (8.1)
```

The effect of the renaming declaration is to associate the identifier with the entity denoted by the name following the reserved word **renames.**

The new name and the old name may have different regions of visibility. The old name must be visible at the point of the renaming declaration, but the renaming declaration—since it is subject to the same scope rules as is any other declaration—may be visible in regions of the program where the old name is not visible.

A task object—that is, a task declared by an object declaration that names a task type—can be renamed. A task object declared by a task declaration cannot be renamed because it is of an anonymous type. Similarly, arrays of an anonymous type cannot be renamed. Finally, generic units cannot be renamed.

8.2.2.1 Renaming of Objects. The renaming of an object is achieved by the use of Statement (8.1) through the choice

```
identifier : type_mark renames object_name;   (8.1.1)
```

There must be type compatibility between the type mark and the type of the denoted object. None of the properties of the object is affected by the renaming. Renaming is not permitted for unconstrained arrays or for generic formal objects of mode **in out.** Examples of renaming of objects are

```
PICTURE : PICTURE_PTR renames FRAME;
--The object FRAME of type PICTURE_PTR is renamed PICTURE.
  Both FRAME and PICTURE denote the same object.

NAME : STRING(1..25) renames ALL_EVENTS(POLITICAL)
                    .LIST(1).ID;
--The object denoted by the expanded name is renamed NAME.
```

In both of these cases, the renaming does not change any characteristics of the object.

8.2.2.2 Renaming of Exceptions. Exceptions can be renamed by the use of Statement (8.1) through the choice

```
identifier : exception renames exception_name;    (8.1.2)
```

The only requirement in renaming an exception is that the exception name be visible. Examples can be found in the predefined package TEXT_IO.

8.2.2.3 Renaming of Packages. A package may be renamed by use of Statement (8.1) through the choice

```
package identifier renames package_name;    (8.1.3)
```

The only requirement in renaming a package is that the package name be visible.

8.2.2.4 Renaming of Subprograms. A subprogram may be renamed by use of Statement (8.1) through the choice

```
subprogram_specification renames subprogram_name;    (8.1.4)
```

The subprogram specification and the subprogram to be renamed must have the same number of parameters, and corresponding parameters must have the same base type and mode. If the subprogram is a function, the result types must also be identical. The names of the parameters in the subprogram specification can be different from those in the renamed subprogram, however, as can default expressions or the absence or presence of default expressions. Subprogram calls using named association must use the new parameter names if the new name for the subprogram is used, and they must use the old parameter names if the old subprogram name is used.

Procedures may be renamed only as procedures, but a function may be renamed as either a function or as an operator; an operator is essentially a function with an operator symbol as a name, as discussed in Section 8.2.1.3. Similarly, an operator can be renamed either as an operator or as a function. Examples of the renaming of subprograms are given below; they are based upon the following declarations:

```
function MAT_SUM(MAT_1,MAT_2 : MATRIX) return MATRIX;
procedure MAT_INVERSE(MAT : in out MATRIX);
function "*"(LEFT, RIGHT : MATRIX) return MATRIX;
```

Renaming declarations are

```
function "+"(LEFT, RIGHT : MATRIX) return MATRIX
             renames MAT_SUM;
--The function MAT_SUM is renamed to the operator symbol
  "+". New parameter names are also declared. Calls to
  both subprograms are valid. Each call must use the
  appropriate parameter names if named association is
  used.

procedure INVERT(MAT : in out MATRIX) renames
                 MAT_INVERSE:
--The procedure MAT_INVERSE is renamed to INVERT. The
  parameter name is not changed.

function MAT_MULT(MAT_1,MAT_2 : MATRIX) return MATRIX
                  renames "*";
--The function "*" is renamed to MAT_MULT. New parameter
  names are provided.
```

In all cases of renaming, the subprogram to be renamed must be visible, and, if its name is overloaded, the parameter list and the result type must suffice to resolve the overloading ambiguity.

8.2.2.5 Renaming of Entries. A single task entry may be renamed through the use of Statement (8.1) by the choice

```
subprogram_specification renames entry_name;    (8.1.5)
```

As indicated, an entry can only be renamed as a subprogram—in particular, it can be renamed as a procedure with the same number of parameters of the same type and mode. An entry of a family can be renamed as a single entry, but a family of entries cannot be renamed as an entire family. A call to the resulting procedure effects an entry call to the renamed entry. These procedure call statements are not permitted in conditional and timed entry calls, in which the syntax requires an entry call statement.

8.2.3 Pragmas

Most modern languages have compiler directives of some kind by which the programmer can issue instructions to the compiler. In the Ada language such a directive is called a pragma. Pragmas can appear at different points in Ada source code, depending upon the particular pragma. Certain predefined pragmas are required of any Ada compiler, but an implementation is free to provide other pragmas as well. Since pragmas are directives to the compiler, they do not compile into executable code.

The pragma provides for some degree of programmer control over the manner in which the compiler forms the source code, or in which the run-time support system provides for the execution of the program. The syntax for a pragma is

```
pragma ::=
   pragma identifier [(argument_association
                      {, argument_association})];    (8.2)
```

where

```
argument_association ::=
   [argument_identifier =>] name
| [argument_identifier =>]
expression.                                        (8.2.1)
```

The identifier in Statement (8.2) is the name of the pragma. Some pragmas have arguments, and, as indicated in Statement (8.2.1), named association may be used. Just where a pragma may appear in a program depends on the pragma itself.

The Ada language has 14 predefined pragmas. Details of these pragmas and their use are contained in Appendix C, but a brief discussion of each is given below.

8.2.3.1 Pragma CONTROLLED. The discussion of access types in Section 3.6.3 implies that objects designated by access objects are created by allocators during execution of a program. Furthermore, the link between an access object and a designated object can be removed by assigning a new allocator, or by assigning the value **null,** to the access object. An implementation is free to reclaim the storage allocated to designated objects that can no longer be referenced. Such a process is termed garbage collection and is almost a necessity in certain applications. If a programmer requires closer control over reclamation of storage allocation for objects designated by objects of a particular access type, the pragma CONTROLLED may be used. The syntax is

```
pragma CONTROLLED(access_type_simple_name);     (8.2.2)
```

The effect of this pragma is to restrain the automatic reclamation of storage allocated to objects designated by values of the access type until execution of the program leaves the innermost block, subprogram body, or task body containing the declaration of the access type. Use of pragma CONTROLLED is not permitted for a derived type. See Section 8.7.2 for further discussion of deallocation.

8.2.3.2 Pragma ELABORATE. The required order of compilation of library units is outlined in Section 3.11.4. It is the responsibility of the programming support environment to ensure the correct order in the compilation or recompilation of library units. Before a main program is executed, all library units required for execution of the main program are elaborated. These library units include those contained in context clauses—indicated by with clauses—both in the main program and in any library unit referenced by the main program in either a direct or indirect manner. The order of elaboration of these library units is normally that implied by the with clauses. In some instances, this normal order of elaboration may be inconsistent with the rules of prior elaboration of the language. In particular, this situation may occur with library unit bodies that require elaboration prior to the point implied by the normal order of elaboration. Such prior elaboration can be requested by use of the pragma ELABORATE, for which the syntax is

```
pragma ELABORATE(library_unit_simple_name
                 {, library_unit_simple_name});     (8.2.3)
```

This pragma appears immediately after the context clause of a compilation unit, and it specifies that the bodies of the named library units must be elaborated before elaboration of the compilation unit.

8.2.3.3 Pragma INLINE. Subprograms in an Ada program are used for two purposes—to encapsulate and therefore to form abstractions of algorithms, and to conserve code statements when a particular sequence is executed repetitively or many times during the execution of a program.

The benefits of the abstraction provided by subprograms is treated in Section 3.10. The advantage in program code reduction provided by the use of subprograms has an overhead cost in the form of the linking of the calling environment to the subprogram. This overhead usually manifests itself in terms of increased execution time, something that may be of critial concern in real-time embedded programs. The pragma INLINE can be used to instruct the compiler to expand a subprogram inline at each point at which a call to the subprogram is made. That is, each subprogram call is to be replaced by the entire subprogram body. The syntax for this pragma is

```
pragma INLINE(name {, name});          (8.2.4)
```

Each occurrence of a subprogram named in the pragma is to be expanded inline at each point of call. If the subprogram names are overloaded, the pragma applies to all subprograms denoted by the name. An implementation is free to follow or ignore the requests made by INLINE pragmas, and furthermore, it is free to follow or ignore them on a call-by-call basis.

8.2.3.4 Pragma INTERFACE. The Ada language permits calls to subprograms written in another language. All communications between the subprogram and the calling environment must be achieved through the use of parameters and, in the case of functions, through the result value. The syntax is

```
pragma INTERFACE(language_name, subprogram_name);
                                              (8.2.5)
```

Pragma INTERFACE is not required of an implementation, and those implementations that do support it may place restrictions on its use.

8.2.3.5 Pragma OPTIMIZE. Efficient Ada compilers will contain optimizers that examine Ada code and perform certain optimization operations. Optimization can relate to maximum execution speed or to minimum storage requirements, or to both. Usually, maximum execution speed and minimum storage requirements are conflicting objectives, requiring a choice to be made between the two. The pragma OPTIMIZE permits the programmer to specify one of two predefined identifiers, TIME or SPACE, as the primary optimization criterion. The syntax is

```
pragma OPTIMIZE(TIME | SPACE);         (8.2.6)
```

This pragma applies only to the block or body in whose declarative part it appears.

8.2.3.6 Pragma PACK. When a record type or an array type is elaborated, an implementation is free to select the mapping between the underlying machine and objects of the type. A programmer can specify the precise mapping—that is, the manner in which the object is stored in memory—by use of a representation clause, to be discussed in Section 8.3. If no representation clause is used, the programmer may specify that storage minimization should be the primary criterion when selecting the representation. Pragma PACK is used to express this instruction to the compiler. The syntax is

```
pragma PACK(type_simple_name);            (8.2.7)
```

The pragma applies only to objects of the named type. Furthermore, only the gaps between storage areas allocated to consecutive components is minimized. Storage of the components themselves can be influenced by further use of the pragma PACK within the components themselves, or by use of representation clauses.

8.2.3.7 Pragma PRIORITY. The use of pragma PRIORITY is discussed in Section 7.4.5. Essentially, this pragma provides a precedence list to be followed by the run-time support system in allocating computational resources to tasks that are eligible for execution. It does not affect the order in which tasks queued at an entry are selected for rendezvous—this order is always first in–first out. The syntax is

```
pragma PRIORITY(static_expression);       (8.2.8)
```

The reader is referred to Section 7.4.5 for further detail.

8.2.3.8. Pragma SHARED. Normally, communication between two concurrently executing tasks is achieved through the use of parameters in the entry call. Other languages that support concurrently executing tasks often use global data—that is, data that is visible to all tasks—to provide this communication. The use of shared data is not normally considered good programming practice, and hence it is not encouraged by the Ada language design. However, pragma SHARED is provided to permit the adaption of Ada code to the use of shared data. The syntax is

```
pragma SHARED(variable_simple_name);      (8.2.9)
```

The effect of this pragma is to make every read and write operation of the specified variable a synchronization point. The reader is referred to Section 7.4.4 for further detail.

8.2.3.9 Pragma SUPPRESS. In Section 3.9, the use of exceptions in Ada programs was discussed. Exceptions can be user-defined, but there is also a set of predefined exceptions that are raised by the run-time support system when an exceptional condition is encountered during the execution of a program. As detailed in Section 3.9.1, these predefined exceptions are

- CONSTRAINT_ERROR
- NUMERIC_ERROR
- PROGRAM_ERROR
- STORAGE_ERROR
- TASKING_ERROR

These exceptions are raised as a result of a run-time check made by the run-time support system. Specifically, the following run-time checks result in the raising of the exception CONSTRAINT_ERROR:

```
ACCESS_CHECK         -- checks that an access value
                        is not null
DISCRIMINANT_CHECK -- checks discriminant constraint
INDEX_CHECK          -- checks index constraint
LENGTH_CHECK         -- checks for matching components
                        of arrays
RANGE_CHECK          -- checks range constraints
```

The following run-time checks can raise the predefined exception NUMERIC_ERROR:

```
DIVISION_CHECK       -- checks for division by zero
OVERFLOW_CHECK       -- checks for overflow in a
                        numeric operation
```

The predefined exception PROGRAM_ERROR is raised when a task activation or a generic instantiation is attempted before the corresponding unit body has been elaborated. This exception is raised by the run-time check

```
ELABORATION_CHECK  -- checks for proper order of
                      elaboration
```

The exception STORAGE_ERROR is raised when the memory space available for a task or subprogram has been exceeded, or when the memory space allowed for the collection of objects designated by objects of an access type exceeds that specified by a length clause. Length clauses are discussed in Section 8.3.2.

The run-time checks, and the subsequent exceptions that they may raise, ensure that an Ada program does not continue to execute when some questionable result has been obtained by the system. The exception-handling features of the language, of course, permit the exceptions raised by these checks to be handled within the high-order language itself. However, the run-time checks performed during program execution consume a considerable amount of time, which may be of critical concern in some real-time embedded-system applications. And there may be instances in which, once a program has been completely debugged, there is no need for some of these checks. The pragma SUPPRESS can be used to give permission to the run-time support system to omit certain run-time checks. The syntax is

```
pragma SUPPRESS(identifier [, [ON =>] name]);
                                        (8.2.10)
```

The identifier is that of the run-time check to be suppressed, and the name is that of an object, a type, a task unit, a subprogram, or a generic unit, for which the check is to be suppressed. If no name is provided, the suppression applies to all entities to which the check applies. The pragma is in effect from the point of its occurrence to the end of the innermost declarative region in which it occurs. If an overloaded subprogram name is used, the pragma applies to all visible subprograms denoted by that name. Details of the use of this pragma are given in Appendix C.

An implementation is free to ignore the SUPPRESS pragma on a check-by-check basis if it is impossible or too costly to suppress the check.

8.2.3.10 Pragmas LIST and PAGE. These pragmas control the printing of the listing of a compiled program. LIST turns the listing on or off, and PAGE starts a new page. The syntax statements are

```
pragma LIST(ON | OFF);          (8.2.11)
```

and

```
pragma PAGE;                    (8.2.12)
```

8.2.3.11 Pragmas MEMORY_SIZE, STORAGE_UNIT, and SYSTEM_NAME. These three pragmas are used to assign values to the three constants

- MEMORY_SIZE
- STORAGE_UNIT
- SYSTEM_NAME

that are declared in the predefined package SYSTEM. Package SYSTEM and its use are discussed in Section 8.6.

8.2.4 Derivable Subprograms

Section 3.2.3 describes the declaration and use of a derived type. A derived type definition defines a new type—distinct from the parent type—that has the same set of values and the same predefined operations as the parent type from which it is derived. In addition, certain subprograms that act as operations on the parent type are derived together with the type, in the sense that a corresponding subprogram acting as the same operation on the derived type is implicitly declared together with the derived type definition. Derived subprograms arise from two situations, as outlined below:

1. When the parent type is declared in the visible part of a package specification and a subprogram that is an operation of the parent type is also declared within the visible part of the specification. The declaration of the subprogram can be the effect of a subprogram specification, a renaming declaration, or a generic instantiation. Any declaration of a type derived from the parent type is then accompanied by an implicit declaration of the associated subprogram.
2. When the parent type is itself a derived type. Then, any subprogram that has been derived by the parent type has a corresponding derived version applicable to the derived type.

The derived subprogram has an implicit specification that can be obtained from the original subprogram specification by replacing the parent type with the derived type. Subtypes are likewise replaced with corresponding subtypes of the derived type.

A generic subprogram declaration cannot be derived, but the subprogram resulting from instantiation of a generic program may be derived, under the conditions specified above.

8.3 RELATING ADA PROGRAMS TO THE UNDERLYING MACHINE

The whole idea of a high-order language is to isolate the programmer and the source program itself from the specific characteristics of the underlying machine. The particular manner in which an object of a given data type is represented in memory, for example, is completely transparent to the programmer. Furthermore, the actual representation may vary from one implementation to another. Usually, an implementation will select a convenient representation. If optimization is in effect, the selection may be based upon time or space optimization, but in any event the selection is made completely independently of any programmer intervention. Embedded-system programming, in particular, may have a requirement for programmer specification of data representation at the machine level, for one of two reasons: (1) to provide more efficient representation or (2) to interface directly with hardware in a manner not provided by the high-order language. In the former case, efficiency may be viewed from the point of view of access speed or of storage minimization. The latter case might arise, for example, in the direct use of a memory-mapped input-output architecture. The Ada languge provides for programmer intervention in the mapping of the high-order language to the underlying machine by permitting the programmer to specify, for various Ada entities, certain characteristics relating to their storage. Specifically, the programmer may provide address specification, length specification, enumeration representation, and record representation. The means by which the programmer conveys these requirements to the compiler is the representation clause, for which the syntax is

```
representation_clause ::=
        type_representation_clause | address_clause     (8.3)
```

where

```
type_representation_clause ::= length_clause
                | enumeration_representation_clause
                | record_representation_clause        (8.3.1)
```

The address clause applies to an object; to a subprogram, package or task; or to a task entry. A representation clause must occur in the same declarative part, package specification, or task specification as does the declaration of the entity to which it applies. Furthermore, the declaration must be elaborated prior to elaboration of the representation clause.

In general, a representation clause cannot appear after an occurrence of the name of the entity to which it applies, if that occurrence implies that the representation must have already been determined. Most occurrences of names of entities are of this kind.

8.3.1 The Address Clause

A programmer may specify the address in memory at which an object is stored; the address at which the machine code of a subprogram body, of a package body, or of a task body begins; or the address of a hardware interrupt to which a specified entry is to be linked. Interrupt handling in an Ada program is accomplished through the tasking features of the language; interrupt handling is further discussed in Section 8.4.

The syntax for an address specification is obtained from Statement (8.3) through the choice

```
address_clause ::= for simple_name use at
                       simple_expression;        (8.3.2)
```

The simple name is the name of the object, subprogram, package, task, or task entry to which the address clause applies. The expression given after the reserved word **at** must be of the type ADDRESS, which is declared in package SYSTEM and which is implementation-dependent. Package SYSTEM is discussed in Section 8.6. In order to make the type ADDRESS visible, the package SYSTEM must be named in a with clause applying to the compilation unit in which the address clause appears. Examples of the use of address clauses appear below.

```
for PRESSURE_READING use at 16#14C58#;
--Specifies that the data object PRESSURE_READING is to be
  stored at memory location hexadecimal 14C58. Such a
  construct might be used in the instance of memory-mapped
  input-output.

for POWER_FAILURE use at 16#7F#;
--Specifies that an interrupt that vectors to machine
  address hexadecimal 7F will constitute a call to entry POWER
  FAILURE. This particular use of an address clause can
  occur only in a task specification. See Section 8.4.
```

These examples have assumed that the based numbers 16#14C58# and 16#7F# are values that are valid for type ADDRESS.

8.3.2 The Length Clause

The length specification can be used by a programmer to control the amount of memory storage allocated to various program entities. The storage that can be affected by a length clause is that associated with a type, the collection of objects designated by objects of an access type, or the declaration of objects in a task. In essence, the length clause specifies the value of a particular attribute of the program entity. Normally, the value of the attribute is selected automatically by the implementation at elaboration time. Those attributes that can be specified by a length clause are as follows:

- for a type, the attribute SIZE
- for an access type, the attribute STORAGE_SIZE
- for a task, the attribute STORAGE_SIZE
- for a fixed-point type, the attribute SMALL

The reader is referred to Appendix B for the precise meaning of these attributes.

The syntax for a length clause is obtained from Statement (8.3) through the choice

```
length_clause ::= for attribute use simple_expression;
                                                  (8.3.3)
```

where the attribute must be either SIZE, STORAGE_SIZE, or SMALL. The effect of the length clause in each of the four cases above is given below:

- Size specification for a type: The value of the expression specifies the upper bound for the number of bits to be allocated to objects of the type.
- Collection size specification for an access type: The value of the expression specifies the number of storage units to be reserved for objects that are designated by objects of the access type.
- Storage specification for a task: The value of the expression specifies the number of storage units to be reserved for the activation of the task. This storage refers only to object elaboration, not to the program code.
- Specification of SMALL for a fixed-point type: The value of the expression is used as the attribute SMALL in representation of objects of the fixed-point type. The value must not be greater than the delta of the type. See Section 3.5.3.

A storage unit is the basic addressable unit of storage. The size of a storage unit is implementation-dependent and is given by the value of the predefined object STORAGE_UNIT in package SYSTEM. See Section 8.6.

Precisely what constitutes the storage required for the activation of a task or for the collection of an access type is implementation-dependent.

Thus, the precise control afforded by length clauses may not be portable from one implementation to another.

Examples of the use of the length clause are given below, and they are based on the following declarations.

```
type HIT_COUNT is range 0..15;
type VOLTAGE   is delta 0.025 range 0..12;
type THREAT    is (UNKNOWN, FRIENDLY, FOE, DANGER);
type POINTER   is access MATRIX;
task SEARCH;
```

Then, example length clauses are

```
for THREAT'SIZE use 2;
--specifies that a maximum of two bits be allocated for
  storage of objects of type THREAT. This value also
  represents the minimum number of bits required; it would
  not necessarily be selected by the implementation.

for HIT_COUNT'SIZE use 8;
--specifies that a maximum of eight bits be allocated for
  storage of objects of type HIT_COUNT. The minimum
  required number of bits is four, which an implementation
  would be free to select even if the length clause were
  not present.

for VOLTAGE'SMALL use 0.025;
--specifies use of 0.025 as the value of SMALL, rather
  than the next smaller power of two that would normally
  be selected by the implementation. See Section 3.5.3.

for POINTER'STORAGE_SIZE use 2048;
--specifies that a maximum of 2048 storage units be used
  to store objects designated by objects of type POINTER.
  If storage exceeds this size, the predefined exception
  STORAGE_ERROR is raised.

for SEARCH'STORAGE_SIZE use 32;
--specifies that 32 storage units be reserved for
  activation of task SEARCH. If storage exceeds this size,
  the predefined exception STORAGE_ERROR is raised.
```

The reader should note that these examples use static values for the expression of Statement (8.3.3). In general, the expression need not be static.

8.3.3 Enumeration Representation

Just how values of an enumeration type are represented by an implementation is a detail that is normally hidden from the programmer. And for good reason, because this kind of abstraction protects values of the type from accidental or intentional intervention at the bit level. There may be instances, however, in which the programmer needs control over the bit representation of values of the type. This requirement may be made necessary, for example, by input-output considerations. Such control is provided by the enumeration representation clause, which is obtained from Statement (8.3) through the choice

```
     enumeration_representation_clause ::=
             for type_simple_name use aggregate;     (8.3.4)
```

The aggregate following the reserved word **use** is an array aggregate, and it contains the integer values that are to be used to represent each of the enumeration literals associated with the enumeration type. The values in the aggregate can use positional or named association. See Section 3.6.1.4 for a discussion of array aggregates.

Examples of enumeration representation clauses are given below, and they are based on the following declarations:

```
type THRUST_VECTOR is (ROLL, PITCH, YAW);
type STATE is (X_VEL, Y_VEL, Z_VEL, X_POS, Y_POS, Z_POS);
```

Example enumeration representation clauses are

```
for THRUST_VECTOR use (2#01#, 2#10#, 2#11#);
--The representation is specified in binary form using
  based numbers. The implementation is still free to
  select the attribute SIZE, so that there is no guarantee
  that only two bits will be used for each value. The
  programmer also may specify SIZE by use of a length
  clause.

for STATE use 6;
for STATE use (X_VEL => 2#000001#,
               Y_VEL => 2#000010#,
               Z_VEL => 2#000100#,
               X_POS => 2#001000#,
               Y_POS => 2#010000#,
               Z_POS => 2#100000#);
--The length clause specifies representation by no more
```

```
than six bits. The values are given in binary in the
representation clause. Named association is used.
```

While these examples use binary representation, in order to display the bit patterns, any allowable number base—including decimal—may be used.

8.3.4 Record Representation

Just as the specific representation of values of an enumeration type can be important in certain instances, so also can the manner in which values of certain record objects are stored in memory. Control over the representation of records comprises control over the order, position, and size of record components and of any discriminants, if present. Such control is obtained from the syntax of Statement (8.3) through the choice

```
record_representation_clause ::=
     for type_simple_name use
        record [alignment_clause]
               {component_clause}
        end record;                      (8.3.5)
```

where

```
alignment_clause ::= at mod static_simple_expression;
                                              (8.3.5.1)
```

and

```
component_clause ::=
     component_name at static_simple_expression
          range static_range;                 (8.3.5.2)
```

The syntax for a range is given by Statement (3.13.2). Basically, the alignment clause specifies the alignment of the starting address of the record value, while component clauses specify the location of the components relative to the starting address. Specifically, the following rules apply:

- The expression following the reserved words **at mod** in the alignment clause must be a static integer expression. The alignment clause forces the starting address of a record of the named type to be a multiple of the value given by the expression. That is, the modular expression

```
(address) modulo (expression)
```

must be zero. This feature can, for example, be used to align records on word boundaries.

- The expression following the reserved word **at** must also be a static integer expression. The range following the reserved word **range** must have static bounds. These expressions locate the component relative to the beginning address of the record. The expression gives the relative location of the storage unit containing the component, and the range gives the bit numbers within the storage unit that represent the component. The first storage unit of a record is numbered zero, as is the first bit of a storage unit. Some details of component location may be implementation-dependent.
- Component clauses may be given for any, for all, or for none of the components of a record. If no component clause is given for any particular component, then the compiler is free to choose the representation for that component, even though the representation for other components may be specified.
- Any constraints on components for which component clauses are specified must be static constraints.

The record representation clause might be used, for example, to provide the proper format for directly addressing input-output device control registers in a system using memory-mapped input-output architecture. To access such a device register from within the Ada language, the programmer would proceed as indicated below:

- Describe the register by means of a record type with record components corresponding to groups of control bits within the register.
- Use a record representation clause to specify how objects of the record type are represented in memory.
- Declare an object of the type.
- Use an address clause to locate the record object at the address in memory occupied by the device.

Thus, assigning a value to the record object loads the control register in the proper manner.

For example, if an application uses a number of identical analog-to-digital converters, each with a single 16-bit register that contains a 12-bit data word and four control bits representing two status codes, the record type used to represent the register might be

```
type A_D_CONVERTER is
    record
       DATA    : INTEGER range 0..4095;
       SWORD_1 : INTEGER range 0..3;
       SWORD_2 : INTEGER range 0..3;
    end record;
```

Suppose that the register is arranged in the manner shown in Figure 8.1.

15	14	13	12	11	10	9	8	7	6	5	4	3	2	1	0
STATUS WORD		DATA												STATUS WORD	

Figure 8.1. Device register.

The record representation clause that maps the storage of objects of type A_D_CONVERTER to the bit format of Figure 8.1. is:

```
for A_D_CONVERTER use
     record at mod 2;
        SWORD_1 at 0 range  0..1;
        DATA    at 0 range  2..13;
        SWORD_2 at 0 range 14..15;
     end record;
```

In this example, the storage unit is assumed to be 16 bits, so that a single storage unit is used. The records are aligned on even addresses.

A more complex instance of a record representation clause is given below. The port control registers of a parallel interface device are shown in Figure 8.2. A record declaration that corresponds to the 16-bit control

7	6	5	4	3	2	1	0
Port A submode		H2 control			H2 interrupt vector	H1 SVCRQ enable	H1 status control

Port A control register

7	6	5	4	3	2	1	0
Port B submode		H4 control			H4 interrupt vector	H3 SVCRQ enable	H3 status control

Port B control register

Figure 8.2. Port control registers of a parallel interface device.

register word is given below:

```
type CONTROL_REG is
   record
      PORT_A_SUB : INTEGER range 0..3;
      H2_CONT    : INTEGER range 0..7;
      H2_INT_EN  : INTEGER range 0..1;
      H1_SVRCQ   : INTEGER range 0..1;
      H1_STATUS  : INTEGER range 0..1;
      PORT_B_SUB : INTEGER range 0..3;
      H4_CONT    : INTEGER range 0..7;
      H4_INT_EN  : INTEGER range 0..1;
      H3_SVRCQ   : INTEGER range 0..1;
      H3_STATUS  : INTEGER range 0..1;
   end record;
```

With this record declaration in effect, and assuming that the storage unit is eight bits, the following record representation clause may be used.

```
for CONTROL_REG use
   record at mod 2;
      PORT_A_SUB at 0 range 0..1;
      H2_CONT    at 0 range 2..4;
      H2_INT_EN  at 0 range 5..5;
      H1_SVRCQ   at 0 range 6..6;
      H1_STATUS  at 0 range 7..7;
      PORT_B_SUB at 1 range 0..1;
      H4_CONT    at 1 range 2..4;
      H4_INT_EN  at 1 range 5..5;
      H3_SVRCQ   at 1 range 6..6;
      H3_STATUS  at 1 range 7..7;
   end record;
for CONTROL_REG'SIZE use 16;
```

Here, the 16-bit control word must begin on an even boundary. If the object declaration

```
PORT_1_CONT: CONTROL_REG;
```

is made, then an address clause such as

```
for PORT_1_CONT use at 16#177FE#;
```

will specify that the record object PORT_1_CONT will be stored at address hexadecimal 177FE. Furthermore, the record will be stored in the format specified by the record representation clause, which is the precise format required for the 16-bit control word.

8.3.5 Change of Representation

If it is necessary within a program to have two different representations of the same data type, a second representation can be obtained by declaring a second type as a derived type and then defining a different representation for the second type. Because the Ada language permits explicit type conversion between a derived type and its parent type, values can be interchanged between objects of the two types by using explicit type conversion. For example, if it is required to have a second representation of type CONTROL_REG of the previous section, then the following declaration and representation clause can be used:

```
type CONTROL_REG_MOD is new CONTROL_REG;
for CONTROL_REG_MOD use
     record
     --second representation specified here
     end record;
```

Then, the two object declarations

```
PORT_1_CONT : CONTROL_REG;
PORT_1_MOD  : CONTROL_REG_MOD;
```

declare objects of two distinct types, but they may be converted by explicit type conversion. For example, the following assignments are permitted:

```
PORT_1_CONT := CONTROL_REG(PORT_1_MOD);
PORT_1_MOD  := CONTROL_REG_MOD(PORT_1_CONT);
```

This example could represent a situation in which the control register contents are read from one device in one format and then written to a second device in a second format.

8.4 INTERRUPT SERVICE

The servicing of interrupts is normally an important feature of any real-time embedded system. In interrupt-driven systems, timer-driven interrupts provide the cyclic executive feature of periodic task execution. In event-driven systems, the asynchronous service requests from system input-output devices are effected through the use of interrupts. Most modern processors provide for one or more *vectored interrupts,* that is, an interrupt mechanism in which the address of the interrupt service routine is provided by a hardware feature rather than by software polling. The Ada language provides for the incorporation of service routines for vectored interrupts through the combination of the tasking feature and the address clause. The syntax of Statement (7.1.1) indicates that a task specification may contain only two kinds of declarations—entry declarations and representation clauses. One of the forms of a representation clause is the address clause, as implied by Statement (8.3) and by the discussion of Section 8.3.1. An address clause given for an entry associates the entry with interrupts that vector to the address specified in the address clause. For example, consider the following task declaration:

```
task READY_INT_HANDLER is
    entry READY;
       for READY use at 16#177F#;
end READY_INT_HANDLER;
```

The entry READY is associated with the interrupt that vectors to address hexadecimal 177F. That is, when an interrupt occurs that vectors to address 177F, the effect is to make an entry call to task entry READY. Thus, the interrupt service routine for the interrupt can be written in the Ada language as an accept statement for entry READY within task READY_INT_HANDLER. Because interrupts have a high priority for the allocation of computational resources, an interrupt that is serviced by an entry call to a task is considered to be issued by an implicit hardware task whose priority is higher than that of the main program or of any user-defined task. Because of the rules of task priority, as outlined in Section 7.4.5, the task containing the interrupt handler assumes the priority of the calling task once the rendezvous has been effected. Thus, the priority of interrupt handling is established.

Modern processors provide for an interrupt structure that permits interrupting devices to pass a priority or other information to the processor along with the interrupt signal. In an Ada program, if control information is supplied along with an interrupt, it is passed to the associated interrupt entry as one or more parameters of mode **in.** Only parameters of mode **in** are permitted for entries that correspond to interrupts.

The precise characteristics of entry calls associated with interrupts through the use of an address clause is somewhat implementation-dependent. In general, the entry call need only produce the results described above—it may actually be implemented by direct hardware execution of the appropriate accept statement. Interrupts that queue behave like queued entry calls, while those that do not queue appear as conditional entry calls.

The precise interpretation of the address specified by the address clause is also dependent upon the implementation. For example, the address may be the actual vector address, or it may be the address in memory where the vector address is found. Thus, use of address clauses in this instance, as in others, may not be portable from one implementation to the next.

8.5 MACHINE CODE INSERTIONS

The Ada language provides the facility for inserting machine code instructions—in the form of mnemonic operation codes—directly within the Ada code. In general, the use of such a feature would defeat the whole purpose of a high-order language, but in certain critical situations a programmer may have to revert to the use of native machine code. Some instances in which such action may be required are

- performing hardware functions that do not map to the high-order language
- accessing registers that are not memory-mapped
- executing special machine instructions that have no high-order language counterpart
- using machine-dependent features to maximize efficiency of storage or of execution time.

Machine code is permitted within an Ada program only in a subprogram whose sequence of statements includes only machine code statements. No declarations and no other Ada statements are allowed within the subprogram. The machine code statements within the subprogram must have the syntax

```
code_statement ::= type_mark'record_aggregate;   (8.4)
```

The right-hand side of Statement (8.4) is a qualified record aggregate. See Sections 3.6.2.3 and 3.7.6.

Each machine code instruction that is to be used must be represented by a record type that contains the operation code mnemonic and the operands as components. These record type declarations must appear in the predefined package MACHINE_CODE, and this package must be named by a with clause that applies to the compilation unit that contains the machine code subprogram. The form of the machine code statement follows the syntax of Statement (8.4). For example, a simple machine code statement might be

```
MACH_INST'(CMP, A1, A7);
```

where the record type MACH_INST is imported from the predefined package MACHINE_CODE. The record aggregate contains the machine code instruction CMP, and the operands are A1 and A7—presumably representing processor internal registers.

An implementation is not required to provide the predefined package MACHINE_CODE. Furthermore, an implementation is free to impose almost any restriction on the record aggregrates constituting machine code statements. Thus, the use of machine code insertion may not even be supported by some implementations; and, if it is supported, the use of such a facility may not be portable. Certainly it would not be portable from one underlying machine to another.

8.6 IMPLEMENTATION FEATURES

In order to write portable Ada code, it is sometimes necessary to query the system in order to determine certain implementation-dependent characteristics. For example, the statement

```
exit when ITEM = MAX_INT;
```

within a loop statement will protect the loop against having the loop index ITEM overflow the values permitted for an integer type, if MAX_INT is the largest integer value supported by the implementation. Furthermore, if MAX_INT is declared in every implementation as the largest representable integer number, then the protection afforded by this statement is portable from one implementation to another, even though the value of MAX_INT may be different. The Ada language provides access to implementation characteristics such as MAX_INT by means of the predefined package SYSTEM. This package consists only of declarations, and the visible part of the specification must contain at least the following declarations:

```
package SYSTEM is
  type ADDRESS is implementation-defined;
  type NAME    is implementation_defined_enumeration_type;
  SYSTEM_NAME  :  constant NAME := implementation_defined;
  STORAGE_UNIT :  constant := implementation_defined;
  MEMORY_SIZE  :  constant := implementation_defined;
```

```
   --System-dependent named numbers:
   MIN_INT       :  constant := implementation_defined;
   MAX_INT       :  constant := implementation_defined;
   MAX_DIGITS    :  constant := implementation_defined;
   MAX_MANTISSA :  constant := implementation_defined;
   FINE_DELTA    :  constant := implementation_defined;
   TICK          :  constant := implementation_defined;

   --Other system-dependent declarations:
   subtype PRIORITY is INTEGER range implementation_defined;
   ...
end SYSTEM;
```

The declarations in package SYSTEM have the following uses:

- Type ADDRESS is the type for addresses contained in address clauses and for the result returned by attribute ADDRESS.
- Type NAME is an enumeration type whose values comprise the names that may be assigned to the constant SYSTEM_NAME.
- The constant STORAGE_UNIT is the number of bits in a storage unit, that is, in the smallest addressable unit of memory.
- The constant MEMORY_SIZE is the number of memory locations in the *target* computer.
- The constant MIN_INT is the most negative value of all predefined integer types.
- The constant MAX_INT is the largest value of all predefined integer types.
- The constant MAX_DIGITS is the largest value allowed for the digits in a floating-point type declaration.
- The constant MAX_MANTISSA is the largest number of bits permitted in the mantissa of the model numbers associated with a fixed-point type declaration.
- The constant FINE_DELTA is the smallest delta allowed in a fixed-point declaration with a range constraint of −1.0..1.0.
- The constant TICK is the system clock period, expressed in seconds.

Package SYSTEM is obviously implementation-dependent. In fact, it describes certain features of the implementation to the user, in that it provides information about the environment to which the implementation is targeted.

While many of the declarations in package SYSTEM cannot be modified, the values of the constants SYSTEM_NAME, STORAGE_UNIT, and MEMORY_SIZE can be assigned values by the programmer through the use of pragmas of the same names. These pragmas are referenced in Section 8.2.3.11; they may only appear at the start of a compilation, and they must appear prior to the first compilation unit. When one of these pragmas is included with a compilation, the effect is as though package SYSTEM is recompiled. This effect, in turn, must be considered with regard to its impact on the order of compilation and recompilation described in Section 3.11.4. The net result is that any other compilation unit that names package SYSTEM in its context clause must then be subsequently recompiled.

Finally, an implementation is free to further restrict the use of these pragmas.

8.7 UNCHECKED PROGRAMMING

Many of the features of the Ada language promote good programming practice. In some instances, it may be necessary for the programmer to override one or more of these features in order to meet some critical requirement of the application program. Instances of how the Ada language provides for the overriding of language features have already been encountered in the use of the pragmas SHARED and SUPPRESS. In this section, two predefined generic subprograms are considered. Function UNCHECKED_CONVERSION permits type conversion to be performed without the usual checking that accompanies explicit type conversion. Procedure UNCHECKED_DEALLOCATION permits the programmer to call for deallocation of storage associated with objects designated by values of an access type, without the usual checking that a run-time support system must make to ensure that the designated object can no longer be referenced.

As is the case in other instances in which normal language characteristics are overridden, the use of unchecked programming requires explicit and specific action on the part of the programmer.

8.7.1 Unchecked Type Conversion

Two of the features of the Ada language that, among others, promote the production of reliable and modifiable software are the strong typing feature and the requirement for explicit declaration of types and objects. These features help detect program errors early in the programming phase of software development, and perhaps immediately in the case of software maintenance. Nevertheless, situations can arise in which the programmer finds it necessary to effect a type conversion without the usual checks that a compiler automatically performs in the case of explicit type conversion. Such a situation occurs when it is desired to make a type conversion not ordinarily permitted by the language. The predefined generic function UNCHECKED_CONVERSION can be instantiated to perform such conversion from one specific data type to another. The specification of this function appears in Appendix C and is shown below:

```
generic
   type SOURCE is limited private;
   type TARGET is limited private;
function UNCHECKED_CONVERSION(S : SOURCE) return TARGET;
```

When this function is instantiated, using two actual generic type parameters which are associated with the formal generic type parameters SOURCE and TARGET, then the resulting function may be called to perform the conversion. For example, consider the declarations

```
type INDEX is INTEGER range 0..127;
CODE : INDEX;
CHAR : CHARACTER;
```

Explicit type conversion is not permitted between integer objects and objects of type CHARACTER, as implied by the discussion of type conversion in Section 3.7.3. Unchecked conversion of objects of type INDEX to objects of type CHARACTER can be provided by instantiating the generic function UNCHECKED_CONVERSION for this specific conversion. Such an instantiation might be

```
function CONV_TO_CHAR is new
  UNCHECKED_CONVERSION(SOURCE => INDEX,
                       TARGET => CHARACTER);
```

The resulting function, CONV_TO_CHAR, can then be called to perform the conversion. For example, the assignment statement

```
CHAR := CONV_TO_CHAR(S => CODE);
```

will assign to the object CHAR the bit pattern contained in the machine representation of the object CODE.

Obviously, the use of unchecked conversion is limited to those cases in which it is applicable. It would hardly be appropriate to convert from an integer type to an array type, for example. Programs that use unchecked conversion in a manner that violates the intrinsic properties of objects in this manner are erroneous.

An implementation is free to place restrictions on the use of unchecked conversions.

8.7.2 Unchecked Storage Deallocation

The use of access types, as discussed in Section 3.6.3, permits the programmer to dynamically create data objects at run time through the use of allocators. A given access object may designate any number of different designated objects at different points in the program execution. If a designated object is no longer accessible through any path of existing access variables, then the run-time support system is free to reclaim the storage allocated to the designated object. This kind of storage reclamation, called *garbage collection,* is not required of an implementation, but it is almost a necessity if minimization of storage requirements is a consideration.

In the process of garbage collection, a run-time support system must ensure that any given designated object is no longer accessible. Checking the accessibility of a designated object entails a detailed search through existing data structures to ensure that no path to the object exists. Since garbage collection is performed periodically at run time, long searches through existing data structures may produce unacceptable delays in program execution. Furthermore, such delays are unpredictable and may occur at random intervals. This kind of intervention into program execution can be intolerable in certain time-critical embedded systems. While the Ada language standard neither requires nor prohibits the use of garbage collection, thus making it an implementation-dependent feature, it does provide means for a programmer to permit deallocation of storage assigned to an object designated by a specific access object. This provision is made through the predefined generic procedure UNCHECKED_DEALLOCATION, for which the specification, taken from Appendix C, is given below:

```
generic
  type OBJECT is limited private;
  type NAME is access OBJECT;
procedure UNCHECKED_DEALLOCATION(X : in out NAME));
```

The generic type parameter OBJECT is associated with the type of the designated object, while the generic type parameter NAME is associated with the access type. When this generic procedure is instantiated, with actual generic type parameters associated with the formal generic type parameters OBJECT and NAME, a call to the resulting procedure will have the following effects:

- The value of the actual parameter associated with formal parameter X is set to **null.**
- The storage allocated to the designated object at the time of call may be reclaimed by the run-time support system.
- If the value of the actual parameter is **null** at the time of call, the procedure has no effect.

If more than one access variable designates the same object, then the effect on one variable of deallocation of the other is not defined by the language rules.

An example is provided by the following declarations:

```
type FIX is
     record
        LATITUDE   : DEGREE;
        LONGITUDE  : DEGREE;
        HOUR       : INTEGER range 0..23;
        MINUTE     : INTEGER range 0..59;
        SECOND     : INTEGER range 0..59;
     end record;
type STELLAR_FIX is access FIX;
STELLAR_1 : STELLAR_FIX;
```

In addition, the generic procedure UNCHECKED_DEALLOCATION is to be instantiated so that the resulting procedure will apply to the object STELLAR_1:

```
procedure DEALLOCATE is new
   UNCHECKED_DEALLOCATION(OBJECT => FIX;
                          NAME => STELLAR_FIX);
```

If a program then assigns a value to the access object STELLAR_1, perhaps by use of an allocator,

```
STELLAR_1 := new FIX;
```

then at the point in the program at which the designated object is no longer needed, it can be deallocated by the procedure call

```
DEALLOCATE(X => STELLAR_1);
```

The run-time support system is then free to deallocate the storage assigned to the designated object without checking to determine whether or not it is accessible. Such deallocation may or may not be a feature of the implementation.

Whereas instantiations of the procedure UNCHECKED_DEALLOCATION permit the run-time support system to deallocate storage associated with designated objects without checking to determine whether or not the object is accessible, the pragma CONTROLLED, which is discussed in Section 8.2.3.1, has just the opposite effect. Pragma CONTROLLED will prevent the run-time support system from deallocating storage even though it has been determined that the designated object is not accessible.

Unchecked deallocation is not permitted for access objects that designate task objects.

8.8 IMPLEMENTATION OPTIONS

The reader may have noted that many of the language requirements discussed in this chapter have been qualified by statements like ". . . the implementation is free to . . . ." When taken to the extreme, these qualifications often make it possible for an implementer to opt out of providing the feature at all. For example, the discussion of task priorities contained in Section 7.4.5, and that of pragma PRIORITY contained in Section 8.2.3.7, imply that an implementation must provide pragma PRIORITY, and that this pragma can be used to establish task priorities. Further reading of Section 7.4.5 indicates that the priority assigned must be of the predefined type PRIORITY, which is declared in package SYSTEM. Reference to the specification of package SYSTEM in Section 8.6 reveals that type PRIORITY is declared as

```
subtype PRIORITY is INTEGER range implementation_defined;
```

Thus, an implementation can conceivably declare type PRIORITY as

```
subtype PRIORITY is INTEGER range 1..1;
```

in which case there is no provision for task prioritization at all. Similar cases can be made with respect to other language features discussed in this chapter, and to other pragmas. In fact, the Ada language standards relating to features of this kind are grouped together as Chapter 13 of the language reference manual, entitled "Representation Clauses and Implementation-Dependent Features." It is generally conceded that Chapter 13 features are optional and that an implementation may provide them to virtually any degree. The Chapter 13 features are

- length clauses
- representation clauses
- address clauses
- interrupt handling
- package SYSTEM
- certain representation attributes
- machine code insertions
- interface to other languages
- unchecked type conversion
- unchecked deallocation

Similarly, many of the predefined pragmas may have no application in a particular implementation. Specifically, the following comments are offered:

- Pragma CONTROLLED has no effect if automatic garbage collection is not implemented.
- An implementation is free to follow or to ignore the recommendation expressed by pragma IN_LINE.
- Pragma INTERFACE is a Chapter 13 feature and is not required of an implementation.
- Pragmas SYSTEM_NAME, STORAGE_UNIT, and MEMORY_SIZE are Chapter 13 features. An implementation is free to impose almost any restriction on their use.
- Pragma PACK is a Chapter 13 feature. It can do nothing more than minimize gaps between components of composite types, but the degree of minimization is not specified.
- Pragma PRIORITY may be completely useless because of the priorities defined in package SYSTEM. See the discussion above.
- Pragma SUPPRESS can be ignored by an implementation if it is impossible or too costly to suppress certain checks.

Thus, each implementation may differ in its response to the requirement for these predefined pragmas. In addition, an implementation is free to provide additional pragmas that may well be implementation-specific.

Because the Ada language standards allow for the machine-dependent variations discussed above, the documentation for each implementation must provide an additional implementation-specific appendix to the language reference manual. This appendix is Appendix F, and it must list at least the following information:

- The form of and use for any implementation-dependent pragmas.
- The name of and use for any implementation-dependent attribute.
- The complete specification of package SYSTEM.
- Any implementation-dependent restrictions on the use of representation clauses.

- Details of any implementation-generated name denoting implementation-dependent components.
- The specific manner in which the expressions appearing in address clauses are related to physical addresses. For example, the relationship between the value of the expression and the vector address of an interrupt must be stated.
- Any implementation-dependent restrictions on unchecked type conversions.
- Any implementation-dependent characteristics of the input-output packages. For example, the details of LOW_LEVEL_IO should be described.

Thus, Appendix F is important to the user of an implementation. In fact, since most other features are standardized and tested by the validation procedures, those described in Appendix F comprise the only real difference, in terms of language features, among different implementations. Of course, the quality of the support systems—the APSE—and the execution speed of the compiled code on the target machine are also vital considerations in comparing implementations.

EXERCISES

1. Discuss the problem of name management in large programs.
2. What features of the Ada language aid in the management of names?
3. What kind of identifiers can be overloaded in an Ada program?
4. What operator symbols can be overloaded in an Ada program?
5. Discuss the overloading of enumeration literals.
6. What are the advantages and disadvantages of renaming?
7. How does renaming affect visibility?
8. Discuss the effect of pragma CONTROLLED.
9. Discuss the effect of pragma INLINE.
10. Discuss the effect of pragma SHARED.
11. Discuss the effect of pragma SUPPRESS.
12. What is a derived subprogram? Under what conditions is a subprogram derived?
13. Why is representation specification sometimes important in embedded-systems applications?
14. What is the relationship between representation specification and the predefined package LOW_LEVEL_IO?
15. Discuss the relationship between the address clause and memory-mapped input-output.
16. Why is enumeration representation sometimes important in embedded-systems applications?

17. Why is record representation sometimes important in embedded-systems applications?
18. How are interrupts handled in an Ada program?
19. What is the relationship between an interrupt and the address clause in the specification of the task that services the interrupt?
20. Explain the manner in which machine code instructions can be embedded in an Ada program.
21. Under what conditions would machine code be used in an Ada program?
22. Explain the significance of the declarations in package SYSTEM. How are the constants declared there used by a program?
23. There are obviously some limitations on the use of the generic function UNCHECKED_CONVERSION. Discuss these limitations.
24. What must appear in Appendix F of the reference manual of any Ada implementation?
25. Discuss the relationship among the strong typing of the Ada language, explicit type conversion, and unchecked conversion.

Chapter 9
SOFTWARE DESIGN AND LIFE-CYCLE SUPPORT

9.1 SOFTWARE LIFE CYCLE

The use of a modern, well-designed language that supports and encourages good software engineering practice does not guarantee that the result of a design process will be software that is reliable, modifiable, and portable. The design methodology must exploit the language features if maximum benefit is to be derived. Using a modern language such as Ada without coupling it to an appropriate design methodology can be frustrating for the programmer and disastrous to the project. Although this text is primarily concerned with Ada as a programming language, it is impossible to consider the Ada language separately from design methodologies and sound software engineering practice. The first eight chapters have presented the Ada language features in a manner that simultaneously illustrates the characteristics of modularization, localization, abstraction, and information hiding supported by those features. In this final chapter, an attempt is made to highlight the salient aspects of how the Ada language and its programming support environment should be used in the design and support of large software projects. Specific design methodologies are not treated here; the reader is referred to the many fine publications in the field of software design for detailed information on any particular design methodology.

Regardless of whose description of the software life cycle is used, there are generally six identifiable phases. These six phases are rather difficult to identify in actual practice, but they are a useful abstraction when attempting to describe the predominant activity at various times from the inception of software until it is removed from service. These phases, as usually identified, are listed below:

1. Requirement analysis, during which the functions to be performed by the software are determined.

2. Requirements specification, during which detailed specifications of the software functions are developed. The software is treated as an abstraction at this point—the input-output functions are specified, but the implementation detail is not given.
3. System design, during which the actual software design is formulated. Detailed executable code is not written during this phase, but instead the data structures and control algorithms necessary for implementation of the design specifications are detailed.
4. Detailed coding, during which the system design is implemented in the chosen language. This phase includes compilation of the implementation programs.
5. Integration and testing, during which the software is executed in order to test its behavior in an actual or simulated environment. Upon completion of this phase, the software becomes operational.
6. Maintenance and modification, which comprises the remainder of the life cycle. Maintenance refers to software changes made in order to correct implementation deficiencies. Modification refers to software changes made in order to implement design changes.

The Ada language, together with the concept of an integrated support environment, was designed with total life-cycle support in mind.

9.1.1 Requirements Analysis

In the requirements analysis phase, operational requirements are synthesized into a realizable concept. Early in this phase is the only point in the entire life cycle at which the problem is stated and the approach to the solution is specified. The initial direction, in which all future development will be oriented, is established here. The three basic characteristics of requirements definition that must be established are (1) why the system is to be developed, (2) what functions the system is to perform, and (3) how the system is to be implemented. The why, what, and how of a system merely serve to establish the bounds of the software design problem, thus leaving more detailed analysis to the system design phase. Just precisely what part the Ada Programming Support Environment (APSE) plays in this phase will vary from one environment to another, but it is clear that the project management features of an APSE will be of great assistance.

9.1.2 Requirements Specification

Ideally, the requirements specification phase of the software life cycle will translate the results of the requirements analysis into a complete, consistent, and unambiguous set of software specifications. Probably one of the most difficult tasks in software development is the generation of software requirements specifications. Unless some systematic approach is used, the result is usually ambiguous and far from concise. Ambiguous specifications make effective management of the project almost impossible, for a variety of reasons. The trend today is toward machine-analyzable software requirements, and one can expect the APSE to move in that direction. The STONEMAN document, briefly discussed in Section 2.2.2, suggests that an APSE may provide tools for tracing requirements specification through to the design and coding phases. Additionally, the APSE data base, documentation system, and project control system can further enhance the automation of this phase.

9.1.3 System Design

In the system design phase, the specifications are translated into a description of the functional system. There are a number of software engineering methodologies that have been developed for the design of large systems. While these methodologies differ in detail and design philosophy, they all have one central theme—the design process serves to (1) decompose the problem into smaller components, each of which can be solved independently to produce a program module; and (2) assemble the developed modules into a functional whole. Only by this process can the complexity of large programs be managed. There are two general lines along which the decomposition can be effected:

1. Functional decomposition, in which the system is divided into major algorithmic components. Often, the division is along procedural lines, entailing certain natural groupings of program code. This is the more traditional view represented by top-down design methodologies.
2. Data structure decomposition, in which the major abstract data structures and the operations defined for those data structures comprise the modules.

In practice, decomposition is rarely purely functional or purely data-oriented, but instead it is defined along lines that permit the division into components that can be treated reasonably independently. The degree of independence of these components, and that of the resulting program modules, is determined in large part by the characteristics of the programming language used for implementation. Language features that support modularization, localization, abstraction, information hiding, and separate compilation—all of which are provided in the Ada language—are important in this respect.

When the independently developed program modules are integrated into a functional program in the coding phase, the process is primarily one of integration and testing. Capable software development tools, such as interactive debuggers and flow analyzers, are essential. The APSE software development tools will prove useful here.

The implementation language does not support the activities in the design phase, but many modern programming environments now use something called a Program Development Language, or PDL. Early versions of PDLs were simply pseudo-code—common English statements implying certain actions that were later translated into computer code—but more recent developments have resulted in PDLs that can actually be compiled in order to check the logical consistency of the developing code. Several APSEs now contain PDLs oriented specifically to the development of Ada code. These PDLs provide the following features, among others:

- an English-language representation of the system design specifications
- top-down structured design format that supports decomposition
- an English-language representation of the functions of system modules
- some sort of compilation of the PDL that checks the logical consistency of the program design
- provision for documentation and configuration management

Some of these PDLs use the format of Ada comments; they can therefore remain with the source code throughout its entire life cycle.

Whatever techniques or tools are used, the design phase should result in a complete system design that contains the following:

- definition of all internal and external interfaces
- specification of all error situations
- identification of all program modules—subprograms, tasks, and packages—together with a description of the services that they provide
- identification of all procedure calls, task entry calls, and accept statements
- definition of any shared or global data
- specification of the processing algorithms of all modules, including those of all rendezvous

Translation of a properly developed system design into high-level source code can be a systematic task, whereas a poor, ill-defined design forces design modifications into the coding phase, where strong interaction among modules may be present.

9.1.4 Detailed Coding

In the coding phase, the abstractions specified in the system design are implemented in the high-order language. If the implementation language is Ada, the specifications of all separately compilable program units should be coded and compiled, with the proper context clauses included. This step may be accomplished in the design phase, and it most likely will be accomplished there if a PDL is used. Each of the modules can be coded independently, and each independent effort can use some appropriate program development methodology. If a PDL is used, some form of stepwise refinement will most likely be appropriate. In general, the resulting code should be structured, self-documenting, and modifiable. These characteristics are easily designed into Ada code because the language supports strong typing, modularization, abstraction, information hiding, separate compilation, and structured control constructs.

The programmer should be aware of the conditions under which *erroneous* programs can arise. Specifically, the Ada language does not define the following:

- the order of evaluation of the operands of a binary operator
- the order of evaluation of the components of an aggregate
- the order of evaluation of expressions in a range
- the order of evaluation of the parameters in a subprogram or entry call
- the order of evaluation of the index expressions in an array component
- the order of evaluation of the when conditions in a select statement
- how open alternatives in a select statement are selected
- the synchronization of concurrently executing tasks except at task activation, rendezvous, and task completion
- whether arrays, records, and private parameters are passed by reference or by value

Additionally, specific documentation should be included when the Chapter 13 optional features are used. Specifically, use of the following features should be noted in the documentation:

- implementation-dependent pragmas
- data types requiring values lying outside the range of 16-bit integer and 32-bit floating-point values

- values from package SYSTEM
- task priorities
- representation specifications
- package MACHINE_CODE
- package LOW_LEVEL_IO
- generic subprograms UNCHECKED_DEALLOCATION and UNCHECKED_CONVERSION

These features, of course, may not be portable from one environment to another.

9.1.5 Integration and Testing

In the integration and testing phase, the independently developed modules are assembled into a single program and tested in an actual or simulated environment. The first concern is that of integration—do the modules interface with one another in the manner anticipated by the design? The second is that of evaluating the functioning program to determine if the requirements have been satisfied. If the implementation language is Ada, the APSE may contain software development tools to aid in both integration and testing.

9.1.6 Maintenance and Modification

During the maintenance and modification phase, the software is employed in its operational environment. Maintenance is required as implementation inadequacies and errors that cause performance that is not commensurate with the requirements specification are discovered in the operational system. Modification occurs when software improvements can enhance the degree to which the requirements are met, or when change and substantial redesign and/or recoding is necessary. In either case, if the original design and coding efforts have stressed the software engineering concepts of understandability and modifiability, the task of recoding is greatly simplified. If Ada is the implementation language, the feature of strong typing—coupled with provisions for abstraction, information hiding, separate compilation, modularization, and localization—permits the programmer in the coding phase to incorporate the characteristic of controlled change into the software. Controlled change and understandability are essential to the production of modifiable software.

Quite often, maintenance and modification occur at a site other than that at which the software was developed and, in the case of modification, at a much later date. Programmers involved in this activity are normally not the same programmers responsible for the original program development. For these reasons, and possibly others, the maintenance and modification phase of the software life cycle is becoming the most costly. It is not surprising that the Ada language supports the development of modifiable software and that the APSE is designed to support the software life cycle through this phase.

9.2 THE ADA PROGRAMMING SUPPORT ENVIRONMENT

The prospect of a common language—and of a common language that readily supports modern software engineering methodologies—makes possible exciting and innovative approaches to software life-cycle support. The use of a common language makes attractive the prospect of a common support environment, and this prospect has prompted the development of the STONEMAN requirements, previously mentioned in Sections 2.2.2 and 9.1.2. The Ada Programming Support Environment, or APSE, outlined in the STONEMAN document provides support for the development, maintenance, and modification of Ada software. That is, support is provided thoughout the entire software life cycle, from the requirements phase through the termination of the operational life of the software. This support extends beyond the provision of the normal software tools such as editors, compilers, and the like; it includes tools for project management, report generation, and configuration management, as well as for other activities necessary to the smooth functioning of a software project over its entire life cycle. The three principal components of an APSE are as follows:

1. The data base, in which resides items associated with each project throughout the entire life cycle. These items may be Ada source programs or fragments of programs, files of data, project requirements specifications, documentation files, data related to configuration management, or any other information required for total and complete life-cycle support.
2. The toolset, which contains—as a minimum—a text editor, a pretty printer, a compiler, a linker, a loader, a file administrator, a configuration manager, and various debugging tools.
3. The interface between the user and the system. This interface includes a control language that gives the programmer control over the support environment. It also includes the means of communications between the toolset and the data base, and among the tools in the toolset.

The APSE concept is oriented to a host-target development environment. That is, the software development takes place on a fairly capable computer that hosts the APSE. This host computer typically is equipped with abundant memory, several traditional input-output devices such as terminals and printers, and a large amount of secondary storage in the form of large disk drives. The host computer exists in a controlled environment that is not considered harsh, and execution speed, while perhaps important from an economic point of view, is not particularly critical. The software that is being developed is to execute—in its operational version at least—on the embedded target computer. The target computer typically has limited memory, requires special input-output device support, has little or no secondary storage, exists in a harsh environment, and may have severe timing requirements. Furthermore, it is not uncommon to find different CPU architectures in the host and target computers. In addition, the APSE tools are intended to be machine-independent. That is, the entire APSE toolset should be portable among APSEs hosted on different machines. To facilitate such portability, the STONEMAN document defines the APSE in three levels:

1. The Kernel Ada Programming Support Environment, or KAPSE. The KAPSE provides for portability by providing the interface between the underlying operating system and the APSE itself. Thus, to port the toolset to another machine requires modification of only the KAPSE. While all software above the level of the KAPSE will be written in the Ada language, the KAPSE may be implemented using native machine code, direct operating system calls, and direct interaction with file handlers or data base facilities as necessary.
2. The Minimal Ada Programming Support Environment, or MAPSE. The MAPSE is intended to provide the minimal set of tools necessary to constitute a useful programming environment. The MAPSE does not emphasize any particular program design methodology at the expense of any other.
3. The APSE itself, which encompasses the KAPSE and MAPSE, and which may encourage specific design methodologies. The APSE is open-ended, permitting and encouraging the inclusion of innovative tools such as program development languages and advanced project management software.

Thus, the KAPSE-MAPSE interface separates the portable and nonportable parts of the support environment, as indicated in Figure 9.1. To move the APSE from one host computer to another—a process known as *rehosting*—requires only the KAPSE to be changed.

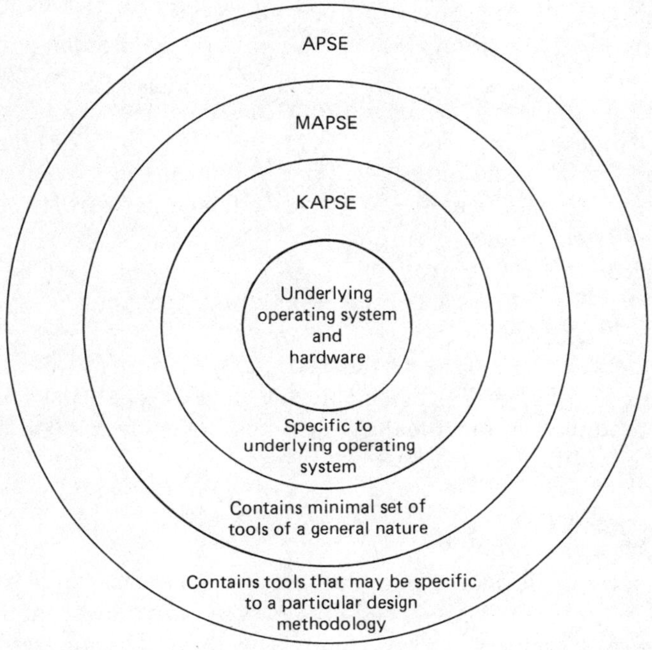

Figure 9.1. The programming support environment.

9.2.1 The KAPSE

The Kernel Ada Programming Support Environment, or KAPSE, isolates the APSE toolset from the underlying operating system. The general functions of the KAPSE are

- to provide the run-time support environment
- to provide the input-output support on the host computer
- to provide the data base access facilities of the APSE
- to provide the means of interaction among APSE tools
- to provide support for the interface between the user and the toolset, and among the tools in the toolset

In particular, the data base function is extremely important to life-cycle software support. Relationships among items in the data base must be maintained, and the items must be retrievable through specification of these relationships. Specifically, the STONEMAN requirements specify that the data base must

- provide for "version groups" among data base items
- support the generation of configuration items as groupings of other items
- provide for the retrieval of all items needed to re-create any item currently in the data base
- provide for the creation of partitions within the data base
- provide for the storage of Ada source code and perhaps for compiled program library units
- provide for access control
- maintain information related to program management

These requirements ensure that the necessary support for all phases of the software life cycle is provided by the data base. In particular, information relating to project management and configuration control must be available within the data base.

9.2.2 The MAPSE

The Minimal Ada Programming Support Environment, or MAPSE, is described in the STONEMAN requirements as providing a minimal but useful Ada programming environment. The MAPSE supports its own extension, however, through the development of additional tools written in the Ada language.

The minimal toolset provided with a MAPSE must contain the following:

- a standard text editor
- a pretty printer program that will format source programs, as well as documentation, according to local standards
- a compiler that will translate Ada source code into native code for the host computer and into native code for at least one target computer
- linkers for both the host and target computers
- loaders for down-loading programs to the target computer
- a static analyzer for generating cross-reference maps for data items in an Ada program
- a flow control static analyzer that can provide charts of control topology of an Ada program
- an interactive debugger
- a file handler for the management of files
- a command interpreter to be used for invoking APSE tools
- a configuration manager for use in maintaining life-cycle support of configuration control

In addition to these minimal requirements, APSE developers can extend the MAPSE by inclusion of additional tools.

9.2.3 Beyond the MAPSE

Those tools in the APSE that extend beyond the MAPSE requirements can support a wide range of methodologies and can provide a much broader support for program management and control. The STONEMAN requirements leave the APSE open-ended, in the sense that no limit to extensions of tools or to the breadth of support are specified. The STONEMAN document itself discusses tools that fill the APSE requirement but extend beyond the MAPSE. Some of these tools are listed below:

- a text editor specifically directed to the preparation of syntactically correct Ada code
- a documentation system for the production and control of project documentation
- a project control system to track the progress of the project with respect to milestone events and budget
- a configuration control system extending beyond those capabilities provided by the MAPSE requirements
- performance measurement tools
- a fault reporting system for tracking error and change reports arising during the operational life of the software
- additional design tools, such as a program development language
- automatic program verification tools
- complex command interpreters that extend the capabilities of the command language

In general, the APSE should be a highly integrated programming environment that exploits specific features of the language that it supports.

9.2.4 The Current Status of Programming Support

The STONEMAN requirements were published in 1980. These requirements are for guidance only—there is yet no standard for the Ada programming support environment, although some work is continuing in this area. Compiler implementers, whether under government contract or funded commercially, provide the support environment along with the compiler. Government-funded implementations tend to be integrated, in the sense that a complete Ada system is developed with the compiler included as one of the tools. Commercial versions usually consist of separately marketed components, so that a user can configure his own support environment. At the current time, only a few compilers have been validated, and even fewer comprehensive support environments have been released. As the Ada language matures through increased use, the support environment requirements can be expected to evolve to meet the developing needs of large-scale software projects.

EXERCISES

1. Discuss the term *life-cycle support.*
2. Indicate how the Ada language and its programming support environment play a part in each phase of the software life cycle.
3. What special characteristics of the maintenance and modification phase are exhibited by Department of Defense embedded systems?
4. What kinds of information should be maintained in the data base of an Ada programming support environment?
5. What kinds of programming support tools should be contained within an Ada programming support environment?
6. What is meant by the term *configuration control*?
7. What are the STONEMAN requirements?
8. What is a program development language?
9. Discuss the differences between functional decomposition and data structure decomposition.

Appendix A
THE PREDEFINED PACKAGE STANDARD

The predefined package STANDARD is provided as an integral part of every Ada compiler implementation. Package STANDARD contains the declarations of those identifiers predefined in the language and of the operations applicable to the types declared within the package. All declarations within package STANDARD are directly visible to any Ada program unit. In addition, package STANDARD plays a conceptual role with respect to the visibility of library units, as discussed in Section 4.3.5.

Within package STANDARD, the following data types are declared and are therefore directly visible in any Ada program unit:

- BOOLEAN
- INTEGER
- FLOAT
- CHARACTER
- NATURAL
- POSITIVE
- STRING
- DURATION

In addition, the following predefined exceptions are declared in package STANDARD.

- CONSTRAINT_ERROR
- NUMERIC_ERROR
- PROGRAM_ERROR
- STORAGE_ERROR
- TASKING_ERROR

Predefined package ASCII is also declared in package STANDARD. This package contains only constant declarations and provides flexibility in dealing with ASCII control characters and other characters not supported by a particular implementation.

The specification of package STANDARD is reprinted here, with permission of the Ada Joint Program Office, Department of Defense, OUSD(R&E), from the *Reference Manual for the Ada Programming Language*, ANSI/MIL-STD-1815A-1983.

```
package STANDARD is

   type BOOLEAN is (FALSE, TRUE);

   -- The predefined relational operators for this type are as follows:

   -- function "="    (LEFT, RIGHT : BOOLEAN) return BOOLEAN;
   -- function "/="   (LEFT, RIGHT : BOOLEAN) return BOOLEAN;
   -- function "<"    (LEFT, RIGHT : BOOLEAN) return BOOLEAN;
   -- function "<="   (LEFT, RIGHT : BOOLEAN) return BOOLEAN;
   -- function ">"    (LEFT, RIGHT : BOOLEAN) return BOOLEAN;
   -- function ">="   (LEFT, RIGHT : BOOLEAN) return BOOLEAN;

   -- The predefined logical operators and the predefined logical negation operator are as follows:

   -- function "and"  (LEFT, RIGHT : BOOLEAN) return BOOLEAN;
   -- function "or"   (LEFT, RIGHT : BOOLEAN) return BOOLEAN;
   -- function "xor"  (LEFT, RIGHT : BOOLEAN) return BOOLEAN;

   -- function "not"  (RIGHT : BOOLEAN) return BOOLEAN;


   -- The universal type universal_integer is predefined.


   type INTEGER is implementation_defined;

   -- The predefined operators for this type are as follows:

   -- function "="    (LEFT, RIGHT : INTEGER) return BOOLEAN;
   -- function "/="   (LEFT, RIGHT : INTEGER) return BOOLEAN;
   -- function "<"    (LEFT, RIGHT : INTEGER) return BOOLEAN;
   -- function "<="   (LEFT, RIGHT : INTEGER) return BOOLEAN;
   -- function ">"    (LEFT, RIGHT : INTEGER) return BOOLEAN;
   -- function ">="   (LEFT, RIGHT : INTEGER) return BOOLEAN;

   -- function "+"    (RIGHT : INTEGER) return INTEGER;
   -- function "-"    (RIGHT : INTEGER) return INTEGER;
   -- function "abs"  (RIGHT : INTEGER) return INTEGER;

   -- function "+"    (LEFT, RIGHT : INTEGER) return INTEGER;
   -- function "-"    (LEFT, RIGHT : INTEGER) return INTEGER;
   -- function "*"    (LEFT, RIGHT : INTEGER) return INTEGER;
   -- function "/"    (LEFT, RIGHT : INTEGER) return INTEGER;
   -- function "rem"  (LEFT, RIGHT : INTEGER) return INTEGER;
   -- function "mod"  (LEFT, RIGHT : INTEGER) return INTEGER;

   -- function "**"   (LEFT : INTEGER; RIGHT : INTEGER) return INTEGER;

   -- An implementation may provide additional predefined integer types. It is recommended that the
   -- names of such additional types end with INTEGER as in SHORT_INTEGER or LONG_INTEGER.
   -- The specification of each operator for the type universal_integer, or for any additional
   -- predefined integer type, is obtained by replacing INTEGER by the name of the type in the
   -- specification of the corresponding operator of the type INTEGER, except for the right operand
   -- of the exponentiating operator.


   -- The universal type universal_real is predefined.

   type FLOAT is implementation_defined;
```

```
-- The predefined operators for this type are as follows:

-- function "="   (LEFT, RIGHT : FLOAT) return BOOLEAN;
-- function "/="  (LEFT, RIGHT : FLOAT) return BOOLEAN;
-- function "<"   (LEFT, RIGHT : FLOAT) return BOOLEAN;
-- function "<="  (LEFT, RIGHT : FLOAT) return BOOLEAN;
-- function ">"   (LEFT, RIGHT : FLOAT) return BOOLEAN;
-- function ">="  (LEFT, RIGHT : FLOAT) return BOOLEAN;

-- function "+"   (RIGHT : FLOAT) return FLOAT;
-- function "-"   (RIGHT : FLOAT) return FLOAT;
-- function "abs" (RIGHT : FLOAT) return FLOAT;

-- function "+"   (LEFT, RIGHT : FLOAT) return FLOAT;
-- function "-"   (LEFT, RIGHT : FLOAT) return FLOAT;
-- function "*"   (LEFT, RIGHT : FLOAT) return FLOAT;
-- function "/"   (LEFT, RIGHT : FLOAT) return FLOAT;

-- function "**"  (LEFT : FLOAT; RIGHT : INTEGER) return FLOAT;

-- An implementation may provide additional predefined floating point types. It is recom-
-- mended that the names of such additional types end with FLOAT as in SHORT_FLOAT or
-- LONG_FLOAT. The specification of each operator for the type universal_real, or for any
-- additional predefined floating point type, is obtained by replacing FLOAT by the name of the
-- type in the specification of the corresponding operator of the type FLOAT.

-- In addition, the following operators are predefined for universal types:

-- function "*" (LEFT : universal_integer; RIGHT : universal_real)    return universal_real;
-- function "*" (LEFT : universal_real;    RIGHT : universal_integer) return universal_real;
-- function "/" (LEFT : universal_real;    RIGHT : universal_integer) return universal_real;

-- The type universal_fixed is predefined. The only operators declared for this type are

-- function "*" (LEFT : any_fixed_point_type; RIGHT : any_fixed_point_type) return universal_fixed;
-- function "/" (LEFT : any_fixed_point_type; RIGHT : any_fixed_point_type) return universal_fixed;

-- The following characters form the standard ASCII character set. Character literals cor-
-- responding to control characters are not identifiers; they are indicated in italics in this definition.

type CHARACTER is

    ( nul,  soh,  stx,  etx,      eot,  enq,  ack,  bel,
      bs,   ht,   lf,   vt,       ff,   cr,   so,   si,
      dle,  dc1,  dc2,  dc3,      dc4,  nak,  syn,  etb,
      can,  em,   sub,  esc,      fs,   gs,   rs,   us,

      ' ',  '!',  '"',  '#',      '$',  '%',  '&',  ''',
      '(',  ')',  '*',  '+',      ',',  '-',  '.',  '/',
      '0',  '1',  '2',  '3',      '4',  '5',  '6',  '7',
      '8',  '9',  ':',  ';',      '<',  '=',  '>',  '?',

      '@',  'A',  'B',  'C',      'D',  'E',  'F',  'G',
      'H',  'I',  'J',  'K',      'L',  'M',  'N',  'O',
      'P',  'Q',  'R',  'S',      'T',  'U',  'V',  'W',
      'X',  'Y',  'Z',  '[',      '\',  ']',  '^',  '_',

      '`',  'a',  'b',  'c',      'd',  'e',  'f',  'g',
      'h',  'i',  'j',  'k',      'l',  'm',  'n',  'o',
      'p',  'q',  'r',  's',      't',  'u',  'v',  'w',
      'x',  'y',  'z',  '{',      '|',  '}',  '~',  del );
```

```
   for CHARACTER use  --  128 ASCII character set without holes
        (0, 1, 2, 3, 4, 5, ..., 125, 126, 127);

   -- The predefined operators for the type CHARACTER are the same as for any enumeration type.


package ASCII is

   --  Control characters:

   NUL        : constant CHARACTER := nul;    SOH        : constant CHARACTER := soh;
   STX        : constant CHARACTER := stx;    ETX        : constant CHARACTER := etx;
   EOT        : constant CHARACTER := eot;    ENQ        : constant CHARACTER := enq;
   ACK        : constant CHARACTER := ack;    BEL        : constant CHARACTER := bel;
   BS         : constant CHARACTER := bs;     HT         : constant CHARACTER := ht;
   LF         : constant CHARACTER := lf;     VT         : constant CHARACTER := vt;
   FF         : constant CHARACTER := ff;     CR         : constant CHARACTER := cr;
   SO         : constant CHARACTER := so;     SI         : constant CHARACTER := si;
   DLE        : constant CHARACTER := dle;    DC1        : constant CHARACTER := dc1;
   DC2        : constant CHARACTER := dc2;    DC3        : constant CHARACTER := dc3;
   DC4        : constant CHARACTER := dc4;    NAK        : constant CHARACTER := nak;
   SYN        : constant CHARACTER := syn;    ETB        : constant CHARACTER := etb;
   CAN        : constant CHARACTER := can;    EM         : constant CHARACTER := em;
   SUB        : constant CHARACTER := sub;    ESC        : constant CHARACTER := esc;
   FS         : constant CHARACTER := fs;     GS         : constant CHARACTER := gs;
   RS         : constant CHARACTER := rs;     US         : constant CHARACTER := us;
   DEL        : constant CHARACTER := del;

   -- Other characters:

   EXCLAM     : constant CHARACTER := '!';    QUOTATION  : constant CHARACTER := '"';
   SHARP      : constant CHARACTER := '#';    DOLLAR     : constant CHARACTER := '$';
   PERCENT    : constant CHARACTER := '%';    AMPERSAND  : constant CHARACTER := '&';
   COLON      : constant CHARACTER := ':';    SEMICOLON  : constant CHARACTER := ';';
   QUERY      : constant CHARACTER := '?';    AT_SIGN    : constant CHARACTER := '@';
   L_BRACKET  : constant CHARACTER := '[';    BACK_SLASH : constant CHARACTER := '\';
   R_BRACKET  : constant CHARACTER := ']';    CIRCUMFLEX : constant CHARACTER := '^';
   UNDERLINE  : constant CHARACTER := '_';    GRAVE      : constant CHARACTER := '`';
   L_BRACE    : constant CHARACTER := '{';    BAR        : constant CHARACTER := '|';
   R_BRACE    : constant CHARACTER := '}';    TILDE      : constant CHARACTER := '~';

   -- Lower case letters:

   LC_A : constant CHARACTER := 'a';
   ...
   LC_Z : constant CHARACTER := 'z';

end ASCII;


-- Predefined subtypes:

subtype NATURAL  is INTEGER range 0 .. INTEGER'LAST;
subtype POSITIVE is INTEGER range 1 .. INTEGER'LAST;


-- Predefined string type:

type STRING is array(POSITIVE range <>) of CHARACTER;

pragma PACK(STRING);
```

```
   -- The predefined operators for this type are as follows:

   -- function "="   (LEFT, RIGHT : STRING) return BOOLEAN;
   -- function "/="  (LEFT, RIGHT : STRING) return BOOLEAN;
   -- function "<"   (LEFT, RIGHT : STRING) return BOOLEAN;
   -- function "<="  (LEFT, RIGHT : STRING) return BOOLEAN;
   -- function ">"   (LEFT, RIGHT : STRING) return BOOLEAN;
   -- function ">="  (LEFT, RIGHT : STRING) return BOOLEAN;

   -- function "&" (LEFT : STRING;    RIGHT : STRING)    return STRING;
   -- function "&" (LEFT : CHARACTER; RIGHT : STRING)    return STRING;
   -- function "&" (LEFT : STRING;    RIGHT : CHARACTER) return STRING;
   -- function "&" (LEFT : CHARACTER; RIGHT : CHARACTER) return STRING;

   type DURATION is delta implementation_defined range implementation_defined;

   -- The predefined operators for the type DURATION are the same as for any fixed point type.

   -- The predefined exceptions:

   CONSTRAINT_ERROR : exception;
   NUMERIC_ERROR    : exception;
   PROGRAM_ERROR    : exception;
   STORAGE_ERROR    : exception;
   TASKING_ERROR    : exception;

end STANDARD;
```

Certain aspects of the predefined entities cannot be completely described in the language itself. For example, although the enumeration type BOOLEAN can be written showing the two enumeration literals FALSE and TRUE, the short-circuit control forms cannot be expressed in the language.

Appendix B
PREDEFINED ATTRIBUTES

Attributes are basic characteristics of Ada data types and data objects, as discussed in Section 3.2.6. In general, the value of an attribute is available at run time under the attribute name. In addition to the predefined attributes listed here, an implementation may provide implementation-defined attributes, in which event a description of the additional attributes must be provided in Appendix F of the implementation reference manual.

This list is reprinted here, with permission of the Ada Join Program Office, OUSD(R&E), from the *Reference Manual for the Ada Programming Language*, ANS1/MIL-STD-1815A-1983.

P'ADDRESS — For a prefix P that denotes an object, a program unit, a label, or an entry:

Yields the address of the first of the storage units allocated to P. For a subprogram, package, task unit,or label, this value refers to the machine code associated with the corresponding body or statement. For an entry for which an address clause has been given, the value refers to the corresponding hardware interrupt. The value of this attribute is of the type ADDRESS defined in the package SYSTEM. (See 13.7.2.)

P'AFT — For a prefix P that denotes a fixed point subtype:

Yields the number of decimal digits needed after the point to accommodate the precision of the subtype P, unless the delta of the subtype P is greater than 0.1, in which case the attribute yields the value one. (P'AFT is the smallest positive integer N for which (10**N)*P'DELTA is greater than or equal to one.) The value of this attribute is of the type *universal_integer*. (See 3.5.10.)

P'BASE — For a prefix P that denotes a type or subtype:

This attribute denotes the base type of P. It is only allowed as the prefix of the name of another attribute: for example, P'BASE'FIRST. (See 3.3.3.)

P'CALLABLE — For a prefix P that is appropriate for a task type:

Yields the value FALSE when the execution of the task P is either completed or terminated, or when the task is abnormal; yields the value TRUE otherwise. The value of this attribute is of the predefined type BOOLEAN. (See 9.9.)

P'CONSTRAINED — For a prefix P that denotes an object of a type with discriminants:

Yields the value TRUE if a discriminant constraint applies to the object P, or if the object is a constant (including a formal parameter or generic formal parameter of mode **in**); yields the value FALSE otherwise. If P is a generic formal parameter of mode **in out**, or if P is a formal parameter of mode **in out** or **out** and the type mark given in the corresponding parameter specification denotes an unconstrained type with discriminants, then the value of this attribute is obtained from that of the corresponding actual parameter. The value of this attribute is of the predefined type BOOLEAN. (See 3.7.4.)

P'CONSTRAINED — For a prefix P that denotes a private type or subtype:

Yields the value FALSE if P denotes an unconstrained nonformal private type with discriminants; also yields the value FALSE if P denotes a generic formal private type and the associated actual subtype is either an unconstrained type with discriminants or an unconstrained array type; yields the value TRUE otherwise. The value of this attribute is of the predefined type BOOLEAN. (See 7.4.2.)

P'COUNT — For a prefix P that denotes an entry of a task unit:

Yields the number of entry calls presently queued on the entry (if the attribute is evaluated within an accept statement for the entry P, the count does not include the calling task). The value of this attribute is of the type *universal_integer*. (See 9.9.)

P'DELTA — For a prefix P that denotes a fixed point subtype:

Yields the value of the delta specified in the fixed accuracy definition for the subtype P. The value of this attribute is of the type *universal_real*. (See 3.5.10.)

P'DIGITS — For a prefix P that denotes a floating point subtype:

Yields the number of decimal digits in the decimal mantissa of model numbers of the subtype P. (This attribute yields the number D of section 3.5.7.) The value of this attribute is of the type *universal_integer*. (See 3.5.8.)

P'EMAX — For a prefix P that denotes a floating point subtype:

Yields the largest exponent value in the binary canonical form of model numbers of the subtype P. (This attribute yields the product 4*B of section 3.5.7.) The value of this attribute is of the type *universal_integer*. (See 3.5.8.)

P'EPSILON — For a prefix P that denotes a floating point subtype:

Yields the absolute value of the difference between the model number 1.0 and the next model number above, for the subtype P. The value of this attribute is of the type *universal_real*. (See 3.5.8.)

P'FIRST — For a prefix P that denotes a scalar type, or a subtype of a scalar type:

Yields the lower bound of P. The value of this attribute has the same type as P. (See 3.5.)

P'FIRST — For a prefix P that is appropriate for an array type, or that denotes a constrained array subtype:

Yields the lower bound of the first index range. The value of this attribute has the same type as this lower bound. (See 3.6.2 and 3.8.2.)

P'FIRST(N) For a prefix P that is appropriate for an array type, or that denotes a constrained array subtype:

Yields the lower bound of the N-th index range. The value of this attribute has the same type as this lower bound. The argument N must be a static expression of type *universal_integer*. The value of N must be positive (nonzero) and no greater than the dimensionality of the array. (See 3.6.2 and 3.8.2.)

P'FIRST_BIT For a prefix P that denotes a component of a record object:

Yields the offset, from the start of the first of the storage units occupied by the component, of the first bit occupied by the component. This offset is measured in bits. The value of this attribute is of the type *universal_integer*. (See 13.7.2.)

P'FORE For a prefix P that denotes a fixed point subtype:

Yields the minimum number of characters needed for the integer part of the decimal representation of any value of the subtype P, assuming that the representation does not include an exponent, but includes a one-character prefix that is either a minus sign or a space. (This minimum number does not include superfluous zeros or underlines, and is at least two.) The value of this attribute is of the type *universal_integer*. (See 3.5.10.)

P'IMAGE For a prefix P that denotes a discrete type or subtype:

This attribute is a function with a single parameter. The actual parameter X must be a value of the base type of P. The result type is the predefined type STRING. The result is the *image* of the value of X, that is, a sequence of characters representing the value in display form. The image of an integer value is the corresponding decimal literal; without underlines, leading zeros, exponent, or trailing spaces; but with a one character prefix that is either a minus sign or a space.

The image of an enumeration value is either the corresponding identifier in upper case or the corresponding character literal (including the two apostrophes); neither leading nor trailing spaces are included. The image of a character other than a graphic character is implementation-defined. (See 3.5.5.)

P'LARGE For a prefix P that denotes a real subtype:

The attribute yields the largest positive model number of the subtype P. The value of this attribute is of the type *universal_real*. (See 3.5.8 and 3.5.10.)

P'LAST For a prefix P that denotes a scalar type, or a subtype of a scalar type:

Yields the upper bound of P. The value of this attribute has the same type as P. (See 3.5.)

P'LAST For a prefix P that is appropriate for an array type, or that denotes a constrained array subtype:

Yields the upper bound of the first index range. The value of this attribute has the same type as this upper bound. (See 3.6.2 and 3.8.2.)

P'LAST(N) — For a prefix P that is appropriate for an array type, or that denotes a constrained array subtype:

Yields the upper bound of the N-th index range. The value of this attribute has the same type as this upper bound. The argument N must be a static expression of type *universal_integer*. The value of N must be positive (nonzero) and no greater than the dimensionality of the array. (See 3.6.2 and 3.8.2.)

P'LAST_BIT — For a prefix P that denotes a component of a record object:

Yields the offset, from the start of the first of the storage units occupied by the component, of the last bit occupied by the component. This offset is measured in bits. The value of this attribute is of the type *universal_integer*. (See 13.7.2.)

P'LENGTH — For a prefix P that is appropriate for an array type, or that denotes a constrained array subtype:

Yields the number of values of the first index range (zero for a null range). The value of this attribute is of the type *universal_integer*. (See 3.6.2.)

P'LENGTH(N) — For a prefix P that is appropriate for an array type, or that denotes a constrained array subtype:

Yields the number of values of the N-th index range (zero for a null range). The value of this attribute is of the type *universal_integer*. The argument N must be a static expression of type *universal_integer*. The value of N must be positive (nonzero) and no greater than the dimensionality of the array. (See 3.6.2 and 3.8.2.)

P'MACHINE_EMAX — For a prefix P that denotes a floating point type or subtype:

Yields the largest value of *exponent* for the machine representation of the base type of P. The value of this attribute is of the type *universal_integer*. (See 13.7.3.)

P'MACHINE_EMIN — For a prefix P that denotes a floating point type or subtype:

Yields the smallest (most negative) value of *exponent* for the machine representation of the base type of P. The value of this attribute is of the type *universal_integer*. (See 13.7.3.)

P'MACHINE_MANTISSA — For a prefix P that denotes a floating point type or subtype:

Yields the number of digits in the *mantissa* for the machine representation of the base type of P (the digits are extended digits in the range 0 to P'MACHINE_RADIX - 1). The value of this attribute is of the type *universal_integer*. (See 13.7.3.)

P'MACHINE_OVERFLOWS — For a prefix P that denotes a real type or subtype:

Yields the value TRUE if every predefined operation on values of the base type of P either provides a correct result,or raises the exception NUMERIC_ERROR in overflow situations; yields the value FALSE otherwise. The value of this attribute is of the predefined type BOOLEAN. (See 13.7.3.)

P'MACHINE_RADIX

For a prefix P that denotes a floating point type or subtype:

Yields the value of the *radix* used by the machine representation of the base type of P. The value of this attribute is of the type *universal_integer*. (See 13.7.3.)

P'MACHINE_ROUNDS

For a prefix P that denotes a real type or subtype:

Yields the value TRUE if every predefined arithmetic operation on values of the base type of P either returns an exact result or performs rounding; yields the value FALSE otherwise. The value of this attribute is of the predefined type BOOLEAN. (See 13.7.3.)

P'MANTISSA

For a prefix P that denotes a real subtype:

Yields the number of binary digits in the binary mantissa of model numbers of the subtype P. (This attribute yields the number B of section 3.5.7 for a floating point type, or of section 3.5.9 for a fixed point type.) The value of this attribute is of the type *universal_integer*. (See 3.5.8 and 3.5.10.)

P'POS

For a prefix P that denotes a discrete type or subtype:

This attribute is a function with a single parameter. The actual parameter X must be a value of the base type of P. The result type is the type *universal_integer*. The result is the position number of the value of the actual parameter. (See 3.5.5.)

P'POSITION

For a prefix P that denotes a component of a record object:

Yields the offset, from the start of the first storage unit occupied by the record, of the first of the storage units occupied by the component. This offset is measured in storage units. The value of this attribute is of the type *universal_integer*. (See 13.7.2.)

P'PRED

For a prefix P that denotes a discrete type or subtype:

This attribute is a function with a single parameter. The actual parameter X must be a value of the base type of P. The result type is the base type of P. The result is the value whose position number is one less than that of X. The exception CONSTRAINT_ERROR is raised if X equals P'BASE'FIRST. (See 3.5.5.)

P'RANGE

For a prefix P that is appropriate for an array type, or that denotes a constrained array subtype:

Yields the first index range of P, that is, the range P'FIRST .. P'LAST. (See 3.6.2.)

P'RANGE(N)

For a prefix P that is appropriate for an array type, or that denotes a constrained array subtype:

Yields the N-th index range of P, that is, the range P'FIRST(N) .. P'LAST(N). (See 3.6.2.)

P'SAFE_EMAX

For a prefix P that denotes a floating point type or subtype:

Yields the largest exponent value in the binary canonical form of safe numbers of the base type of P. (This attribute yields the number E of section 3.5.7.) The value of this attribute is of the type *universal_integer*. (See 3.5.8.)

P'SAFE_LARGE — For a prefix P that denotes a real type or subtype:

Yields the largest positive safe number of the base type of P. The value of this attribute is of the type *universal_real*. (See 3.5.8 and 3.5.10.)

P'SAFE_SMALL — For a prefix P that denotes a real type or subtype:

Yields the smallest positive (nonzero) safe number of the base type of P. The value of this attribute is of the type *universal_real*. (See 3.5.8 and 3.5.10.)

P'SIZE — For a prefix P that denotes an object:

Yields the number of bits allocated to hold the object. The value of this attribute is of the type *universal_integer*. (See 13.7.2.)

P'SIZE — For a prefix P that denotes any type or subtype:

Yields the minimum number of bits that is needed by the implementation to hold any possible object of the type or subtype P. The value of this attribute is of the type *universal_integer*. (See 13.7.2.)

P'SMALL — For a prefix P that denotes a real subtype:

Yields the smallest positive (nonzero) model number of the subtype P. The value of this attribute is of the type *universal_real*. (See 3.5.8 and 3.5.10.)

P'STORAGE_SIZE — For a prefix P that denotes an access type or subtype:

Yields the total number of storage units reserved for the collection associated with the base type of P. The value of this attribute is of the type *universal_integer*. (See 13.7.2.)

P'STORAGE_SIZE — For a prefix P that denotes a task type or a task object:

Yields the number of storage units reserved for each activation of a task of the type P or for the activation of the task object P. The value of this attribute is of the type *universal_integer*. (See 13.7.2.)

P'SUCC — For a prefix P that denotes a discrete type or subtype:

This attribute is a function with a single parameter. The actual parameter X must be a value of the base type of P. The result type is the base type of P. The result is the value whose position number is one greater than that of X. The exception CONSTRAINT_ERROR is raised if X equals P'BASE'LAST. (See 3.5.5.)

P'TERMINATED — For a prefix P that is appropriate for a task type:

Yields the value TRUE if the task P is terminated; yields the value FALSE otherwise. The value of this attribute is of the predefined type BOOLEAN. (See 9.9.)

P'VAL — For a prefix P that denotes a discrete type or subtype:

This attribute is a special function with a single parameter X which can be of any integer type. The result type is the base type of P. The result is the value whose position number is the *universal_integer* value corresponding to X. The exception CONSTRAINT_ERROR is raised if the *universal_integer* value corresponding to X is not in the range P'POS (P'BASE'FIRST) .. P'POS (P'BASE'LAST). (See 3.5.5.)

P'VALUE

For a prefix P that denotes a discrete type or subtype:

This attribute is a function with a single parameter. The actual parameter X must be a value of the predefined type STRING. The result type is the base type of P. Any leading and any trailing spaces of the sequence of characters that corresponds to X are ignored.

For an enumeration type, if the sequence of characters has the syntax of an enumeration literal and if this literal exists for the base type of P, the result is the corresponding enumeration value. For an integer type, if the sequence of characters has the syntax of an integer literal, with an optional single leading character that is a plus or minus sign, and if there is a corresponding value in the base type of P, the result is this value. In any other case, the exception CONSTRAINT_ERROR is raised. (See 3.5.5.)

P'WIDTH

For a prefix P that denotes a discrete subtype:

Yields the maximum image length over all values of the subtype P (the *image* is the sequence of characters returned by the attribute IMAGE). The value of this attribute is of the type *universal_integer*. (See 3.5.5.)

Appendix C
THE PREDEFINED ADA ENVIRONMENT

Package STANDARD, which is contained in Appendix A, constitutes that part of the predefined Ada environment that is directly visible to any Ada program unit. As discussed in Section 4.3.5, package STANDARD has the rather special characteristic that declarations within the package are global to every Ada program unit. There are other parts of the predefined Ada environment that do not share this special characteristic. The use, by a program unit, of any entity declared in this remaining predefined environment is possible only if the appropriate predefined package or subprogram containing the declaration of the entity is named in a with clause by the using program unit. The predefined packages and subprograms constituting the remainder of the predefined environment are given below:

- `generic package SEQUENTIAL_IO`
- `generic package DIRECT_IO`
- `package TEXT_IO`
- `package LOW_LEVEL_IO`
- `package SYSTEM`
- `package IO_EXCEPTIONS`
- `generic procedure UNCHECKED_DEALLOCATION`
- `generic procedure UNCHECKED_CONVERSION`
- `package MACHINE_CODE`

This appendix contains the specifications of these predefined program units, together with the list of predefined pragmas. They are reprinted here, with permission of the Ada Joint Program Office, Department of Defense, OUSD (R&E), from the *Reference Manual for the Ada Programming Language,* ANSI/MIl-STD-1815A-1983.

GENERIC PACKAGE SEQUENTIAL_IO

This package provides a program unit with input-output operations involving sequential-access files, as outlined in Section 6.2.1.1. The generic package must be instantiated for each specific data type for which input-output support is required. The program unit in which such instantiation is declared must have SEQUENTIAL_IO named in a with clause within its context clause.

```
with IO_EXCEPTIONS;
generic
  type ELEMENT_TYPE is private;
package SEQUENTIAL_IO is

  type FILE_TYPE  is limited private;

  type FILE_MODE is (IN_FILE, OUT_FILE);


  -- File management

  procedure CREATE (FILE   : in out FILE_TYPE;
                    MODE : in FILE_MODE := OUT_FILE;
                    NAME : in STRING := "";
                    FORM : in STRING := "");

  procedure OPEN   (FILE   : in out FILE_TYPE;
                    MODE : in FILE_MODE;
                    NAME : in STRING;
                    FORM : in STRING := "");

  procedure CLOSE  (FILE : in out FILE_TYPE);
  procedure DELETE (FILE : in out FILE_TYPE);
  procedure RESET  (FILE : in out FILE_TYPE; MODE : in FILE_MODE);
  procedure RESET  (FILE : in out FILE_TYPE);

  function MODE    (FILE : in FILE_TYPE) return FILE_MODE;
  function NAME    (FILE : in FILE_TYPE) return STRING;
  function FORM    (FILE : in FILE_TYPE) return STRING;

  function IS_OPEN (FILE : in FILE_TYPE) return BOOLEAN;

  -- Input and output operations

  procedure READ  (FILE : in FILE_TYPE; ITEM : out ELEMENT_TYPE);
  procedure WRITE (FILE : in FILE_TYPE; ITEM : in ELEMENT_TYPE);

  function END_OF_FILE(FILE : in FILE_TYPE) return BOOLEAN;

  -- Exceptions

  STATUS_ERROR  : exception renames IO_EXCEPTIONS.STATUS_ERROR;
  MODE_ERROR    : exception renames IO_EXCEPTIONS.MODE_ERROR;
  NAME_ERROR    : exception renames IO_EXCEPTIONS.NAME_ERROR;
  USE_ERROR     : exception renames IO_EXCEPTIONS.USE_ERROR;
  DEVICE_ERROR  : exception renames IO_EXCEPTIONS.DEVICE_ERROR;
  END_ERROR     : exception renames IO_EXCEPTIONS.END_ERROR;
  DATA_ERROR    : exception renames IO_EXCEPTIONS.DATA_ERROR;

private
  -- implementation-dependent
end SEQUENTIAL_IO;
```

GENERIC PACKAGE DIRECT_IO

This package provides a program unit with input-output operations involving direct-access files, as outlined in Section 6.2.1.2. The generic package must be instantiated for each specific data type for which input-output support is required.

The program unit in which such instantiation is declared must have DIRECT_IO named in a with clause within its context clause.

```
with IO_EXCEPTIONS;
generic
   type ELEMENT_TYPE is private;
package DIRECT_IO is

   type FILE_TYPE   is limited private;

   type      FILE_MODE is (IN_FILE, INOUT_FILE, OUT_FILE);
   type      COUNT      is range 0 .. implementation_defined;
   subtype   POSITIVE_COUNT is COUNT range 1 .. COUNT'LAST;


   -- File management

   procedure CREATE ( FILE   : in out FILE_TYPE;
                      MODE   : in FILE_MODE := INOUT_FILE;
                      NAME   : in STRING := "";
                      FORM   : in STRING := "");

   procedure OPEN   ( FILE   : in out FILE_TYPE;
                      MODE   : in FILE_MODE;
                      NAME   : in STRING;
                      FORM   : in STRING := "");

   procedure CLOSE  (FILE : in out FILE_TYPE);
   procedure DELETE (FILE : in out FILE_TYPE);
   procedure RESET  (FILE : in out FILE_TYPE; MODE : in FILE_MODE);
   procedure RESET  (FILE : in out FILE_TYPE);

   function MODE    (FILE : in FILE_TYPE) return FILE_MODE;
   function NAME    (FILE : in FILE_TYPE) return STRING;
   function FORM    (FILE : in FILE_TYPE) return STRING;

   function IS_OPEN (FILE : in FILE_TYPE) return BOOLEAN;

   procedure READ  (FILE : in FILE_TYPE; ITEM : out ELEMENT_TYPE; FROM : POSITIVE_COUNT);
   procedure READ  (FILE : in FILE_TYPE; ITEM : out ELEMENT_TYPE);

   procedure WRITE (FILE : in FILE_TYPE; ITEM : in   ELEMENT_TYPE; TO : POSITIVE_COUNT);
   procedure WRITE (FILE : in FILE_TYPE; ITEM : in ELEMENT_TYPE);

   procedure SET_INDEX(FILE : in FILE_TYPE; TO : in POSITIVE_COUNT);

   function INDEX(FILE : in FILE_TYPE) return POSITIVE_COUNT;
   function SIZE  (FILE : in FILE_TYPE) return COUNT;

   function END_OF_FILE (FILE : in FILE_TYPE) return BOOLEAN;

   -- Exceptions

   STATUS_ERROR  : exception renames IO_EXCEPTIONS.STATUS_ERROR;
   MODE_ERROR    : exception renames IO_EXCEPTIONS.MODE_ERROR;
   NAME_ERROR    : exception renames IO_EXCEPTIONS.NAME_ERROR;
   USE_ERROR     : exception renames IO_EXCEPTIONS.USE_ERROR;
   DEVICE_ERROR  : exception renames IO_EXCEPTIONS.DEVICE_ERROR;
   END_ERROR     : exception renames IO_EXCEPTIONS.END_ERROR;
   DATA_ERROR    : exception renames IO_EXCEPTIONS.DATA_ERROR;

private
   -- implementation-dependent
end DIRECT_IO;
```

PACKAGE TEXT_IO

This package provides a program unit with input-output facilities for text files, as outlined in Section 6.2.2. Package TEXT_IO is not a generic unit, as are SEQUENTIAL_IO and DIRECT_IO, but declared within TEXT_IO are the four generic packages:

- INTEGER_IO
- FLOAT_IO
- FIXED_IO
- ENUMERATION_IO

The function of each of these generic packages is discussed in Section 6.2.2. Input-output operations for objects of types STRING and CHARACTER are provided in the nongeneric part of package TEXT_IO, and no instantiation is required. Input-output operations for other data types are provided by the four generic packages, and these packages must be instantiated for each specific data type for which input-output support is required. Since the generic packages INTEGER_IO, FLOAT_IO, FIXED_IO, and ENUMERATION_IO are declared within package TEXT_IO, only TEXT_IO need be named in a with clause within the context clause of a program unit in which one or more of the generic units are instantiated. A use clause applied to TEXT_IO will make the generic units directly visible. Without a use clause, any instantiation must reference the expanded name, such as TEXT_IO.INTEGER_IO.

```
with IO_EXCEPTIONS;
package TEXT_IO is

  type FILE_TYPE  is limited private;

  type FILE_MODE is (IN_FILE, OUT_FILE);

  type COUNT  is range 0 .. implementation_defined;
  subtype POSITIVE_COUNT  is COUNT range 1 .. COUNT'LAST;
  UNBOUNDED : constant COUNT := 0; -- line and page length

  subtype FIELD          is INTEGER range 0 .. implementation_defined;
  subtype NUMBER_BASE is INTEGER range 2 .. 16;

  type TYPE_SET is (LOWER_CASE, UPPER_CASE);

  -- File Management

  procedure CREATE  ( FILE   : in out FILE_TYPE;
                      MODE : in FILE_MODE  := OUT_FILE;
                      NAME : in STRING      := "";
                      FORM : in STRING      := "");

  procedure OPEN    ( FILE   : in out FILE_TYPE;
                      MODE : in FILE_MODE;
                      NAME : in STRING;
                      FORM : in STRING := "");

  procedure  CLOSE   (FILE : in out FILE_TYPE);
  procedure  DELETE  (FILE : in out FILE_TYPE);
  procedure  RESET   (FILE : in out FILE_TYPE; MODE : in FILE_MODE);
  procedure  RESET   (FILE : in out FILE_TYPE);
```

```
function    MODE    (FILE : in FILE_TYPE) return FILE_MODE ;
function    NAME    (FILE : in FILE_TYPE) return STRING;
function    FORM    (FILE : in FILE_TYPE) return STRING;

function    IS_OPEN(FILE : in FILE_TYPE) return BOOLEAN;

-- Control of default input and output files

procedure   SET_INPUT   (FILE : in FILE_TYPE);
procedure   SET_OUTPUT (FILE : in FILE_TYPE);


function    STANDARD_INPUT      return FILE_TYPE;
function    STANDARD_OUTPUT     return FILE_TYPE;

function    CURRENT_INPUT       return FILE_TYPE;
function    CURRENT_OUTPUT      return FILE_TYPE;

-- Specification of line and page lengths

procedure   SET_LINE_LENGTH    (FILE : in FILE_TYPE; TO : in COUNT);
procedure   SET_LINE_LENGTH    (TO : in COUNT);

procedure   SET_PAGE_LENGTH    (FILE : in FILE_TYPE; TO : in COUNT);
procedure   SET_PAGE_LENGTH    (TO : in COUNT);

function    LINE_LENGTH  (FILE : in FILE_TYPE) return COUNT;
function    LINE_LENGTH   return COUNT;

function    PAGE_LENGTH (FILE : in FILE_TYPE) return COUNT;
function    PAGE_LENGTH  return COUNT;

-- Column, Line, and Page Control

procedure   NEW_LINE      (FILE : in FILE_TYPE; SPACING : in POSITIVE_COUNT := 1);
procedure   NEW_LINE      (SPACING : in POSITIVE_COUNT := 1);

procedure   SKIP_LINE     (FILE : in FILE_TYPE; SPACING : in POSITIVE_COUNT := 1);
procedure   SKIP_LINE     (SPACING : in POSITIVE_COUNT := 1);

function    END_OF_LINE  (FILE : in FILE_TYPE) return BOOLEAN;
function    END_OF_LINE   return BOOLEAN;

procedure   NEW_PAGE      (FILE : in FILE_TYPE);
procedure   NEW_PAGE;

procedure   SKIP_PAGE     (FILE : in FILE_TYPE);
procedure   SKIP_PAGE;

function    END_OF_PAGE (FILE : in FILE_TYPE) return BOOLEAN;
function    END_OF_PAGE  return BOOLEAN;

function    END_OF_FILE  (FILE : in FILE_TYPE) return BOOLEAN;
function    END_OF_FILE   return BOOLEAN;


procedure   SET_COL (FILE  : in FILE_TYPE; TO : in POSITIVE_COUNT);
procedure   SET_COL (TO    : in POSITIVE_COUNT);

procedure   SET_LINE (FILE  : in FILE_TYPE; TO : in POSITIVE_COUNT);
procedure   SET_LINE (TO    : in POSITIVE_COUNT);


function COL  (FILE : in FILE_TYPE) return POSITIVE_COUNT;
function COL    return POSITIVE_COUNT;
```

```
function LINE  (FILE : in FILE_TYPE) return POSITIVE_COUNT;
function LINE return POSITIVE_COUNT;

function PAGE (FILE : in FILE_TYPE) return POSITIVE_COUNT;
function PAGE  return POSITIVE_COUNT;

-- Character Input-Output

procedure  GET(FILE   : in   FILE_TYPE; ITEM : out CHARACTER);
procedure  GET(ITEM   : out  CHARACTER);
procedure  PUT(FILE   : in   FILE_TYPE; ITEM : in CHARACTER);
procedure  PUT(ITEM   : in   CHARACTER);

-- String Input-Output

procedure  GET(FILE   : in   FILE_TYPE; ITEM : out STRING);
procedure  GET(ITEM   : out  STRING);
procedure  PUT(FILE   : in   FILE_TYPE; ITEM : in STRING);
procedure  PUT(ITEM   : in   STRING);

procedure  GET_LINE(FILE : in    FILE_TYPE;  ITEM : out STRING; LAST : out NATURAL);
procedure  GET_LINE(ITEM : out  STRING; LAST : out NATURAL);
procedure  PUT_LINE(FILE : in    FILE_TYPE; ITEM : in STRING);
procedure  PUT_LINE(ITEM : in    STRING);

-- Generic package for Input-Output of Integer Types

generic
   type NUM is range <>;
package INTEGER_IO is

   DEFAULT_WIDTH   : FIELD := NUM'WIDTH;
   DEFAULT_BASE    : NUMBER_BASE := 10;

   procedure GET(FILE   : in   FILE_TYPE; ITEM : out NUM; WIDTH : in FIELD := 0);
   procedure GET(ITEM   : out NUM; WIDTH : in FIELD := 0);

   procedure PUT( FILE     : in  FILE_TYPE;
                  ITEM     : in  NUM;
                  WIDTH    : in  FIELD := DEFAULT_WIDTH;
                  BASE     : in  NUMBER_BASE := DEFAULT_BASE);
   procedure PUT( ITEM     : in  NUM;
                  WIDTH    : in  FIELD := DEFAULT_WIDTH;
                  BASE     : in  NUMBER_BASE := DEFAULT_BASE);

   procedure GET( FROM  : in   STRING; ITEM : out NUM; LAST : out POSITIVE);
   procedure PUT( TO    : out STRING;
                  ITEM  : in NUM;
                  BASE  : in NUMBER_BASE := DEFAULT_BASE);

end INTEGER_IO;

-- Generic packages for Input-Output of Real Types

generic
   type NUM is digits <>;
package FLOAT_IO is

   DEFAULT_FORE   : FIELD := 2;
   DEFAULT_AFT    : FIELD := NUM'DIGITS-1;
   DEFAULT_EXP    : FIELD := 3;

   procedure  GET(FILE : in FILE_TYPE; ITEM : out NUM; WIDTH : in FIELD := 0);
   procedure  GET(ITEM : out NUM; WIDTH : in FIELD := 0);
```

```
   procedure PUT(FILE   : in FILE_TYPE;
                 ITEM   : in NUM;
                 FORE   : in FIELD := DEFAULT_FORE;
                 AFT    : in FIELD := DEFAULT_AFT;
                 EXP    : in FIELD := DEFAULT_EXP);
   procedure PUT(ITEM   : in NUM;
                 FORE   : in FIELD := DEFAULT_FORE;
                 AFT    : in FIELD := DEFAULT_AFT;
                 EXP    : in FIELD := DEFAULT_EXP);

   procedure GET(FROM   : in STRING; ITEM : out NUM; LAST : out POSITIVE);
   procedure PUT(TO     : out STRING;
                 ITEM   : in NUM;
                 AFT    : in FIELD := DEFAULT_AFT;
                 EXP    : in FIELD := DEFAULT_EXP);
end FLOAT_IO;

generic
   type NUM is delta <>;
package FIXED_IO is

   DEFAULT_FORE  : FIELD := NUM'FORE;
   DEFAULT_AFT   : FIELD := NUM'AFT;
   DEFAULT_EXP   : FIELD := 0;

   procedure GET(FILE  : in FILE_TYPE; ITEM : out NUM; WIDTH : in FIELD := 0);
   procedure GET(ITEM  : out NUM; WIDTH : in FIELD := 0);

   procedure PUT(FILE   : in FILE_TYPE;
                 ITEM   : in NUM;
                 FORE   : in FIELD := DEFAULT_FORE;
                 AFT    : in FIELD := DEFAULT_AFT;
                 EXP    : in FIELD := DEFAULT_EXP);
   procedure PUT(ITEM   : in NUM;
                 FORE   : in FIELD := DEFAULT_FORE;
                 AFT    : in FIELD := DEFAULT_AFT;
                 EXP    : in FIELD := DEFAULT_EXP);

   procedure GET(FROM   : in  STRING; ITEM : out NUM; LAST : out POSITIVE);
   procedure PUT(TO     : out STRING;
                 ITEM   : in NUM;
                 AFT    : in FIELD := DEFAULT_AFT;
                 EXP    : in FIELD := DEFAULT_EXP);

end FIXED_IO;

-- Generic package for Input-Output of Enumeration Types

generic
   type ENUM is (<>);
package ENUMERATION_IO is

   DEFAULT_WIDTH    : FIELD := 0;
   DEFAULT_SETTING  : TYPE_SET := UPPER_CASE;

   procedure GET(FILE    : in FILE_TYPE; ITEM : out ENUM);
   procedure GET(ITEM    : out ENUM);

   procedure PUT(FILE    : in FILE_TYPE;
                 ITEM    : in ENUM;
                 WIDTH   : in FIELD     := DEFAULT_WIDTH;
                 SET     : in TYPE_SET  := DEFAULT_SETTING);
   procedure PUT(ITEM    : in ENUM;
                 WIDTH   : in FIELD     := DEFAULT_WIDTH;
                 SET     : in TYPE_SET  := DEFAULT_SETTING);
```

```
   procedure GET(FROM  : in  STRING; ITEM : out ENUM; LAST : out POSITIVE);
   procedure PUT(TO    : out STRING;
                 ITEM  : in  ENUM;
                 SET   : in  TYPE_SET := DEFAULT_SETTING);
 end ENUMERATION_IO;

 -- Exceptions

 STATUS_ERROR  : exception renames IO_EXCEPTIONS.STATUS_ERROR;
 MODE_ERROR    : exception renames IO_EXCEPTIONS.MODE_ERROR;
 NAME_ERROR    : exception renames IO_EXCEPTIONS.NAME_ERROR;
 USE_ERROR     : exception renames IO_EXCEPTIONS.USE_ERROR;
 DEVICE_ERROR  : exception renames IO_EXCEPTIONS.DEVICE_ERROR;
 END_ERROR     : exception renames IO_EXCEPTIONS.END_ERROR;
 DATA_ERROR    : exception renames IO_EXCEPTIONS.DATA_ERROR;
 LAYOUT_ERROR  : exception renames IO_EXCEPTIONS.LAYOUT_ERROR;

private
  -- implementation-dependent
end TEXT_IO;
```

PACKAGE LOW_LEVEL_IO

The predefined package LOW_LEVEL_IO is a highly implementation-dependent input-output package that will be determined by the characteristics of the target computer and by the specific input-output requirements of the target environment, as implied by the discussion of Section 6.3. More specific details of the use of LOW_LEVEL_IO must be included in Appendix F of an implementation reference manual.

```
package LOW_LEVEL_IO is
  -- declarations of the possible types for DEVICE and
  -- DATA;
  -- declarations of overloaded procedures for these
  -- types:
  procedure SEND_CONTROL    (DEVICE : device_type; DATA :
                             in out data_type);
  procedure RECEIVE_CONTROL (DEVICE: device_type; DATA :
                             in out data-type);
end;
```

PACKAGE SYSTEM

Package SYSTEM contains only type and object declarations. Specifically, it contains the declaration of certain implementation-specific constants and data types, as discussed in Section 8.6.

```
package SYSTEM is
  type ADDRESS   is implementation_defined;
  type NAME      is implementation_defined_enumeration_type;

  SYSTEM_NAME    : constant NAME   := implementation_defined;
```

```
   STORAGE_UNIT     : constant := implementation_defined;
   MEMORY_SIZE      : constant := implementation_defined;

   --  System-Dependent Named Numbers:

   MIN_INT          : constant := implementation_defined;
   MAX_INT          : constant := implementation_defined;
   MAX_DIGITS       : constant := implementation_defined;
   MAX_MANTISSA     : constant := implementation_defined;
   FINE_DELTA       : constant := implementation_defined;
   TICK             : constant := implementation_defined;

   --  Other System-Dependent Declarations

   subtype PRIORITY is INTEGER range implementation_defined;

   ...
end SYSTEM;
```

PACKAGE IO_EXCEPTIONS

This package contains only the declarations of exceptions. Specifically, these exceptions relate to those conditions that can arise during input-output operations. All three input-output packages—SEQUENTIAL_IO, DIRECT_IO, and TEXT IO—rename these exceptions, thus making the renamed exceptions visible to users of the input-output packages.

```
package IO_EXCEPTIONS is

   STATUS_ERROR : exception;
   MODE_ERROR   : exception;
   NAME_ERROR   : exception;
   USE_ERROR    : exception;
   DEVICE_ERROR : exception;
   END_ERROR    : exception;
   DATA_ERROR   : exception;
   LAYOUT_ERROR : exception;

end IO_EXCEPTIONS;
```

GENERIC PROCEDURE UNCHECKED_DEALLOCATION

This generic procedure can be instantiated to provide the means of permitting a run-time support system to deallocate storage dedicated to designated objects of a particular access type, as discussed in Section 8.7.1. Any program unit containing an instantiation of the generic procedure must have UNCHECKED_DEALLOCATION named in a with clause within its context clause.

```
generic
   type OBJECT is limited private;
   type NAME   is access OBJECT;
procedure UNCHECKED_DEALLOCATION(X : in out NAME);
```

GENERIC PROCEDURE UNCHECKED_CONVERSION

This generic procedure can be instantiated to provide type conversion from a source type to a target type, as discussed in Section 8.7.1. Any program unit con-containing an instantiation of the generic procedure must have UNCHECKED_CONVERSION named in a with clause within its context clause.

```
generic
   type SOURCE is limited private;
   type TARGET is limited private;
function UNCHECKED_CONVERSION(S : SOURCE) return TARGET;
```

PACKAGE MACHINE_CODE

This package, if provided by an implementation, will declare a record for each machine instruction supported, as described in Section 8.5.

PREDEFINED PRAGMAS

The predefined pragmas listed below must be supported by every implementation but, as discussed in Section 8.8, the degree to which they are supported can be quite implementation-dependent. Most of the pragmas listed here are discussed in Section 8.2.3.

Pragma	*Meaning*
CONTROLLED	Takes the simple name of an access type as the single argument. This pragma is only allowed immediately within the declarative part or package specification that contains the declaration of the access type; the declaration must occur before the pragma. This pragma is not allowed for a derived type. This pragma specifies that automatic storage reclamation must not be performed for objects designated by values of the access type, except upon leaving the innermost block statement, subprogram body, or task body that encloses the access type declaration, or after leaving the main program (see 4.8).
ELABORATE	Takes one or more simple names denoting library units as arguments. This pragma is only allowed immediately after the context clause of a compilation unit (before the subsequent library unit or secondary unit). Each argument must be the simple name of a library unit mentioned by the context clause. This pragma specifies that the corresponding library unit body must be elaborated before the given compilation unit. If the given compilation unit is a subunit, the library unit body must be elaborated before the body of the ancestor library unit of the subunit (see 10.5).
INLINE	Takes one or more names as arguments; each name is either the name of a subprogram or the name of a generic subprogram. This pragma is only allowed at the place of a declarative item in a declarative part or package specification, or after a library unit in a compilation, but before any subsequent compilation unit. This pragma specifies that the subprogram bodies should be expanded inline at each call whenever possible; in the case of a generic subprogram, the pragma applies to calls of its instantiations (see 6.3.2).

INTERFACE Takes a language name and a subprogram name as arguments. This pragma is allowed at the place of a declarative item, and must apply in this case to a subprogram declared by an earlier declarative item of the same declarative part or package specification. This pragma is also allowed for a library unit; in this case the pragma must appear after the subprogram declaration, and before any subsequent compilation unit. This pragma specifies the other language (and thereby the calling conventions) and informs the compiler that an object module will be supplied for the corresponding subprogram (see 13.9).

LIST Takes one of the identifiers ON or OFF as the single argument. This pragma is allowed anywhere a pragma is allowed. It specifies that listing of the compilation is to be continued or suspended until a LIST pragma with the opposite argument is given within the same compilation. The pragma itself is always listed if the compiler is producing a listing.

MEMORY_SIZE Takes a numeric literal as the single argument. This pragma is only allowed at the start of a compilation, before the first compilation unit (if any) of the compilation. The effect of this pragma is to use the value of the specified numeric literal for the definition of the named number MEMORY_SIZE (see 13.7).

OPTIMIZE Takes one of the identifiers TIME or SPACE as the single argument. This pragma is only allowed within a declarative part and it applies to the block or body enclosing the declarative part. It specifies whether time or space is the primary optimization criterion.

PACK Takes the simple name of a record or array type as the single argument. The allowed positions for this pragma, and the restrictions on the named type, are governed by the same rules as for a representation clause. The pragma specifies that storage minimization should be the main criterion when selecting the representation of the given type (see 13.1).

PAGE This pragma has no argument, and is allowed anywhere a pragma is allowed. It specifies that the program text which follows the pragma should start on a new page (if the compiler is currently producing a listing).

PRIORITY Takes a static expression of the predefined integer subtype PRIORITY as the single argument. This pragma is only allowed within the specification of a task unit or immediately within the outermost declarative part of a main program. It specifies the priority of the task (or tasks of the task type) or the priority of the main program (see 9.8).

SHARED Takes the simple name of a variable as the single argument. This pragma is allowed only for a variable declared by an object declaration and whose type is a scalar or access type; the variable declaration and the pragma must both occur (in this order) immediately within the same declarative part or package specification. This pragma specifies that every read or update of the variable is a synchronization point for that variable. An implementation must restrict the objects for which this pragma is allowed to objects for which each of direct reading and direct updating is implemented as an indivisible operation (see 9.11).

STORAGE_UNIT Takes a numeric literal as the single argument. This pragma is only allowed at the start of a compilation, before the first compilation unit (if any) of the compilation. The effect of this pragma is to use the value of the specified numeric literal for the definition of the named number STORAGE_UNIT (see 13.7).

SUPPRESS Takes as arguments the identifier of a check and optionally also the name of either an object, a type or subtype, a subprogram, a task unit, or a generic unit. This pragma is only allowed either immediately within a declarative part or immediately within a package specification. In the latter case, the only allowed form is with a name that denotes an entity (or several overloaded subprograms) declared immediately within the package specification. The permission to omit the given check extends from the place of the pragma to the end of the declarative region associated with the innermost enclosing block statement or program unit. For a pragma given in a package specification, the permission extends to the end of the scope of the named entity.

If the pragma includes a name, the permission to omit the given check is further restricted: it is given only for operations on the named object or on all objects of the base type of a named type or subtype; for calls of a named subprogram; for activations of tasks of the named task type; or for instantiations of the given generic unit (see 11.7).

SYSTEM_NAME Takes an enumeration literal as the single argument. This pragma is only allowed at the start of a compilation, before the first compilation unit (if any) of the compilation. The effect of this pragma is to use the enumeration literal with the specified identifier for the definition of the constant SYSTEM_NAME. This pragma is only allowed if the specified identifier corresponds to one of the literals of the type NAME declared in the package SYSTEM (see 13.7).

INDEX

INDEX